Acronym sheet

NEA - National Educati

D0935122

NCWC- National Catholic Welfare
           Council

HEW- Dept. of Health, Education
          & welfare

ESEA - Elementary & Secondary
          Education Act of 1965

NDEA - National Defense
          Education Act

See
Government
Grow

See Government Grow

Education Politics from Johnson to Reagan

Gareth Davies

UNIVERSITY PRESS OF KANSAS

© 2007 by the University Press of Kansas

All rights reserved

Published by the University Press of Kansas (Lawrence, Kansas 66045), which was organized by the Kansas Board of Regents and is operated and funded by Emporia State University, Fort Hays State University, Kansas State University, Pittsburg State University, the University of Kansas, and Wichita State University

Library of Congress Cataloging-in-Publication Data

Davies, Gareth, 1965-
   See government grow : education politics from Johnson to Reagan / Gareth Davies.
      p.   cm.
   Includes bibliographical references and index.
   ISBN 978-0-7006-1532-2 (cloth : alk. paper)
   1. Education and state—United States—History—20th century. 2. Federal aid to education—United States—History—20th century. I. Title.
   LC89.D38 2007
   379.73′09045—dc22   2007021999

British Library Cataloguing-in-Publication Data is available.

Printed in the United States of America

10 9 8 7 6 5 4 3 2 1

The paper used in this publication is recycled and contains 50 percent postconsumer waste. It is acid free and meets the minimum requirements of the American National Standard for Permanence of Paper for Printed Library Materials Z39.48-1992.

To the memory of Hugh Davis Graham

CONTENTS

ACKNOWLEDGMENTS

This book has taken a long time to write, and I should begin by expressing my gratitude to Fred Woodward at Kansas for his forbearance, as well as to his colleagues, especially Susan McRory and Susan Schott, for the care that they have taken with my manuscript. My early thinking about the project, back in the twentieth century, was greatly assisted by Hugh Davis Graham and Diane Ravitch, who provided full and insightful peer reviews of my initial proposal. Graham also had a decisive impact on the subsequent development of the book, through a series of penetrating and immensely learned email messages, and by commissioning the conference policy that turned into the bilingual education chapter (the first to be written). Hugh's interventions, together with those of my most important academic mentor, Martha Derthick, encouraged me to pay much greater attention to the institutional characteristics of American democracy than I had displayed in my first book.

I am extremely grateful to the friends, colleagues and father who read every single chapter of the book in an earlier—and often distinctly rudimentary — form: Edward Berkowitz, Nigel Bowles, Christopher Cross, Mervyn Davies, Martha Derthick, Sian Findlay, Otis L. Graham, Jr., Samuel Halperin, Michael Heale, David Mathews, Shep Melnick, and John David Skrentny. Conscious that simply naming them scarcely does justice to their contribution, I nevertheless thank them equally for encouraging me to think more deeply about education politics, for sharpening my prose, and for catching errors. In the case of Sam Halperin, I benefited not simply from his deep knowledge of education politics and outstanding copyediting skills, but from his generosity in putting me in touch with a large number of colleagues, including Gerald Bracey and Paul Barton, who helped with school achievement data.

I am also happy to have the opportunity to record my gratitude to those participants in the events described within these pages who kindly consented to revisit times long gone by reading particular chapters: John Brademas, Francis Hurley, Albert Quie, Roy Millenson, Don White, Stephen Joel

Trachtenberg, Jack Jennings, Emerson Elliott, Charles Saunders, Stanley McFarland, August Steinhilber, Leonard Garment, George Shultz, Frank Dunbaugh, William Taylor, James Turner, St. John Barrett, the late Jerris Leonard, Fred Graham, Leon Panetta, Chester Finn, Edwin Martin, Anne Hocutt, Ira DeMent, Frederick Weintraub, Chris Koyanagi, Tom Shannon, Jack Coons, Stephen Sugarman, James Kelley, Arthur Wise, Larry Hammond, Allan Cohen, Elam Hertzler, Charles Radcliffe, Rich DiEugenio, Milton Goldberg, Bruce Boston, James Harvey, Gerald Holton, and Gary Jones. Thanks too to fellow-historians and political scientists Andrew Adonis, Mark Brilliant, Linda Kerber, David Mayhew, Stephen Tuck, Michael Klarman, Charles Jones, and Carlos Kevin Blanton, whose feedback on individual chapters was enormously helpful. And I am particularly indebted to Byron Shafer, whose penetrating critique of what I had thought to be the final version of the Introduction led me to rewrite it entirely.

I appreciated the opportunity to present parts of my argument to a number of scholarly audiences. In particular, thanks to Tony Badger, who twice invited me to speak at his Cambridge American history research seminar; Byron Shafer, whose impressive graduate students at the University of Wisconsin at Madison helped me to think about the relationship between this project and my first book; Robert Mason, who invited me to address the Edinburgh University history seminar; and David Mathews, who, together with his colleagues at the Kettering Foundation, encouraged me to think more deeply about the present-day implications of my research.

My most important institutional debts are rather similar to those that I incurred in writing my first book. Both were written while I was based at Oxford University but were made possible in important respects by a year spent immersed in the extraordinary intellectual community that is the University of Virginia. At Oxford, I thank the many colleagues in St. Anne's College, the History faculty, the Bodleian Library, the Rothermere American Institute, and the American history group, for having provided such a friendly and intellectually rich environment. Although I can not enumerate them all, I would be remiss if I did not record my particular gratitude to Nigel Bowles, who has been as superbly supportive a colleague as he was previously a doctoral supervisor. Warm thanks too to Richard Carwardine, Stephen Tuck, Jay Sexton, Lawrence Goldman, Peter Ghosh, Janet Howarth, Jane Rawson, Peter Thompson, and Isabel Holowaty.

It is thanks to the generosity of the Leverhulme Trust that I was able to spend the year 2004–2005 in Charlottesville, allowing me to make big strides toward completing a project that had previously seemed becalmed. I am grateful to Brian Balogh, Sid Milkis, and Chi Lam for having arranged a visiting professorship at the Miller Center of Public Affairs, a unique and superb resource for scholars of American political development. I thank Brian additionally for having lent me his history office in Randall Hall, and Charles McCurdy and his colleagues in the Corcoran Department of History for having made me so welcome. Guian McKee, Kent Germany, and Mike Greco, all of the Miller Center, helped me to use LBJ's taped phone conversations. And I am deeply indebted to the wonderful staff of the Alderman Library, especially to the interlibrary loan department, and to whoever conceived the extraordinary "Leo" service, whereby any member of the UVA faculty can have books and journal articles delivered free of charge to his or her office on grounds. I hope that I did not abuse this privilege. Thanks too to the many other U.S. librarians and archivists who have helped me with my research during the past decade, especially Claudia Anderson of the LBJ library, Dottie Gray of the National School Boards Association, and Trudy Kerr of the Council for Exceptional Children. On a different note, I feel duty-bound to acknowledge the tenacity of Olivia Gattis, who resolutely refused to give me access to the archive of the National Education Association, despite all my best efforts.

Returning to Charlottesville, one of my other great and most serendipitous debts from that year is to the staff of the Venable elementary school. As well as looking after our five-year-old son Peter, who spent his kindergarten year under the expert and warm tutelage of Brenda Payne and Doris Smith, principal Malcolm Jarrell and his colleagues gave me a vivid personal glimpse of American elementary education at its very best. And from conversations with these staff, and by reading the school's newsletter, *Venable Buzz*, I also gained some appreciation for the extraordinary pressures that American public school teachers and administrators face as they strive to cope with the transformed world of education politics that is recorded in this book.

I am pleased to have an opportunity to express my deep personal debt to my wife, Liz; to our two children, Peter and Rhys; to my parents, Mary and Mervyn Davies; and to my sister, Kate. They have varying degrees of enthusiasm for American history and education politics, but I cannot imagine having brought this project to a conclusion without their warm and loving support. Thanks too to my father-in-law, Otto, for his hospitality during our visits to Washington. Although she is not narrowly speaking a part of my family, I nevertheless want to record in this same space how much I have cherished the friendship, as well as the intellectual inspiration, that Martha

Derthick has provided over the past near two decades. I also have Martha to thank for the title to this book. (For the benefit of fellow non-Americans, U.S. children between the 1930s and 1960s commonly learned to read with the help of the Dick and Jane series, whose books featured phrases such as "see Spot run." Dick and Jane have long been superseded, but this catch-phrase remains widely known.)

This book is dedicated to Hugh Davis Graham, whose death in 2002 (on the very day that the *Wall Street Journal* published the first review of his final book) robbed the profession of one of its most foremost practitioners. Having known Hugh is one of the great privileges of my career. None of us who feel his continuing influence can expect to match the sustained brilliance of his masterwork, *The Civil Rights Era*. I hope that this book is at least worthy of his memory.

INTRODUCTION

Historians commonly conceive of American politics since the 1960s as a sustained reaction against Great Society liberalism. There is plenty of evidence to support the notion of a rightward shift, be it in the form of election results, poll data (declining numbers of Americans identifying with "liberalism," levels of trust in government), growing inequalities of wealth and income, rates of incarceration, the proliferation of conservative think tanks and lobby groups, the decline of organized labor, the composition of the Supreme Court, the growth of evangelical Protestantism, welfare reform, or the declaration by Democratic president Bill Clinton that "the era of big government is over." The list could easily be extended.

In this book I am concerned with the other part of the story, namely the persistence and even growth of big government during a supposedly conservative era. Specifically, I examine the case of elementary and secondary education, an area in which conservatives came to embrace conceptions of federal responsibility that would have been considered daring had they been proposed by liberals in 1965, when Lyndon Johnson's Great Society was at its zenith. When Congress passed the landmark Elementary and Secondary Education Act of 1965 (ESEA), the idea that the federal government had any responsibility for schools was controversial; this was the quintessentially local function, and every previous effort to enact large-scale federal aid had run aground. Four-fifths of Republicans in the House of Representatives voted against ESEA, primarily on local control grounds. It could only have passed in an exceptionally Democratic year.

Four years later, Richard Nixon became president, inaugurating a long era of Republican dominance of the White House. He won office in part by appealing to public dissatisfaction with liberalism. What would GOP control of the presidency mean for ESEA, which had been controversial even in 1965, when liberalism was at its zenith? Supporters of federal aid were convinced that Nixon would seek to eviscerate the program, and their capacity to resist this expected attack was weakened by evidence that ESEA was falling short of its primary goal, which was to improve educational opportunities for disadvantaged children. Yet in these unpropitious circumstances, the strong, bipartisan roots that ESEA had begun to put down during the Johnson presidency became much deeper, such that by the time that it came up for renewal in 1974, conservative opposition had all but disappeared. The first four chapters of this book explore the process whereby this once bold principle of federal aid to schools was established and won broad acceptance.

Part of the reason was that ESEA required very little of the states. Programs funded under Title I, which accounted for more than 80 percent of the initial $1.2 billion authorization, were supposed to be "designed to meet the special educational needs of educationally deprived children," but no great effort was made to monitor how the funds were spent, and there was no mechanism for terminating aid to school districts whose initiatives failed to help the poor. In these circumstances, fears of federal control began to subside, and school districts came to rely on the roughly 8 percent of their revenues that came from Washington. If federal dollars ceased, states and localities would have to pick up the tab, an unwelcome prospect amid the difficult fiscal circumstances of the 1970s.

In addition, the growing popularity of federal aid to education during the Nixon-Ford years exemplifies a basic reality of American politics that is easily lost if one views the story simply in terms of cycles of reform and reaction: there are powerful inertial forces in American political life, and they can work to preserve the liberal legacies of periods of reform ferment in less propitious times just as much as they constrain innovation. Initially bold departures in policy become embedded in the fabric of American politics, acquire a constituency back home and supporting lobbies in Washington, and become, if not impregnable, then at least firmly resistant to assault. Conservative opponents can turn with surprising speed into conservative champions.

Although part of the appeal of ESEA resided in the fact that it required little of the states, in other respects the federal role in education became much more assertive and intrusive during the Nixon-Ford years. The engine for this development was civil rights enforcement, and the story begins with the passage of the Civil Rights Act of 1964, Title VI of which forbade discrimination on grounds of "race, color, or national origin" by any recipient of federal funds. Washington was permitted to cut off funds to those who transgressed, and that became a potentially powerful vehicle for attacking racial discrimination in schools when Congress enacted ESEA the following year. The Johnson administration enforced Title VI with determination, despite a clamor of protest from the South, and Nixon was elected in part because white southerners expected him to ease the pressure. Yet even though Nixon duly tried to meet those expectations, it was during the Nixon-Ford presidency that Title VI became a vehicle for reconfiguring the broader federal-state relationship in elementary and secondary education. In 1970, civil rights officials in the Department of Health, Education, and Welfare (HEW) declared that Title VI prohibited discrimination against "language-minorities": school districts must take special measures to help children with limited English proficiency or risk losing federal dollars. And by the time that Ford left office, Congress had charged these same officials with policing discrimination against women, the aged, and Americans with disabilities.

Chapters 5 through 8, in Part II, consider the changes in American government that allowed this more assertive federal role to develop. In part, it is concerned with the way that southern massive resistance to desegregation undermined the principle of "states' rights," legitimizing projections of federal authority that would have been unthinkable in earlier years. Many conservatives voted for the Civil Rights Act of 1964, their worries about big government trumped by the moral force of the African American freedom struggle. And during the 1970s they would support the rights claims of other minority groups, whose representatives often strove to present their plight as being in some way analogous to the black case.

The main focus in this book is not on the power of ideas per se, however, but rather on the institutional changes in American government that accompanied the civil rights revolution. One obvious change was divided government: although Republicans dominated the White House after 1968, the Democrats continued to dominate Congress. The most striking feature of education reform politics during the 1970s, though, was its comparative detachment from the world of electoral politics. The highly intrusive Education for All Handicapped Children Act of 1975, for example, was achieved through the actions of a congeries of unelected political actors: federal district judges, public interest law firms, antipoverty lawyers, congressional subcommittee staffers, foundation executives, career civil servants, and interest group lobbyists. These actors also played a decisive role in the other cases explored here: bilingual education and school finance reform. By comparison, the role of presidents and legislators in these reform causes was limited.

Political scientists have long been familiar with the institutional changes in the American political system that allowed the banner of liberal reform, though assailed, to remain aloft during an era of rising disillusionment with government. Some have gone so far as to argue that a "new American political system" came into being during the late 1960s and 1970s.[1] Among its characteristics, they have said, were divided government, a proliferation of "public interest" and minority-oriented pressure groups, a marked tendency on the part of federal judges and administrators to endorse the constitutional and statutory claims of such groups, a decentralization of power within Congress, a new relationship between the federal government and the states, and a tremendous increase in the amount and intrusiveness of federal regulation.

With the outstanding exception of Hugh Davis Graham, historians of recent American politics have been slow to reflect on the way that these institutional changes complicated the task of those who sought to reverse the policy trajectory of the 1960s.[2] Instead, they have frequently assumed that the next third of a century was marked by a sustained and largely successful conservative reaction against liberalism. Synthetic overviews of the period bear titles such as *America's Right Turn, Right Turn,* and *The World Turned Right Side Up*.[3] And works on particular topics feature subtitles such as *Race in the Conservative Counter-Revolution, From the War on Poverty to the War on Welfare, The Rise of Modern American Conservatism,* and *The Transformation and Decline of Great Society Liberalism*.[4]

Perhaps that emphasis reflects the fact that historians of the United States tend to think of "progressive" political change as arising either out of pressure from bottom-up social movements (the civil rights movement being the paradigmatic example) or through strong presidential leadership (ESEA, Medicare).[5] Those dynamics of reform were comparatively weak after 1970, whereas many of the other political indicators that historians tend to emphasize (the electoral fortunes of the two major parties, presidential agendas, political rhetoric, opinion poll data) suggested that the nation was in the throes of a sustained reaction against liberalism.

Such a reaction *did* take place, and it would be foolish to claim that the liberal impulse was gaining in strength. Still, the case of education politics suggests the difficulty of asserting that these were decades of triumph for the antigovernment right.[6] The limits to its success are illustrated by the ease with which supporters of federal aid, including many conservatives, rebuffed the intended Reagan Revolution in education during the early 1980s. Coming into office when public dissatisfaction with liberalism and government was at its zenith, Ronald Reagan pledged to abolish the newly created federal Department of Education (ED), slash federal spending, and replace the

Great Society's panoply of "categorical" programs for specific purposes with a no-strings-attached block grant to the states.

Reagan enjoyed some success with the second and third of these objectives in 1981, when his political standing was enormous, but during the rest of his presidency his achievements were steadily eroded, until by the time that he left office the status quo ante had been almost fully restored. As for the first objective, the abolition of ED, that got nowhere, even though Reagan's predecessor, Jimmy Carter, had struggled mightily to secure its creation just three years previously. By the end of Reagan's first term, when this book ends, any prospect that the federal role in education might diminish had entirely disappeared. More than that, the Reagan administration had issued *A Nation at Risk*, a government report on the condition of American schooling that catapulted education near to the top of the national political agenda, helping to pave the way for a further extension of the federal role in the nation's school districts.

Still in the future at the point where this book ends lay the No Child Left Behind Act of 2002 (NCLB). Any book about the federal politics of education since the 1960s is, inescapably, written in the shadow of this dramatic measure, which requires states to ensure that *all* public school children achieve competency in English, math, and science by the year 2014 and threatens schools that fail to make "adequate yearly progress" toward these goals with tough sanctions. What is the relationship between NCLB and the events described in the present book? The fact that so prescriptive a measure was sponsored by President George W. Bush, a Republican, and enacted by a GOP-dominated Congress illustrated anew that conservatives had traveled a long way since the enactment of ESEA, decisively abandoning the small government faith of their forefathers. The events described in this book afford some insights into how that happened. At the same time, as is discussed in the Conclusion, NCLB was primarily a product of events in American politics since the mid-1980s, most especially during the presidency of Bill Clinton. The purpose of this book, in other words, is not to explain NCLB but rather to illuminate the long shadow that the Great Society years continued to cast over American politics during the 1970s and 1980s.

By way of further disclaimer, this book does not purport to provide a general or comprehensive history of federal education policy between the 1960s and the Reagan presidency. Instead, its goal is more specific: to explain why the federal role in schools continued to expand after Lyndon Johnson left the White House, despite the political reaction against the Great Society, and even though four of his five immediate successors were Republicans, while the fifth—Jimmy Carter—was a "post–New Deal" Democrat.[7] Although the approach is broadly chronological, the book comprises a set of case studies, rather than a blow-by-blow narrative, with the cases selected because they illuminate the broader institutional character of American political development particularly well.[8] My particular concern is with the dynamics of policy innovation, and with the process whereby initially bold departures in policy became embedded in the fabric of American politics, irrespective of who occupied the White House. The book is much less concerned with policy implementation, or with program evaluation, even if much of the analysis is predicated on the assumption that compensatory education programs such as Title I have fallen short of the buoyant expectations of the mid-1960s.[9]

The Passage and Consolidation of the Elementary and Secondary Education Act

Race, Religion, and Reds

Numerous scholars have detailed the three or four factors that regularly combined to kill seemingly promising federal aid to education bills during the first two post–World War II decades, and there is little disagreement among them.[1] As the contemporary quip went, when it came to the *politics* of education, the "three Rs" were Race, Religion, and Reds. There were comparatively few American politicians who opposed federal aid in *any* form, but the support of most was constrained by one or more of those combustible factors. In the case of religion, some—advocates of strict church-state separation, public school interests, and anti-Catholic nativists—opposed aid to parochial schools in any form, while others—Catholic schools and bishops, legislators with large Catholic constituencies—insisted on "parochaid." Msgr. Francis Hurley of the National Catholic Welfare Conference (NCWC) summarized the resultant stalemate: "Better no federal aid than that parochial schools be included, said one faction. Better no federal aid than that parochial schools be excluded, said another faction." Disputes between them played the largest role in defeating general aid during the Truman and Kennedy administrations.

As for the case of race, supporters of African American civil rights were reluctant to endorse general aid bills that benefited segregated school districts, and during the Eisenhower presidency, Rep. Adam Clayton Powell, a

Democrat from Harlem, regularly added an amendment to school aid measures denying federal funds to segregated school systems. But even comparatively liberal southerners were unable to support measures containing the Powell amendment, even though it was poor southern districts that stood to gain the most from federal aid in financial terms. That dispute heated up dramatically after the *Brown v. Board of Education* decision of 1954, and it played the leading role in defeating the school construction aid bills of the Eisenhower era, especially in 1957 and 1960, when there had seemed to be a real prospect of success.[3]

The other "R," Reds, was shorthand for the concerns about federal control.[4] Of the three Rs, it is the one that has tended to receive least attention in historical accounts of the long travail of federal aid. That is justifiable, as it was the other two that contributed most dramatically to successive legislative failures. If there was any single factor that was salient in every single battle and that allowed congressional majorities to form against general aid, however, it was the opposition of antistatist conservatives to the specter of federal intrusion and to federal taxation in support of an assumed state function. The Johnson administration's continuing concern about its force—even in 1965, when conservatism was at a low ebb—was evident from the painstaking fealty that ESEA's legislative draftsmen paid to the doctrine of local control. From a post–No Child Left Behind vantage point, that is, in a policy world where most conservatives have embraced strong federal mandates on the states, the strength of localism during this earlier period stands out.

Even at the time, it stood out. After all, in so many other policy areas where the states had traditionally been dominant, the successive political earthquakes of the Great Depression, World War II, and the Cold War had powerfully increased the federal presence.[5] In the area of elementary and secondary education, however, the story was different. Until 1965, for example, the National School Boards Association (NSBA) opposed general aid. Even though many districts—buffeted by rising salaries, schoolroom shortages, and the growing federal taxation burden—were hard pressed to finance their schools, the local worthies who dominated these boards prized local control and feared federal encroachment.[6] As Thomas Shannon, a subsequent executive director of the association, has noted, "school board members were skeptical that the federal government would provide the funds and then passively back off when decisions about actual programming would have to be made. They viewed federal guidelines, policies, rules and regulations, conditions, and suggested operating approaches . . . as nothing short of preemption of local authority and a subversion of the American institution of local representative governance of the schools." At its 1962 delegate assembly, the NSBA voted by a more than two-thirds majority to oppose any general federal aid legislation. Its president insisted that "our task is not to stop or obstruct the splendid efforts to provide excellence in education." The key to success, though, lay not in federal aid but "in re-awakening our local communities to the importance of the principle of self-autonomy."[7]

localism

Perhaps the very fact that the federal role had expanded in so many other areas increased the determination of school board members to preserve this last remaining bastion of traditional American federalism. At a time when the NSBA lacked even a branch office in Washington, the main pressure group putting forward this line was the United States Chamber of Commerce (many of whose members served on school boards).[8] Stewart McClure, a liberal Senate staffer from this period, recalls with frustration an attitude that to him seemed almost inexplicable:

> They clung on to some mythical constitutional principle: the last thing that could happen in the United States was for the federal hand to be laid on local education, which belongs to the hands of the school boards and local council of education or whatever they're called—which, of course, are all controlled by the Chamber of Commerce. . . . Now what all this was supposed to prevent or forestall I never could figure out, but it was a religious faith. They'd get white and scream and wave their hands in the air about the *horrible* prospects of this vicious, cold hand of federal bureaucracy being laid upon these pristine, splendid local schools that knew better than anyone what needed to be done, and so forth and so forth. . . . I don't know, it's a real mythology, but it was real and senators and congressmen had to deal with it.[9]

That basic impulse, together with a desire to rein in federal spending, complicated President Eisenhower's approach to the question of school construction aid, the federal aid issue that dominated his years in office, at least until the Soviet Union sent its Sputnik satellite into orbit around the earth in 1957, sparking a different set of concerns. On the one hand, he recognized that the Depression and World War II had delayed needed construction projects and that the efforts of school districts to make good that backlog were being immensely complicated by enrollments that were increasing by one million children each year. Because of those circumstances, he sup-

| Sputnik came change)

ported a modest five-year program of federal construction aid. On the other hand, he did not push very hard for its passage, and he was blamed by Democrats for the failure of three promising construction bills in the mid-1950s.

They had a point but were probably wrong to ascribe Eisenhower's behavior to a purportedly casual, disengaged style of leadership. More likely, Eisenhower—like leading congressional Republicans such as Charles Halleck of Illinois, the House minority leader, and Jeffersonian Democrats such as Howard Smith of Virginia, who chaired the House Rules Committee—deprecated the growth of federal power and federal spending.[10] At press conferences, Eisenhower told reporters: "I don't believe in the general theory of Federal Government supporting education throughout our country all the time." He *could* support emergency aid for a finite period of time, but when the emergency had passed, "then [we should] turn the whole thing back to the States, and have nothing more to do with it."[11] In private, he worried about even this limited aid, seeing it as being part of "a world trend toward socialism." Maybe, though, he mused, "we cannot get out of it. Perhaps we are like the armed guard with rusty armor and a broken sword, standing at the bridge and trying to stop progress."[12]

When the House failed by a five-vote margin to pass construction aid in 1957, it seemed clear that Eisenhower could easily have forced it through. Challenged on this point, he explained that this was not his style and claimed not to have been made aware of the unusual parliamentary maneuver by Halleck and Smith that had precipitated the defeat. But he went on, in characteristically prolix style, to make clear that he was not entirely unhappy about the outcome:

> If you try to make every State believe that they are getting something for nothing out of such a bill, then I would doubt your ability to terminate the operation of the bill at the end of the five-year period. At least, I would be fearful, and certainly at the end of that time I am not going to be around to veto any extension of the thing. . . . I am getting to the point where I can't be too enthusiastic about something that I think is likely to fasten a sort of an albatross, *another one*, around the neck of the Federal Government—I don't believe it should be done.[13]

Two months later, however, Sputnik went into orbit, and supporters of federal aid to education were able to harness national alarm about this development to their cause. October 1957 was not the first time that Cold War concerns had permeated the debate about American education. Hitherto, though, one of its main effects had been to heighten the desire of some "schoolmen" (the contemporary term) to preserve decentralized arrangements that seemed to them to exemplify all that was best in American democracy. Now, its main effect was to legitimize an expansion in the federal role. Why had the Soviet Union succeeded with Sputnik, whereas the American Vanguard rocket had been a flop? Why was the United States not producing engineers and mathematicians capable of sending a satellite into orbit around the earth?

[margin note: global competition]

Stated thus, there was a compelling conservative rationale for federal school aid. Many conservatives had been fretting for a while about the baneful spread of Progressive methods of teaching: child-centered learning, for example, and the idea of the comprehensive high school.[14] Now, following Sputnik, there was a national security dimension to these concerns: alleged deficiencies in the teaching of science, mathematics, and foreign languages were placing the survival of the free world in jeopardy. Deftly exploiting these concerns, supporters of federal aid wrapped their proposal in the flag and gave it the title National Defense Education Act (NDEA).

[margin note: exploitation of national alarm]

National Defense Education Act

The idea that the federal government should work to stimulate better teaching in academic subjects with particular pertinence to national security preceded Sputnik; indeed, the idea may have come from Elliot Richardson, a patrician, moderate Republican from Massachusetts whose long career of federal public service began in the mid-1950s, when Eisenhower made him an assistant secretary at the Department of Health, Education, and Welfare (HEW).[15] But it was Sputnik that led the issue to catch fire, enabling Democrats on the Hill to transform Richardson's very modest proposal into a substantial vehicle for federal aid. The leading role was played by two powerful Alabamians: Senator Lister Hill, chair of the Labor and Public Welfare Committee, and Rep. Carl Elliott, who chaired the House education subcommittee. Each was a long-time passionate supporter of federal aid whose ardor had been increasingly blunted during the 1950s by the racial question: neither could support any aid measure that seemed likely to hasten the demise of segregation. To them, and to other progressive southerners, NDEA was manna from heaven, the kind of education measure that they could defend back home on Cold War grounds without invoking *Brown*.[16]

[margin note: Sputnik trumps racial issues]

The chief clerk to Hill's committee, Stewart McClure, recalls the way that supporters of NDEA (he claims credit for the title) wrongfooted conservatives by hearing testimony from "the cream of the brains of this country," including such noted Cold War figures as Admiral Hyman Rickover and physicist Edward Teller.

> When we went on the floor we could say, "Well, now, does the senator mean that he challenges the distinguished leader of the National Council on Science, Detlev Bronk, who says. . . ." We hammered them into the ground. And, of course, if anybody brought up socialism or something like that, the dreadful specter of socialism, we had Edward Teller and the Hydrogen Bomb to clobber them with! Well, hearings . . . really can shape the form of anything. You get the right witnesses and ask the right questions and they give the right answers, your opposition is slaughtered before they can open their trap. That's one of the tactical secrets of functioning on this Hill. Well, I really pulled together an incredible array of talent, of not only Ph.D.'s but Nobel Prize winners and so forth. And, of course, the press was paying a great deal of attention to this. We were getting headlines every day, and all of that has an impact, too.[17]

How the "Hill" works... *Political games*

NDEA allotted federal money for a number of ostensibly Cold War–related purposes: loans to college scholarship funds for students intending to teach in elementary or secondary schools or with defense-related specialties; graduate fellowships for students interested in college teaching; seed money to induce states to establish programs for testing, guidance, and counseling in secondary schools; money to allow colleges to increase provision for advanced foreign language training. Title III, meanwhile, authorized the expenditure of $75 million per year for the purchase of equipment that would enhance the teaching of science, mathematics, and foreign languages.

The specific content of NDEA, as opposed to its overall packaging, owed much to interest group pressures. Although federal aid on a large scale did not yet exist, where it had gotten underway the relevant interests had been swift to exploit their opening, building useful clientele relationships with the relevant staff and committee members in a hierarchical, committee-dominated Congress. Their names rarely appeared in the papers, but lobbyists such as Russell Thackery (land-grant colleges), Oscar Rose (impact aid), Germaine Krettek (public libraries), and William Geer and Elizabeth Boggs (handicapped children) had become familiar figures on Capitol Hill some years before ESEA transformed the politics of education. While the much larger National Education Association (NEA) enjoyed only indifferent success, these smaller groups fared quite well, by being realistic in their goals and by cultivating connections with the sometimes relatively small number of key legislators and staffers who controlled the fate of their programs.

In the case of NDEA, lobbyists representing the major universities, guidance counselors, student aid advocates, and teachers of science, math, and modern languages seized their opportunity and swarmed over the Hill, as soon as the broad purposes of the bill had been adumbrated by Richardson, Hill, and Elliott. Although it was only a small program, the role played by lobbyists is particularly well illustrated by Title III, which was the brainchild of Donald (Don) White, executive vice president of the National Audio Visual Association (NAVA). This trade group represented manufacturers and distributors of such technologies as television, film, slide and overhead projectors, and language laboratory equipment. White, then in his early forties, had come to Washington the previous year, at a time when the potential educational market for these educational tools was vast but when—as he recalls—"there was virtually no money available for their purchase."[18] With the federal role increasing in so many other areas of national life, White went to work on the Hill, getting to know the legislative process and becoming friendly with some of the key players in the small world of education politics, such as Senator Norris Cotton of New Hampshire, an influential Republican on the Appropriations subcommittee that handled HEW funds; Adam Clayton Powell, who was the number two Democrat on the House Education and Labor Committee; Jack Forsythe, the top Democratic staffer on Lister Hill's committee; and Stewart McClure.[19] It helped, White thinks, that he was from Georgia; he got on well with the senior southerners who dominated the key committees and especially well with their staff members, who took him under their wing and taught him some of the tricks of the trade.[20]

By the time that NDEA came before Congress, White was well established and in a good position to take advantage of Sputnik. There had been no audiovisual equipment title in the original bill, but White managed to change that, drafting a form of words and having them inserted in the Senate bill by his contacts on the committee staff. For the industry he represented, it was an important beginning: national spending on audiovisual equipment doubled during the first year of Title III. But it was only the start of what was to be an extraordinarily successful career on the Hill for White, facilitated by a combination of tactical acumen, good connections, and deep pockets (many legislators expected to be entertained by lobbyists, and appreciative NAVA members ensured that White was able to satisfy those expectations).[21] Arrangements for purchasing audiovisual equipment were included not just in NDEA but in each of the other three big education measures of the next decade or so: the higher education acts of 1963 and 1965 and ESEA.

NDEA was, as *Congressional Quarterly* later noted, "by far the largest federal commitment to the national general educational level" in history, authorizing expenditures of over $1 billion.[22] Eisenhower, who viewed the measure with apprehension, nevertheless had no option but to sign it. He told reporters that he approved of its core objective "to inspire the people who have normally been responsible for [the] educational process to do better." But he was also worried: "If you try to take it in such a sweeping way that the whole country is looking merely to the Federal Government to do this now for the coming years, I think we have lost a very great and vital feature of our whole free system. Now, that is exactly what I think." In signing it into law, he hoped that NDEA did not represent a fundamental change of direction: "Much remains to be done to bring American education to levels consistent with the needs of our society. The Federal Government having done its share, the people of the country, working through their local and State governments and through private agencies, must now redouble their efforts toward this end."[23]

But it did...

Eisenhower's sense that the nation might be crossing some kind of Rubicon in passing NDEA looks well founded in retrospect. Although it was presented as an emergency measure, due to expire in the early 1960s, it was renewed during the Kennedy administration in a considerably expanded form. Still, if most conservatives were prepared to go along with narrowly targeted categorical aid (aid to public libraries and to the handicapped each won bipartisan backing), they remained opposed to general aid. The thinking here was that general aid was unconstitutional and that it was likely to result in federal control. Vice President Richard Nixon, for example, delivered a tie-breaking vote against the 1960 general aid bill, on the grounds that some of the funds would go for teacher salaries, opening up the possibility of federal control over who taught and what was taught.[24]

issue w/ constitutionality

That vote concerned a technical amendment, and the bill went on to clear the Senate. A similar measure passed the House, too, raising the expectations of supporters of federal aid to new heights. However, those expectations were dashed again by the wiliness of Howard Smith, whose Rules Committee declined to send the House version to conference. Parliamentary efforts to force it on to the floor failed. On the one hand, it was enormously frustrating to have come so close to victory, only to fall at the last hurdle. On the other hand, this was the first time ever that the House and Senate had passed a general aid bill in the same year, and that augured well for the future, provided that a desegregation amendment could be avoided—it was the inclusion of the Powell amendment that led Smith's committee to block the 1960 bill—or, alternatively, that the Rules Committee could somehow be brought to heel. The momentum for federal aid increased further during the 1960 presidential campaign, during which John F. Kennedy and Lyndon Johnson repeatedly pilloried Nixon for having voted against general aid.[25] In comparison to previous elections, the education issue enjoyed an unusually high profile, and when Kennedy entered office in 1961 he listed federal aid to schools as one of his five top domestic priorities. One month into his presidency, he unveiled a $2.3 billion, three-year proposal for construction aid and teachers' salaries.

*[margin note: *60's — education became a top issue]*

Education and the Kennedy Presidency

By this time, prospects seemed brighter still, for the new administration and House Speaker Sam Rayburn had engineered an enlargement of the Rules Committee that appeared to leave it with a pro-aid majority. But those expectations rapidly turned to frustration, as the religious issue that had defeated federal aid in 1949 came roaring back, displacing race as the most treacherous obstacle. (Powell, the new chairman of the House Education and Labor Committee, was persuaded not to introduce his amendment during the Kennedy years.) The crucial factor was Kennedy's Catholicism, which compelled him to go to unusual lengths to oppose parochial aid. Unveiling his bill, he told Congress that "in accordance with the clear prohibition of the Constitution, no elementary and secondary school funds are allocated for constructing church schools or paying church school teachers' salaries."[26] This stance provoked an angry response from Archbishop Karl Alter of Cincinnati, speaking on behalf of the Catholic bishops. They felt that to speak of a "clear prohibition" of parochial aid went much farther than the courts had done and that Kennedy had essentially "slammed the door on us."[27] Kennedy's statement and Alter's response doomed the 1961 general aid proposal to failure. As NCWC's Msgr. Hurley recalled in 1965, when he was trying to ensure that ESEA did not go the same way, "a church-state explosion reverberated across the entire country."[28]

Frustratingly, it was in the Rules Committee—again—that the bill ran aground, as conservatives who opposed general aid in any form allied with two northern Catholic Democrats who opposed the exclusion of parochial schools. One was the future speaker, Thomas P. O'Neill of Massachusetts, who represented Kennedy's old House seat and was a dependable party man

*[margin note: *issue of parochial schools + aid (church + state)]*

on most questions. The other was James Delaney, whose constituency was the New York borough of Queens but who was thought within the administration to owe his primary allegiance to his archbishop, Francis Cardinal Spellman.[29]

The White House had badly mishandled the bill, and the danger was that the consequence might be even deeper antagonism between supporters and opponents of parochial aid.[30] It was not easy to see how that problem could be circumvented, given that NEA, on one side of the divide, and NCWC, on the other, each seemed to have the power to kill any general aid proposal. That impression deepened the following year, when the NEA was blamed for torpedoing a higher education bill whose passage had seemed certain, on the grounds that it permitted limited aid to Catholic colleges and universities. This was disheartening, given that aid to Catholic higher education institutions had a number of precedents, including NDEA and the GI Bill and had not been thought to be especially controversial.

By the autumn of 1962, the Kennedy administration's education program lay in ruins. Adding to the sense of disarray was the resignation of the HEW secretary, Abraham Ribicoff, who left to run for the Senate, and the virtually simultaneous departure of Sterling McMurrin, the commissioner of education. Just at this time, political scientists Frank Munger and Richard Fenno published *National Politics and Federal Aid to Education*, which reviewed the legislative record of the previous decade and a half and asked "whether the effort to build consensus for federal aid has made any headway whatsoever."[31] As Hugh Davis Graham put it in his classic historical account, *The Uncertain Triumph*, "to propose federal 'intrusion' into the sanctity of the state-local-private preserve of education was to stride boldly into a uniquely dangerous political mine field that pitted Democrat against Republican, liberal against conservative, Catholic against Protestant and Jew, federal power against states rights, white against black, and rich constituency against poor in mercurial cross-cutting alliances." The issues of federal control and separation of church and state, in particular, "seemed fiendishly designed to raise one another, and then to cancel one another out."[32]

Waking Up the Office of Education: Francis Keppel Becomes Commissioner

In retrospect, though, 1962 was a turning point in the struggle for federal aid. The most important development was the appointment of Francis Keppel to be U.S. commissioner of education. Keppel was an influential educator: for fifteen years he had headed the Harvard Graduate School of Education. He was well connected in other ways, too. His father, Frederick, had been dean of Columbia College and then president of the Carnegie Corporation. (In that capacity, he had commissioned Gunnar Myrdal's celebrated report on race relations, *The American Dilemma*.) His acquaintance Henry James had observed that the elder Keppel "possessed a gift for getting quickly to the nub of a matter. His genius was . . . cooperative. He lubricated, and facilitated, and fostered."[33] The same could be said of the son, and this fact was to have an important bearing on the fight for federal education aid.

Keppel was appointed to the Harvard position at the age of thirty-two, at the personal request of the university's president, James B. Conant, returning to the university where he had once been a classmate of John Kennedy's elder brother, Joe, and had gotten to know the family slightly. When Keppel and John Kennedy first met during his presidency, Kennedy grinned, and asked Keppel if he was not the person who "used to run against Joe for Harvard offices?" When Keppel acknowledged the fact, Kennedy said "didn't he beat you?" to which Keppel replied "yes, Sir."[34] Swearing him in at the end of 1962, Kennedy declared: "No free society can possibly survive unless it has an educated citizenry . . . we are particularly fortunate to have Mr. Keppel give leadership to this cause." Keppel, contemplating this daunting assignment, joked to the audience of journalists and educators: "This ought to be fun."[35]

Taking up the Office of Education (OE) position, Keppel told his new colleagues that he was decidedly an administrator, rather than an academic (McMurrin had been a professor of philosophy at the University of Utah). "I should prefer to be called *Mr.*," he told them, "for the simple reason that I have no doctorate."[36] Perhaps that sounded like modesty, but in truth Keppel was sending OE staff a signal that his appointment represented a break with the past. Traditionally, the office had been a sleepy backwater, churning out statistics, enjoying collegial relations with the major education interest groups, having very few programmatic responsibilities, and possessing— in Keppel's jaundiced view—something of the atmosphere of a second-tier school of education. McMurrin's approach to education, he considered, had been to "sit back and think high thoughts in the Office of Education."[37] Such was McMurrin's consequent anonymity that when his departure was announced in the press, President Kennedy expressed surprise, exclaiming to White House aide McGeorge Bundy: "What's going on! I never heard of the fellow."[38] His departure, coming as it did shortly after the failure of the higher education bill, resulted, Keppel later noted, in much "stuff in the press about how no man in his right mind would take the job."[39] Perhaps he felt the same way when, shortly after having accepted the job, he was sitting in his office and received a personal call from the president. This was apparently so unprecedented—Keppel guesses that "the President hadn't called since before Franklin Roosevelt"—that Kennedy "damn near frightened the office to death."[40]

As the appointment of Keppel and that phone call indicated, Kennedy was looking for a new approach to the politics of education. From the new commissioner's perspective, it seemed that "this administration hadn't passed a damn thing" and that "Mr. Kennedy wanted to get *something* on the books."[41] The main White House man on education policy, Theodore Sorensen, was of course especially worried about the religious issue, which—naively, one might think—had caught the White House by surprise the previous year.[42] After the failure of the higher education bill and with a new team at the head of both OE and HEW, he pondered possible ways through the morass.[43] On the one hand, as Sorensen told an audience at Columbia University in the fall of 1962, it was peculiarly difficult for the nation's first Catholic president to embrace aid to parochial schools. On the other hand, as he told Keppel, early on in their relationship, it was imperative that the administration should begin a behind-the-scenes dialogue with the Catholic bishops and monsignors, hopefully forging a relationship of trust with some of the more influential ones and gaining a better sense of their minimum demands. Perhaps he might be able to persuade the NCWC to accept something short of absolute equality of treatment, which had been the group's demand ever since World War II. With that in mind, Keppel recalls that "one of the first things Ted Sorensen did was to take me off to see the local Bishop."[44]

Keppel set about this diplomatic assignment with characteristic energy, deploying to the full those inherited gifts of tact, patience, and synthesis. It is doubtful that he would have had much prospect of success, however, had it not been for the dramatic changes that were occurring within the Roman Catholic Church between 1962 and 1965. These were the years of the Second Vatican Council, convened by Pope John XXIII in October 1962 to consider the relationship between the church and the modern world and continued by his successor, Paul VI. American bishops and theologians played a prominent role in the council's deliberations, which were characterized above all by a new ecumenicism.[45]

In this environment, the younger staff at NCWC, in particular, were more open to Keppel's overtures than they would otherwise have been.

In addition, Keppel surmises that they were pleased to receive *any* attention from OE, which had never had "a direct communications line with the Catholic Church." For his part, Keppel found the new monsignor in NCWC's Washington office, Father Francis T. Hurley, to be "charming" and developed a good rapport both with him and with the council's chief lawyer/lobbyist, Robert Consedine.[46]

The second diplomatic task facing Keppel was at least as formidable: to get education interest groups that viewed each other with heightened distrust following the failure of the higher education bill to talk to one another. It was not just that the NEA and the NCWC opposed one another. In addition, the American Council on Education (the principal higher education lobby group) blamed NEA for having sunk its bill, creating an obvious danger that it would retaliate in kind when the administration introduced a new measure for schools. Finally, some of these groups were strongly divided internally.[47]

[handwritten margin note: 2nd - Mediate Special interest groups]

Keppel's first move in trying to heal these wounds came at his swearing-in ceremony. So angry was Kennedy at the NEA's role in defeating the higher education bill that he adamantly refused to allow its executive secretary, William Carr, to attend. Indeed, he was initially unwilling for *anyone* from NEA to come along, eventually allowing its president-elect, Robert Wyatt, to participate only on the grounds that he was a loyal Indiana Democrat.[48] The next task was to reconcile Carr with the head of the higher education lobby. Keppel claims to have facilitated this rapprochement:

> The higher education fellows were so mad at the NEA fellows they wouldn't speak to them. In fact, I can recall negotiating a private meeting between Mr. Logan Wilson representing the higher education interests, and William Carr. . . . These two men had worked with each other for probably five or ten years [but] were so cross at each other in early 1963 that I personally had to invite them to dinner, and they didn't dare turn me down. This was literally the case.[49]

NEA's role in the defeat of the higher education bill had been a bad error, creating immense ill will against it on the part of the White House and other education groups. Looking back, though, it was also an error that helped to pave the way for the successful federal aid struggle of 1965. In the second big turning point of 1962 (the first being Keppel's appointment), reform elements within NEA started to challenge Carr's dogmatic insistence on "general aid or nothing" and his equally adamant refusal to consider parochial aid in any form. If the NEA persisted with this line, these elements noted, the outcome would always be no federal aid at all. With the same argument gaining ground in NCWC following its implication in the defeat of the 1961 education bill, an opportunity existed for the Kennedy administration. Here is how Keppel reconstructs his approach:

> The problem was not so much to get the lobbyists to agree on supporting anything as to agree on not killing each other's interests. The first task was to try to get the lobbyists—Catholic, NEA, American Council on Education, land grant college, and all the others[—]to shut up about things they didn't like and only talk about things they did like. . . . So we tried to build that kind of a lobbying situation, the most delicate part of it being the relations between the higher education world and the elementary, secondary world on the one side, and the Catholics and everybody else as another cut-across.[50]

With this in mind, the administration decided to abandon the general aid approach that had been pursued in 1961, in favor of a categorical, omnibus bill that contained something for every constituency. And in order to make it seem less daring, Keppel and Sorensen harnessed the new proposals to existing programs that were already established and popular. Accordingly, Kennedy's fourteen-point 1963 education package included elementary and secondary aid, higher education, libraries, aid to the handicapped, and the renewal of NDEA, vocational education, and impact aid, all in the same bill.[51]

The strategy did not work: as soon as the bill got into Powell's Education and Labor Committee, he split it into its component parts and sent each element to the relevant subcommittee. This was a deft move by Powell in terms of the internal politics of his committee, giving each of his senior colleagues a piece of the action.[52] But it doomed elementary and secondary aid, the most controversial aspect of the omnibus bill. Graham notes, however, that the politics of education on Capitol Hill were much less acrid in 1963 than they had been the previous year.[53] Predictably, impact aid, vocational aid, and NDEA extension went through (shortly after Kennedy's assassination). Less predictably, so did higher education, helped by the self-restraint exercised by NCWC and NEA. The Catholic Conference's Msgr. Hurley recalls having been at the end of a White House receiving line in 1963, and President Kennedy's having told him that "we have to get the higher education bill through. We've got to keep the Bishops quiet." To that, Hurley replied: "You notice they haven't spoken yet?" and they kept their silence.[54] At the same time, Keppel notes, "the NEA, bless its beads, kept its word."

Even though the higher bill was going through, they didn't shoot it down because of anger that it wasn't an "El-High" bill. They kept their word. So that when the following year came, after the tragic assassination, the higher education fellows kept their word and didn't shoot down the lower bill.[55]

Lyndon Johnson: The First Education President

Prospects for federal aid to elementary and secondary schools, already improving, were further enhanced when Lyndon Johnson became president. First, there was the strong emotional mood in the country following John Kennedy's assassination, including the sense that Congress should enact legislative monuments in his memory. In this climate, Johnson and his legislative liaison chief, Lawrence (Larry) O'Brien, were able to circumvent parliamentary blocking maneuvers by GOP minority leader Charles Halleck and force significantly broadened versions of vocational education and NDEA through Congress during the first three weeks after Dallas, together with higher education.[56] On the phone to Wayne Morse of Oregon, who chaired the Senate's education subcommittee, Johnson exulted that "you're going to have the best education year since the beginning of the Republic."[57]

Also, as even hostile biographers have been willing to concede, Johnson had an authentic and passionate faith in the power of education, rooted in his own youth, including most obviously his experiences as a schoolmaster in Cotulla, Texas, during the early years of the Great Depression. Paul Conkin refers to "his lifelong perception of education as the main pathway to opportunity, a theme rooted in his own experience and his earliest career choice."[58] In this, he differed from Kennedy, for whom education mattered as a political question, but—as with most domestic questions—had less visceral resonance.[59]

Finally, President Johnson approached the world of legislative politics with rare knowledge, zest, and skill. By contrast, his predecessor had not enjoyed cajoling legislators or plotting parliamentary strategy. Lawrence O'Brien, who was chief lobbyist for both, observed that "Jack Kennedy could not bring himself to strong-arm members of Congress to secure their vote."[60] When an interviewer asked Keppel about Kennedy's approach to the business of "getting hold of Congressmen and twisting arms," he responded: "well, he certainly didn't seem to like it," citing the case of Rep. Edith Green.[61]

Green, a former teacher and Oregon Education Association official, was an influential member of the House Education and Labor Committee. A strong supporter of federal aid to schools and a highly astute legislative tactician, she was nevertheless viewed with antagonism by fellow Democrats on her committee, for she had an abrasive, iconoclastic personality, tended to stand on principle rather than accept compromise, and maintained irritatingly close ties to prominent committee Republicans such as Albert Quie of Minnesota.[62] She was, however, a great admirer of John F. Kennedy, having headed his 1960 campaign in Oregon. Pondering how to reward her loyalty, Kennedy had considered nominating her to head HEW, but that idea went down very badly within the department, and he dropped it.[63] Thereafter, says Keppel, the president went out of his way to avoid contact with Green:

> Obviously, the President wanted to deal with her as little as possible. I remember at some meeting or other, the President turned and said, "Well, now [Wilbur] Cohen, you haven't succeeded with her, and Sorensen hasn't, Keppel is a new boy in town, and it's his turn." I got the sense that he was delighted that there was some new boy in town to take her on.[64]

According to Charles Radcliffe, GOP staff member on Education and Labor, and someone who enjoyed good relations with Green, this presidential attitude was unfortunate for the Democrats:

> She was a Kennedy loyalist to the core. I think if President Kennedy had picked up the phone and called her on occasion, rather than having one of his flunkies do it, he would have gotten good results. But unlike Johnson, he didn't seem to understand the Congress and its sensitivities.[65] *Kennedy vs. Johnson*

Johnson's approach was indeed quite different from that of his predecessor. As vice president, one of his great disappointments had been his *lack* of involvement in Capitol Hill politics. Having become minority leader of the Senate after only one term and then having wielded exceptional power as majority leader during the last six years of Eisenhower's presidency, he had hoped that his new role as presiding officer of the Senate would permit him to keep his office and retain power on the Hill.[66] Rebuffed on both counts, and feeling acutely his diminished stature, he tore eagerly into the task of coaxing Congress into action during the early part of his presidency.[67]

Despite this, Johnson and his aides recognized that passing a big federal aid to education bill remained a formidable task. During 1963, it had not been easy to persuade the NEA not to kick up a fuss about the higher education bill: angered that higher education and vocational education seemed to

have been emphasized at the expense of elementary and secondary schooling, they had seriously contemplated trying to torpedo the measure again.[68]
And any fond hope that ecumenicism and administration diplomacy had put
the religious issue to bed was extinguished by the legislative debate over the
War on Poverty the following spring, which featured an acrimonious fight
over parochial school aid.

Education and the War on Poverty

If any one legislative measure during Johnson's first year bore his distinctive stamp, then it was the War on Poverty. As one biographer has observed:
"Throughout his life, nothing in politics appealed more to him than mar-
rying his ambition to help for the poor."[69] Given his similar passion for education, the virtual absence of any reference to school aid in the Economic
Opportunity Act is striking. Certainly, there was a considerable rhetorical
emphasis on "turning tax-eaters into tax-payers," and education was presented as being the decisive weapon that would allow the antipoverty war to
be won. In programmatic terms, though, the main vehicle for boosting educational levels was to be New Deal–style work-study camps (the Job Corps)
rather than aid to schools. The explanation is not hard to find: Religion was
the most formidable of the three Rs, and in an election year, Johnson was not
prepared to risk another church-state storm by making a big push for federal aid to education. The only mention of school aid in the Economic Opportunity Act was discreet: inconspicuously tucked away in Title II, which
related to community action programs, was a reference to remedial instruction projects, to be administered by the local school district.

Although the reference was inconspicuous, it was sufficient to trigger yet
another church-state row, and at one time Johnson was concerned that it
might even sink the whole bill. The episode is worth recounting, in part because it reveals that Keppel's diplomatic overtures to NCWC and NEA had
yet to yield a tangible reward, in part because it is unusually well documented
in Johnson's recorded telephone conversations.[70]

Under this proposal, private and parochial schoolchildren were among
those eligible to enroll in remedial education programs, provided that the
funds were administered by a public educational agency. It was hoped that
this arrangement would pass constitutional muster on child-benefit grounds,
that is, because federal funds benefited the child rather than a religious institution. When the House Education and Labor Committee began hearings
on the Economic Opportunity Act, however, Catholic groups complained
of discrimination and demanded direct aid. The spokesman for this view on

the committee was Hugh Carey, a Catholic, liberal Democrat from Brooklyn who, like James Delaney, was considered to be close to Cardinal Spellman, despite the latter's conservatism.[71]

Quite apart from wishing to be helpful to Spellman, Carey needed the issue for electoral reasons. He had won his Brooklyn district in 1960 against the odds (his constituents voted for Nixon rather than Kennedy), had barely clung to it two years later, and was worried in the spring of 1964 not only by the prospect of another close fight in the fall but also by an even more imminent primary contest. What made the situation worse was mounting speculation in New York that the federal government was on the point of closing down the Brooklyn Navy Yard. With his primary opponent using that issue against him, he feared for his political future and called Johnson to explain his "political facts of life." He told the president that he "got elected in my district because I went in and made it an issue that I was going to do something for the kids in all the schools," including those that attended parochial school. Although he appreciated that the issue was a sensitive one, Carey argued that Johnson could afford to amend the bill to give equitable treatment to these schools. A recent poll, he claimed, revealed a "tremendous shift" in favor of parochial aid.[72]

Johnson tried to reassure him that Sargent Shriver—the Catholic whom he had chosen to run the War on Poverty—was strongly opposed to religious discrimination but was otherwise noncommittal. Later that day, though, when Johnson spoke to O'Brien, he expressed alarm that Carey should "want to bring in this Cardinal Spellman question," complaining that "he's gonna mess me all up in the parochial poverty fight."[73] His preferred solution was to leave the bill unchanged while "tucking away" language in the House report that gave Shriver the administrative discretion that he needed in order to ensure equitable aid to parochial schools.[74] But Carey was not buying that approach, and as he played the issue for all it was worth, NEA inevitably got involved on the other side, threatening to derail the Economic Opportunity Act if it were amended to include direct aid.[75] If such language were *not* included, though, the bill might well fall in Rules, where Tip O'Neill and James Delaney were each likely to side with Carey.[76]

Johnson's anxiety peaked after a lunch-time meeting with the Texas congressional delegation.[77] In conversations with Shriver and O'Brien, he remarked that parochial aid had been the first issue that they wanted to talk about, that they had been "frothing mad," and that "in Al Smith's day you never heard anything so vicious." To amend the bill in this context would be fatal, he felt: "You're just gonna have a war if you try to rewrite the bill we sent up there. They're gonna say that Spellman rewrote it. It's that simple. They'll say we had a bill for all the country, all the people, treated them all well, but Spellman rewrote it. He sent down the word from the Pope, and that's it."

Undeterred, Shriver sought to persuade him that the Carey amendment should be adopted, floating the possibility that its Democratic opponents might be swayed by appeals to party unity. Disdainfully, Johnson shot him down, remarking that, if it passed Rules, it would only be because the conservatives who teamed up with O'Brien and Delaney in committee had seen the amendment as the best way of defeating the Economic Opportunity Act on the House floor, where few southerners were prepared to vote for a parochial aid bill.[78] Even majority whip Carl Albert would have to oppose the administration, Johnson told O'Brien, so great was anti-Catholic sentiment in his rural Oklahoma district.[79]

Speaker John McCormack, a staunch Catholic, was inclined to blame "the goddamn NEA" for this mess, telling Johnson that he had "hoped that they had grown somewhat" after the 1962 higher education fiasco but had evidently been mistaken. Johnson, however, demurred, feeling that it was Carey and his confederates whose grandstanding had "got it screwed up," inflaming the "crackpot preachers," and giving a gleeful Charles Halleck an opportunity to "defeat this bill and divide the party." In this sulphurous atmosphere, administration officials worked hard with Carey and Philip Landrum of Georgia to find legislative language that might satisfy both sides. (The respected Landrum, sponsor of the Economic Opportunity Act, was central to Johnson's strategy for wooing southern support.)

Meanwhile, Johnson worked the phones. On one occasion, when he called the Speaker, McCormack was in a meeting with two of the seven Catholic Democrats on the education committee—Frank Thompson of Camden, New Jersey, and James O'Hara of Macomb County, in suburban Detroit. Talking to Thompson, Johnson recalled that as Texas director of the National Youth Administration during the Depression, he had used his administrative discretion to divert funds to Catholic institutions and that Shriver could be trusted to tell public education agencies that they would not receive federal funds "unless you do something for St. Anne's, or do something for St. John's." At the same time, however, the absence of any explicit reference to parochial aid in the text of the bill would allow Johnson to reassure southern Democrats that "the Pope's not coming here to take over yet."

Characteristically, he leavened his hard pitch for political support with an anecdote, telling Thompson that the intransigent head of the Southern

Baptists had recently turned up at the White House, demanding to see the president so that he could express his outrage about papal influence on the administration. On arrival, however, his fellow Baptist, White House aide Bill Moyers, told him that he could not reach the president at that time because he was "in a meeting." When the suspicious minister asked what kind of meeting it was, Moyers had the perfect answer: "He's out swimming with Billy Graham." Mollified, the minister remarked: "Well, there must not be much in this Pope story."[80]

Still, as in 1961 and 1962, once the religious genie had escaped, it proved impossible to put back in the bottle. At one point, things got so bad that Johnson wondered if Title II should be completely deleted. "To *hell* with community action," vented the president to Landrum, who shared his doubts about the idea, and his greater enthusiasm for the work-study concept, with its Depression-era resonances.[81] Shriver and Moyers talked him out of such radical surgery. Instead, Title II remained, while its remedial education provision was stricken.

If so small an initiative could generate this kind of a religious storm, even after eighteen months of hard work by Keppel and despite the constructive approach of people like the NCWC's Francis Hurley and NEA's Robert Wyatt, then clearly prospects for large-scale education aid remained indifferent. In his 1964 book, *Obstacle Course on Capitol Hill*, the veteran reporter Robert Bendiner surmised that "it may happen, but it is not a good bet." The defeat of general aid, he observed, "has become almost as much a tradition as bean soup in the Capitol restaurants and free haircuts in the Senate."[82]

Making History

THE PASSAGE OF ESEA

Having decided not to make a big push for federal aid to education during a presidential election year, the administration sought in a number of ways to prepare the way for a major initiative in 1965. First, Johnson made education a central theme in the fall campaign against Barry Goldwater.[1] "On the horizon," he warned an audience in Atlantic City, "are problems so huge that only a national effort of vast dimensions can meet them." School enrollments, he went on, continued to increase at a million a year, "and unless we act now our education system will crack under the pressure."[2] Second, John W. Gardner, head of the Carnegie Corporation, was chosen to lead a White House task force on education, charged with identifying programmatic priorities for an expanded federal role (the remarks in Atlantic City had rather a stale air, recycling arguments from a decade earlier that now had doubtful pertinence).[3] Third, Francis Keppel stepped up his existing effort to reach out to the Catholics and the public school groups, in an effort to find a way through the parochial aid morass.

In this last effort, Keppel received important support from John Brademas, a three-term congressman from South Bend, Indiana, who was well placed to be helpful in these negotiations. Through Indiana Democratic Party channels, he was acquainted with Robert Wyatt, president of NEA. At the same time, before joining Congress, Brademas—himself a Methodist—

had taught at Holy Cross, a Catholic college in his district, which also included the University of Notre Dame.[4] Partly for that reason, he had good contacts with the NCWC too, not least with the long-standing director of its education division, Msgr. Frederick Hochwalt. Brademas knew Keppel through Harvard. Finally, this former Rhodes Scholar had a strong interest in education, and during his brief career in Congress had already emerged as an influential member of the House Education and Labor Committee.

Toward the end of 1963, and continuing into 1964, Brademas hosted a series of behind-the-scenes dinner meetings with lobbyists and administration officials, at his house in Georgetown and at his club. The NCWC's Francis Hurley recalls them as having been exceptionally convivial affairs that helped participants to forge important personal relationships, despite the deep divisions that continued to exist between, and even within, their organizations.[5] Above all, though, they allowed Keppel and others at HEW to float various ideas that ended up being central to ESEA, such as an emphasis on the educational needs of the poor and the "shared-time" concept, whereby parochial school children might use federally funded public school resources outside of regular school hours. NEA and the NCWC did not explicitly endorse these ideas: to the contrary, public school groups were unenthusiastic about the antipoverty approach, and the Catholics felt that "shared-time" still left them second-class citizens. Keppel remarks that "no documents ever were distributed" and "there was no formal agreement that 'my group will support your program, if your group will support mine.'"[6]

Nevertheless, Keppel learned through these meetings that the NCWC was keenly interested in the nascent federal antipoverty initiative, with Francis Hurley one of two officials whom the Catholic bishops had asked to coordinate the Church's response.[7] In subsequent meetings at HEW, Samuel Halperin, head of OE's legislative liaison team, worked closely with the two officials and with the NCWC's counsel, Robert Consedine, seeking to develop a legislative proposal that both developed the "shared-time" concept and exploited this common interest in poverty. Interviewed four decades on, Hurley recalled the tenacious, direct, and knowledgeable Halperin as having been "the greatest help that we had."[8]

Interest in poverty was less obvious at NEA, where the focus remained squarely on measures that would result in higher teacher salaries. That said, its big research division *had* recently produced a survey of current efforts to help disadvantaged children, suggesting at least some interest in the topic.[9] In this environment, as one participant in the discussions at Brademas's house remarked, "the administration in effect said, 'Do you dare oppose this one?' In fact, the parties did not."[10] That was also the impression of Johnson's chief education aide, Douglass Cater: in the year in which a War on Poverty was getting underway, the Catholics "admitted that they could not make an all-out stand against" a poverty-centered bill, especially in light of the ecumenical spirit engendered by Pope John.[11]

November 1964: A Political Earthquake

These discussions might not have mattered, though, had it not been for Johnson's smashing electoral victory in November. First of all, he secured 61.1 percent of the vote against Barry Goldwater, besting even Franklin Roosevelt's performance in 1936. Still more important were his long coattails: the Democrats now enjoyed better than a two-thirds majority in both the Senate and the House, for the first time since the height of the New Deal. In the House, there were fifty-eight northern Democratic freshmen. It was one of those moments, rare in American politics, when dramatic change seems possible, a sense that was only increased by the epochal developments that were simultaneously taking place in the African American struggle for political equality. Four months earlier, the 88th Congress had passed the Civil Rights Act, banning discrimination in employment and public accommodations and strengthening the enforcement powers of the federal government in cases of noncompliance, together with its power to enforce the *Brown* ruling.

It was these profoundly altered political circumstances that made the passage of ESEA possible: Johnson had an extraordinary mandate; liberal gains had greatly depleted the ranks of those who disapproved of federal aid on principle; and the key interest groups had the worrying feeling that perhaps the president no longer needed to listen to them. Still, scholars who argue that the election made the passage of ESEA *inevitable* go too far.[12] Certainly, that was not the feeling within the administration. Instead, as historian Edward Berkowitz has observed, they "were haunted by the possibility of a sudden shift in scene in which consensus turned to conflict. . . . Everyone who tracked the bill was concerned that it would fall apart, just as it always had."[13] Halperin confirms that assessment, remembering that "we were *all* running scared all the time."[14] In particular, the church-state issue continued to loom large, not least because the 89th Congress was the first in history in which Catholics were the largest single religious group, following the big gains that the Democrats had made in the urban North.[15]

ESEA was put together during November and December of 1964. Because the administration remained uncertain about the legislative outcome, its content owed less to philosophical or programmatic considerations than to political calculation. For that reason, the importance of the Gardner task force should not be overstated, even though it issued its report at this time. John Gardner himself asserts that "most of the Elementary and Secondary Education Act came out of the task force report," but other participants tend to downplay its significance. Halperin, who was centrally involved in the effort to find a way through the church-state and formula distribution issues, argues that the Gardner group had little impact on the content of ESEA.[16] That is also Keppel's view: it had little to do with Title I, the "diesel engine . . . for the train," which accounted for $1 billion of the $1.3 billion first-year price tag, despite a shared emphasis on the educationally disadvantaged. Instead, he says, Title I emerged out of negotiations between his team at HEW, the familiar interest groups, and a cluster of influential legislators and their staffs.[17] Meanwhile, the concept for the second biggest item, Title II, which distributed federal funds for library resources, apparently came from Hugh Carey.[18] Title IV, for federal education research, simply absorbed the Cooperative Education Act of 1954. And Title V, whose purpose was to enable state education agencies to improve their operations, reflected the priorities of Commissioner Keppel, who doubted that many of them were currently equipped to spend Title I funds money wisely. Only Title III, for supplemental education centers, emerged directly out of the work of the Gardner task force.[19]

In addition to Keppel and Halperin, the administration figures most closely involved in putting ESEA together were Wilbur Cohen and Douglass Cater. At this time, Cohen was an assistant secretary at HEW, responsible for developing legislation and helping it through Congress (in 1965 he would be promoted to second in command at HEW, and by the end of the administration he was secretary). As his biographer observes, "for Cohen, education policy was a matter of finding the right deal, not the right idea."[20] For three decades, both from within government and from his academic perch at the University of Michigan, Cohen had nurtured the expansion of the Social Security program, as well as being intimately involved in successive failed efforts to pass federal health insurance and education aid. These experiences had given Cohen both a deep knowledge of Congress and a bedrock belief in the advantages of patience and incrementalism in pursuing grand legislative objectives. As he told his son on one occasion: "politics is not like an athletic event. . . . There is always a tomorrow when you must try to get support from someone who has opposed you today." After the failure of education aid in 1961, Cohen apparently thought that Sterling McMurrin would be cheered by the observation that it had taken seventeen years for him to win disability insurance.[21]

When Larry O'Brien was asked in retirement to mention figures within government whom he had admired for their grasp of legislative politics, he immediately thought of Cohen, observing that he was the "perfect" person to have working on legislative liaison and that both the Kennedy and Johnson administrations would respond to difficulties on the Hill by saying "let's go to Wilbur."[22] Keppel confirms that Johnson thought Cohen "a darned good legislative tactician," and the president's admiration and affection certainly come across in their recorded phone conversations. When Johnson read that Cohen was thinking of resigning, he called HEW to reassure himself that the story was false, complaining: "I can't lose you. You been with me since long before I was President." Relieved by Cohen's response, he joked "I'd just as soon lose Miz Johnson. . . . When you get ready to resign, you let me know and you can take my place."[23]

Douglass Cater was the education and health specialist in the Johnson White House. He had become known to Johnson during the 1950s, when he was Washington correspondent for the liberal political magazine, *The Reporter* (his first story on Johnson, entitled "Lyndon Johnson: Rising Democratic Star," had appeared in 1953).[24] Among other stories, he had covered the loss of the 1962 higher education bill. Naturally, he had developed good contacts in Congress. They included a number of powerful southerners, such as his fellow Alabamian, Lister Hill, who chaired both the Labor and Public Welfare Committee and the Appropriations subcommittee that dealt with HEW funding. During the winter of 1964–1965, Cater was closely involved with Keppel and Cohen in the tasks of working with interest groups, talking to congressional staffers, liaising with the Gardner task force, and crafting a bill. He also helped to write Johnson's education speeches during the campaign, together with the address that he delivered when ESEA was unveiled in January.

As Cater and the HEW people were working on the bill, a number of political questions came to the fore. First among them, obviously, was the religious issue. Although there was some concern at NCWC that Johnson no longer needed to listen to them, given his new mandate, this was not the president's view: When Cohen ran into him at a State Department party shortly after the election, Johnson told him to "be sure to keep him out of the parochial school issue."[25] Behind that warning lay not just the lessons of history but the particular promises that he had made to Catholics during the antipoverty controversy. In private conversation with Speaker McCormack, for example, he had predicted: "I'll do more for the religious people than anyone ever has, and ten times as much as Kennedy did, I can tell you that. But I can't do it until the election."[26] And the Democratic platform at Atlantic City had advocated "the channelling of federally collected revenues to all levels of education, and, to the extent permitted by the Constitution, to all schools."[27] Accordingly, when Keppel outlined an education package that he hazarded might apportion 12 percent of federal funds to the 15 percent of Americans who sent their children to nonpublic schools, Johnson wondered whether that was good enough. Why, he asked Cater, should they not receive a fully equal share?[28] Based on their contact with public school groups such as NEA and the Council of Chief State School Officers (CCSSO), Keppel and Cater knew that this was entirely unrealistic.[29] Quite what level of parochial school support might satisfy both NEA and NCWC, though, was difficult to discern.

A second tricky political issue concerned the distribution formula. Past legislative efforts had been complicated by congressional disagreement over the degree of "equalization" that should be employed.[30] Simply on grounds of educational need, there was a strong case for funneling funds disproportionately to the poorer states. That also made some political sense, at least in the Senate, where the rural South was strongly represented. But how could legislators representing more affluent parts of the country be persuaded to back such a measure? From the perspective of urban Democrats in the House, it might seem that their constituents, already paying high taxes to support their *own* schools, could not reasonably be expected to subsidize the education of children in the South as well. How could that be justified, especially when those children attended illegally segregated schools and when the result might be to give the low-wage South a further competitive advantage economically vis-à-vis the high-wage North? These questions were bound to be raised, especially in the House, and most particularly in its Education and Labor Committee, which—because of its concentration on labor issues in the past—was dominated by Democrats from northern industrial states. Could a formula be found that would satisfy both camps?

In comparison to these considerations, two other long-standing barriers to federal school aid had less salience than in previous battles. The second of the three Rs, race, loomed much less large, because Title VI of the recently enacted Civil Rights Act barred federal aid to institutions that practiced racial discrimination. Lawrence O'Brien continued to worry that some southern Democrats would be tempted to play the race card, but at least there were not going to be any more Powell amendments. As for the third R, "reds," the federal control issue was less important, given the composition of the 89th Congress. But it had not gone away: the administration would still need support from some Republicans and southern Democrats who worried about Washington meddling. Keppel, then, still needed to find a way of packaging ESEA that would diminish the sense that it represented a sharp break with traditional models of federalism. Given that Johnson was proposing to more than double federal spending on schools in one fell swoop, that might take some doing.

At the heart of the administration's response to these various political challenges was the decision to present ESEA as a major instrument of the War on Poverty. Such an approach was, of course, congenial to Johnson and flowed naturally out of the broader aspirations of Great Society liberalism. For someone like Wilbur Cohen, however, the beauty of Title I, which distributed federal funds to school districts containing concentrations of poor children, lay not in its programmatic purpose but in the way that it allowed Washington to distribute federal dollars to almost every congressional district in the nation. A poor child was defined as one whose family earned less than $2,000 per year.[31] To calculate a county's entitlement, the number of children in this category was to be multiplied by 50 percent of the state's per capita spending on education. Any county with 200 poor children qualified for aid. That meant that 94 percent of the counties would be eligible for Title I money.

Meanwhile, in terms of the church-state question, the crucial fact was that a focus on poor children rather than on schools allowed the administration to invoke the "child-benefit theory" that the Supreme Court had seemed to endorse in 1947: it was constitutional for public funds to be used to benefit children attending private schools, so long as the *institution* did not directly benefit.[32] In this case, all Title I funds would go to public school districts (hopefully heading off NEA protests), but poor children attending parochial and private schools would be counted in calculating the level of federal support, and school districts would be required to ensure that the compensatory programs that they established with those funds benefited *all* poor school-age children, not just those attending the public schools.

The emphasis on poverty also helped in terms of the federalism issue. When Congress had passed the Economic Opportunity Act it had clearly declared poverty to be a national problem, one in which the federal government had a legitimate role. As part of the war on poverty, ESEA looked less stark and revolutionary than a $1.3 billion school aid proposal would otherwise have done. Although it is hard to imagine that many legislators were taken in by the claim, perhaps it also helped that Title I was packaged as an amendment to the popular, decade-and-a-half-old impact aid program.

ESEA and Impact Aid

Had ESEA been shaped by philosophical or programmatic considerations, this pairing would not have been an obvious one because, within the executive branch, impact aid was widely viewed as a bad program. At its inception in 1950, it had been designed to help school districts that housed large numbers of military personnel who did not have to pay property tax, but whose children went to the local public schools. Since then, however, impact aid had been altered out of all recognition, as school superintendents led by the gifted lobbyist, Oscar Rose, succeeded in broadening its coverage, and legislators worked to ensure that their districts were included.[33] Very soon, the claim that it was targeted at the districts most in need started to look dubious: one of the biggest beneficiaries by the 1960s, Montgomery County, Maryland, was also one of the wealthiest districts in the nation, thanks to an expanding federal workforce whose members were, for the most part, comfortably off, property tax–paying civilians. Starting with Truman, every president had sought to rein in the program, which was always on the Bureau of the Budget's A-list for cutbacks. But precisely because the scope of the program had broadened, it had become increasingly invulnerable to these executive branch assaults on the Hill.

impact aid

Keppel viewed this policy trajectory with a certain wry amusement, telling one interviewer that although the program had been designed to help districts "impacted" by the military, it had "always seemed to me to have rather a dental meaning; it hurts to try to pull out a tooth which is impacted."[34] ESEA attenuated the rationale for the program still further, leading the budget bureau and program planners at HEW to recommend a renewed effort to scale it down. But the focus on poverty opened up a more politically realistic, indeed enticing possibility: *expanding* impact aid by adding concentrations of poverty to the list of factors that qualified a district for aid. Not surprisingly, this plan originated on Capitol Hill, with two staffers on the Labor and Public Welfare Committee: Stewart McClure, its chief clerk, and Charles Lee, who was majority staffer on Wayne Morse's education subcommittee. Here is how McClure recalled their deliberations, a quarter of a century later:

> One night, . . . I had bought a bottle of Irish whiskey called "Kennedy," which by the way is very good. Charlie liked to sip a bit at the end of

the day, as did I, so I brought this pint of "Kennedy" Irish whiskey into his office and we just sat around chewing the fat, as goes on every day up here. We had just gotten through, I think, a session on the federal impacted aid program. . . . I don't know whether it was Charlie or I who broached the subject, could have been either of us, so let's just say that *we* agreed that the principle of federal impact was a damn good idea [and] a child going to a poor school in a poor district should be considered suffering a national impact caused by the failure of the whole society to upgrade his disadvantaged area. . . . We put it together and went to see Morse. He thought it was great.[35]

[handwritten margin note: ✱ new way of framing aid]

Senator Morse and Rep. John Dent—a Democrat from Pennsylvania who served on the Education and Labor Committee—introduced "poverty impact" bills in 1964, but the administration response was lukewarm, in part because the antipoverty formula proposed was unwieldy but also because Johnson thought that the timing was wrong.[36] Still, the seed was planted, and when Keppel recorded his oral history with the Kennedy library in September 1964, it had clearly begun to germinate. Having recalled that Kennedy "didn't like" impact aid and "used to growl at it," the commissioner suggested that "I think in heaven he's probably watching with an amused smile now, because we're going to keep on using it. That thing is a political booster. OK, let's hitch some instruments on it. . . . I think we'll do it next session too. I hope so. But, it's a reverse all right."[37]

A Swift but Rocky Ride through Congress

ESEA went through Congress in eighty-nine days and emerged from that process with only modest changes. That reflected both the strength of Lyndon Johnson's political position at the start of 1965 and the lengths to which the administration had gone to clear it with key legislators and interest groups before sending it to the Hill.[38] Reviewing the archival sources, though, together with the disappointingly limited number of ESEA-related phone conversations that Johnson recorded, it is clear that its passage did not seem straightforward at the time. Rather, almost until the last, Johnson worried that it might come unstuck, especially on church-state grounds.

[handwritten margin note: ESEA Passed but not easily]

At first, everything went well: the chairman of the House subcommittee on general education, Carl Perkins of Kentucky, was an administration loyalist, who represented one of the poorest congressional districts in the country. On both counts, he was anxious to expedite ESEA's passage. By holding Saturday sessions and packing large numbers of witnesses into each session, he was able to complete hearings within two weeks and mark up a bill within three. That delighted the White House, where it was felt that any delay increased the likelihood of a damaging church-state controversy. Even in this brief time, though, there were some danger signs: spokesmen for the American Civil Liberties Union and the American Jewish Committee objected to parochial school aid in any form, and subcommittee Republicans led by Charles Goodell of New York eagerly pounced on their arguments, casting doubt on the constitutionality of the first three titles of the bill, each of which used a child-benefit rationale to justify aid to parochial school children.

They were aided in that endeavor by Edith Green of Oregon, who doubted that ESEA—for all its undoubted ingenuity—would do much for American education. Whereas Perkins, Morse, and the administration saw ESEA primarily as a political compromise, she was by temperament inclined to view such deals with suspicion, worrying not just about parochial aid (which she strongly opposed) but also about the likely effectiveness of an antipoverty formula that distributed more aid to affluent but populous Westchester County, New York, than to some much poorer districts in the South.[39]

Meeting in executive session at the close of the hearings, the Perkins subcommittee drew up a set of modest amendments to the first three titles of the bill, each designed to reassure opponents of parochial aid.[40] Catholics, naturally, were unhappy at this, and Daniel Patrick Moynihan would later go so far as to claim that "the Catholics got nothing out of" the final bill, "save a few trailers parked across the street from St. Agnes or whatever where students could learn mathematics without fear of papal influence."[41] Still, at the time NCWC lobbyists took a more optimistic view, seeing the changes as cosmetic and seeing ESEA as a useful foot in the door, quite apart from being politically difficult to oppose.[42]

When ESEA reached the full committee, though, its progress ground to a halt, even though Adam Clayton Powell had agreed to dispense with further hearings and move straight to executive markup sessions. Two new problems arose. First, chairman Powell reneged on a promise to begin those sessions immediately, delaying them for more than two weeks in what was for him a characteristic display of political blackmail. Ostensibly, the question at issue on this occasion was committee expenses: Powell indicated that he would not move to consider ESEA until the House increased his operating budget by $400,000. Within the committee, however, there was some suspicion that the real issue was his ongoing effort to stop the Internal Revenue Service (IRS) from disclosing his record of income tax evasion.[43]

If that *was* Powell's real agenda, then the administration outsmarted him, combining with the House leadership to force the committee-funding bill out of a deeply hostile Rules Committee and then securing the speedy passage on the floor of a bill that went *beyond* what Powell had demanded.[44] Simultaneously, Larry O'Brien started conspiring with other senior Democrats on the committee to take the bill away from the chairman and made sure that Powell knew about these plans. As O'Brien later recounted with glee to Johnson, the first of these tactics "pulled out his props," and the second forced "Powell . . . to rush to get in front of the troops."[45] Finally, Powell convened the first markup session.

At this point, the second problem arose. In a development that highlighted the extraordinary delicacy of the formula question, northern Democrats who had kept quiet during the Perkins hearings started complaining that Title I gave too much money to the rural South, just the *opposite* of the Green/Goodell complaint. They cited HEW calculations suggesting that Texas was to receive more funds than California, North Carolina more than Pennsylvania, Louisiana more than Illinois, Georgia more than Michigan, and Mississippi as much as New Jersey and Massachusetts combined.[46] The problem for members such as William Ford and James O'Hara of the Detroit suburbs and Roman Pucinski of Chicago was that the $2,000 poverty figure was simply too low to capture many of their families. Cohen and Halperin, anticipating that problem, had sought to get around it by including the multiplier that related federal aid to per capita spending on education in the state. But the northerners were not satisfied, wanting to add some new index of socioeconomic need that would do more for their districts.

Given that these northerners dominated the committee and that time was marching on, the administration recognized the need to make some concession. Halperin recalls the "wonderful crew of civil servants . . . who labored nightly to prepare . . . charts" that estimated the impact of different options on each state. Keppel referred to these charts as "ask what your country can do for you" tables.[47] O'Brien hoped to persuade the northerners to accept a change that would add just $50 million to the price tag. But when Halperin entered the committee room with his thick notebook containing the various alternative fund distribution tables, Pucinski—a tough product of Chicago ward politics—physically grabbed it away from him; quickly found the data relating to his preferred alternative, which included families receiving Aid to Families with Dependent Children (AFDC) in the formula, whatever their income; and successfully moved to insert it in the bill.[48]

Another problem that faced the administration during this fraught week-long markup process was the difficulty of assembling a committee quorum. That difficulty might have arisen in part because Powell, despite having finally allowed the committee to convene, was not always physically present, and—when he was absent—he made Hugh Carey his proxy. Although Carey was able and well liked, he inevitably lacked Powell's stature (when he was around, Powell was very good at cracking the whip, and colleagues were loath to incur his displeasure). The indiscipline that Munger and Fenno identified in their 1962 book, *National Politics and Federal Aid to Education*, as having been characteristic of the committee is nicely illustrated by an anecdote from Halperin, who recalls that "one of my jobs when the White House was trying to assemble a quorum for committee action was waking two Members who were 'sleeping,' accompanied, in the old Congressional Hotel . . . and rushing them back to the committee room."[49]

After a week of these tussles, Johnson learned that Powell was up to his familiar tricks.[50] With the Democrats divided by the formula and by the religious question, the chairman left a message with White House aide Jack Valenti, saying that he was currently unable to force ESEA out of committee: the latest vote to adjourn the markup session had been defeated by a single vote, as six Democrats voted with the ten Republicans.[51] When Valenti returned the call, he began by saying "I hope this is a josh," but Powell told him "my committee is up in arms," affecting a tone of helplessness. He went on to imply, though, in a subtly indirect way, that he *might* be able to secure a positive outcome if the administration removed what he claimed was an "anti-Negro" feature of the Appalachia bill (which was going through Congress at the same time). This was presumably a contrived objection, concealing some new, undisclosed price that Powell wished to exact for reporting ESEA.[52] Seemingly baffled by Powell's elaborate charges, but recognizing that the struggle for ESEA had reached a critical juncture, Valenti called in the president.

It was 9:30 P.M., the end of a long day that had been dominated by the launch of the Operation Rolling Thunder bombing campaign in North Vietnam. When Johnson came on the line, he sounded furious, cutting short Powell's opening pleasantries and heatedly demanding: "What the hell has been happening to your committee? I thought you told me two months ago that you were going to pass a bill for me." When Powell sought to respond, Johnson interrupted, referring back to the recent controversy over committee expenses ("what the hell are you doing blackmailing me?") and protesting that "you damn near defeated the best education bill I've got." At this point, Powell sought to raise his ostensible objections to the Appalachia bill, but this precipitated another explosion from Johnson, who told the Harlem Democrat that "Appalachia ain't got a damn thing to do with you," adding in a regretful tone that "I sure thought I had better leadership on that committee than what I got. I'm *awfully* disappointed." Responding to Johnson's earlier point, Powell defended his actions during the controversy over committee expenses:

> Powell: Don't you think I was entitled to the money?
>
> LBJ: No, I don't think you're entitled to a damn thing! . . . You looked me straight in the eye and said, "I'll report this bill and I'll get it on the floor," and you *did not do it*. . . .
>
> Powell: By March first, I told you.
>
> LBJ: Oh, *hell no!* [shouting] You didn't say March first. You told me you were going to *do* it. Then you ran off for three weeks and they couldn't even locate you.[53] I asked the Speaker to call you and tell you that this was serious. This is bad. This is the thing we ran on all over the country. Your people are being damn well taken care of in it.

As he tended to do when confronted with Democratic obstruction, Johnson then went on to accuse Powell of having been an unwitting pawn in a dastardly GOP plot to defeat the bill. "For *God's sake*, Adam," he entreated Powell, "don't get sucked into it. They *used* you for three weeks and murdered me! They got *thirty-two* amendments written while you were gone. They got the *hell* raised in the Senate. . . ." Now, following the latest committee vote, "Bill Ayres and Charles Goodell are *laughing* at you."[54] "I want that bill reported out tomorrow morning, like the administration wanted," Johnson demanded. In return, he added opaquely, "what you want me to do I'll try to do." Powell responded with alacrity, promising to have ESEA reported out of Education and Labor the next day. In this, he was successful: a new motion to adjourn the markup passed by a single vote.

Writing to Johnson a few days later, Larry O'Brien observed that "the victory in the House Education and Labor Committee last week and the difficulty in obtaining it" were "not generally understood." "Certainly the press understands neither," he added, "which, at this point, is just as well."[55] He was hopeful that—although other problems doubtless lay ahead—the biggest barrier to ESEA's passage had been safely negotiated. Two weeks later, Howard Smith's Rules Committee sent it to the floor, again by a bare, one-vote margin. In conversation with George Meany, whose potent American Federation of Labor–Congress of Industrial Organizations (AFL-CIO) lobbyists were helping the administration on the Hill, Johnson reported that the decisive vote came from John Young, a Catholic from Corpus Christi who had been appointed to Rules the previous year precisely because he promised never to oppose the leadership line, save for procedural reasons.[56] Probably exaggerating the difficulty in a bid to persuade Meany to call out all the stops on behalf of the bill, Johnson claimed that "we had to beg, and borrow, and bribe, and take John Young . . . and promise him the world with a fence around it."[57]

The stage was now set for what proved to be a bruising floor fight centering in part on the Title I formula but much more on the religious question. In both cases, education committee Republicans, ably led by Charles Goodell of New York and Albert Quie of Minnesota, teamed up with Edith Green and subjected ESEA to uncomfortable scrutiny. Charles Radcliffe, the key education aide on the committee's minority staff, had produced statistics contrasting the seemingly generous Title I allotments to some of the wealthiest counties in the nation to the smaller sums going to some of the poorest.[58] He recalls that William Ayres of Ohio (whom Johnson had fingered in his conversation with Powell as a "goddamn outlaw") leapt on these figures and rode them for all they were worth. If the issue gathered momentum, there was the real risk that southerners on whose support Johnson was counting would decide to oppose the bill, making its passage unlikely. Philip Landrum of Georgia, whose support had done much to bolster southern support for the War on Poverty the previous year, worked hard to try to keep them on board.

The religious issue was more difficult, not least because exactly what ESEA would mean for Catholic schools was not certain. What would happen, for example, in the thirty-two states that barred state aid to private schools? If public school agencies declined to include Catholics in compensatory programs or in the library and audiovisual equipment program, how would the federal government respond? If the Office of Education stepped in to administer Title II directly in such cases, what would that mean for local control? Did the wording of Title I permit public school special needs teachers to help needy parochial school children in their own schools? If so, was that constitutional? Some of these questions were hard to answer, and they caused immense discomfort to the administration, and satisfaction for its opponents, as committee Democrats led by Carl Perkins and Hugh Carey struggled to provide answers that would satisfy both northern Catholics and southern Protestants. Eidenberg and Morey cite an unnamed administration source who recalled that "Perkins was obviously weak and Carey had the religious ax to grind." The source added that "Goodell and Quie started taking Perkins and Carey apart" and that "we had to put together a more competent team to handle the floor debate."[59]

From that point on, the lead was taken by three other committee Democrats: John Brademas, Frank Thompson, and James O'Hara, backed up by position papers and rebuttals supplied by Halperin's team at HEW. Among other things, they sought to head off the threat of a judicial review amendment that would result in the constitutionality of parochial aid being determined by the Supreme Court. Were such an amendment to be included, it was likely that the NCWC would have to oppose the bill: alarmed by *Engel v. Vitale*, the 1962 ruling that outlawed prayer in schools, they worried that a court test might bar parochial aid in *any* form.[60]

Writing to Johnson at the end of the first day of the House floor debate, Valenti passed on O'Brien's report that "it's been hell today." Many Democrats, he added, were still undecided, with two days still to go and much time for things to unravel. In this frenzied atmosphere, Carl Albert had been "shoring up Carl Perkins," and the leadership more generally were "cashing in their IOU's with these waverers."[61] Meanwhile, HEW officials in the galleries were giving Thompson, O'Hara, Perkins, and Brademas memos to use in response to Goodell's tough questions without alienating either northern Catholics or southern Protestants.[62] It worked, and in the event the margin of victory was comfortable, 263 votes to 153, much larger than the White House and HEW headcounts had anticipated.[63]

A delighted Johnson called both Perkins and Powell to congratulate them. "I didn't think it could be done," LBJ told Powell. Powell (who, in truth, had not played a prominent role in the floor fight) grandly told the president that "I had to be rough" to circumvent the obstacles. "I'll tell you one thing, Mr. President," he added with feeling, "I hope you'll never do a favor in your *life* for Miz Green." When Johnson noted querulously that Powell should have cut her down to size earlier, while agreeing that she was thoroughly "mean," Powell responded with feeling: "Oh my God. You never seen a woman with such a vicious face. You should ask your aides. The look on her face the whole time. . . ."[64]

In the Senate, it was barely conceivable that ESEA would not pass, given how comparatively receptive the body had been to federal aid proposals for the past decade. But that did not mean that the administration was home free. Given how difficult the bill's passage had been to this point, Johnson worried that it might come unstuck in conference. And perhaps, he feared, it would not even reach conference. What if, as had happened in 1960, it proved impossible to secure the necessary House rule the second time around?[65]

These anxieties seem to have first surfaced some time earlier, during the long wait for Powell to act on the subcommittee bill. At that time, the White House had begun to discuss with Senate staffers Charles Lee and Jack Forsythe whether Wayne Morse might be prepared to pass the House version, without changing even a comma, thereby obviating a conference and a second rule. This was, of course, a considerable affront to the dignity of the Senate, but Morse and the full committee chairman Lister Hill went along.[66] That did not mean that the committee was willing to leave matters entirely to their colleagues in the House: as one staffer told the *Wall Street Journal*, "it has to proclaim its independence, you know."[67] Rather, it meant that the committee had to find novel means of placing its imprint on ESEA.

This happened in a number of ways. When Senator Robert Kennedy of New York announced his intention to propose an amendment that subjected federally funded education programs to monitoring and oversight, Wilbur Cohen persuaded him that it should be added to the House bill instead, by Brademas.[68] A second challenge was presented by staffer Jack Forsythe's desire to help two interest groups to which he had particularly strong ties: the handicapped children's lobby and Don White's audiovisual lobby.[69] Here, the threat of conference-inducing Senate amendments was avoided by a variety of methods. First, language helpful to both the handicapped and the audiovisual lobby was inserted into the Senate report (Lee referred to this as the "silent amendment" strategy[70]). Second, as well as working through Forsythe, White used his friendship with Powell (they used to go to Bimini together) to secure the rest of what he wanted out of ESEA, right at the end of the House markup session.[71] During a legislative battle that was otherwise notable for the inability of lobbyists to leave much of an impact on the legislation, White was a notable exception, securing language in each of the first three titles that allowed federal funds to be used for the purchase of audiovisual equipment.[72] And third, it was agreed that a separate measure incorporating the handicapped into ESEA in a more comprehensive fashion would be introduced later in the session.[73]

That left one remaining hurdle, in the form of Senator Ralph Yarborough of Texas, a longtime political adversary of the president who, in Johnson's jaundiced view, was "not too stable a lot of the time."[74] When the Morse subcommittee opened proceedings, Yarborough threatened to undermine the administration's elaborate strategy by introducing an amendment that would have modified the Title I formula, giving some $2 million more to Texas and also benefiting other southern and border states. This had Johnson worried: if they voted their states, Hill of Alabama and Jennings Randolph of West Virginia would support him, and so too would the Republicans, save for Jacob Javits of New York. Drawing the worst case scenario, Johnson warned O'Brien that "if we get an amendment, we won't get a rule."[75] Shortly before it was to come to a vote, Johnson made another phone call, this time to George Meany, whom he asked to contact Randolph, Hill, and Yarborough. "If you'll get us this bill without amending it," he wanted Meany to tell them, "then next year I'll take you down to the President and we'll improve the formula if you want it, but don't make us go back to Howard Smith."[76] When Randolph voted against the amendment, which was therefore defeated, ESEA had surmounted its final obstacle.[77] On the Senate floor, the unamended bill passed by an overwhelming margin: 73 votes to 18.

That set the stage for an emotional bill-signing ceremony outside the one-room schoolhouse in Johnson City that Johnson had attended as a boy.[78] It was the Sabbath, and only two days after the Senate vote (normally it took ten days for a bill to be prepared for a president's signature), but Johnson explained that he had not wished to waste any time and that the attorney general had assured him "that it is legal and constitutional to sign this act on Sunday, even Palm Sunday." Standing next to him at the ceremony was his first teacher, Kate Deadrich Loney. Greeting her, he observed that "I started school when I was four years old, and they tell me, Miss Kate, that I recited my first lessons while sitting on your lap." In the audience, meanwhile, were his own former pupils from Cotulla and Houston, together with associates from his college days at San Marcos teacher training college. By way of explanation, he mentioned that he had "felt a very strong desire to go back to the beginnings of my own education—to be reminded and to remind others of that magic time when the world of learning began to open before our eyes." "No law I have signed or will ever sign," he averred, "means more to the future of America." If there was an element of "hokum" to remarks such as these, his speechwriter Harry McPherson observed, they were also from the heart.[79]

Conclusion

Although large-scale federal aid to education had been hard to achieve, even in the liberal *annus mirabilis* of 1965, Johnson was confident that once it was on the statute books it would soon put down strong roots. Just before his angry phone conversation with Powell, at the beginning of March, Johnson had met with a group of education leaders who were on their way to the Hill to lobby for ESEA and delivered the following extemporaneous remarks:

> The education bill we picked out can be improved. The T-Model Ford could be improved and has been. The first train that ran from Fredericksburg, a little town I lived close to, went to San Antonio—it has been improved a great deal. But I remember the story that they told about it the day it took off—from one of the founding fathers. He said, "Well, they will never get her started, and if they do they will never get her stopped."[80]

Whether the train could be stopped or reversed, or whether it would accelerate in the way that Johnson anticipated, would depend in part on the fortunes of Great Society liberalism, at its very zenith in the spring of 1965 and almost certain to lose at least some of its luster during the years ahead. Just as Franklin Roosevelt had conceived of the Social Security program as a system that would be able to withstand the vicissitudes of political fortune, so Lyndon Johnson must have hoped that ESEA would survive the next conservative tide and become embedded in the fabric of American politics. That expectation would meet its first big test in 1967, by which time the fortunes of the Great Society appeared to be in free fall. What would happen to ESEA in these new political circumstances?

3

Putting Down Roots, 1965–1968

During the rest of the Johnson presidency, ESEA became increasingly popular in Congress, despite the broader political travail of the Great Society. By 1966, the administration was already struggling to restrain those who wished to expand it more rapidly. And in 1967, despite the more conservative composition of the 90th Congress, a promising GOP effort to turn ESEA into a block grant was rolled back. Why did this happen, given that enacting the legislation had been difficult when liberalism was at its peak? It was certainly not a reflection of ESEA's success in policy terms; to the contrary, early evaluations were deeply discouraging, and some academic research was calling into question the whole concept of "compensatory education" upon which the big Title I program rested.[1] Rather, it is primarily a story of Capitol Hill politics.

Congress and the First Vietnam Budget

Nineteen sixty-five was a year of extraordinary legislative success for Johnson, but by the end of the year, the prospect for liberalism had dimmed. During the summer, 75,000 ground troops had been committed to Vietnam, and when he unveiled his new budget in January 1966, anticipated spending on the war exceeded the previous year's forecast for fiscal year 1967 by $10.5 billion, 9.1 percent of the entire federal budget.[2] Because he had to pay for the war, Johnson was already unable to satisfy the domestic appetites that he had whetted during the previous year, and as 1966 ran on, his need to rein in spending only deepened, as the specter of inflation loomed on the horizon. By midyear, federal spending threatened to unbalance the hitherto controlled and inflation-free expansion of the past five years.

In January 1966, Johnson was not prepared to submit a war budget comprising higher taxes and higher borrowing.[3] Instead, his economic advisers crafted a hold-the-line package: it included no significant tax hike, predicted only a modest deficit, and—in consequence—had to keep expenditures for Great Society programs at essentially standstill levels. In the case of education, he sought to fund modest increases in ESEA by saving money on four older programs: the impact aid program of 1950, the NDEA of 1958, the school milk program of 1954, and the Morrill land grant act of 1862.

Johnson's proposed cuts were obviously unrealistic. To be sure, he insisted with every appearance of conviction that Congress must not exceed his budgetary requests, that to do so would destabilize the economy. But, if he meant it, why had he proposed cuts that even some of the most conservative members of Congress would find unacceptable?[4] After all, NDEA, the Morrill Act, the school lunch program, and impact aid were all popular, well established, and uncontroversial. The main controversy centered on impact aid. Johnson thought it a waste of money, especially now that ESEA was on the books. When he called his mentor, Senator Richard Russell (D-Ga.), to discuss the program, Johnson said that he favored cuts and asked Russell what he thought of the idea:

> RUSSELL: I'd leave that alone. I wouldn't fool with that. That's part of the school system in this country and has been for fifteen years.
>
> JOHNSON: Yes, but a third of it goes to rich people.
>
> RUSSELL: (Wearily) I know it's all wrong . . .
>
> JOHNSON: (Interrupting) It's not to the poor districts—it's in fact [going] to these goddamn districts where . . .
>
> RUSSELL: (Interrupting) . . . these districts with the highest per capita income.
>
> JOHNSON: [Districts like] Alexandria and Arlington get a third of it. It's just outrageous.[5]

In part, impact aid was successful because it distributed aid to more than 4,000 school districts, with very few strings attached. Also, it boasted a singularly formidable, if unorthodox, lobby operation, led by one Oscar V. Rose, superintendent of schools for Midwest City, Oklahoma. That was an unprepossessing-sounding title, but a veteran education staffer on the Hill recalls Rose as having been "the most effective lobbyist I ever met."[6] When Ralph Huitt, head of HEW's legislative liaison team, learned that the Bureau of the Budget was recommending cuts, he dispatched an urgent note to the White House, warning of Rose's power:

ADMINISTRATIVE-CONFIDENTIAL

MEMORANDUM TO HONORABLE DOUGLASS CATER

Attached is a list of the school superintendents principally relied on by Oscar Rose in his lobbying efforts for federally impacted school districts. Rose's group has neither name nor organization. Nevertheless it can get telegrams or phone calls from many of the more than 4000 school superintendents whose districts qualify for money under P.L. 874 and 815. Those listed here are highly effective.

Rose and his group, it should be noted, can be relied on to help with our other education bills.

In attempting to put some limits on expenditures for these districts, I think we need to talk realistically about what we have a chance to pass. If our suggestions are too drastic the legislation will be written by Rose's superintendents and the committee members.[7]

The particular cuts proposed by the administration were entirely *un*realistic. Among those disproportionately affected were Senator Lister Hill (D-Ala.), head of both the Labor and Public Welfare Committee and the appropriations subcommittee responsible for HEW; Rep. John E. Fogarty (D-R.I.), chair of the House appropriations subcommittee; and Rep. Adam Clayton Powell (D-N.Y.), chairman of the House Education and Labor Committee.[8] When Hill's appropriations subcommittee met in March, its members talked of little else, comparing notes regarding how their respective states would be affected and berating HEW secretary John W. Gardner for the proposal's obvious political absurdity. Conservative Senator Norris Cotton (R-N.H.) indicated that it would pass only "over my dead body."[9] At the equivalent meeting of the House subcommittee, chairman Fogarty was withering.[10]

As Huitt had warned, legislators could not conceive that such a proposal might have been seriously intended and took its inclusion in Johnson's education budget as an invitation to write their own bill. Perhaps some of them were more pleased than offended by the administration's misstep. Having played second fiddle to the executive branch the previous year, senators and representatives were anxious to show their independence.[11] The political

shift in alliance to Johnson

mood was very different from the year before, even though the personnel were the same. Among the former political allies who were now seeking to distance themselves from the White House was Wayne Morse, chair of the Senate Labor and Public Welfare Committee's education subcommittee.

VIETNAM AND THE CHANGING POLITICS OF EDUCATION

Despite his reputation as a loose cannon, Morse had proved to be a tactful and considerate chairman, good at forging alliances, and attentive to minority party colleagues.[12] His value to the White House had never been more apparent than during the previous year's ESEA debate, when he had demonstrated great restraint in agreeing that the House bill should move through the Senate unamended, obviating a conference. Until now, the fact that he was an outspoken critic of the war had not damaged his broader relationship with the White House. According to Vice President Hubert Humphrey, Morse and Johnson "had a strange relationship. Wayne would constantly implant his foot right in Johnson's groin and a few days later they would be bosom buddies."[13] When he and Johnson spoke, they would reminisce about their years together in the Senate, poke fun at one another, and compare notes on their respective livestock holdings.[14] Johnson apparently respected him as a principled opponent of the war, in a way that he did not respect other critics, such as Senators William J. Fulbright (D-Ark.) or Robert Kennedy.[15]

To some extent, this "strange relationship" persisted after 1965. When Johnson was looking for help in settling a damaging airline strike, he turned to Morse (a former labor lawyer), and the Oregonian accepted the assignment.[16] And there were occasions when they continued to work together on education too. HEW staffer Samuel Halperin recalls having been in Morse's office one day, discussing tactics for an education bill, when the senator picked up the phone and dialed the White House. Morse and Johnson proceeded to conspire amicably on the same topic, worrying in particular about how to get Morse's fellow Oregonian, Edith Green, "on board" (a perennial concern). When that discussion was concluded, though, Morse abruptly shifted gears and started "screaming" at Johnson for backing fascist colonels and juntas in Latin America.[17]

Still, Morse's ever more strident condemnation of Johnson's policies in Vietnam during the early months of 1966 did affect the politics of education, not least because he was increasingly being joined in his criticisms of the war by two Democratic colleagues on the education subcommittee: Robert Kennedy and Joseph Clark (D-Pa.). In early February, Ralph Huitt found Morse "highly cooperative and ready to push the education program."[18] When his subcommittee commenced ESEA hearings a few weeks later, though, the chairman's mood had changed.

The catalyst for the change was Senator Fulbright, chairman of the Foreign Relations Committee. During February, he convened hearings on the administration's conduct of the Vietnam War, and soon they were attracting a television audience of some 30,000,000 Americans as well as exhaustive coverage in the newspapers. Morse intervened aggressively in the debate, in a move that reportedly generated "thousands" of "congratulatory telegrams, encouraging letters, and imploring speaking invitations" and made him "Washington's busiest platform speaker."[19] As he competed with colleagues such as Kennedy and Clark for the approbation of the growing antiwar movement, Johnson's proposed Vietnam-related cuts emerged as one element of their attack. When John Gardner, secretary of HEW, appeared before Morse's committee, it was Kennedy who took center stage. Clearly addressing a wider audience, he berated Gardner and the new education commissioner, Harold Howe, in strikingly belligerent, emotional, and at times incoherent terms, excoriating the administration for its inattention to the needs of children, racial minorities, and the poor. "We are spending $12 billion each year extra in Vietnam," Kennedy charged, "and most of that is dealing with killing people, and it doesn't seem to me [sic], I think it is shortsighted at the same time not to be doing what we have to do in our own country to educate people."[20]

INTEREST GROUPS AND THE PRESSURE TO EXPAND ESEA

To administration officials such as Huitt and Douglass Cater, the other notable feature of the Senate subcommittee's treatment of the education bill was the intensive interest group activity. The previous year, lobbyists had not had much opportunity to shape ESEA, in part because of Johnson's political strength but also because it was recognized that any amendment might disrupt the precarious entente that existed among supporters of the bill. Then, the lobbyists had been reduced to foot soldiers in the administration's successful effort to force ESEA through Congress. Their willingness to discharge that role, however, had been contingent on their understanding that, once the program was up and running, they would have a greater opportunity to adjust it in the interests of their constituents. Reauthorization hearings provided them with their first big opportunity, and textbook publishers, librarians, the handicapped, and research universities were among those who leaped in, exploiting the administration's new vulnerability and petitioning legislators and their staffers regarding their particular needs.

Their conduit to the committee was Charles Lee, who had been the professional staff member to the education subcommittee throughout Morse's years as chair. During that period, he had become an influential figure in education politics, with a consummate mastery of education law and committee politics and unrivaled contacts among the lobby groups. He was talented in other ways too, according to Stewart McClure, chief clerk to the full committee: "He was a brilliant guy. . . . He was a rotund, slightly effeminate, hilariously witty man who had read everything there ever was and could quote it all. 'As Carlyle said,' or Shakespeare, or Moliere. Wonderful guy and a superb parallel with Morse, who was just as bright but in a different way. They made a great team. Charlie Lee was just a superb person to work with."[21]

Morse, who was a tough boss, sometimes took unfair advantage of Lee. Although Lee was formally employed by the committee, for example, Morse also expected him to help out with his livestock business. On occasion, says Morse's biographer, Lee would find himself "hauling cows to the Carolinas and horses to Oregon."[22] But when it came to education politics, the senator was heavily dependent on his staffer, whom he trusted implicitly for his policy knowledge, his contacts, and his shrewd political brain.[23] Such was his reliance on Lee, that at one meeting with them, Edith Green—who detested Morse—snapped, "If Senator Morse doesn't know the answer, maybe Senator Lee does."[24]

While Johnson worried about the prospect of a ballooning budget deficit, his aides struggled to restrain the strong pressures to expand education spending. During the markup sessions, Douglass Cater warned him that "Charlie Lee . . . has been blissfully compiling one expensive amendment after another."[25] His capacity to do so was enhanced by the abject failure of the administration's attempt to cut back impact aid. As Huitt told the White House—in a memo whose language perhaps hinted at his other life, as a political scientist—"the Administration's failure in this and other attempted changes and reductions has hurt its prestige."[26] Johnson warned Wilbur Mills (D-Ark.), chair of the House Ways and Means committee, that Fogarty would add "five or six hundred million over the budget" and that "when Morse and Bobby Kennedy get through it may be a billion."[27]

The first prediction was accurate, but the second proved too sanguine. In fact, when Lee had finished his work, the committee bill exceeded the administration proposal by $2 billion. HEW and White House officials had been working hard to try to dissuade the subcommittee from this budget-busting bill, Cater told the president, but "there is no reasoning with Morse."[28] That was also the impression of Henry Hall Wilson, Johnson's top House liaison man: "Senator Morse's attitude appears to be budgetary considerations are meaningless and that you should save money by cutting down spending in Vietnam."[29]

Unable to sway Morse, they tried to persuade Lister Hill, chairman of the full committee, to crack the whip. Hill, though, was increasingly disinclined to get involved in education politics, even though this had been one of his real passions during the first half of his long political career.[30] As Stewart McClure explains, "the *Brown* decision came down and the segregationists went mad. George Wallace wasn't [yet] governor, but the mood in Alabama was that it was no time for the federal government to put its fingers into public education. He was driven off of it, except for the NDEA, which was wrapped in the flag and safe."[31] Accordingly, Hill had been unwilling to get involved in the fight for ESEA in 1965, which coincided with the Selma crisis, and although Johnson had badly wanted his support, he also understood Hill's predicament, telling Moyers: "I imagine he's upset in Alabama [sigh]. I imagine he's afraid of us. I imagine that they're giving him hell, poor man."[32]

By March of 1966, it was if anything still *less* likely that Hill would want to get involved in education politics: HEW had just issued tough new desegregation guidelines, and this was creating a firestorm of protest across the South.[33] In that environment, he opted out of the ESEA debate entirely, refusing to return Douglass Cater's phone calls. Budget director Charles Schultze reported that with "Senator Morse and his influential subcommittee staff piling expensive amendment on top of expensive amendment, Hill was 'taking no part.'" Indeed, he had not attended a single session, despite being a member of the subcommittee.[34]

With the final markup session about to take place, Schultze asked the president to intervene. Specifically, he suggested that Johnson make the following three points to Hill, designed to appeal to his instincts as an appropriations subcommittee chairman:

- Call attention to the *huge* and *irresponsible* increases which are involved.
- Point out that school districts cannot conceivably increase their spending this rapidly without being wasteful and extravagant.

- Indicate that increases of this magnitude are *completely unacceptable*—especially in the light of current inflationary pressures.[35]

Evidently alarmed, Johnson ordered Cater to summon Lister Hill to the White House the following day and won from him a public commitment that he would try to cut the bloated subcommittee bill back in full committee.[36] Meanwhile, HEW officials tried to work on other members of the Senate education subcommittee, including its chairman. Since Morse had just announced in higher education hearings that he intended "to place the responsibility for the Vietnam war where it belongs—on the doorstep of the White House," it was clearer than ever that he would not be impressed by economy arguments of the kind that Schultze was commending to Johnson.[37] He had indicated his willingness to listen to educational arguments, however.[38] In response, Francis Keppel's replacement as education commissioner, Harold Howe II, told Morse that "large additional appropriations" would lead to waste and that this would "discredit the program in the long run—and even bring the entire concept of Federal aid to education into disrepute."[39]

In support of their case, Howe and Secretary Gardner told Morse of mounting evidence that school districts were struggling to formulate ESEA Title I proposals, putting them together hurriedly and in some cases submitting bids that had little obvious relevance to compensatory education. In particular, following Don White's energetic efforts in behalf of the audio-visual lobby the previous year, large amounts had been spent on equipment purchases. At HEW, the feeling was "that a number of school districts are using Title I funds to stockpile costly electronic apparatus and other items they cannot fully utilize now."[40]

Morse was not persuaded, and neither were his subcommittee colleagues, who reported a bill that more than doubled the cost of the administration's proposal.[41] The bulk of the increase—$1.5 billion—came from the decision to raise the poverty level used in the Title I formula from $2,000 to $3,000. This was an idea that the administration had supported until recently, but which it now viewed as being unaffordable, given the deteriorating budgetary picture. Responding to Johnson's entreaties, Lister Hill managed to have the subcommittee bill pared back in full committee, but only by half a billion dollars: the Title I poverty bar was raised to $2,500 instead of $3,000. The White House indicated that it would support an increase to $3,000 in 1967. The bill approved by the full Senate the following week still authorized $1 billion in excess of the administration's request.

The funds still had to be appropriated, of course, and the appropriations committees were dominated by conservatives. Still, as Ralph Huitt had re-marked a few months earlier, "the appropriations committees are not happy about being made the 'goats' by failing to appropriate what the majority of the Congress has authorized."[42] Given the extent of the add-ons and the strong political support for education spending that had been apparent dur-ing the Senate hearings, it was not at all clear that they would wish to risk the obloquy of sticking to Johnson's budget. Much would depend on what hap-pened in the House.

ADAM CLAYTON POWELL KEEPS HIS WORD — EVENTUALLY

Of the two authorizing committees that handled education legislation, it was the House body that had the reputation for being unruly and hard to manage.[43] In particular, no one could predict how Chairman Powell would behave. The previous year, where Morse had been the team-player par excel-lence, Powell had been a loose cannon, holding ESEA hostage in exchange for personal favors from the administration. How would he behave now, with the administration's political standing palpably diminished?

Proceedings got off to an inauspicious start. Just before he was to meet an HEW delegation headed by Secretary Gardner, Powell left town without explanation.[44] And when hearings got underway, the administration came under sustained attack. Huitt reported that there was "scarcely a Demo-cratic member who is interested in 'holding the line.'"[45] Still, when Johnson and Powell spoke on the telephone at the end of May, just before the bill was scheduled to be reported, the chairman seemed cooperative. Characteris-tically whimsical, Powell—celebrated pastor of the huge Abyssinian Bap-tist church in Harlem—introduced himself as "your humble parish priest." When they got to the subject of ESEA, however, Johnson's tone was serious and urgent, reflecting his intense anxiety about the deficit and his desire to get his message through to the mercurial chairman. Powell reported his in-tention to get ESEA out of committee the following week, at which point Johnson told him (in an insistent tone): "Make them stay with it. Don't let them run wild." Powell reassured him: "Oh no," and repeated the phrase twice more for emphasis.[46]

Perhaps Johnson was not entirely surprised when the next week, and in-deed the next *seven* weeks, came and went without the bill being reported. During this period, as Henry Hall Wilson told Johnson, it was "pretty dif-ficult to talk with House members" about cuts, given what was going on in the Morse subcommittee. Still, two weeks later, Powell belatedly kept his word: the budgetary increase was kept to $400 million. It was an impressive demonstration of what one close observer referred to as his "rare ability to keep a number of rather cantankerous individuals . . . in line."[47] His motivation for cooperating is less clear, but a move was under way in the House to split his committee into two parts, and perhaps in resisting this unwelcome prospect Powell needed the administration's cooperation as much as it needed his.[48] Whatever the explanation, Cater told Johnson that this was "a surprisingly responsible result," adding that a "number of costly amendments were avoided by narrow margins." With luck, he surmised, the committee's move "provides us with a strong talking point to bring about reductions in the Hill committee and in Conference."[49]

That confidence turned out to be justified. In conference in October, the most expensive element of the Senate-passed bill, the increase in the poverty standard to $2,500, was removed, and the total authorization reduced by $1 billion. That was still half a billion in excess of what the administration had requested, but clearly the prospects for avoiding an appropriation that greatly exceeded Johnson's budget had materially improved.

A CHANGE OF MOOD: CONGRESS EMBRACES FISCAL RESTRAINT

A portentous turning point in overall congressional attitudes toward spending took place during the fall of 1966, shortly before that year's midterm elections. Earlier in the year, legislators had chafed at what they considered to be the modesty of the administration's budgetary requests for Great Society programs. By the late summer, though, the cost of the war and Johnson's repeated entreaties to legislators to stay within his budget were having some effect: although the liberal majority of the 89th Congress remained keen to fund new Great Society programs more generously, conservative advocates of spending restraint were now less isolated than before.[50] In the House, for example, there were seventy-one freshman Democrats, many of whom represented normally Republican districts. Whereas in November of 1964, they had benefited from Lyndon Johnson's long coattails, now their chances of reelection were imperiled by his deepening unpopularity.[51] To stay in office, some of them needed to distance themselves from the White House, soft pedal their support for civil rights and the war on poverty, and bang the drum for spending restraint.

One sign of the new mood in Congress was its failure to enact "fair housing" legislation.[52] Another was its new willingness after the summer recess to contemplate cuts in Johnson's budget. It was a very sudden change that, in retrospect, prefigured the big battles over spending and taxation that would occur during the last two years of the Johnson presidency. It had more immediate implications for education, for the mood change came shortly after the Senate and House education committees had each reported their ESEA reauthorization bills. In October, very late in the session, the two spending committees went to work.

Of the two Appropriations Committees, the more important was the House body, chaired by George Mahon of Texas.[53] Although the overall composition of the committee was highly conservative, its Labor-HEW subcommittee was comparatively liberal, and its chairman, John Fogarty of Rhode Island, especially so. Since the full committee normally abided by decisions reached in its subcommittees, there was no individual in Congress who mattered more to HEW than Fogarty, who played a larger role in determining how much money each of John Gardner's agencies had to spend.[54] Gardner recalls having found him quite formidable, characterizing him as "a hard-drinking Irishman, very truculent, rough in his manner and often appearing hostile."[55] At the same time, he greatly appreciated Fogarty's staunch support for social spending, which helped him to combat White House demands for retrenchment, and HEW program administrators strove to win the Rhode Islander's approbation.[56]

President Johnson recognized Fogarty's power too, and during the first half of 1966, when the pressure in Congress for boosting Great Society spending had been at its height, Johnson had lobbied Fogarty intensively. In February, for example, he had presented the Rhode Islander with the American Heart Association's Heart of the Year award, given to figures in public life who had suffered a heart attack and gone on to champion the association's cause.[57] Two months later, he had spent an hour with Fogarty at the White House, trying in vain to dissuade him from raising appropriations for education and (especially) health. Finally, in June, the president had dropped in unannounced at Gallaudet University's commencement exercises, having discovered that both Fogarty and Lister Hill were to receive honorary doctorates.[58]

It is not clear that Johnson's personal diplomacy made any difference to Fogarty's behavior. At the White House meeting, for example, Johnson reported that "all he'd do is sit there, puffed up, wouldn't debate, he just said 'we don't do enough for health and education.'" Frustrated, Johnson told Wilbur Mills that chairman Mahon had "lost control" of the Fogarty subcommittee.[59] In conversation with budget director Schultze, the president assailed legislators wanting more money for HEW as "greedy" and as "bastards."[60] By the fall, though, Mahon was very worried about the budgetary situation, knew that Congress in general was more receptive to spending restraint than earlier in the year, and put greater pressure on his colleagues—including Fogarty—to make cuts.[61] Accordingly, when the House Appropriations Committee reported out its supplemental appropriation for Labor-HEW in October, it ignored the authorizing committees and gave the administration exactly what it had asked for back in January, even to the point of specifying that each title of the bill should receive the precise amount that Johnson had requested.[62] The Senate followed suit, in its last action before Congress adjourned for the midterm elections.

In conversation with Wilbur Mills, the president took a share of the credit for this development, telling the powerful chairman of Ways and Means that "I held them [to] just what I recommended." He went on:

> Congress backed me up. They had up to 8 billion [dollars] reported there at one time, and in the final days because we all raised so much hell and started talking about cutting and everything, Congress acted *very* responsible last week—and I think it's largely because of the campaign we put on talking about how much they were going over.[63]

But even though the mood had shifted from expansion to retrenchment, these last actions of the congressional session also attested anew to the relative popularity of education spending on the Hill. Of the fifteen appropriations bills that Congress deliberated on toward the end of the session, thirteen had gone below the administration's request.[64]

THE RIGHT GAINS GROUND: THE MIDTERM ELECTIONS OF 1966

After the midterm elections, Johnson confronted a dramatically altered congressional landscape. The key change had occurred in the House: half of the big Democratic freshman class of 1964 was wiped out, a number of southern moderates were defeated, and the net result was a Republican gain of forty-seven seats. The Democratic edge declined from 295–140 in the 89th Congress to 238–187 in the 90th. Most of the more prominent Republican victors were ideological moderates, such as Senators Edward Brooke (Mass.), Charles Percy (Ill.), Mark Hatfield (Ore.), and Howard Baker (Tenn.). Critical of the excesses of Great Society liberalism, they had also presented themselves as modern Republicans who accepted that the federal government had a role to play in improving the education system, reducing poverty, and eliminating racial discrimination.[65]

The Republican Party was resurgent, and when Gerald Ford and Everett Dirksen—GOP leaders in the House and Senate, respectively—delivered a "state of the union" address in January 1967, their self-confidence and ambition were palpable. They too sought to present the image of a positive, modern, constructive Republican Party, one that rejected not government per se, but rather red tape, excessive centralization, welfarism, and waste. In the case of education, they did not propose to stop the flow of federal funds to the nation's school districts but to spend the money differently, in a way more respectful to federalism:

> The Elementary and Secondary Act . . . at minimum requires substantial revision to simplify forms, reduce excessive paperwork and eliminate the heavy-handed Federal intrusions. . . . Republicans trust local school boards to formulate policy and set priorities far more than we trust bureaucrats in Washington.
>
> Congress should take the federal handcuffs off our local educators. The best way to do this is by tax sharing and tax credits. If the Democrats, who control Congress, refuse to consider tax sharing legislation, Republicans will seek to substitute block education grants, without federal earmarking or controls.[66]

That approach left ESEA much more vulnerable than an outright, Goldwaterite attack on the enlarged federal role in education would have done. Still, replacing ESEA with block grants would certainly not be easy, given the difficulty of dislodging established federal programs. Much would depend on the political adroitness of the advocates of reform, who would be up against talented White House and HEW congressional relations operations.

The Great Society in Hard Times: Education Politics in 1967

Although the Republican Party's midterm gains were deeply unwelcome, another adverse development loomed still larger in President Johnson's thinking as he put together his 1967 legislative program and his 1968 budget. The war in Vietnam was now putting the nation's finances under tremendous strain: the projected budget deficit for the current fiscal year stood at $25 billion, compared to the president's initial projection of less than $5 billion. And whereas inflation had stood at 2.5 percent twelve months before, now the figure stood at 4 percent, owing mainly to increased federal spending and a series of expensive wage settlements. In the case both of the deficit and inflation, worse was feared.[67] Johnson felt constrained to recommend a 6 percent tax surcharge and to produce a budget that—again—kept domestic discretionary spending far below what congressional liberals had anticipated. Absent evidence of a serious effort by the president to save money, it was unlikely that conservatives would agree to a tax increase: many of them shared Ford's stated belief that the budget could be balanced simply by cutting non-essential spending.[68]

What did all this mean for education? The most important thing was that the budget bureau felt that it was not possible to fund the liberalized Title I formula that the administration had promised Congress the previous year. That brought cries of anguish from John W. Gardner. In mid-December, midway through the FY 1968 budget round, he warned Johnson about the likely effect of the proposed cuts on "your image and the image of the Administration." "Briefly," he said, "budget allowances on a number of items (chiefly in education) are going to be so dramatically below authorizations we asked for two years ago, that you will be *extremely vulnerable* to charges of gutting the Great Society. *You will be subjected to severe and continuing criticism as a result of these items.*"[69]

Johnson was unmoved, siding with Schultze, who had explained to him that education was where most of HEW's discretionary funds were concentrated.[70] At that point, Gardner issued a second appeal, noting that "we will be funding the 1968 program at the level authorized for 1966" and pleading that the president at least request the Title I funds necessary to raise the poverty threshold from $2,000 to $2,250. If that were done, HEW could at least make the case to Congress that there was some "forward momentum."[71] Again, his appeals fell on deaf ears. One can imagine the feelings of trepidation and disappointment that Gardner must have experienced as he returned to his department with this bad news and contemplated the prospect of another round of appearances before the same liberal-dominated authorization committees that had savaged the administration the previous year. Then, he had claimed that school districts needed a little time to absorb the new arrangements and had held out the promise of greater largesse in 1967. What was he to say this time?

Gardner was right in predicting that the administration's education budget would be poorly received. As soon as it had been unveiled, Charles Lee called OE to complain, and when Gardner and Howe appeared before the House Education and Labor Committee in March, its Democratic members expressed outrage and dismay, just as they had in 1966.[72] This year, however, the complaints were less politically important, given the inescapable budgetary realities and the much greater pressure that the administration was under from the Right. That threat took shape on March 20, when Congressman Albert Quie of Minnesota, the leading Republican education spokesman in the House, unveiled the GOP's block grant proposal.

ALBERT QUIE AND MODERN REPUBLICANISM

Quite early in his career, the national party had singled out Albert Quie, a Minnesota farmer and former navy pilot, as the kind of attractive young face that the GOP needed if it were to combat the appeal of Camelot. The Republican National Committee had sent him around the country in 1961 as one of four "Paul Reveres," deputed to expose the failings of the new Kennedy administration.[73] He had an agreeable personality. One profile in a Minnesota newspaper, later in the decade, described him like this: "He wears a big friendly grin. His crewcut in the Era of the Mop doesn't make him look square, just earnest with a touch of All-America. His voice and diction are crisp and smooth. He sounds like television's Hugh Downs and could probably get a network job if Congress became a bore."[74]

If the Paul Revere venture had yielded little, Quie had emerged in the years since as one of the sharpest critics of Great Society liberalism and especially of the War on Poverty, which he labeled "vacuous and partisan."[75] When he attacked the war on poverty, however, it was significant that Quie did not simply suggest that the Economic Opportunity Act be repealed. Rather, he proposed a Republican Opportunity Crusade in its place. In other words, he already epitomized before 1967 the kind of constructive, modern brand of Republicanism that his minority leader was looking to promote in the aftermath of the midterm elections.

Because of Quie's strong criticisms of Great Society programs and because the Republican leadership admired him so, administration figures such as Larry O'Brien and Douglass Cater tended to regard him as an out-and-out partisan and assumed that the Quie amendment was motivated primarily by a desire to embarrass the administration and score political points.[76] That was an understandable assessment but probably also unjust. One aspect of Quie's political personality that does not come through in the newspaper profiles but emerges very strongly in his private correspondence and in interviews with his associates is his studious, painstaking approach to public policy. Doubtless he was opportunistic in the way that all successful politicians must be opportunistic, but—those sources suggest—he was in other respects unusual, especially in the time that he devoted to mastering policy detail and worrying about broad principles.[77]

That was reflected in his approach to education policy, a subject that had engaged him since his time in the Minnesota state legislature, during the mid-1950s. In 1965, despite his belief that the federal government had a legitimate role to play in elementary and secondary schooling, he had opposed ESEA.[78] The following year, however, he switched sides, voting to reautho-

[Quie + Esea]

rize the legislation. He outlined his pragmatic rationale in a letter to a constituent who had expressed misgivings about the new federal role in education: "I note that you have the same conflicts which I do in regard to Federal assistance to education. Now that the Federal Government assists education to the extent it does, I believe there is little likelihood that the level of support will decrease[,] mostly because of the difficulty local education systems have raising their funds from non-Federal sources in the event Federal funding should be reduced."[79] At the same time, he worried that "if the categorical approach continues for any length of time I believe it unbalances our education system," tending to diminish the power of the states to set their own priorities and making them overly dependent on Washington. To avert this danger, he felt that categorical programs should be converted into general aid, once they had been in operation for a few years.[80]

The fruit of these ruminations about the federal role in education was the Quie amendment. It would replace four of ESEA's five categorical titles (all but Title IV, which gave federal grants for education research) with a single grant to the states, according to a formula that would funnel rather greater resources to the poorer states. Since Quie did not propose to reduce federal funding, one might ask why the White House should have regarded the amendment with apprehension. After all, a few years earlier it had been the *liberal* position to support such "general" aid (for example, the 1961 Kennedy proposal), whereas conservatives had viewed this concept with suspicion, seeing in it the potential for federal control over every aspect of local schooling. Back then, conservatives had much preferred categorical aid for specific purposes, on the grounds that it allowed them to confine the federal role to those limited areas where there was a clear national interest in education (for example, in the context of national security).

Since the early 1960s, however, conservatives and liberals had switched sides. Now, liberals tended to support categorical aid: partly on the grounds that the federal contribution was small and would have no effect on the educational priorities of local school districts unless the funds were directed toward specific purposes; partly because the particular lobbies that benefited from categorical aid (librarians, equipment manufacturers, and research universities, for example) would have a greater stake in fighting for higher federal spending if the money were earmarked for their constituents. Meanwhile, conservatives increasingly worried about categorical aid for the very same reasons: it was prescriptive in ways that offended the principle of local control, and it subordinated national problems to the parochial preferences of an emerging "educational-industrial complex."[81]

The Quie amendment represented a potent challenge to the Johnson administration, at least in the House, whose complexion had been so significantly altered by the recent elections (liberals remained dominant in the Senate). It could be expected to appeal to southerners on the grounds that its distribution formula would benefit poorer states, whereas diminished federal bureaucracy might reduce the pressure on school districts to desegregate. Also, the big education interest groups (unlike their more specialized colleagues) claimed to prefer general aid to categorical aid, because the funds could be used for immediately pressing local needs (school construction, for example, or higher salaries), rather than to advance the more abstract social policy priorities of the Johnson administration, and because general aid would involve a lot less paperwork.[82]

Within the Johnson administration, the Quie amendment caused deep apprehension. It was not so much that the White House feared that ESEA was about to unravel: the block grant proposal might well succeed in the House, but it would have an uphill struggle in the Senate, where the administration's political position was much stronger. Rather, defeat in the House would be a devastating psychological blow, further weakening Johnson's already diminished standing and boosting an already buoyant conservative movement. According to the *Wall Street Journal*, this would be "the first clear test in the 90th Congress of President Johnson's ability to hold his domestic course against a Republican call for 'new directions.'" Observing that "school aid is among the most popular of all of his Great Society programs," the *Journal* felt that "a successful GOP move to remold it would alter other legislative prospects." It quoted an unnamed administration official who felt the same way: "While it's always dangerous to draw sweeping conclusions from the voting on a single bill, the results on this one could set the tone of the entire Congressional session. If the Republicans put over their substitute, they're clearly the masters of the House, and anyone who wants a bill passed will be inclined to take their terms."[83]

THE ADMINISTRATION COUNTERATTACKS

Faced with this prospect, an unnamed Johnson official conceded that "we're running scared."[84] Determined to avoid further erosion in its political standing, the administration mounted a fierce, sustained effort to defeat the Quie amendment. It was led by Larry O'Brien, now postmaster general, but still called in by the president to coordinate the really big legislative fights, of which this was one. Formally in charge of the White House lobbying effort, meanwhile, was Henry Hall Wilson, who was admired by O'Brien and Johnson, especially for his skill at working with southern Democrats.[85] Douglass Cater's role was also important. Two years after the passage of ESEA, in which he had played an important role, he remained Johnson's White House education expert, although his time was increasingly taken up with defending the administration's policies in Vietnam.[86] Like Wilson, he had good links to the southerners.

The White House challenge was complicated by turmoil within the Education and Labor Committee. At the beginning of the year, Adam Clayton Powell had been expelled from the House for abuse of privileges, leaving Carl Perkins in charge (a position that he would retain until his death in 1984). Although Perkins went on to become an immensely accomplished chairman, the short-term effect of Powell's departure was to create something of a vacuum of leadership within this always fractious committee. Responsibility for coordinating the ESEA fight on the floor ended up being shared by four senior committee Democrats (Perkins, John Brademas, James O'Hara, and Roman Pucinski), while Edith Green, excluded from that group, wielded greater political power than any of them, thanks to her close ties to southern Democrats and Republicans and to the additional fact that neither her colleagues nor the administration was privy to her intentions.

In this environment, the intrinsically difficult task of turning back the challenge of the Quie amendment became even more complicated, with administration officials shouldering responsibilities that might in other contexts have been handled by allies on the committee. Although O'Brien and Cater played an important role, their HEW colleagues were also at the heart of the fight to save ESEA, with Samuel Halperin recalling "a great deal of head-counting, marshalling of forces, a great deal of political propaganda."[87] The crucial achievement of the HEW team was to turn Catholic and other private school groups against the amendment.

TURNING THE CATHOLICS AGAINST QUIE

Although Catholics had not done as well out of ESEA as they might have hoped, all of its first three titles had resulted in some funds reaching parochial school children, and a new title for the handicapped, approved the previous year, promised to do the same.[88] An additional result of the act was that state boards of education, local school boards, and pressure groups such as the NEA had to learn how to work with Catholic school groups. Already, groups that had previously viewed one another with deep suspicion were starting to develop amicable working relationships, to the satisfaction of Catholic superintendents and lobbyists.[89] When the Quie amendment surfaced, someone at HEW warned Msgr. James C. Donohue, director of the U.S. Catholic Conference's (USCC) department of education, that it might lead to Catholic school children losing their ESEA funds.[90]

That claim rested on the fact that more than thirty states barred any form of state aid to private schools, even under the child-benefit theory. If federal funds were distributed by the states, rather than passed straight through to individual districts, aid to parochial and private school students would be in jeopardy in those states. Donohue told Quie that he viewed the proposal "with deep apprehension and concern."[91] Three days later, on the day that the amendment was introduced, the executive director of a leading private school pressure group distributed a doom-laden form letter to its membership. It began with the stark warning that

> Unless immediate and drastic steps are taken, nonpublic school children are about to be eliminated from all future federal aid to education programs.

Having outlined the details of Quie's proposal, the letter goes on, with emphasis:

> *Thus, general federal aid to education without participation by nonpublic school children will be achieved.*

All recipients of the letter were urged to phone their congressmen, send telegrams, and arrange for fifty associates to act similarly. The letter concluded in apocalyptic terms:

> Accept no compromise from Congressmen which does not provide for full and equal participation on an equal basis in *all* portions of the bill. By May 1 the ball game may be over! I cannot overemphasize the danger of this emergency or the long-range disaster that will result if we fail. PLEASE ACT NOW![92]

This letter mobilized parochial and private school interests into high gear.[93] Taken aback, Quie invited Huitt and Halperin to his house one Sunday and asked them to "call off the dogs."[94] With this fight having become a credibility test for the administration's entire domestic program, though, the cordial relations that Quie normally enjoyed with the HEW men counted for little.[95] More plausibly, he moved quickly to try to reassure the Catholics, amending his proposal to prevent commingling of federal and state funds. (That meant that although the states would be distributing the aid, the funds would still be labeled "federal" moneys, getting around the state prohibitions on parochial aid.) When that failed to appease Donohue and the private school lobby, Quie went further, proposing that if a state failed to distribute funds for the benefit of private school students, responsibility should revert to Washington. That, however, significantly undermined the devolutionary intent of the measure and exposed Quie on another front: administration officials started arguing that he was actuated not by principle but simply by a partisan desire to hurt the Democrats.

Quie's general aid proposal was vulnerable in other ways too, ways that highlighted the political advantage of the categorical approach. Precisely because funds would be distributed at the discretion of the state, no district or interest could be certain that it would receive as much money under the Quie substitute as it received under the ESEA formula grant. Johnson, Gardner, and Harold Howe, in public, and the HEW and White House liaison teams, in private, hammered home this message, weaning the big education groups away from their stated preference for general aid. Four weeks into the campaign, a Republican newsletter had Quie remarking that "Johnson has got the big city superintendents thinking they'll get less money under my plan, and the rural school people thinking they'll be cheated. He's got the private and parochial people afraid they'll lose out, the civil rights backers afraid of less action against segregation, and the segregationists afraid my plan will cause more rigid enforcement."[96] It was a comment both on the political sagacity of the administration's attack and the intrinsic vulnerability of Quie's proposal.

The administration's other line of attack centered on Quie's alleged opposition to an active federal role in education. On the face of it, that was a hard argument to make, given that the Minnesotan had voted for the renewal of ESEA in 1966 and was sponsoring a proposal whose authorization first matched that of the bill reported by the Perkins committee, and then exceeded it.[97] Pointing to his record, however, administration officials noted that he had opposed the school construction bills of 1960 and 1961, the Health Professions Educational Assistance Act of 1963, the Vocational Education Act of the same year, two library construction bills in 1964, and ESEA and the Higher Education Act in 1965. Highlighting that record, an administration "fact sheet," prepared for distribution on the Hill, concluded: "Truly, it would be difficult to find a more consistent opponent of the Federal aid to education [sic] than the man who now claims to be its best friend."[98] At other times, the administration accentuated not his consistent opposition but rather his *in*consistency, as in the sheet that gleefully recited the five successive versions of the Quie substitute that had appeared in recent weeks, concluding with a snide "Isn't this all 'a *Quie* bit too much?'"[99]

Returning from a visit to Germany, Johnson weighed in, extolling the achievements of ESEA, and warning that everything could be about to unravel:

> Now some so-called "friends of education" want to go back to where we started. They claim they know a better way to spend the money. They propose to discard the Elementary and Secondary Education Act of 1965—to scrap it before it is two years old—and to substitute a different kind of legislation.
>
> No one can tell for sure how they plan to change the law. Each day they trot out a new version. But already they have accomplished a great deal. They have stirred up the suspicions of the poor states toward the wealthy states. They are reviving ancient and bitter feuds between church and public school leaders. They have aroused fears of the big city school superintendents. They are raising the same road blocks which halted federal aid to education for twenty long years. I hope Members of Congress will stop, look, and listen before they march down this blind alley.
>
> It is a time of testing for American education. The gains we have made so far are only the beginning. We must build on them. But we must not lose all we have gained by this reckless effort to rewrite our laws for partisan political advantage.[100]

Administration officials were pleased with the results of this campaign. It was now clear that the Catholic and private school groups would oppose Quie and that Republican members of Congress representing heavily Catholic districts would be under pressure to do likewise. It seemed too that—despite their preference for general aid—the other big education pressure groups would back the administration. Initially, NEA intended to stay on the fence, unwilling to jeopardize its relations with the administration but not wishing to oppose a bill that comported with its stated preferences.[101] Just ten days later, however, it was characterizing the Quie amendment as "a massive assault on the Great Society program."[102] Also opposing the proposal by this time were NSBA, the National Parent-Teacher Association (PTA), and the superintendents of a number of big city school systems.[103] The only major education group to have endorsed Quie was the Council of Chief State School Officers.

THE WHITE HOUSE WOOS THE SOUTH

These groups were motivated in part by the danger, emphasized by Gardner and Howe, that if Quie succeeded in substituting his amendment for the administration bill, the Catholic groups would kill it, leaving school districts back where they had been before 1965.[104] Nevertheless, the Republican proposal remained alive. GOP members of Congress still saw this as a test of their party's new vitality, believed that victory here would portend other triumphs, and worked hard to build a majority coalition with southern Democrats. Larry O'Brien, in a confidential telex to the LBJ ranch early in May, could detect only modest Republican erosion: somewhere between twelve and twenty. It was clear to him that "the intense Catholic effort is paying off," but his best estimate was that "we are in the range of 190 'right' combining Democrats and Republicans with a considerable way to go." It still looked like an "uphill struggle," he judged, despite the prodigious effort of the past three weeks.[105] Henry Wilson agreed, telling Johnson that although the "battle through pressure groups over the past two weeks has been extremely helpful," it had not been enough to "win this fight" or "warrant an all out showdown," that is, a vote on the floor.[106] That vote was put off for another two weeks while the administration hunted around for the additional thirty or so votes that—by O'Brien's calculation—were still needed.

Everything now depended on the southern Democrats. The administration had circulated tables showing that the southern states would lose funds under the Quie substitute, but as Wilson explained to Johnson, "the application of integration guidelines frightens Southerners far more than Administration pressure."[107] To win them over, HEW finally announced a decision that it had been trying to avoid for over a year: responsibility for enforcing civil rights guidelines was to be moved from OE to Secretary Gardner's own office. With luck, that would make OE less unpopular in the South and would make it easier for southern moderates such as Philip Landrum to vote for the renewal of ESEA. Quie's close ally Charles Goodell detected "a transparent maneuver to appease Southerners."[108]

ENTER EDITH GREEN: STALKING HORSE FOR QUIE?

At this point, shortly before the postponed floor debate was to begin, the unpredictable Edith Green offered three amendments to ESEA. The first required that the civil rights enforcement activities of HEW apply equally to all the fifty states. The second gave the states almost complete discretion over how to use Title III funds, which funded supplemental educational centers. And the third gave similar discretion to the states over Title V, a smaller program designed to improve the performance of state departments of education. All three amendments were opposed by the administration, the first on the grounds that it would undermine the desegregation pressure in the South, the other two because HEW felt that state education departments would waste the money.

Green's motivation in offering these amendments is not entirely clear. As she recalled the circumstances in a 1985 oral history, she went to see Carl Perkins in his office, "told him that I was going to offer this series of amendments, and we both agreed that without the amendments the bill couldn't possibly pass." Encouraged by his support, Green says, she went to work on Republicans and southerners, with whom she enjoyed excellent relations because of her record as a strong critic of Great Society programs.[109] Skeptics, though, ascribed Green's actions to personal pique (Perkins having denied her a role in managing the bill on the floor, despite her seniority), together with a desire to reduce the federal role in education and undermine civil rights enforcement.[110] The second and third of those explanations were some way off the mark: Green had a strong record of support for civil rights and favored a big *increase* in federal aid to education.[111]

As for the first, the muckraking columnists Jack Anderson and Drew Pearson were echoing prejudices against Green that were widely held in the administration and on her committee, when they claimed that she "takes a conspiratorial view of the world. She thinks everyone is ganging up against her—except in recent years the Republicans and Dixiecrats."[112] According to Samuel Halperin, Green "was openly hostile to LBJ's program and eager to see how far Quie could get." Even if Quie were defeated, the passage of her proposals would ensure that he achieved at least some of his policy objectives, whereas Johnson would have sustained a bloody nose.[113]

The most important of the three Green amendments was the one concerning civil rights, for it was considered before Quie's broader block grant proposal came to a vote and may have helped to determine its political fate. Because a subcommittee that she chaired had berated OE the previous year for going beyond the letter of the law in its approach to desegregation, she had a lot of credibility with southerners. Accordingly, when she proposed her equal-enforcement amendment, they applauded what they took to be an effort to rein in the department, while some liberal Democrats from the North attacked it on the same basis.[114] As the debate continued, however, its meaning seemed less and less clear, and civil rights proponents gradually came to the conclusion that it could be taken as a spur to greater enforcement activities in the North rather than an effort to reduce desegregation efforts in the South.

Green neither encouraged nor discouraged either interpretation, simply restating, again and again, that she favored equal enforcement across the country. According to one account, "Mrs. Green, sitting demurely in a green dress with a pained expression on her face, was bombarded by questions from all sides on what she was trying to accomplish."[115] (An HEW official from this period recalls that when Green was passionately concerned that one of her bills should become law, she would appear dressed in a "Kelly Green" suit. If the matter was less pressing, she would wear red.[116])

An important moment in the debate came when Perkins, probably responding to a signal from the administration, stood up and declared that Green's proposal seemed consistent with recent judicial decisions, that it was "innocuous," and that he could not "personally see any objection" to it.[117] When the majority leader, Carl Albert, followed suit, the tenor of the debate began to change.[118] First, Frank Thompson, an administration loyalist on the Education and Labor Committee, announced that he would be supporting Green. Then John Conyers, a black congressman from Detroit who had earlier opposed the proposal, returned to the microphone to say that he too had changed his mind.[119] At the same time, Dixiecrats still liked the amendment: In the view of one, it would rein in "the presently unrestrained, educational fantasies of Dr. Harold Howe II."[120]

After three hours, the legislative record was utterly confused, with James O'Hara complaining that "one member is clear that one thing is so, and another member is clear that exactly the opposite is so."[121] That suited Carl Albert and the administration, and with "the House . . . in uproar" a voice vote was called, whereupon the Green amendment was approved, backed by both the strongest supporters of civil rights and its strongest enemies.[122]

Then the House took up the Quie amendment. The passage of Green's civil rights amendment made it easier for moderate southerners to support ESEA, but the administration remained uncertain that it had the votes to defeat Quie, whose block grant proposal was debated long into the next day. Waving his arms, an impassioned Speaker McCormack charged that it would "upset the delicately balanced compromises" on the church-state issue that had been painstakingly achieved in 1965.[123] Late in the evening, the proposal finally came to a vote and was defeated by the comfortable margin of 197 votes to 168.

Because it was an unrecorded teller vote, the precise breakdown of support is unknown, but *Congressional Quarterly* recorded that "the Republicans failed to pick up substantial support from Southern Democrats."[124] With just fifteen additional southern votes, the block grant proposal would have passed the House, setting up a battle royal with the more liberal Senate and ensuring that ESEA would have been, at the least, heavily modified. Whatever Green's motivation in offering the civil rights amendment, its main consequence was to ensure that Johnson's landmark education bill retained its essential character. By contrast, the passage of her *other* two amendments, the ones giving the states greater control over the disbursal of Title III and Title V funds, deprived two of ESEA's five categorical programs of their teeth and were rightly construed by Republicans as "mini-Quie amendments" that helped them to achieve some of their objectives through the back door.

When the House approved a fourth amendment, proposed by Sam Gibbons (D-Fla.), that gave a larger share of Title I funds to the poorer states, ESEA looked more attractive than ever to southerners.[125] Half an hour later, the House finally voted on the administration bill, passing ESEA by its biggest margin yet: 294 votes to 122. The previous year, a majority of southerners had voted for ESEA for the first time. This time, following the defeat of the Quie amendments and the success of the Green amendments, it was Republicans who crossed the Rubicon. In 1965, three-quarters of them had opposed ESEA. Now, they voted to reauthorize it by a margin of 99–80.[126]

THE SIGNIFICANCE OF THE QUIE AMENDMENT FIGHT

In the Senate, passage of ESEA was much more straightforward, reflecting the fact that the political balance of power had not shifted to anything like the same extent in November of 1966. Although Morse subcommittee members remained deeply unhappy about funding levels, there was no equivalent to the previous year's rebellion against the administration. Rather, attention focused on civil rights enforcement, on the distribution formula, and on the future of the Teacher Corps. The biggest development on the Senate side was the addition of yet another title to ESEA: Title VII, which provided funds in support of bilingual education programs. As with Title VI for the handicapped, which had been created the previous year, it was initially a small program, but it created yet another constituency for federal aid in its current, categorical form.[127] Every time that happened, the prospects for general aid receded further into the distance.

What did all this mean for the future of ESEA? Despite the irritation of the Green amendments, which liberals saw as having emasculated Title III and Title V, the administration was exuberant at having defeated Quie. Henry Hall Wilson told Johnson that it had been "very much touch and go," to the point that the administration might have lost in the House had the vote been held even an hour earlier. Despite what has been said about Green's role, it is also surely the case that the role of people like Wilson, O'Brien, and their colleagues at HEW had been critical to the survival of ESEA. In a reflective mood, Wilson considered that this had been the most "difficult, delicate, complex" operation that he could recall and that he could not think of any victory that had given him "more personal satisfaction."[128] Looking back on the episode toward the end of his life, Larry O'Brien—veteran of a great many titanic legislative struggles during the New Frontier–Great Society period—also felt that this one had been peculiarly satisfying: "That was exciting—I don't often say that about legislative proposals, because much of it was sweat, blood and tears and you found it difficult to find the excitement quotient."[129]

In a memo dated "May 25, 1967—The Morning After," Samuel Halperin looked beyond the immediate legislative triumph and pondered its broader meaning for the federal politics of education. The memo began as follows:

1. Federal aid to education is here to stay. Major alternatives were a $3.3 billion Administration bill and a $3 billion GOP substitute. On final passage, the vote was [294] to 122. There is obviously strong bi-partisan support for substantial Federal aid to elementary and secondary education.
   The big issue is not "whether" but "how." The basic consensus of 1965, though rattled, has survived essentially intact.

2. Private school power is at an all-time high. Catholic pressure was the essential ingredient in defeating Quie. The Republicans will probably never offer private school interests less than the Quie bill. . . . On the other hand, I cannot anticipate this Administration ever turning its back on private school interests by the proposal of a "public schools only" bill, as under JFK in 1961. A striking feature of the 3-day debate was the solicitude on all sides for the participation in Federal programs by the [Catholic] school children.

3. Mrs Green is the master of all floor action on education and related measures. With Powell gone—the only one who could contain her—Mrs Green has shown an ability to construct a Republican–Southern Democrat coalition which is capable of overriding committee

recommendations. Although many of the Members would like to back Perkins they now doubt that he is strong enough to run a most difficult committee. Mrs Green may be harassed in committee but she will be a major force to reckon with on the House.[130]

That was a perceptive set of reflections. The first point was the most important, and its accuracy was confirmed in December, at the end of another protracted legislative session. Considering the somewhat liberalized ESEA amendments that had just emerged from conference, the House voted in favor by the commanding margin of 286–73. The number of opponents had more than halved since the liberal glory year of 1965. More than 80 percent of Republicans were now voting in favor of categorical federal aid to education, and the ranks of those voting for ESEA for the first time included Minority Leader Gerald Ford and such doughty conservatives as William Ayres, Mendel Rivers (D-S.C.), George Mahon, W. R. Poage (D-Tex.), and John Byrnes (R-Wisc.).[131]

So it seemed that the "whether" question had indeed been answered. But as Halperin observed, the "how" question remained alive. Yes, the outcome of the 1967 fight had suggested the intrinsic political difficulty that would face any general aid proposal: if the efficacy of the categorical approach in policy terms was open to question, its political advantages had been strikingly demonstrated. But those questions of policy efficacy were real, growing, and potentially troublesome in political terms down the road. To be sure, when federal dollars were so limited (8 percent of total spending on schools), a strong case could be made on programmatic as well as political terms for a categorical approach that targeted those dollars for specific purposes. But what of the evaluative research showing that Title I funds were not reaching the poor, or that even small grant applications imposed a crushing bureaucratic burden on school districts, or that the results of federal grants were hard to determine? What, still more worrying, of a growing body of academic research suggesting that schools could not compensate for societal inequality or that there was very little correlation between educational "inputs" (i.e., money spent) and educational "outputs" (i.e., academic performance)?[132]

When the Nixon administration turned its mind to the question of federal aid to education, a couple of years later, it tried to reopen the "how" question and resuscitated the block grant idea. Partly, that was because of the questions over ESEA's effectiveness. The main motivation, though, was budgetary. During the Nixon-Ford administration, the main question was neither "whether" nor "how," but rather "how much." As the White House strove to hold down spending in a deteriorating economic environment, the education interest groups that had worked with the Johnson administration to defeat the Quie amendment forged an increasingly strong relationship with one another to combat Nixon.

How Much? Budget Battles, 1969–1977

The Nixon-Ford years were ones of drama, uncertainty, and intense institutional conflict in education politics, just as in American politics more generally. Every year, the president tried to rein in Great Society programs such as ESEA and Head Start, arguing that they were not working and that spending increases would stoke inflation and unbalance the budget. Meanwhile, members of Congress responded to the popularity of education spending back home by advocating big increases in spending on schools. Before 1969, no president had ever vetoed the education appropriations bill. Nixon and Ford, by contrast, vetoed seven out of nine.[1] Table 4.1 shows the figures for budget requests and actual appropriations for OE between FY 1969 (the last budget that Johnson controlled) and FY 1977.

Divided government is a major part of the explanation for this new era of institutional conflict. Nixon was the first president in 120 years to assume office with the opposition party in control of Congress. It was not just Democrats in Congress who were voting for big increases in education spending, however: Republicans did so too, including some who were quite ideologically conservative. As that suggests, other considerations were at work besides partisanship. Among the more important were the new economic setting, the mobilization of a powerful education lobby, and institutional change in Congress. Still, the place to start is with partisanship and

TABLE 4.1. The Battle over the Education Budget, 1969–1977 (in $ billions)

Fiscal Year:	1969	1970	1971	1972	1973	1974	1975	1976	1977[a]
Administration request	3.49	3.18	3.97	4.95	5.49	5.28	6.57	6.13	4.32
Congressional appropriation	3.62	4.20	4.42	5.28	6.31	6.02	6.60	7.48	5.93
Sign/veto?	Sign	Veto	Veto[b]	Sign	Veto[c]	Sign	Sign	Veto[b]	Veto[b]
Final appropriation	—	3.81	—	—	6.28[d]	—	—	—	—
Excess over request	0.13	0.63	0.45	0.33	0.79	0.74	0.03	1.35	1.61

Sources: Table i in Robert W. Frase, "Five Years of Struggle for Federal Funds," *Publishers Weekly,* January 21, 1974, 65; *Congressional Quarterly: 1974* (Washington, D.C.: *Congressional Quarterly Almanac,* 1975), 97–98, 110; *Congressional Quarterly Almanac: 1975* (Washington, D.C.: Congressional Quarterly, 1976), 784, 788; *Congressional Quarterly Almanac: 1976* (Washington, D.C.: Congressional Quarterly, 1977), 791; House Committee on Appropriations, Subcommittee on Labor-HEW, hearings, *1976 Appropriations—Education Division* 93rd Cong., 1st Sess., pt. 1, March 7, 1975, 100. Figures include higher education.

[a]Excludes higher education and library programs, for which authorizing legislation had yet to be enacted.
[b]Veto overridden.
[c]Veto sustained but circumvented by continuing resolution.
[d] Amount set by continuing resolution.

with Carl Perkins's response to the arrival of Richard Nixon in the White House.

The Democratic Response to the Nixon Presidency

Perkins had entered the House in 1949, when Nixon was a second-term congressman, best known for his pursuit of Alger Hiss and his defeat of Helen Gahagan Douglas. Perkins presumably shared the distaste for the red-baiting Nixon that was characteristic among Democrats of his vintage. Quite apart from that, many Democrats assumed in 1969 that Nixon was out to dismantle the Great Society. If that was right, then ESEA looked distinctly vulnerable: how would it fare, absent Lyndon Johnson's strong and effective support and beset as it was by negative evaluations of its effectiveness?[2] With the program's authorization due to expire in 1970, perhaps a new battle for block grants was about to ensue, with the White House this time leading the charge for reform.

Perkins did not wait to find out, moving swiftly to take the initiative away from those who might wish to cut or reorient the federal role in education. Far from giving the incoming administration the customary opportunity to present its legislative proposals, his committee began hearings on the reauthorization of ESEA before Nixon had even taken office, on January 15, 1969. That meant that the first government witness would be out-going HEW secretary, Wilbur Cohen, rather than his GOP successor, Robert Finch.[3]

Had Cohen been speaking on behalf of a new Democratic administration, it would have been an uncomfortable encounter, for after three stand-still budgets in a row, Johnson's 1970 budget—designed to maintain the previous year's surplus and restrain inflationary pressures—had requested a small *cut* in OE funds.[4] Freed of this responsibility, Cohen spoke expansively of the success of ESEA and the need for a much greater federal share of school costs. That set the tone for two months of hearings, carefully choreographed by Perkins to reinforce the same message. When Finch was finally invited to appear before the committee, on the last day of hearings, he made the case for budgetary restraint and a two-year extension of ESEA while the administration evaluated its performance and weighed up alternative ways of spending the money. Ignoring that request, the committee reported a bill that extended the ESEA for five years. Powerless minority members complained that Democrats had ignored "all kinds of evidence . . . that ESEA is falling far short of congressional hopes."[5]

The Nixon administration reacted slowly. It did not in fact possess a blueprint for overhauling the Great Society, and neither did it approach the task of developing one with much urgency. The president's attention was elsewhere, focused on the overwhelmingly urgent task of trying to extricate the nation from Vietnam.[6] And no high-ranking official in his administration was giving much attention to education: there had been a transition task force devoted to the subject, but its impact was nugatory. Until the fall, when the White House was forced by events on the Hill to pay attention to education politics, the one agency taking a close interest in the subject was the Bureau of the Budget, which was pondering ways of reducing Johnson's 1970 package.

Applying the Ax: Nixon's First Education Budget

In that final Johnson budget, a slight increase in the sum requested for Title I had been offset with larger cuts in impact aid, library assistance, and educational equipment purchases, all felt to be areas of lower priority. When the House appropriations subcommittee for Labor-HEW invited Robert Finch to appear before it in March, the budget review was still underway, meaning that there was little for them to talk about. Still, Chairman Daniel Flood did express some qualms about Johnson's proposed OE cuts, warning that they had generated an unusual volume of adverse mail.[7] Attention then turned to health matters, culminating in a brief discussion of one of Flood's favorite topics, the dangers of smoking. That discussion concluded, Finch was on his way, unscathed, and expressing appreciation for "the tender loving care of the committee, and the very fine treatment I have been accorded by the chairman."[8]

Within a few weeks, the mood had changed decisively. Shortly after Finch's appearance, the administration, worried by inflationary pressures, decided to pare Johnson's budget by $3 billion, and Finch was told to find $500 million in additional education savings, a tall order in a budget of $3.6 billion. He successfully fought back cuts in vocational education (which was especially popular with GOP legislators) but had to concede an overall reduction of $360 million, including further cuts in impact aid and library assistance.[9] Had the administration been more attuned to the politics of education, it would have realized that these objectives were entirely unobtainable. That said, it cannot be blamed for having failed to anticipate the enormous reaction that the cuts provoked, which was quite unprecedented. Its force reflected not just the popularity of the programs in question but also the particular financial pressures that school districts across the country were facing in the spring of 1969.

Rising Costs/Angry Taxpayers:
The Politics of School Finance in 1969

Throughout the post–World War II period, school costs had been rising precipitously.[10] Student enrollments doubled during the baby boom years, peaking in 1971. The number of teachers, meanwhile, *more* than doubled, as did their salaries.[11] School construction costs also shot up, initially because of the need for new schools and buildings to house all the new students, then (by the late 1960s) because of the rising cost of borrowing.[12] As these costs rose, finding the money became more difficult. The big problem here, from the point of view of school administrators, was that taxpayers got to vote on increases in the property tax rate and on construction bond issues. They were increasingly saying no, less because they thought that schools were doing a poor job than because this was the only opportunity that the roughly 15 percent of Americans who participated in such elections had to indicate their displeasure at high taxes, inflation, and big government. In 1964, 74.7 percent of bond issues were approved. By November 1968, the figure had plummeted to 45 percent.

To officials at the budget bureau, poring over Johnson's 1970 budget in search of $3 billion in cuts, the education budget was full of promising possibilities: the NDEA equipment purchases program, the various small titles giving federal funds to school and public libraries, and impact aid could all be presented as wasteful congressional sops to favored constituencies. Had they instead been poring over newspapers, though, they might have wondered about the political practicability of cuts. One front page story in the *Wall Street Journal* was headlined "Strangled Schools: Rebellion by Taxpayers and Rising Costs Force Curtailment of Classes." Schools in Youngstown, Ohio, were closed because voters had defeated a tax levy; a new school in Grand Ledge, Michigan, was empty because the district could not raise the funds to hire teachers; and teachers in Champaign, Illinois, were "being paid with vouchers that local banks have agreed to cash on the assumption that the hard-pressed school district eventually will sell enough bonds to redeem them."[13] Those were extreme cases, but as the *Journal*'s reporter noted, the "basic problems" were "far from rare." In proposing a 10 percent reduction in the federal education budget in that environment, the Nixon White House was taking a significant political risk. Soon, it would look to have been a bad miscalculation.

The Democratic majority in Congress was no longer in the awkward position of bemoaning the parsimony of a Johnson education budget: now it had a Nixon budget to kick around. When Finch returned to the House appropriations subcommittee to defend his shrunken education budget, Flood complained that he and his colleagues had already "received personal visits, stacks of mail, and telephone calls about the Johnson budget in which education programs were cut $87 million." Now, he remarked, "along comes the Nixon budget and it cuts education another $376 million. How can you or we or anybody explain to these educators that this budget does not deliberately and grossly discriminate against education as contrasted with health and welfare?"[14]

That Nixon's proposal would fail was predictable. Prospects for increasing spending beyond Johnson's budget were also poor, however. During the past three years Congress had moved sharply away from the expansionist tendencies that had so vexed Johnson during the first half of 1966. Back then, he had been making the case for budgetary restraint while impatient legislators had clamored for higher Great Society spending. But even before the midterm elections of 1966, that had begun to change, and the 90th Congress had gone further than Johnson in advocating restraint. In 1968, for example, it had passed the Revenue and Expenditure Control Act, which contained painful cuts in Great Society programs and a ceiling on overall spending, as its price for approving Johnson's tax surcharge. With the 91st Congress very similar in composition, and the House in particular dominated by a resurgent conservative coalition, the political outlook for Nixon was not quite as bleak as one might have assumed, divided government notwithstanding. According to some on the Hill, a reliable political majority in the House was within his grasp, provided he played his cards well.[15]

Concluding that this was a standstill year for education, Flood warned educators appearing before his subcommittee not to expect too much from Congress. When a spokesman for the higher education community put the case for a massive increase in spending, the chairman put him in his place, observing that it had increased fivefold since 1960 and that "that ain't hay."[16] And when the education commissioner, James Allen, made clear his unhappiness about the proposed cuts, Flood remarked that "you have been eating higher and higher on the hog for about ten years, but this ain't your year." (These were characteristic turns of phrase for Flood, who was one of the House's great eccentrics, perhaps best known for his extravagant waxed moustache and black cape but also renowned for a highly self-conscious rhetorical style that blended down-home colloquialisms and quotations from Shakespeare.[17])

Flood's prediction was soon cast into doubt, however, by an unprecedented development in American politics, namely the emergence of a powerful and cohesive education lobby. In the past, there had been something of a mismatch between the appeal of education as a political issue, which was considerable, and the power of the education lobby on the Hill, which was much less strong. True, its members had been able to work together during the fight for ESEA in 1965 and in opposition to the Quie amendment in 1967, but only because the White House was pulling the strings. Now, in this moment of seeming political peril, education lobbyists took the initiative, forming an eclectic coalition of eighty organizations with a stake in federal aid. By the end of the year, the political influence of this Emergency Committee for Full Funding of Education Programs was such that the chairman of the House Appropriations Committee, George Mahon, was referring to educators as "the second most powerful lobby in Washington," and Edith Green espied an emergent "education-industrial complex."[18]

Origins of the Full Funding Coalition

According to the architects of the new coalition, the most damaging failure of the education groups until then had been their inability to get federal programs adequately funded.[19] Since 1958, when NDEA was passed, they had enjoyed considerable success in winning congressional support for their programmatic ideas and in securing generous authorizations for those programs. But when it came to appropriating funds, they either failed to mobilize or squabbled among themselves for a larger share of the education budget, rather than working together to increase total spending. As a result, the gap between authorizations and appropriations got bigger each year, and the federal share of education spending remained stuck at around 8 percent, where it had been since FY 1966. To the organizers of the Emergency Committee, it seemed that the way out was for educators to focus more on the appropriations process and unite around the concept of "full funding."[20] That meant persuading Congress to fund every education program at the authorized level. In effect, it was asking for a $5 billion increase in education spending and an increase in the federal share from 8 to almost 20 percent.

The committee emerged out of a conversation among a small number of education lobbyists, including Stanley McFarland of the NEA, August Steinhilber of the NSBA, Germaine Krettek of the American Library Association, Don White of the National Audio-Visual Association, and William Simmons of the impact aid lobby. Meeting on Capitol Hill in the Democratic Club, they pondered how best to respond to the Nixon administration's cuts and decided to seek counsel from the astute Charles Lee. The following week, McFarland's boss, John Lumley, convened a meeting of education lobbyists at NEA headquarters, with Lee in attendance. Representatives of most of the major education groups were there. So too was Kenneth Young, the congressional lobbyist for the AFL-CIO whose portfolio included education.[21]

That last fact alone conveys the novelty of the venture. One of the main arguments that NEA officers used in opposing a merger with the rival American Federation of Teachers (AFT) was the latter's affiliation to the AFL-CIO.[22] That they should be working hand-in-glove like this was unusual. The participation of White and Simmons was also surprising. During the past decade, White had won a string of important victories on the Hill for equipment manufacturers, always acting as a lone operator. As for the impact aid superintendents, they managed to secure "full funding" for their programs every year by picking off weaker competitors during the appropriations process (one budget bureau official charged that it "cannibalized" them).[23] This year, however, White and Simmons felt exposed: in an adverse budgetary climate, their programs were coming in for an unusual amount of criticism. To preserve their programs in their current form, they might need allies.[24]

In addition to their sense of shared vulnerability, cooperation was facilitated by the friendly relations that lobbyists representing the individual organizations often enjoyed, irrespective of the disagreements that might exist between their employers. NEA and NSBA were often at odds, but McFarland and Steinhilber were friends, sometimes going hunting together (occasionally they would be joined by Albert Quie). In a similar fashion, McFarland got on well with James Kirkpatrick of the American Association of School Administrators (AASA) and Carl Megel of the AFT, despite the sharp differences that separated their organizations.[25] The Emergency Committee emerged initially out of these personal relationships among lobbyists, rather than from initiatives taken by the leadership of their organizations.

Having agreed on objectives, the committee needed a budget. This was a politically delicate matter. According to Jack Morse, who was then top lobbyist for the higher education community, "It was clear that it could be permanently and well funded simply through contributions from industry (audio-visual manufacturers, book publishers, et al.)." "A number of us felt," however, "that this would be disastrous and lend credence to [the] charge . . . that this was the handmaiden of the industrial-educational complex." Anxious to avoid that taint, "we firmly ruled out *any* contributions from the profit-making sector."[26] Despite Don White's participation in the meetings that led to the creation of the Emergency Committee, for example, NAVA was not even listed as a member.[27] The committee's operating budget came instead from relatively small contributions by each of the constituent elements.

Those contributions allowed the coalition to hire Charles Lee as its executive secretary, and he set up shop in a suite at the Congressional Hotel. In June, the group made its political debut, appearing before Flood's subcommittee. To emphasize the bipartisan character of the venture, Arthur S. Flemming, secretary of HEW under Eisenhower, had been approached to be its chairman. Flanked by no fewer than ten colleagues, representing the full range of the coalition's concerns, his appearance made quite an impact on Flood. "I might say," he remarked, "I have been sitting here for a number of years and this is the biggest claque I have seen come into the room so far."[28] But Flood found Flemming's message *less* impressive, wondering what the point of the appropriations process was if Congress adopted the "full funding" approach. His query highlighted the obvious danger of the coalition's approach. At a time when their authority was already being challenged on other fronts (by the existence of the spending ceiling, for example, and by the growth of entitlement spending), Daniel Flood, and his Senate counterpart, Warren Magnuson (D-Wash.), were bound to have qualms about a group whose success could only come at their expense.[29]

The Labor-HEW subcommittee had quite a conservative complexion in 1969. That reflected the close working relationship between Flood and ranking minority member Robert Michel (R-Ill.), both of whom were more conservative than the men they had replaced, John Fogarty and Melvin Laird (R-Wisc.). Also, when Fogarty died, George Mahon had drastically revised the membership of the majority to rein in what he saw as its big-spending proclivities.[30] It now behaved more like an appropriations subcommittee was meant to behave: looking for places to save money. So while Flood and his colleagues took note of the unusual lobbying campaign to which they had been subject, they largely ignored it when it came to marking up a bill, adding only $100 million to Nixon's education budget. Clearly they did not think that the coalition posed much of a threat: they were accustomed to getting their way on the floor, and in 1969 the House had a generally conservative disposition. Had Flood, Michel, and Mahon sensed a threat, they would undoubtedly have responded to it, for if there was one thing that threatened their customary status even more than profligacy it was being "rolled" on the floor of the House. One way that Mahon's committee had maintained its standing had been by knowing when it had to yield.[31] On this occasion, however, Mahon got it wrong: the rest of the session would yield three legislative successes for the full-funding coalition, and they had the cumulative impact of substantially eroding the authority of his committee.

The first reverse came in the Senate. It voted in June to protect all OE programs from cuts that the budget bureau had proposed in response to the expenditure ceiling. This was a remarkable development, inasmuch as the proposal originated on the floor, where the Appropriations Committee's right to set spending levels was hardly ever questioned. Warning colleagues against establishing a dangerous precedent, Everett Dirksen complained that "any Senator can stand up here and pick out something in the bill, and say, 'I would like to have that exempted,' and he can make a pretty good case for it." The entire integrity of the appropriations process, he felt, rested on that not happening. Warren Magnuson, a strong liberal, indicated that he felt the same way.[32]

But while they were speaking on the floor, the decisive action was taking place in members' offices and in the corridors of the Senate, where Charles Lee coordinated the education coalition's lobbying effort. "If it turned out that a Senator had misgivings," he later recalled, "I'd see to it that he was talked to by some people back home—a librarian, a school board member, or some teacher."[33] The technique that had been deployed without success before Flood's committee—appearing in a group to demonstrate solidarity—was more effective in this setting. In the past, lobbyists for parochial schools, librarians, and chief school officers would have been working against one another. When they entered a member's office together, the legislator got a jolt. NSBA's Steinhilber recalls that if school board members and teachers from a district showed up in a legislator's office together, the sight "blew people's minds."[34] With Dirksen acknowledging the political acumen of the "very effective school lobby," the new coalition carried the day, winning the vote by 53 votes to 42.

Rolling the House Appropriations Committee

The coalition won a much more important victory in the House the following month. When its attempt to add a billion dollars to Flood's education bill on the floor was first mooted, it was not even certain that such a move could be attempted in parliamentary terms, for the convention until then had been to permit a single, limited amendment on the floor, at the discretion of George Mahon. The House parliamentarian had to be persuaded that there was some precedent for a more comprehensive amendment, such as the coalition was proposing. James O'Hara of the Education and Labor Committee and Jack Reed (a staffer to Perkins) began an urgent search for a precedent. Fortunately, they found one.[35]

That left the question of how high the coalition forces should aim. Kenneth Young, skilled lobbyist for the AFL-CIO, reckoned that anything in excess of $1 billion would be "just asking for trouble." Following consultation with Perkins and others, a figure of $895 million above the Mahon bill was agreed on. As for how the cake should be divided, that decision was—as Lee frankly acknowledged—"entirely pragmatic." Impact aid got nearly half of the funds ($398 million), and the rest was shared between vocational education ($131.5 million), equipment and library funds ($110.4 million), higher education ($73.8 million), and ESEA, Title I ($180.8 million).[36] That figure was roughly proportionate to the vote-pulling capacity of the respective interests.

The task of "rolling" the committee promised to be a formidable one. Before the procedural reforms of the early 1970s, House floor amendments were decided by unrecorded "teller" votes: the overall vote was recorded, but the decisions of individual members were not. That was one of the sources of the Appropriations Committee's authority and something that limited the power of interest groups: members who did not wish to offend either could simply stay away or alternatively vote with the committee and (when convenient) claim to have voted against it. The absence of roll-call votes also meant that tallies were often taken at short notice, making it hard for the supporters of an amendment to mobilize their troops.[37]

Faced with this challenging situation, Young and Lee choreographed a remarkable operation. Contemporary accounts described Capitol Hill as having been awash with home district amateurs—superintendents, teachers, school board members, nuns, librarians—who had paid their own way to Washington and who sported bright yellow buttons reading "Save Education and Library Funds."[38] In the chamber, the main challenge facing volunteers in the gallery was to monitor how the members below were voting on each amendment. But the bulk of the action was going on elsewhere, in the Rayburn, Longworth, and Cannon House office buildings. According to one report, Young "stationed one or two men in a friendly lawmaker's office on each floor of the three House office buildings. Each agent had a list of the nearby lawmakers who had promised to vote the educators' way." Another Young confederate occupied a phone booth and kept a line open to Lee back at the Congressional Hotel. On getting the word that an important vote was coming up, Lee volunteers contacted the Young people in the House buildings, who "dashed into offices to urge the Congressmen to rush to the House chamber to vote."[39] And as they walked toward the floor, the corridors of the office buildings were reportedly lined with coalition representatives who were there "to add their encouragement." Finally, when they reached the chamber, some found educators from their districts waving down at them.[40] Lee recounted that one congressman changed his vote "when he saw his bishop looking down at him from the gallery."[41]

On the floor, responsibility for managing the amendment rested with Charles Joelson, a five-term congressman from Paterson, New Jersey. He served on the Appropriations Committee but had been excluded from its Labor-HEW subcommittee because Mahon's predecessor, Clarence Cannon, had felt that he was too much of a big spender.[42] Recently, considering that his decade in the House had yielded few achievements, he had decided to quit in favor of a state judgeship. Accordingly, he had nothing to lose by spearheading this revolt against Mahon. His previous contribution to the debate having reportedly been limited to "tension-easing quips," however, preparing him to manage the $895 million amendment involved three days of intense cramming. Introducing the measure, he declared: "I hope after I am through today and tomorrow, I will have a school named after me, and perhaps even a college."[43]

As the full scale of the education coalition's effort became apparent, supporters of the committee bill had to think on their feet. Michel sought to head off the Joelson proposal by introducing an amendment that limited the increase to impact aid. A strong proponent of spending restraint, he worried about even *that* increase, telling colleagues that "if I had heard anybody say two weeks ago that I would take such action, I would have said he was crazy. I cannot believe it myself. I awakened this morning at 5 o'clock, and I was distressed about this action of mine."[44] In truth, though, it was too *cautious*, and failed by 160 votes to 197.

Then Flood took the floor, declaring himself "amazed" that such a proposal had even been bruited, given that it "violates by its presence the intent and the spirit of the rules of this House for generations." While his affection for his departing New Jersey colleague was unbounded, he added, he did not consider that he deserved "a going away present of $1 billion."[45] But none of his arguments worked: Joelson's amendment passed by the resounding margin of 294 votes to 119. Southern Democrats voted in favor by 48–36, Republicans by 99–81.[46]

Democrats were jubilant. Patsy Mink (D-Hawaii), a member of the Education and Labor Committee, shouted "Whoopee" when the vote was announced, and Majority Leader Carl Albert celebrated what he called "the greatest Democratic victory since the 89th Congress."[47] Lloyd Meeds (D-Wash.), another member of Perkins's committee, told a constituent that this was "a historical turning point in Congressional attitudes toward education" that had "put the Appropriations Committee on notice."[48] Seemingly sharing that view, the organizers of the full-funding coalition prepared a certificate of merit for all the educators who had come to Washington to lobby for the Joelson amendment.[49] Michel, by contrast, was despondent that most Republicans had voted for the extra $1 billion and particularly displeased with those who had opposed his effort to head it off. When he raised his disquiet with Albert Quie, though, the Minnesotan explained that "your main difficulty came from the fact that the Administration completely misjudged the Congress' attitude toward education expenditures." Conceding that Joelson's amendment went too far, he nevertheless objected that Michel's amendment had not gone far enough. When the teller vote on the Joelson amendment started, he had still been undecided, but "when the vote went well over 200, I decided I might just as well vote yes. . . . I knew that I would vote for it on the record."[50]

By October, though, it appeared that the triumph on the Joelson amendment might have been for naught, for the Senate had not even begun committee work on the Labor-HEW bill. In the meantime, schools were being funded via continuing resolutions, at the spending levels proposed by Nixon, and the likelihood was that this would remain true into 1970. By that time it would be hard to make the case for the extra billion dollars, with the fiscal year more than half gone.

Faced with this situation, the Emergency Committee swung into action again, crafting an amendment to George Mahon's latest continuing resolution that required the administration to start spending at the higher level immediately. Its sponsor was Jeffrey Cohelan, of Berkeley, California, another junior member of the Appropriations Committee whose career in politics was drawing to an early close (although he did not know that yet).[51] The powerful Mahon was reduced to an almost pitiful appeal: "I do not want to see the Committee on Appropriations discredited. Like other Members in this House, I do not want to be humiliated, or have the feeling myself, or have others feel, that I have failed to do my job, or that the 51 members of the Committee on appropriations have failed to do their job."[52]

But Mahon, while a fiscal conservative, was also a consensus seeker. With the debate not going his way, he proposed an amendment to limit the increase to $600 million. Gerald Ford, the minority leader, then stepped in to say that to go higher would be an exercise in futility, since the president had no intention of spending the extra money. Other opponents, including the majority leadership, complained that the Cohelan amendment was an egregious affront to the comity of the Senate.[53] Nevertheless, it passed, by 177 votes to 124, and it was at this point that Mahon made his remark about educators being the second-most-powerful lobby in Washington.

The Nixon Approach to Congressional Relations

The White House remained largely aloof from the battle about education spending between April, when the revised budget was unveiled, and October, when the House voted on the Cohelan amendment. Doubtless White House and HEW liaison staff were working hard between the scenes, but there is nothing in the archives or in the press coverage to suggest high-level White House interest in what was happening on the Hill. There is a striking contrast between the extensive memo traffic generated by the Johnson administration's efforts to head off the Quie amendment in 1967 and the lack of material on the education budget fight in the papers of Nixon and his closest advisers.

Part of that, no doubt, reflected the different priority that the two presidents attached to education. But it is also consistent with what legislators and pundits were saying at the time about the administration's overall congressional relations effort. One end-of-year newspaper analysis referred to its "ambiguous leadership on key issues, marked by a tendency to remain aloof from the battle and apparent willingness to allow both the initiative and the responsibility for legislation to remain on Capitol Hill." The same reporter cited "impatient Republicans" who felt that Nixon's approach had "been marked by poor liaison, insufficient attention to Congressional needs, misguided strategy and poor intelligence on Congressional sentiment on some key issues." Time and again—on the antiballistic missile (ABM) system, the nomination of Clement Haynsworth to the Supreme Court, tax reform, renewal of the surcharge, and the war on poverty—GOP legislators had been dismayed by the administration's legislative performance.[54]

In 1971, when Rowland Evans and Robert Novak published a caustic but well-informed analysis of the administration's first two years, congressional relations stood out as the greatest failure. In their view, Bryce Harlow, who headed the White House team, was overstretched. In part that was because he had insufficient help: taking insufficient heed of the enormous growth in government that had occurred during the last decade, he sought to recreate the lean staff operation that had worked so well for him when he performed the same function for Eisenhower. But the bigger problem was that legislators and lobbyists wishing to contact the administration did not know who else to call. As soon as Harlow walked into his room at transition headquarters— the Pierre Hotel in New York—the phone started ringing. For the next few hours, he was "chained to the telephone," having no time even to unpack his suitcase.[55] When the 1969 congressional session began, he found himself still more overwhelmed, receiving more than 200 calls a day. Even when he was able to return the calls, he often had little to say, given the lack of clarity regarding the new administration's program and legislative priorities and the inadequacy of his channels to the White House.[56]

In choosing Harlow, William Timmons, and Kenneth Belieu to head his congressional liaison team, Nixon had come up with a talented team. Perhaps it bears comparison to the exceptional Johnson operation of Larry O'Brien, Mike Manatos, and Henry Hall Wilson. The big difference between the two groups has to do with the people to whom they reported. The Johnson team reported to White House aides who possessed an intimate knowledge of and appreciation for the world of Washington politics (Joseph Califano, Harry McPherson, Douglass Cater, Bill Moyers). By contrast, the individuals who had most to do with day-to-day politics in the Nixon administration had no such background. The chief of staff, H. R. Haldeman, was an advertising man, and so were many of his deputies. They seem to have seen governing as simply an extension of campaigning, rather than as a distinct art requiring specialized knowledge of political institutions and conventions. Meanwhile, John D. Ehrlichman, who emerged during 1969 as Nixon's main domestic adviser, was a West Coast lawyer, and most of his aides were also lawyers. In almost every case, their experience of politics too was confined to the world of campaigning. Neither did any of Nixon's principal speechwriters have any background in politics, outside of that specific milieu. The one exception to this generalization about the Nixon White House may have been Charles Colson, who had been a legislative assistant to Senator Leverett Saltonstall (R-Mass.). But he, better than anyone, came to exemplify an approach to politics based on combat and public relations.[57]

The Haldeman diaries are full of disdainful references to Harlow, who is presented as being too soft on the administration's "enemies," deeply insecure about his standing with the president, and irritatingly keen to get Nixon personally involved in legislative arm-twisting. They also drip contempt for Congress and its members. The best source for the latter, however, is Ehrlichman's memoir, *Witness to Power*, which is studded with withering assessments of top legislators, including such powerful Republicans as House minority leader Gerald Ford and his opposite number in the Senate, Hugh Scott of Pennsylvania.[58] As for the institution more generally, Ehrlichman betrays a fundamental ignorance of its procedures and culture and an almost total incapacity to acknowledge that it might play any useful or legitimate role in the American political system. Here is one of his many disdainful references:

> The Members consume time in enormous quantities in their quaint Congressional processes. They recess; they junket; they arrive late and leave early; they attend conferences out of time, fly off to give speeches, sip and chat and endlessly party. And only sometimes do they focus on legislation.

He compares this leisurely rhythm to the very different pattern at the other end of Pennsylvania Avenue:

> The Nixon White House and the Congress were different worlds. We went to work every day—often on Sundays. We operated on schedule. There was an elaborate Haldeman staff *apparat* which enforced assignment deadlines, followed up with memos and phone calls, insisted on prompt performance and ratted on you if you were late. Domestic

legislation came off the Domestic Council assembly line according to a schedule that dovetailed with the [Ron] Ziegler news plan, the President's activity calendar and the Haldeman PR strategy.[59]

Taking on Congress: The Labor-HEW Veto Decision

Given that mentality, it is not surprising that the education budget first crops up in both Ehrlichman's papers and the Haldeman diaries in the context of the need to "take on" Congress. That was a growing theme during the fall of 1969, reaching particular intensity in mid-November, when the Senate rejected the Haynsworth nomination by 55 votes to 45, the first time that this had happened since 1930. Following that defeat, Haldeman recorded Nixon's view that "the whole exercise is proof that we should take a harder line with Congress, not waste so much time with the leaders, and with the ones who are always against us, and really work closely with our solid friends."[60] From that point on, the administration generally welcomed opportunities to dramatize its differences with the Democratic Congress, hoping that confrontation between a spendthrift, obstructionist legislature and a thrifty, inflation-taming president might lead to GOP gains in the midterm elections and to greater legislative accomplishments thereafter.

When the Senate approved the extra billion dollars for education in mid-December, Nixon was presented with one such opportunity and took it, announcing that he would veto the Labor-HEW bill unless Congress backed down when it came to voting on the conference report. Quite apart from the politics, there were plausible budgetary and educational reasons for doing so. How could he stay within the expenditure ceiling that Congress had insisted upon, if education spending ballooned? Could HEW distribute the funds wisely, or school districts make good use of the money, now that the school year was half gone? Were programs such as Title I and vocational education achieving their stated purposes? What would the markets make of the administration's anti-inflationary resolve, if it went along with such a profligate measure?

The administration's task in advancing these respectable questions was complicated by the fact that it had previously had so little to say about education. In a year when the subject had been of such pressing interest on the Hill and in school districts around the country, that silence had been conspicuous. By the fall, when the White House started to speak out against the extra billion dollars, it had resulted in growing talk that the administration was "antieducation." Finch and Daniel Patrick Moynihan—the senior White House adviser who was most closely interested in education—sought to counter that by having the president give a major speech about education reform. Perhaps, Moynihan hoped, the administration could change the national conversation about education from being about "how much" to being about "how." Nixon initially liked that idea, which comported well with his desire to be seen as an ideas president and a reformer. But drafting an address that was acceptable to the budget bureau, HEW, and the White House proved to be impossible: there was no money for grand new projects, inexpensive proposals would look stingy when set beside the billion dollars, and it was hard to emphasize reform without sounding negative about existing efforts, thereby reinforcing the "antieducation" charge. The address was shelved and not delivered until March 1970. But that decision too entailed further criticism: the administration still had no positive message about education.[61]

In part for that reason, there was a real risk that a veto might be overridden, something that had not happened for a decade. The Senate was almost certain to override, and—despite Nixon's warning—the relatively conservative House had approved the conference bill by a veto-proof vote of 261–110. In mid-January, with the bill about to reach his desk, Nixon briefly wavered, worrying about what defeat would mean for his administration's standing. He had committed himself a month earlier, however, and backing off now would arguably be more damaging than defeat. In his veto message, delivered in front of a prime-time television audience, he emphasized the common stake that all Americans had in the fight against inflation, highlighted the "unfairness" of the impact aid program, and averred that there were "no goals which I consider more important for this nation than to improve education and to provide better health care for the American people."[62]

It was the first veto of Nixon's presidency, and the first time ever that a veto message had been televised. After the speech, Nixon was reportedly in good spirits, albeit grumbling that he had to compose the message himself (he had reviewed several drafts, but none had satisfied him).[63] The full resources of the administration were deployed in an effort to sustain the veto in the House, with the bulk of the effort centering on the eighty Republicans who had voted against the president on the conference bill. Such was the extent of the pressure being applied from the White House that some Republicans became resentful, but they were getting similarly disproportionate attention from the full funding forces, which badly overplayed their hand, unwisely threatening reprisals against members who voted the "wrong" way.

Two other factors helped tip the balance in the administration's favor.

First, the White House presented the issue as a vote of confidence in the administration. Second, it issued private assurances that it would yield the bulk of the billion dollars in subsequent negotiations, if only the House would sustain its will on this crucial symbolic vote. That proved to be enough to secure a comfortable margin of victory for Nixon. The White House was ecstatic, holding an impromptu reception for all those who had voted the right way. Haldeman's note read: "Got 191, a great victory! And a sensational way to start off the second year, with strong action and a major Congressional coup." His note on the party is also worth recording: "[Nixon] in top form at Congressional gathering. A real victory celebration, with that feeling in the air, both Republicans and Democrats. Had several of the leaders speak after he did, and all were very enthusiastic, built some pretty good equity and shafted the 'anti' press. Dan Rather thought the party was incredible. Really hates to see P win anything."[64]

Two months later, Nixon quietly signed a revised Labor-HEW measure that still exceeded his education budget by $600 million, nearly 20 percent. What was unclear, as he did so, was whether this still-significant victory for the full funding coalition presaged a new era in federal education politics. Perhaps it was an aberration, reflecting mistakes by an error-prone new administration that would not be repeated. Perhaps too the extraordinary effort mounted by the full funding force in 1969–1970 might turn out to have been a flash in the pan. It was uncertain that so eclectic a coalition would be able to sustain its unity. Its Republican titular head, Arthur Flemming, was unhappy at the "strongarm" tactics that lobbyists had deployed during the recent veto fight, and so too was the higher education community, whose principal lobbyist, Jack Morse, confessed to "quite acute" doubts as to whether it should continue.[65] On the Hill, even some influential friends of expanded federal aid had been alienated by the coalition's tactics and by the threat that they posed to established congressional procedure.[66] That did not augur well for the education lobby. Finally, it was not clear what conclusions should be drawn from the fact that the House Appropriations Committee had been rolled for a billion dollars. Given its record and reputation, it was plausible to think that it would regain its customary authority.

The "Emergency Committee" Becomes Permanent

During the remainder of the Nixon-Ford presidency, the education coalition stayed in business. Its survival reflected a mixture of camaraderie and self-interest among its members, born amid the triumphant events of 1969 and sustained by adversity during the challenging years that followed. In

1969—hoping for a post-Vietnam peace dividend and assuming that the long postwar boom would continue—they had dreamed of a massively increased federal contribution to education. As those fond hopes receded, during the remainder of the Nixon-Ford presidency, the objective changed from "full funding" to maintaining the status quo, in the face of continuing presidential pressure for belt-tightening.

For all their periodic tensions, coalition participants worried that if they did not hang together, they might hang separately. When a college leader suggested that the American Council of Education withdraw from the coalition, Jack Morse contended that "of all the segments of education, higher education was in the weakest bargaining position." "When one talks about muscle," he added, "a lobby has only two things to offer: a lot of votes or a lot of money. We have neither."[67] The chief lobbyist for the school boards, on the other hand, believed that the higher education people possessed considerable political clout and was anxious to have them on board. Representatives of colleges and universities were respected local figures, he felt, and when they came to Washington to argue their case, legislators from their district or state would generally sit up and take note.[68] It was as well that the two groups should be on the same side.

In 1972, the Emergency Committee for Full Funding of Education Programs formally dropped "emergency" from its title, becoming the Committee for Education Funding (CEF), and soon thereafter it departed its suite at the Congressional Hotel, moving into more permanent quarters.[69] For political and tax reasons, it remained financially dependent on small, voluntary contributions, meaning that it continued to lead a somewhat precarious existence. But in other respects it was becoming institutionalized, recognized as an important player in the annual battle over the education budget. In 1971, when a Nixon HEW official was striving to defend the administration budget, and Daniel Flood responded by inquiring, "you are not unacquainted with the phrase, 'full funding,' are you?" his witness replied: "We would be very myopic indeed if we had not recognized the full impact of that phrase for the past two years."[70]

By then, Flood, like Mahon, recognized that he had to make concessions to the education coalition to retain his authority. He implored another OE official, Terrel Bell, to recognize his predicament:

> Don't forget when the time comes for this bill to go on the floor, you will be sitting with your cohorts smiling happily in the balcony while Flood and his colleagues will be down in the well of the House trying

to handle this thing. I can just imagine the types of questions and where they will come from. . . . When somebody says, "Will the gentleman from Pennsylvania yield," what is my act? What do I do? What do I say?[71]

The sole purpose of the CEF was to influence education appropriations, but its existence also had implications for program content. The ESEA debate of 1965 and the Quie amendment debate of 1967 had served already to highlight the political advantages of the categorical approach over general aid, the model that most of the big education groups had claimed to favor throughout the 1960s. Those advantages became still more apparent when the CEF went to work. In administrative and policy terms, it was not always easy to justify the proliferation of narrowly targeted programs in behalf of libraries, gifted children, high school drop-outs, the poor, math education, ethnic studies, and metric education, for example. But in political terms it made a lot of sense for educators whose main concern in the 1970s was not program content but funding levels. Even as universities and school boards complained of red tape and excessive prescription, their political representatives in Washington recognized that a shift to general aid would likely result in reduced funding: the more specialized education groups would have less incentive to lobby on the Hill, for they would have no control over how the money was spent at the state and local level.[72] Given that likelihood, an important task for members of the education coalition was to preserve the categorical character of aid.[73] In these circumstances it is not surprising that periodic efforts by Nixon and Ford to replace categorical aid with "special revenue-sharing" did not get very far.[74]

The Institutional Conflict Deepens:
Nixon and Education Spending in 1970

The annual battle of the education budget between 1970 and 1977 illustrates not just the changing world of education politics but also a number of important broader developments, beginning with one of the big turning points in Nixon's domestic presidency, namely the moment in the summer of 1970 when he decided to tack sharply to the right, largely forswearing the comparatively liberal domestic initiatives that had punctuated his early presidency.

Nixon's strong desire to confront Congress, evident already at the end of his first year in office, deepened markedly as the midterm elections of 1970 drew near, as he concluded that institutional conflict might serve his political interest better than cooperation. The turning point came in July and August, just as Congress was considering his FY 1971 education budget. Earlier in the year, the administration had accommodated the strong sentiment on the Hill for increased education: his request exceeded that for the previous year by 25 percent. And although the White House was not happy when the House Appropriations Committee added $300 million, he was initially inclined to go along with the OE spending bill that reached him in July. Keen to register his anxiety about inflationary pressures in some way, he decided to do it less provocatively, by vetoing the housing appropriation bill instead.[75]

Then, though, he abruptly changed his mind. Part of his reasoning was budgetary: Office of Management and Budget (OMB) director George Shultz, and his deputy, Caspar Weinberger, warned that vetoing just one of the two rogue bills would send an unclear message to Congress. The main rationale, however, appears to have been political. In the summer of 1970, Nixon was in the process of reevaluating what he now considered to have been the excessively liberal domestic policies of the administration during its first eighteen months. Haldeman recorded the president's "new conclusion" that the "policy of sucking after Left won't work, not only can't win them, can't even defuse them."[76] His flagship progressive domestic initiative, the Family Assistance Plan, was stuck in Congress, as was his proposal to provide financial assistance to school districts undergoing desegregation. Other bold moves—in areas such as tax reform, revenue-sharing, hunger, affirmative action, and minority business assistance—had received little recognition. The Senate had rejected the Supreme Court nomination not just of Haynsworth but also of the administration's second candidate, Harrold Carswell. Finally, the same body had just approved the Cooper-Church amendment, an effort to force Nixon to end military operations in Cambodia and Laos.

With the midterm elections now less than three months away, Nixon was less concerned with establishing a cooperative relationship with Congress (not that he had been overly solicitous before) and more preoccupied with appealing to a putative new majority that was reacting against the excesses of big government liberalism. To quote Haldeman again: "We have now learned we have gained nothing by turning to the other side. . . . [W]e have to build our own establishment. We're in a deadly battle with the establishment on many fronts: press, civil rights, education, political."[77]

Two days after that message was recorded, the surprise decision to issue a veto was made. Among those most surprised was Elliot Richardson, who had recently replaced Robert Finch as Secretary of Health, Education, and

Welfare and who learned about the decision from the Associated Press, having strongly argued against a veto. Congress overrode the president by commanding margins: 289 votes to 114 in the House and 77 to 16 in the Senate. In the House, 77 Republicans voted to override, compared to fewer than 20 in January.[78]

Meltdown: The Budget-Making Machinery Collapses

The presidential election year of 1972 generated even greater acrimony in education politics. With Democrats in Congress portraying Nixon as antieducation and Nixon charging them with destabilizing the economy, the budget-making machinery broke down entirely. And after the election, when one might have expected the partisan tension to diminish, it only heightened, as the Watergate scandal came to dominate the political landscape. In 1973, education spending was at the heart of an acrid broader controversy that centered on the president's right to impound funds.

The seeds of the controversy were sown when, ten weeks before the election, Congress sent Nixon a Labor-HEW budget that exceeded his request by $1.7 billion.[79] The bulk of these funds were added by Representative Flood and Senator Magnuson, keen to avoid being rolled again and considering Nixon's budget to have been unrealistically and provocatively modest. When Nixon vetoed the bill, and Congress failed to override him, legislators belatedly embarked on a serious effort to assemble a bill that the president might sign: it exceeded the budget by the same amount but gave Nixon the authority to impound up to two-thirds of the funds. By this point, however, with the election just three weeks away, Nixon was more interested in having the issue than the bill: after holding on to it for two weeks, until a week before polling, he issued a pocket veto, part of a series of highly publicized measures designed to emphasize his inflation-fighting credentials.[80]

After the election, there was remarkably little will on either side of the institutional and partisan divide to find a modus vivendi. Instead, Nixon, having defeated George McGovern in forty-nine of the fifty states and secured 61 percent of the vote, was in a belligerent, combative mood, more determined than ever to face down his enemies in Congress. And it was now that the Watergate scandal, successfully contained by Nixon during the recent campaign, suddenly caught fire. At the end of January 1973, federal judge John J. Sirica found two former Nixon aides, G. Gordon Liddy and James W. McCord, guilty of conspiracy, burglary, and illegal wiretapping. And a week later, the Senate created a Select Committee on Presidential Campaign Activities, chaired by Senator Sam Ervin (D-N.C.).

It was in this environment that Congress and the White House were supposed to renew their effort to agree on a Labor-HEW budget for the 1973 fiscal year, now almost two-thirds gone. In a dramatic sign of how poisonous the relationship had become, each branch eschewed budgetary compromise, electing instead to try to govern without the other. First, Congress decided not to bother with a third attempt at setting a budget.[81] Instead, legislators crafted a continuing resolution that would stay in effect not for a couple of weeks (the usual arrangement) but for the entire remainder of the fiscal year. And whereas these resolutions normally funded programs at the lowest available figure (for example, the previous year's appropriation), this one required Nixon to fund education and health programs at $1.3 billion above his budget, with no impoundment clause. Nixon signed the resolution but announced that he would not spend any funds above those that he had requested a year earlier.

Nixon and Impoundment

Nixon embarked on his second term armed with a big mandate, reflecting on the many frustrations of his first term in office and determined to cow Congress by appealing to middle America. The "bring us together" theme of 1969 had yielded, for the most part, to the New Majority theme of the recent campaign. Central to this was the idea that Americans had had enough of high taxes and big government and that the president alone represented their perspective, whereas Congress responded simply to the narrow preferences of entrenched, special interests. Thus defined, the New Majority approach implied an even more confrontational relationship between the White House and Capitol Hill, especially since Nixon's coattails in November had been so modest (the GOP had gained only thirteen seats in the House and had actually lost two in the Senate).

But even had someone other than Richard Nixon occupied the White House, the basis for conflict would still have been substantial. When Nixon complained that the budgetary process had broken down, the complaint fit nicely with his overall second-term message. But he also was articulating an institutional perspective. From the vantage point of the White House, a number of aspects of the congressional budget process seemed indefensible: Most members thought in particularist terms, ignoring the overall budgetary impact of their actions. Even the appropriations process suffered somewhat from this defect, with each subcommittee considering one of thirteen parts of the budget in isolation. And most spending bills did not arrive at Nixon's desk until well into the fiscal year. What was a president to do? One solution was to impound funds: all Nixon's modern predecessors had done so, and according to the budget office, Kennedy and Johnson had used the tactic more often than he.[82]

Impoundment had always been unpopular on the Hill, but for most of his first term Nixon had been protected from serious attack by the relative modesty of the sums that he was withholding and by the fact that Congress had simultaneously instructed him to stay within an expenditure ceiling and sent him appropriations bills that exceeded those levels.[83] In 1969, when NEA contemplated testing impoundment in the courts, Warren Magnuson was unpersuaded:

> I do not know how you can make an executive spend it. This is not only true with Mr. Nixon: I have been around with seven Presidents and they have withheld funds, six of them now. I don't know what the court can do. You can't put them in jail, can you? You can't put the Secretary of the Treasury in jail. You can't go down there and take it out of the till if they close the door. But I think they have been reasonable. I think the withholding of funds has been reasonable.[84]

Three years later, when Nixon impounded $1.8 billion in health and education funds in the aftermath of the continuing resolution, Magnuson did *not* think that was reasonable. For one thing, $1.8 billion was a large sum. For another, the administration was withholding even larger sums for other programs: an astonishing $6 billion, in the case of the water pollution law that Congress had passed the previous year. Third, Congress had no obvious way of getting around the problem. When Lyndon Johnson had withheld impact aid and equipment purchase funds in order to stay within the first congressional ceiling, Congress had exempted all OE funds from impoundment, and Johnson had reluctantly released the funds. But by 1973, Nixon's use of the practice was much more daring. On occasion, he used it not simply to pare spending on particular programs but to eliminate them entirely, as with two rural electrification schemes that Congress had endorsed without dissent.[85]

Whatever one thought of the merits of each case, they seemed like departures from past practice and were extremely imprudent in political terms. Among those who were appalled were many conservative Democrats who had been among Nixon's strongest allies in the first term on issues such as Vietnam, the Haynsworth vote, and the ABM system. Perhaps the strongest critic was Sam Ervin, who, as well as chairing the select committee on Watergate, headed the Senate Judiciary Committee's subcommittee on the separation of powers. In response to people like Ervin, Nixon fell back on the unsatisfactory argument that the right to impound funds existed under the Constitution: he told journalists in January 1973 that the "constitutional right for the President of the United States to impound funds . . . when the spending of money would mean either increasing prices or increasing taxes for all the people . . . is absolutely clear."[86] Other presidents and budget directors had mumbled that argument too and had been allowed to get away with it, but Nixon had to make it much more forthrightly, in the full glare of publicity and in the context of the wider questions that were swirling around his administration.[87]

Education and Impoundment

In this context, "full funding" acquired a new meaning: forcing the president to spend all appropriated funds.[88] Education lobbyists were among the multitude of interests that challenged Nixon's right to impound funds in the federal courts during 1973. The key education case was *Commonwealth of Pennsylvania v. Weinberger*, which was brought by eleven states, together with a number of education groups, including the chief state school officers and NSBA.[89] In November, after a four-month trial, Judge Joseph Waddy of the District of Columbia district court handed them a big victory, declaring that the impoundment of education funds by the Nixon administration had been "unlawful and unconstitutional."[90]

That was the forty-fifth impoundment decision to be handed down, and all but five had gone against the White House. Until now, HEW had dismissed the possibility that defeat in a lower federal court might lead the administration to release the funds: its new secretary, Caspar Weinberger, insisted that he would wait for a definitive ruling by the Supreme Court. By the end of 1973, though, the administration was completely consumed by the Watergate investigation, bold ideas of forcing a New Majority having yielded to a desperate fight to stay in office. Vice President Spiro Agnew and domestic policy chief John Ehrlichman had each been forced to resign, and their replacements were Gerald Ford and Melvin Laird, men of Congress who understood and respected its mores and were anxious to build bridges between the White House and Capitol Hill.[91] When Laird counseled Nixon to go along with Judge Waddy, as part of this bridge-building exercise, the president accepted the recommendation, and the funds were finally released.

Finally, almost five months into FY1974, the *previous* year's budgetary fight had at last been settled, with Congress having defeated a by now almost mortally wounded President Nixon. It was a big win for the CEF, one of whose lobbyists, Robert Frase, celebrated "the great victories of the education and library coalition" in his employer's trade publication, *Publishers Weekly.* Looking back over the battles of the past five years, he concluded that friends of education had finally "found a way to counteract the Nixon Administration strategy of vetoes upheld by one-third of the House of Representatives."[92]

Education Funding in a Deteriorating Economy

By this time, though, Frase and his colleagues faced a new foe: sharp economic decline. As well as featuring the virtual disintegration of the Nixon presidency, 1973 was the year of the Yom Kippur war and the OPEC crisis, which saw oil prices increasing fourfold between October and December. This deepened a recession that had started soon after the 1972 election and that would last until 1975. Historian James T. Patterson identifies this as the period when the "grand expectations" of the postwar period were replaced by a mood of acute anxiety about the future. This, he recorded, was a time of "sagging productivity, declining competitiveness in world markets, accelerating inflation, rising unemployment, especially among minorities and the millions of baby boomers seeking work, and a slowing down in the creation of good-paying, career-enhancing jobs outside of the increasingly dominant service sector."[93] Another historian of the 1970s, Edward Berkowitz, remarks that "it looked at the time as though a crucial climacteric had been reached."[94]

Anxiety about the budget deficit and the threat of inflation had helped shape education politics since the escalation of the Vietnam War in the mid-1960s. Now, though, they were of an entirely different order of magnitude. The deficit reached $53 billion in FY1975 and $74 billion the following year (the previous post–World War II high had been $23 billion, in 1971).[95] Inflation, meanwhile, reached 11.3 percent in 1974 (when Johnson era fears about prices had been at their height, the figure had been 4.2 percent).[96] Unemployment, during this same period, reached a post–Great Depression high of 8.5 percent. And real gross national product fell by 2 percent in 1974 and 3 percent in 1975.[97]

Prospects for a substantial, real increase in federal education spending were nil, especially given the enormous increase that had taken place in entitlement spending (Social Security, food stamps, Supplemental Security Income) during the Nixon administration. Discretionary spending was squeezed, and the larger number of constituencies chasing those discretionary dollars, following the various health and environmental laws of the early

1970s, made the challenge facing the education lobby greater still. More than ever, success for the CEF would be measured in terms of preserving the gains of the glory years, rather than boosting appropriations.

Ford versus Congress

Prospects for achieving that limited goal brightened appreciably with the Watergate election of November 1974. Three months into Gerald Ford's caretaker term, and one month after his politically damaging decision to pardon his predecessor, the Democrats won two-thirds majorities in both House and Senate, for the first time in a decade. Compared to 1964, moreover, the Democratic caucus was much more liberal, especially in the House. Throughout the Nixon years, ambitious young reformers in Congress had helped to chip away at the conventions and procedures that had sustained the hierarchical, seniority-based system of the past half century and had won some important victories: recorded teller votes, greater autonomy for subcommittees, full caucus votes on committee chairmanships, the opening up of committee hearings and markup sessions to the public. Now, the full impact of those earlier victories began to be felt, as an enormous and unusually cohesive freshman class of seventy-five Democrats began to flex its muscles.

One consequence was that the Labor-HEW subcommittee shifted to the left, complicating the Ford administration's attempt to cut education spending. Ever since the Joelson amendment, one staff member observed, it had "changed from trying to find cuts to deciding what [*sic*] of the budget's cuts to restore."[98] Now, that process accelerated, in part because the liberal-dominated Democratic caucus had won the power to replace appropriations subcommittee chairmen such as Flood, further diminishing their already attenuated authority and making them keener than ever to accommodate majority sentiment. Also, the ideological composition of Flood's subcommittee had changed: three strong liberals had joined it since 1972—David Obey of Wisconsin (added by Mahon in a bid to win the approbation of the reformers), Louis Stokes of Ohio, and Edward Roybal of California (both added in 1975).

Still, these changes did not result in a new period of congressional government. In part that was because the devolution of power in Congress made it harder for the Democratic leadership to provide effective leadership.[99] More important, though, was Ford's use of the veto strategy and the skill with which he and his congressional aides kept the loyalty of the depleted coalition of Republicans and conservative Democrats. As of late July,

Ford had sustained all seven of his vetoes. In mid-September, when the Senate sustained his veto of an important energy bill, a frustrated Senator John Pastore (D-R.I.) complained that "this has become a government by veto. We've got the minority dragging the majority by the nose."[100]

When Ford vetoed the 1976 OE appropriation bill, which exceeded his budget by an enormous $1.3 billion, Democrats were not at all confident of an override.[101] Because of that, the House leadership postponed the vote until after the month-long summer recess. During that month, the CEF mounted one of its biggest lobbying campaigns yet, and when Congress reconvened, an estimated 1,000 to 1,500 educators came to Washington to make the case for a vote against the president. Congress voted to override by startling margins: 379 to 41 in the House, and 88 to 12 in the Senate. It was the biggest win for the education coalition since 1969. Spectators in the galleries reacted by breaking into applause, until Speaker Carl Albert admonished them for their lack of decorum.[102]

The following year, five weeks before the presidential election, Congress overrode Ford's Labor-HEW veto again. This time, the bill exceeded his budget by a massive $4 billion, with education spending accounting for $1.6 billion of that figure. For the first time, Flood was on the same side as the insurgents: the bulk of the extra funds had been added by his subcommittee. When Robert Michel implored Republican colleagues to stand with the president and hold down government spending, Flood reportedly responded with a "dramatic reading" of all the programs that Michel's proposal would affect, following each item "with a short whistle or exclamatory sound." Getting into the spirit of things, the GOP minority "took up the chant, echoing each of Flood's dramatic flourishes with good natured mimicry." Flood won, with Michel's amendment being defeated by a margin of seventy-five votes.[103] The Senate largely went along with the House bill. When Ford's veto was comfortably overridden, it was only the seventh time that this had occurred during his brief presidency, in thirty-two attempts.

Given the congressional arithmetic, that was not a bad record for Ford. That two of those overrides should have concerned education appropriation bills confirmed again the particular power of that lobby. It helped that, as Max Friedersdorf, head of Ford's congressional relation team, observed, education was a "motherhood issue."[104] In 1965, Republicans could vote against federal aid without too much fear of being labeled as "antieducation." A decade later, that was no longer the case. Also, education groups that either had previously shown little interest in federal politics, or had competed with one another for the attention of legislators, had now learned how to work together. It was no longer possible for George Mahon to hold down education spending by playing the impact aid lobby against the NEA.

What had been the impact of the education coalition? Clearly, all those big congressional add-ons did not greatly increase the amount of federal spending. Rather, they simply negated efforts by Presidents Nixon and Ford to reduce spending. Set against the expectations of the late 1960s, when representatives of the Big Six education groups had fondly anticipated a rise in the federal share of elementary and secondary education spending to a fifth, or perhaps even one-third, this was a modest achievement.[105] But when one considers how great the pressure on discretionary spending had become by the mid-1970s, even holding one's own was an accomplishment. In another sense, moreover, the impression of stagnation conveyed by a flat 8 percent federal share through the Nixon-Ford years is misleading, for this was 8 percent of a substantially expanded total. In a time of diminishing enrollments, total education spending per pupil increased in constant 2002 dollars from $3,800 in 1969 to $5,100 in 1977. And federal spending per pupil in unadjusted dollars increased by 250 percent during the same period.[106]

Education and Regulatory Federalism

Chapters 3 and 4 were concerned with an enduring, basic truth about American political democracy, namely the difficulty of dismantling any federal program that has acquired a strong constituency. Supporters of ESEA were able to preserve its categorical character and to maintain funding levels during the decade after 1965, despite the disappointing results of Title I and in the face of an increasingly adverse budgetary climate. Even so, the *direct* impact of ESEA on local schooling was constrained both by limited funding—the federal share of education spending never reached 10 percent of the total—and by the tenacity of the idea that education policies should be set locally.

The *indirect* impact of ESEA on the local politics of education was enormous, however. To understand why, one needs to begin with Title VI of the 1964 Civil Rights Act. This provides in Section 601 that "no person in the United States shall, on the basis of race, color, or national origin, be excluded from participation in, be denied the benefits of, or be subjected to discrimination under any program or activity receiving federal financial assistance."[1] Where a school district or other entity was found to be in violation, the relevant federal agency was empowered to terminate funding. At the time, that did not seem very important, because federal funds were so small.

The passage of ESEA, though, made Title VI much more significant: by

1967, many southern districts received more than 20 percent of their funds from Washington, and in some cases the figure exceeded 30 percent. In most instances, the federal share had doubled during the preceding twelve months.[2] Moreover, HEW administrators went about the task of administering Title VI with greater zest than southern educators can ever have anticipated. "Within a year after President Johnson signed the Civil Rights Act," Gary Orfield has remarked, "unknown bureaucrats were drawing on the authority granted by Title VI to administer a major social revolution in thousands of southern school districts."[3]

The results of this attempt at "social revolution" were mixed (see Chapter 5), but in terms of the broader history of federal education policy since the 1960s, Title VI looms as large as ESEA. During the 1970s, a series of other federal antidiscrimination initiatives were launched in the area of elementary and secondary education, the most important of them focusing on the rights of language minorities and children with disabilities. In the first of those cases, HEW administrators construed Title VI as conferring a right to bilingual education, and the Supreme Court ratified that interpretation (see Chapter 6). In the second case, the initiative was taken by the lower federal courts, and Congress then enshrined their rulings on behalf of children with disabilities into statutory law (see Chapter 7). In a third case, school finance experts worked through the courts to force states to equalize spending on the poor, but fell at the last hurdle, after a long run of eye-catching legal victories (see Chapter 8).[4]

In fact, with the possible exception of education for the handicapped, it would be problematic to present any of the four cases treated in this section as having yielded unambiguous, enduring victories for the group on whose behalf action was launched: even in the three cases that seemed to be victories, the story is, to at least some extent, one of dashed hopes. That is not to say, however, that their consequences have been trivial or ephemeral. On the contrary, their cumulative impact was to legitimize a much more intrusive federal role than policymakers had imagined when they were putting together ESEA in 1965. The crossing of this "legitimacy barrier" (to use James Q. Wilson's term) during the 1970s came about in the specific context of civil rights enforcement, where the principle of localism had been sharply devalued by massive resistance to desegregation in the South.[5] But the fact that a legitimacy threshold was crossed in one context of education policymaking, and crossed by conservatives as well as liberals, paved the way for other deviations from the traditional pattern of American federalism in subsequent years, notably the extraordinarily prescriptive No Child Left Behind Act of 2002.

This was all part of the broader minority rights revolution of the late 1960s and 1970s, whereby a whole variety of groups drew inspiration from the black civil rights movement and sought to duplicate its political success. Historians are wont to construe American politics during the 1970s in terms of a conservative reaction against the liberal 1960s. By contrast, the cases in education policymaking considered here allow one to probe the ways in which the liberal reform impulse endured during the 1970s, having dramatically changed in character since 1965. As sociologist John David Skrentny has argued, ideas played a central role here: minority rights claims tended to prosper to the extent that the group in question could draw a plausible analogy to the black example. In the cases considered below, advocates for language minorities, the disabled, and children in poor school districts each sought to draw such analogies when arguing before the courts, with varying degrees of success.[6]

At least as important were changes in the political process. The cases of education policymaking considered below should be understood not just in relation to the minority rights revolution but as embodying the new pattern of "regulatory federalism" that students of American political development see as having characterized the Nixon-Ford years.[7] Reviewing its impact in 1984, the Advisory Commission on Intergovernmental Relations (ACIR) found that "over the past two decades . . . —and since 1969 in particular— there has been a dramatic shift in the way in which the federal government deals with states and localities. . . . Federal policymakers . . . turned increasingly to new, more intrusive, and more compulsory *regulatory* programs to work their will."[8] Among the leading cases were such policy areas as environmental protection, occupational safety and health, and consumer rights. In each case, advocates of social regulation were animated by a new understanding of the proper role of the federal government.

Education politics offers a good illustration of the new politics of regulation, for the number of pages of federal regulations affecting education increased more than tenfold between 1965 and 1977, from 92 to nearly 1,000.[9] Sometimes these regulations were in response to legislation, but—as with American politics more generally—what was particularly notable was the growing role of the courts in shaping social policy. More federal court cases affecting schools were decided between 1967 and 1971 than during the entire previous history of the Republic.[10] If the federal government was not giving very much more money to school districts during the 1970s, then clearly it was setting a lot more instructions about how they were to behave.

Back in 1965, when the Great Society was at its zenith, the three big engines of social reform had been presidential leadership, the Warren Court, and bottom-up social protest. In the 1970s, reform often emanated from less conspicuous places: from within the federal bureaucracy, from the lower federal courts, and through the energetic efforts of congressional staffers, lobbyists, and public interest law firms. Only rarely did their activities make the national newspapers, but their cumulative impact was to utterly transform the world of education politics. The next four chapters explore the changes in American governance that allowed liberal reformers to build on, and in some cases far transcend, the policy record of the Johnson years.

When we broaden our gaze beyond the White House and beyond the actions and rhetoric of elected officials, ESEA remains central to the story of federal education policy during the 1970s. The view of American liberalism that one would gain from dwelling exclusively upon them—defensive in character, struggling to hold on to the gains of the 1960s, unhappily conscious that the glory days are long gone—ceases to be sufficient, however. In its place, one needs a version of events that captures both that story *and* a more complicated one, in which reformers faced with the passing of the glory days find new ways of keeping the banner of reform aloft.

The place to begin such a story is back in 1964, with the enactment of Title VI. The next two chapters explore the process by which an initially inconspicuous feature of the Civil Rights Act paved the way for a basic shift in the federal role in education.[11]

5

Ending Massive Resistance

THE FEDERAL GOVERNMENT AND SOUTHERN

SCHOOL DESEGREGATION, 1964–1970

Few opponents of the Civil Rights Act of 1964 saw Title VI as one of the more objectionable features of the bill.[1] In part, that was because supporters were so reassuring regarding its likely impact. Hubert Humphrey (D-Minn.), who was Senate floor manager for the bill, exclaimed that "if anyone can be against [Title VI], he can be against Mother's Day." "It does not confer any new Federal authority," he promised, "it merely states how the authority conferred by other laws is to be administered. It is not a regulatory measure but an exercise of the unquestioned power of the Federal Government to 'fix the terms on which Federal funds shall be disbursed.'"[2] When John Sparkman (D-Ala.) objected that "nowhere . . . in this great omnibus bill is the term 'discrimination' defined," Humphrey emphasized administrative deference to the courts, going on to note that they currently construed racial discrimination quite narrowly. "While the Constitution prohibits segregation," he reminded colleagues, "it does not require integration. . . . The bill does not attempt to integrate the schools, but it does attempt to eliminate segregation in the school systems."[3]

The most controversial aspect of Title VI was the clause empowering the federal government to cut off funds in the case of noncompliance. But when Sam Ervin and Richard Russell (D-Ga.) charged that this gave excessive power to federal bureaucrats, the claim attracted remarkably little attention. In the case of school desegregation, that doubtless reflected the facts that federal aid to education was small and that political prospects for larger-scale aid looked indifferent.[4] Also, elaborate and time-consuming procedural safeguards were included.[5] Finally, the OE administrators charged with exercising this discretion had long enjoyed amicable relationships with local school officials, including southern superintendents and state chiefs. Orfield remarks that it would be "difficult to imagine any agency less prepared in terms of temperament, tradition, and philosophy to forcefully set in motion a major social revolution."[6]

HEW and Desegregation

According to one careful analysis of Title VI, most federal agencies gave "little more than rhetorical attention" to its enforcement, justifying the relatively relaxed attitude that southerners had taken in 1964.[7] The big exception, oddly enough, was OE, which took its responsibilities seriously right from the start. Why should this have been? The first reason is prosaic: Unlike any other agency at HEW, OE had a civil rights budget, and that gave commissioner Keppel the option of creating a specialist civil rights staff within the agency.[8] A strong supporter of integration, Keppel exercised this option and established a discrete Equal Educational Opportunities Program (EEOP) within OE, rather than adding civil rights to the responsibilities of every program officer.[9]

Naturally, this body attracted individuals with a personal commitment to civil rights, including veterans of the Congress of Racial Equality and the Student Nonviolent Coordinating Committee. EEOP head David Seeley was a graduate of Yale Law School who had studied under Keppel at the Harvard Graduate School of Education, prior to going to work for the U.S. Civil Rights Commission. Although he strove to rein in his more militant colleagues and to retain the trust of the more moderate element at EEOP, his personal sympathies were captured by a 1967 memo in which he declared that "our program is different from all others in the Office. . . . It is *not* just a small grant program. It is a form of *warfare*."[10]

In 1965, though, Keppel and Seeley hoped that "warfare" would be unnecessary, thinking that ESEA might be a sufficient carrot to obviate too much recourse to the stick. Their optimism was reflected in the first desegregation guidelines that OE issued: all that a district had to do to receive ESEA funds was sign a piece of paper certifying that it did not discriminate on grounds of race. Segregated districts across the South blithely provided such assurances, and the federal dollars started flowing. In reality, their "freedom of choice" plans tended to remove the legal edifice of Jim Crow while preserving rigid racial segregation by informal mechanisms. Looking back, Seeley acknowledged a "general lack of appreciation of the monstrousness of the task before us."[11]

A more sober mood developed during the summer of 1965, as EEOP field officers first encountered the fierce determination of southern whites to resist anything other than token compliance. Orfield remarks that they began the summer "with naivete, optimism, and idealism" but ended it "as a corps of professional school desegregators, able to realistically estimate local attitudes and accurately outline the requirements for protection of the constitutional rights of southern Negro students."[12] Activists at the Student Nonviolent Coordinating Committee (SNCC) and the American Friends Service Committee pressed for action against the techniques that whites used to preserve segregation, and HEW and Justice officials started to contemplate new guidelines that would make substantial integration a prerequisite for receiving federal school dollars.

Even before those guidelines were promulgated, in the spring of 1966, Title VI started to cause political headaches for the Johnson administration. Surprisingly, the first big controversy occurred not in the South, but in Chicago. In a bad political miscalculation, Keppel and Seeley decided to defer ESEA payments to Chicago, following complaints from a local civil rights group. The city's powerful mayor, Richard Daley, went straight to his political ally at the White House, and a furious Johnson insisted that the maladroit decision be reversed. Title VI administrators were left demoralized by his intervention, newly uncertain of the White House commitment to integration.[13]

Far from diminishing, though, the enforcement effort gained new intensity during the months after Chicago. That owed something to the fact that Harold Howe II, who replaced Keppel as commissioner shortly after the debacle, was a passionate advocate of civil rights. That commitment had deep roots: his father had been president of one of the premier black higher education institutions in the South, the Hampton Institute; his maternal grandfather, Samuel Chapman Armstrong, had founded the institute, having previously commanded a unit of black soldiers during the Civil War; and his grandmother was "one of the New England schoolmarms who went South in the 1880s to help educate the freed slaves."[14] Throughout his stormy three-year tenure at the head of OE, Howe was an outspoken, unflinching champion of racial integration, enduring an unceasing torrent of abuse from southern politicians.

The abuse started in earnest in March 1966, when John W. Gardner promulgated new Title VI guidelines. Whereas the previous HEW secretary, Anthony Celebrezze, had little interest in civil rights, the patrician Gardner shared Howe's strong commitment.[15] Reflecting their shared determination to undermine massive resistance, the guidelines stated that districts where a small amount of integration had taken place to date would be expected to treble the number of African Americans attending integrated schools that fall and that districts where a somewhat more substantial start had been made should aim to at least double the current figure. Where no integration at all had taken place, a district was expected to make "a very substantial start." In order to break down the racial identification of schools, meanwhile, districts would be required to assign teaching staff on an integrated basis.[16]

The southern reaction was fierce, gaining particular intensity during the summer of 1966, when an overstretched Seeley sent hundreds of law student volunteers down South to negotiate agreements with school officials. One Alabama congressman charged that "Harold Howe has pressed down upon the brow of the South a crown of thorns as cruel and as torturous as that pressed upon the head of the Prince of Peace when they crucified Him on the cross."[17] Johnson never publicly criticized Howe or Gardner and staunchly resisted calls for Howe's dismissal, but in private he was dismayed at the political fallout.[18] So was John Fogarty: OE's association with the guidelines complicated his effort to secure more federal money for schools. The powerful appropriations subcommittee chief told Gardner that HEW would be much less politically exposed if the EEOP were transferred to the Justice Department.[19]

Gardner resisted that idea, but other top officials at HEW and Justice shared Fogarty's dismay at what they took to be Seeley's ham-fisted approach. Undersecretary Cohen, whom Lyndon Johnson had deputed to solve the Chicago problem, blamed Seeley for having riled Mayor Daley. Looking back, he described the EEOP chief in unflattering terms:

> Dave Seeley, who had been there [in Chicago], was very immature; he was "gung ho" for all this. But he had no political knowledge, no real administrative ability, and a fine fellow, but he wasn't dry behind the ears in terms of how to handle these things.

Warming to his subject, Cohen then broadened the attack:

> And another thing: most of the other people who were with him, were all these young lawyers who had good ideas, but their concept

of enforcement and administration was juvenile. And, just like I've said of Medicaid, if you're going to have a program, you've got to give thought to recruitment of personnel, you've got to have a management approach; you've got to have a battle plan; you've got to know where to go forward; you'd got to know where to retreat. There was none of that in it. Just a bunch of amateurs with real good ideas and very socially minded, wandering around in the desert of Sinai.[20]

By the time that Cohen became secretary of HEW, continuing pressure from the Hill had forced HEW to lodge the responsibility for Title VI in the Office for Civil Rights (OCR), which was located in the office of the secretary, where legislators could keep a closer eye on its activities. But the move did not make very much difference to the politics of desegregation, which became ever more acrimonious. Constrained by segregationist fervor in their districts and by local resentment of Harold Howe, many southern school officials were politically unable to comply with the 1966 guidelines, but their resistance caused OCR officials to seek a still *stronger* federal response. HEW started cutting off funds to uncooperative districts in 1967, and by the time that Johnson left office this sanction had been applied in almost 200 cases.[21]

As secretary, the workaholic Cohen found his life dominated by civil rights, remarking that "if I hadn't worked twelve hours a day during that period of time, it would have taken fifty percent of my time."[22] Resenting this fact, and feeling that it had poisoned HEW's relationship with important southern legislators, he came to regret not having made a strong case for Fogarty's original proposal: that the responsibility for enforcing civil rights be transferred to Justice. During the Nixon transition, he urged his successor, Robert Finch, to take this step.[23]

HEW under Nixon: Great Society in Exile

During the 1968 presidential campaign, Richard Nixon won support in the South by opposing busing and judicial activism and by remarking that "I don't believe you should use the South as a whipping boy." He told southern delegates to the Republican National Convention that when children were bused "into a strange community . . . I think you destroy that child." And he added that "it is the job of the courts to interpret the law, and not make the law" and that no judge "is qualified to be a local school district and make the decision as your local school board." Finally, he opposed the "dangerous" idea of withholding funds "to force a local community to carry out what a

Federal administrator or bureaucrats may think is best for that local community."[24]

When Nixon narrowly won the election, thanks to the support of the upper South, southern backers such as Senator Strom Thurmond (R-S.C.) looked to him to convert campaign words into presidential deeds. But that proved difficult. As in a number of other policy areas, Nixon's effort to place a distinctively Republican stamp on his administration was complicated by a strong commitment within the federal bureaucracy to preserving the Great Society. Whereas Nixon's foreign policies gave liberal contemporaries the sense that his was an "imperial" or even a "revolutionary" presidency, in the area of social policy he often had strikingly little ability to impose his policy priorities.[25] Frustrated by his seeming inability to influence the policies of his domestic agencies, Nixon grumbled that "the way I have influence on this government . . . is to make notes in the margins of memoranda which gradually leak to the columns."[26]

No episode did more to shape Richard Nixon's hostility to the federal bureaucracy than his inability to get HEW to respond to his political needs. Nixon entered the White House with little interest in the substance of civil rights policy: his record on race was moderately progressive, but it was not a subject that engaged him.[27] As with other aspects of domestic policy, he looked to his cabinet appointees to ensure that his campaign commitments were carried out and keep him out of political trouble so that he could get on with more important business, such as ending the Vietnam War—the challenge that promised to make or break his presidency—and establishing a new relationship with the Soviet Union and the People's Republic of China.[28]

In the case of civil rights, the task of keeping Nixon out of trouble fell principally to two close political allies: Attorney General John Mitchell and HEW secretary Finch. Mitchell had been Nixon's law partner in New York during the past four years, and Nixon saw him as a shrewd, tough strategist, hence his decision to ask him to run the 1968 campaign. In that role, he had been principal architect of Nixon's southern strategy. As for Finch, he came to Washington from California, where he had been lieutenant governor, and was a trusted, longtime political associate for whom the generally remote Nixon felt real affection.[29] At the White House, meanwhile, the initial responsibility for gauging the political impact of their decisions lay with Harry Dent, a partisan champion of southern republicanism who had been chief of staff to Thurmond. But when Nixon appointed Leonard Garment, a liberal Democrat, to his staff a few months into the administration, with the vague responsibility of reaching out to "non-traditional" GOP constituencies, he provided a counterweight to Dent.[30]

When Finch started work at HEW, he immediately confronted a tricky civil rights decision. Cannily, Wilbur Cohen had delayed a politically difficult set of five Title VI cut-off decisions so that the final announcement would have to be made by his successor, during his second week in office. From the point of view of Dent, this was a good opportunity to show the South that HEW was adopting a new approach. For Finch it meant something else. A forty-four-year-old liberal Republican, he had assembled a hybrid political coalition during his race for the lieutenant governorship, easily outpolling his running mate, Ronald Reagan. Powerfully impressed by the promise of the "new politics," he was on record as believing that 1968 would be "the last election that will be won by the un-black, the un-poor and the un-young." Offered first the vice presidency and then the Justice Department by Nixon, he had turned down both in favor of HEW, believing that it would be "the action department of the administration." His long-term ambition was to become a senator in the mold of such other progressive California Republicans as Earl Warren and Thomas Kuchel.[31]

Nixon gave Finch considerable latitude over his appointments. As undersecretary he selected John Veneman, a former Californian assemblyman who shared his political convictions and was distrusted by Governor Reagan.[32] The job of top lawyer went to a conservative, Robert Mardian, but not before it had been turned down by Roger Wilkins, nephew of the NAACP executive director and one of the more militant African American appointees in the Johnson administration.[33] Reflecting the same desire to reach out to minorities, James Farmer, former head of the Congress of Racial Equality (CORE), became assistant secretary for administration. In the area of education, Finch selected a particularly liberal team. James Allen, head of the New York school system and a forthright supporter of busing, became commissioner.[34] And Leon Panetta, an aide to Senator Kuchel, was chosen to head OCR.[35]

By comparison to Wilbur Cohen, Finch was committed to strong HEW civil rights enforcement. When the outgoing secretary urged him to reassign the responsibility to Justice, he rejected the advice, presumably feeling that bringing about speedy desegregation was the inescapable number one responsibility for a New Politics–oriented "action department." According to Panetta, he exclaimed: "That would only water down the enforcement process." Asked by journalists whether HEW was intending to modify LBJ's Title VI guidelines, he said no.[36]

In arriving at these positions, Finch's personal instincts would have been reinforced by the overall political milieu at HEW, where there was strong suspicion of Nixon within the permanent bureaucracy. Wishing to win the approbation and trust of his new colleagues, but needing too to respond to the political interests of the Nixon White House, Finch found himself in an impossible political dilemma. HEW resistance to the Nixon White House was not driven simply by ideological distaste. Also, programmatic agencies were constrained to respond to the will of the Democratic Congress, whose spending committees controlled their funding and whose authorizing committees determined how those funds were spent. Even when the same party controlled both ends of Pennsylvania Avenue, having two masters was a recipe for institutional conflict, and in the case of divided government it was likely to be particularly intense.

In addition, high-ranking career officials in the agencies naturally developed ongoing and fruitful associations both with subcommittee staffers on the Hill and with interested pressure groups. Take, for example, Alden Lillywhite, the New Deal veteran who had administered the impact aid program since its inception during the Truman administration. Described by a colleague as a tall, lanky, foppish man who wore a different-colored flower in his lapel each day, Lillywhite was disliked by some at HEW because he had such a strong power base outside of the department.[37] By the same token, however, he had close ties to Oscar Rose's lobby and was widely respected in Congress. When the budget bureau sought to cut the program that Lillywhite had helped to create, he could not be expected to lobby on behalf of the proposal. To the contrary, he was part of the iron triangle network that regularly repelled such assaults.

In a 1974 book dedicated to "the unsung career employees of HEW," the department's former top career official, Rufus Miles, pondered the political implications of such networks. Regardless of party, he noted, White House officials "seem to expect . . . that the Secretary ought to stamp out these unholy alliances. They fail to comprehend that this would be an extremely unwise use of the Secretary's time and power," likely to result "in an utter quagmire." "Wise Secretaries," in his view, "seek to create an atmosphere of mutual trust and loyalty that will minimize 'end runs' rather than creating an espionage system for 'getting the goods' on persons suspected of disloyalty."[38]

Precisely because he tried to take this advice, however, Finch soon found himself in trouble with the White House, especially with Dent, Ehrlichman, and Harry Flemming (whose responsibilities included screening political appointees for loyalty). When Mardian was appointed general counsel, a few weeks into the administration, the pressure had come from a White House that was already becoming worried about obstructionism within HEW, the Department of Housing and Urban Development (HUD), the Office of Economic Opportunity (OEO), and other Great Society–oriented departments and agencies. An Arizona Republican who had played a leading role in Barry Goldwater's 1964 campaign, Mardian and L. Patrick Gray (who was deployed in the secretary's office) were the White House men at HEW, deputed to prevent Finch's liberal tendencies from getting out of hand.

The White House officials were right to think that raw ideological hostility, as well as institutional self-interest, shaped HEW resistance to policy redirection. For a Goldwater Republican, arriving at HEW in the spring of 1969 must have seemed like landing on an alien planet. Mardian's personal papers bring his encounters with oppositionism at HEW vividly to life, as well as conveying the febrile circumstances in which Nixon came to power, with antiwar activism at its zenith. He recorded, for example, the activities of the HEW chapter of Federal Employees for a Democratic Society (FEDS). Its Thursday Discussion Group met on government property to discuss such matters as draft-avoidance, ways of opposing the administration's Antiballistic Missiles program, and the value of "demonstrations, sit-ins, slow-downs or any of the other forms of protest used by SDS on the campuses" in bringing about institutional change within HEW. At one of these gatherings, a staffer to James Farmer entertained his colleagues with mocking references to "Tricky Dick," reportedly joking that "you can imagine how much I enjoy working for *this* administration."[39]

A sympathetic Harry Dent responded to reports from behind enemy lines by imploring Mardian to "be brave." "Help," he added mysteriously, "is on the way."[40] To judge from a 1970 survey by Fred Malek of the White House, the cavalry was slow to arrive. Asked by H. R. Haldeman to undertake a broader Project to Upgrade Personnel, Malek uncovered eye-catching instances of dissent at HEW:[41]

- Robert Berlinner, a GS-18 official at the National Institutes of Health, had recently told a television interviewer that "Nixon is trying to take medical research back to the Dark Ages."
- Thomas Kennedy of the National Institutes of Health (NIH) (like Berlinner, a holdover from the Johnson administration) was reportedly involved in organizing the Vietnam Moratorium

movement and sported a "McCarthy for President" bumper sticker on his car.

- Harold Suskin, director of personnel at OE, was, like Kennedy, associated with the Moratorium and reportedly unwilling to hire Republicans.
- James Abert, deputy assistant secretary for program evaluation, had recently tried to hire a Democratic activist who, when being sworn into office on a previous occasion, had used the autobiography of Malcolm X, instead of a Bible.[42]

The fact that so detailed a catalog of anecdotes was compiled suggests the kind of surveillance and suspicion to which HEW became subject during the early years of the Nixon administration. When such tidbits reached Nixon, his initial indifference to HEW activities rapidly gave way to a preoccupation with its opposition culture.[43] He was particularly outraged by the activities of Leon Panetta's Office for Civil Rights.

OCR under Nixon

When OCR took over the task of enforcing Title VI from OE in 1967, John Gardner feared that the move would be seen as a retreat from civil rights. He need not have worried, for OCR rapidly acquired the same kind of militant commitment to strong enforcement that had characterized David Seeley's EEOP. Panetta recalls his reception in March of 1969, two months into the Nixon administration:

> I could sense more than a little reserve, if not hostility. This was the small bureaucracy—less than three hundred staff members—which had begun one of the most significant, controversial social revolutions in the Nation's history. They didn't know whether the task begun with such pain would be concluded in the South in the next year or two and expanded in the North, or whether Richard Nixon and his agents like me would bring it all to a grinding halt, undo the work of these fifteen years, and restore separate but equal to its time-honored standing. . . .
>
> It was a close office, with a staff prepared to work ungodly hours, travel untold miles and endure their share of insults from unhappy officialdom in order to desegregate schools, hospitals and welfare agencies. Many were motivated by personal experience by this time, even if they were not black.[44]

Panetta could "feel the tension" and had to struggle to win their support.[45] He succeeded by resisting White House pressure to soft-pedal Title VI enforcement and urging Finch to stay true to his principles. But this made him a bête noire at the White House, where John Ehrlichman felt that Panetta "symbolized the bureaucrat-ideologue who persisted in rubbing people's noses in a social mess that was not their fault."[46] In the South, he became the Harold Howe of the Nixon administration, symbol of unfeeling, bureaucratic diktat.

Things had seemed to get off to a good start for the southern strategists when the five terminations due to come into effect at the end of January 1969 were suspended for two months. Days later, though, HEW announced the immediate withdrawal of federal funding from three additional districts, including one in Thurmond's South Carolina. Southern Republican chairmen meeting in Washington felt confused and even betrayed, and Thurmond was reportedly "furious" with the administration, charging that there had been "absolutely no change" in HEW policy since the election.[47]

On occasion, Nixon would lash out at his southern critics, expressing irritation to Haldeman at their "constant right-wing bitching, with never a positive alternative."[48] More commonly, though, he vented at HEW, fomented by right-wingers in the administration such as Dent, speechwriter Patrick Buchanan, and Vice President Spiro Agnew, who drew each OCR outrage to his attention in an effort to prompt him to decisive remedial action. Dent was particularly assiduous, muttering darkly about the "outsiders, apparent pro-hippie types, and Negroes" who were being sent by HEW to his beloved Southland. Grandly inviting Nixon to "consider these observations by one who understands the Southern mind, the problem, and the law," he declared that "the basic ideology among personnel" at HEW was "much left of center—zealots."[49]

The longer the Johnson administration's tough HEW guidelines remained in force, the greater the White House pressure on Finch. Apprised of newspaper speculation that Finch was under pressure to relax the guidelines "in a furtive and quiet manner," Nixon instructed his friend: "Bob— I want them relaxed in a *direct, forthright* manner."[50] But if Finch responded to such pressure (as he did in an interview with *U.S. News and World Report*, a few days after that nudge), Panetta and like-minded colleagues would mobilize a concerted countereffort. Nancy Dickerson of NBC referred to "an underground of HEW officials who get the word to friendly liberals who then initiate pressure of their own."[51] There were plenty of pro–civil rights

Republicans in Congress, including Senate minority leader Hugh Scott and minority chief whip Robert Griffin (R-Mich.).[52] With Scott taking the lead, Dickerson observed, "they send letters to the White House and make speeches demanding strict adherence to desegregation guidelines, thus stiffening the resolve of those who are asked to weaken them."[53]

Unable to persuade HEW to ease the guidelines, Nixon finally forced Finch to issue a joint statement with Mitchell on July 3, 1969, in which they announced new measures to improve coordination between their two departments. From the language of the statement, it was not obvious that much had changed, but journalists attending a press conference at the Justice Department were told that the administration envisioned a diminished reliance on Title VI of the Civil Rights Act and a growing emphasis on Title IV, which authorized Justice to bring lawsuits against segregated school districts and HEW to provide them with "technical assistance." That interpretation suited the White House, for southern school officials generally preferred judicial enforcement, feeling that it left them less politically exposed and that southern judges were less likely than federal bureaucrats in Washington to require substantial integration.

The July 3 statement was widely portrayed as a victory for Dixie. The next day's newspaper headlines read: "President Eases School Deadline on Desegregation" (*New York Times*) and "President Keeps Promise of His 'Southern Strategy'" (*Washington Post*). Addressing the NAACP annual convention, its executive director, the normally even-tempered Roy Wilkins, accused the Nixon administration of "breaking the law," declaring that "it's almost enough to make you vomit." When HUD secretary George Romney, who had not been apprised of the statement, stood up to address the assembly, he was booed and shouted at.[54]

The Complex Legacy of Title VI

At this stage, the notion that Title VI might provide the model for some new brand of "regulatory federalism" would have appeared far-fetched. On the face of it, HEW enforcement had been not just a political albatross for two presidents but a policy failure. More than two-thirds of African American children in the South continued to attend all-black schools, fifteen years after *Brown* and five years after the Civil Rights Act.[55] The contribution of Title VI to the ultimate desegregation of southern schools was much greater, however, than this might suggest.[56] Although it was true that 68 percent of black children in the South still attended segregated schools in 1969, it was also the case that 89 percent of districts in the region had come fully into compliance with Title VI.[57] The task that remained, of course, was by far the hardest one: black-majority districts where white resistance to integration was most severe. Still, the South had traveled a long way during the years since 1964, a lot further than during the decade of judicial enforcement that had preceded the Civil Rights Act. When political scientist Gary Orfield published an account of OCR's activities in 1969, he felt justified in titling it *The Reconstruction of Southern Education*. And at OCR, according to Rufus Miles, the general view by 1968 was that "the collapse of the segregation system was rapidly approaching, and, when it came, it would probably come with a rush."[58]

That prediction turned out to be accurate, for when the 1970 school year began, the proportion of African American children attending integrated schools had shot up to 85.9 percent.[59] Any attempt to assess the respective contributions of administrative, judicial, and local action to this development is complicated by the fact that the three elements were so intimately interwoven.[60] For example, it was administrative enforcement at HEW that pushed the courts toward bolder interpretations of the *Brown* decision. Until 1966, federal judges remained attached to the *Briggs* dictum, a 1955 ruling according to which "the Constitution . . . does not require integration. It merely forbids . . . segregation."[61] Even when they were not personally committed to segregation, southern judges had to live in the communities on which they were casting judgment, and they shrank from rulings that would endanger their local reputations. More than that, they felt poorly equipped to evaluate or develop detailed plans for desegregation, absent authoritative guidelines from educators.[62] In these circumstances, they tended to accept even token desegregation plans. As of 1965, just 0.019 percent of African American children in districts covered by court-ordered desegregation plans were attending previously "white" schools.[63]

That helps to explain why segregationists preferred judicial action. By 1969, however, this preference was no longer so well founded, because the 1966 HEW guidelines had prompted judges to go beyond the *Briggs* dictum and to demand actual integration. To HEW's critics the guidelines seemed impolitic and unenforceable, but in retrospect they facilitated a decisive acceleration in the rate of *judicially* imposed desegregation. In the summer of 1966, lawyers at the Justice Department's Civil Rights Division filed a Title IV suit against the school district of Jefferson County, Alabama, with the specific intent of winning constitutional backing for HEW's recent guidelines.

The choice of venue meant that *U.S. v. Jefferson County* was decided by the relatively liberal Fifth Circuit Court of Appeals, whose members had already indicated some inclination to defer to administrative standards.[64] The judge who wrote its opinion, John Minor Wisdom, a Republican from the historically Unionist hill country of northern Alabama, had been appointed to the court by President Eisenhower. Wisdom handed down a ringing endorsement of the HEW guidelines, declaring that they were entirely consistent with both Title VI and the Fourteenth Amendment and adding that "the standards of court-supervised desegregation should not be lower than the standards of HEW-supervised desegregation." Noting that southern school officials had long had the *Briggs* dictum "dinned into their ears," he dramatically repudiated it, declaring that *"the only adequate redress for a previously overt system-wide policy of segregation directed against Negroes as a collective entity is a system-wide policy of integration."*[65]

Wisdom hoped that his ruling would strengthen Title VI and diminish the intolerable pressure that his circuit had been under in recent years.[66] No longer could superintendents look to the courts for lax enforcement.[67] With school officials in black-majority districts continuing to defy HEW, however, the main effect of *Jefferson County* was to encourage those who felt that judicial action was the most promising route to desegregation.[68] That belief was further bolstered in May 1968, when the Supreme Court handed down its decision in the case of *Green v. New Kent County.* Justice William Brennan, writing on behalf of a unanimous court, decreed that "the burden on a school board today is to come forward with a plan that promises realistically to work, and promises realistically to work *now.*" This plan must result in "a system without a 'white' school and a 'black' school, but just schools."[69]

In the light of these decisions, NAACP's dismay at the Finch-Mitchell statement was overstated. It was possible, indeed, that it would speed up compliance in the 11 percent of southern districts that remained utterly intransigent in their resistance to integration. In many of these often black-majority districts, Panetta had told Finch two months previously, "HEW has negotiated with them for close to four years." Even he felt that "it therefore makes sense that these majority Negro districts (120 remaining) should be brought into court to combine the power of the court with HEW assistance in achieving compliance."[70]

The Nixon Justice Department and School Desegregation

Following the July 3 statement, President Nixon must have hoped that he had now paid his debt to the South and was free to get on with more rewarding business: basking in the glory of the Apollo XI landing, promulgating a new Nixon Doctrine in foreign affairs, embarking on a much-anticipated Asian and European tour, working with Henry Kissinger on a new, high-stakes initiative to bring the Vietnam War to a speedy conclusion. To his frustration, however, the school desegregation issue just would not go away.

From John Mitchell's point of view, the best way to make it go away was to bring the Deep South into speedy compliance by demonstrating his commitment to the law while simultaneously requesting limited flexibility over dates where immediate integration appeared impossible to achieve. The head of his Civil Rights Division (CRD), Jerris Leonard, acknowledged in an interview that the attorney general did not necessarily possess "a philosophical commitment to the civil rights movement" but added that Mitchell "knows the job has to be done" and was "interested in what works." "We don't get involved in the emotion of it at all," Leonard explained, "but we understand how important it is to get results."[71]

For Mitchell, "getting results" meant treating southern educators and politicians with greater tact than had been shown by the "zealots" at OCR. He predicted that his approach would have "a hell of a lot more impact" on school desegregation than the policies of previous administrations.[72] Within four days of the Finch-Mitchell statement, the Justice Department had brought six new Title IV lawsuits and announced plans to file additional suits in other districts. The *New York Times*'s reporter remarked that the department had "taken more school desegregation action in this one week than in the . . . preceding five months."[73] The next day, Jerris Leonard made an even more dramatic move, announcing that the federal government was intending to sue the entire state of Georgia, on the grounds that it had the power to compel its 195 school districts to comply with *Brown* but had failed to use it.[74]

Despite the *Times* comment, the extent of the shift in policy should not be overstated. Senior civil rights officials at CRD did not detect any great change in their role after July 3.[75] Leonard had been encouraged to develop a new plan for achieving desegregation through the courts since his first meeting with President-elect Nixon, at the Pierre Hotel in New York. When he asked Nixon for his "marching orders," he was told: "Jerris, enforce the law but use your head, and get that damn school desegregation over before the 1972 election."[76] Considering that "our predecessors had not accomplished a lot," Leonard had responded by hiring more lawyers and developing a new litigation strategy.

That strategy was founded on the conviction that "almost every school superintendent had a workable and constitutional school desegregation plan sitting in their desk drawer," but that local conditions prevented voluntary implementation. Choosing Louisiana as his test case for this proposition, Leonard told its federal judges that he was planning to file suits requiring selected schools in the state to integrate in the fall of 1969. Then, CRD attorneys worked with local school officials behind the scenes to get those desegregation plans out of the desk drawer and into the courtroom. According to Leonard, the experiment was a success, and "the selected districts in Louisiana opened with little disturbance." If the July 3 statement provided one trigger for the accelerated pace of CRD activity in the summer and fall of 1969, then the Louisiana experiment was another.

To judge from Leon Panetta's account, the July 3 statement had a more substantial impact at HEW, substantially undercutting OCR's raison d'être. Even here, though, the visible effects were not dramatic. Within four weeks, OCR had announced new funding terminations in Florida, Georgia, and South Carolina.[77] In a vintage display of invective, Senator James Allen (D-Ala.) excoriated "the unbearable arrogance of Federal bureaucrats and education extremists," declaring that "the people of Alabama and the people of this Nation are fed up with federally financed revolutions."[78] Clarke Reed, chairman of the Mississippi GOP, warned Harry Dent that a mood of severe disappointment was spreading in the South: "The Finch-Mitchell statement we gently cheered is within only a few days proving to be real damage to our credibility. It looks to the leadership down here like the same old story, Harry. The administration moves one degree to help us, then the Times, Post, etc. scream. The administration over-reacts in irresolute panic." Ruefully contemplating the passion with which HEW and CRD integrationists went about their task, Reed observed that "with their zeal for politics, it's too bad they're not on our side."[79]

Alexander v. Holmes

In Reed's Mississippi, the most urgent problem was the recent decision of the Fifth Circuit in the case of *Alexander v. Holmes County*, which required thirty Mississippi counties to undergo complete integration that fall and told their school officials to seek technical assistance from HEW. The White House came under strong political pressure from Senator John Stennis (D-Miss.) to try to get the court order modified, and his bargaining power was considerable, because he was floor manager for the administration's controversial $22 billion military procurement bill.[80] With antiwar sentiment rising in the Senate, this measure was coming under strong criticism, particular controversy centering on the deployment of the Safeguard

Antiballistic Missiles system. Almost fifty senators had declared their opposition, and the administration needed all of Stennis's considerable parliamentary skill if it were to prevail. How would he react when HEW filed its detailed plans for the thirty districts, certifying that desegregation that fall was entirely practicable in each case? The White House pressured Finch to delay filing the plans until after the ABM vote, which the administration won on a 50–50 vote, with Vice President Agnew breaking the tie.

The administration still needed Stennis's cooperation, quite apart from being indebted to him for his role in securing the ABM victory, for the defense procurement debate in the Senate continued for two more months. According to contemporary accounts, the courtly Stennis did not explicitly tell Nixon that he would not help unless the administration pushed for a delay in desegregation. Rather, he wrote a letter to the president indicating that its implementation was likely to create so much turmoil that he would probably have to "go down and be with my people."[81] The timing was awkward, for HEW had now gone ahead and filed its Title IV plans with the court. Still, Nixon felt constrained to respond and instructed Finch to write to the chief judge of the Court of Appeals for the Fifth Circuit, John R. Brown, arguing that HEW had not had sufficient time to give adequate guidance to the districts and that implementation would "produce chaos, confusion and a catastrophic educational setback."[82]

A week later, Leonard appeared before Brown to put the case for delay. He admitted being "somewhat embarrassed" at the apparent reversal in the government's position.[83] That feeling was alleviated, however, by the intervention of Hurricane Camille, a devastating storm that ripped through the Mississippi Gulf Coast on August 17, causing enormous property damage and loss of life. Before going down to Jackson, Leonard had met with Title IV people investigating the effects of Camille on Mississippi schools and learned that hurricane damage made it "impossible to move the many hundreds of students around the schools in the various districts and have any semblance of order." Leonard was initially skeptical, but found the level of detail that they then supplied regarding the damage to individual schools persuasive. His deputy, Frank Dunbaugh, a passionate civil rights advocate, concurred, feeling additionally that some of the plans had been impracticable even without Camille.[84] Leonard and Dunbaugh argued that a one-semester delay in implementing the court order would allow the damage to be repaired and better plans to be developed.[85]

Their case was sufficiently persuasive that the Fifth Circuit endorsed the government case. But when the NAACP Legal Defense Fund appealed its decision, arguing that the ruling would encourage delay across the South, the Supreme Court found *that* argument compelling and unanimously reversed the decision. The new chief justice, Warren Burger, declared that "the Court of Appeals should have denied all motions for additional time because continued operation of segregated schools under a standard of allowing 'all deliberate speed' for desegregation is no longer constitutionally permissible. Under explicit holdings of this Court the obligation of every school district is to terminate dual school systems at once and to operate now and hereafter only unitary schools."[86]

This affected not just the Mississippi districts, but federal judges throughout the South who faced the difficult task of applying the previous year's *Green* decision to the particular circumstances in their districts. In a succession of follow-up rulings, lower courts across the region decreed that, because *Alexander* had been so unequivocal, it was not good enough for districts to wait until the start of the 1970 school year to bring about constitutionally required changes in the student and faculty composition of their schools. Rather they must begin the process right away, in midsession. The school board in Atlanta was ordered to ensure that all of its schools had a faculty ratio of 57 black:43 white by the beginning of February. Elsewhere in Georgia, eighty-one school districts were told that the student ratio in each of their schools must be between 50 percent and 150 percent of the overall ratio for the district, regardless of the racial composition of the neighborhood.[87] In Charlotte, North Carolina, a still tougher regime was imposed: all schools had a May 4 deadline for establishing a student composition that came within 15 percent of the district's overall ratio of 70 percent white: 30 percent black.[88]

The White House Weighs Its Response

The long battle over the desegregation of southern schools had reached a critical juncture. Publicly, Nixon declared that "I believe in carrying out the law even though I may have disagreed as I did in this instance with the decree that the Supreme Court . . . came down with."[89] In private, though, he was dismayed, raging at the "clowns" on the Supreme Court and charging that their behavior had been "childish" and "irresponsible."[90] "Why should we continue to kick the South," Nixon asked Ehrlichman, "and hypocritically ignore the same problem in the North?"[91] "Whites in Mississippi can't send their kids to schools that are 90 percent black," he declared. "They've got to set up private schools."[92] Leonard Garment's interactions with the president on this issue left him convinced that Nixon "really feels the school desegregation process is the agony of the South."[93]

With George Wallace claiming Nixon had done more to bring about desegregation than Johnson, a political case could be made too for throwing down the gauntlet to the judiciary in some way, as Franklin Roosevelt had done back in 1937. Spiro Agnew and Pat Buchanan favored defiance, with the latter particularly well placed to press their case, given his role in preparing the daily news summaries that the president hungrily consumed.[94] The selection seems often to have been designed to stoke Nixon's anger. Summaries for the third week in January 1970, for example, included four inflammatory items on schools, including an incendiary column by arch-segregationist James J. Kilpatrick and some wounding remarks by Wallace ("the Administration has done more to destroy the public school system in one year than the last Administration did in four"). Fuming, Nixon had two questions for Ehrlichman:

1) What is our answer to this?
2) Can't we do or say something to bring some sense into the dialogue?
I just disagree completely with the Court's naïve stupidity—
I think we have a duty to explore ways to mitigate it.[95]

Options for Defying the Court

Nixon asked Mitchell to consider filing appeals against the more far-reaching lower court rulings. Conceding that they might be "a futile act," given that federal judges had no choice but to follow the instructions of the Supreme Court, it would at least place the administration "on the right side of the issue."[96] Outraged by the Charlotte decision, he argued that "there is nothing to be gained and much to be lost by going along with the courts" and hoped to "put some daylight" between the White House and the courts by at least issuing a statement of disapproval.[97] The Justice Department objected strongly to this idea, however, calling it "most inappropriate," and neither did it wish to launch an appeal. Nixon was perturbed, telling Bryce Harlow that "it appears that Justice needs to examine the realities as well as the legal technicalities."[98]

Buchanan suggested a second possibility: a rhetorical attack on the South's enemies by Agnew. Portraying the South as being in a state of near insurrection, he quoted one excited South Carolinian as looking out of his window at Fort Sumter and remarking that "if the federal government didn't have

the atomic bomb, we'd be firing on it." Three of the region's governors—
John McKeithen of Louisiana, Lester Maddox of Georgia, and Claude Kirk
of Florida—were counseling outright defiance of the courts, and Buchanan
clearly believed that a new era of massive resistance had begun.[99] He told
Nixon that "the second era of Reconstruction is over; the ship of integration is going down . . . and we ought not to be aboard. For the first time
since 1954, the national civil rights community is going to sustain an up-
and-down defeat."[100]

Even Buchanan recognized that a president could not take the Lester "Ax
Handle" Maddox approach, but he felt that Agnew was less constrained and
should go down South to launch an unrestrained assault on the courts.[101] A
copy of one draft speech by Buchanan survives in the National Archives and
fully justifies his boast to an uncomfortable Leonard Garment that it would
"tear the scab off the issue of race in this country."[102] It was titled "A Brief
Against Compulsory Integration," and the peroration went as follows:

> There are Americans who still insist that we continue stubbornly along
> the same road we have travelled; they insist that HEW continue to write
> its guidelines for integration North and South, that the Courts continue
> to hand down their court orders to bring the races more together in
> the public schools; that the Department of Justice move swiftly and
> vigorously to enforce those orders—not some time in the future,
> but now.
>
> To these Americans I now say: the burden of proof has now shifted
> upon you to tell us, the rest of America, what tangible further benefits
> can be realized by continuing along this same road.
>
> For the life of me, I cannot see ahead any benefits to justify the
> terrible costs we are paying and that we shall pay in the future, if we
> move toward racially unified school systems throughout this country.[103]

Nixon had deployed Agnew in a similar way in the recent past (in attacks
on the press and on antiwar protestors) and would do so again. On this occasion, too, he was tempted, and Agnew judged the speech an excellent idea.[104]
It might blunt George Wallace's attack on the administration and dissuade
influential southerners such as Richard Russell from blaming Nixon for the
ferment in the South.[105]

In the event, however, the speech was not delivered.[106] Instead, Nixon deployed a very different strategy, placing the White House at the forefront of
a concerted effort to bring about swift southern compliance with *Alexander
v. Holmes*. In January 1970, he established a Cabinet Committee on Educa-

tion (CCE) to coordinate the administration's desegregation strategy, operating out of the White House and headed by Secretary of Labor George Shultz.[107] In March, Nixon issued a lawyerly 8,000-word statement in which he emphasized his determination to carry out the law. Over the summer, he met members of the biracial state committees that the CCE had established to facilitate compliance and urged them on. Perhaps most remarkably, in July he approved an IRS ruling that denied tax-exempt status to segregated private academies, a move that the Johnson administration had refused to take. In the view of Leonard Garment, "Nixon did what had to be done and did so with an extraordinarily adept exercise of his considerable political skills."[108]

Explaining Nixon's Decision

Why did Nixon accept Garment's argument that he must take personal charge of this effort? Clearly it was not because the president shared Garment's pro–civil rights views: on the contrary, he resented his more liberal advisers for defending Leon Panetta and accused Garment of being "emotionally . . . committed to a course which the President does not agree with."[109] Part of his motivation was political. Although Nixon repeatedly told aides that going along with the courts damaged his political prospects in the South, to "tear the scab off the issue of race" might be even more harmful. Specifically, he worried that Wallace would run against him in 1972 and would poll strongly in the South if desegregation were still the number one issue. Embarking on a primary campaign against Albert Brewer, the incumbent moderate governor of Alabama, Wallace accused Nixon of leading an "all-out onslaught to force integration regardless of the consequences."[110] Clearly, he was positioning himself for 1972. When a *Washington Star* columnist argued that "Wallace is emerging as a greater threat to Richard Nixon than any which arises from the Democratic side," Nixon indicated that he thought this an "astute analysis."[111]

Strom Thurmond warned Nixon against heeding a "group of liberal advisers" who could turn the South against him and lose him the election, but the president worried that the Buchanan approach would have the same effect.[112] It was not clear that he could do anything to reverse the process that *Alexander v. Holmes* had started, and he was unable as president to match Wallace's level of invective. In that environment, Nixon told Ehrlichman and Garment, it was "in our interest, politically, to get the issue behind us now," to have the "confrontations this year rather than '72."[113]

That reference to invective raises a broader consideration that made it impossible for Nixon to take the Buchanan line, namely his particular conception of the presidency and the responsibilities of a leader.[114] By the start of his second year in office, he had come to regard school desegregation as the biggest domestic issue facing the country. Recognition of that fact had dawned slowly, reflecting his comparative lack of interest in the subject of civil rights and his consequent tendency to think of it in political rather than substantive terms. But by early 1970 the struggle to desegregate the South had apparently reached one of those crystallizing moments of decisive change, a point comparable to Little Rock in 1957, Birmingham in 1963, and Selma in 1965. When Nixon met Richard Russell in February, the Georgia senator warned that the people of his state were more "worked up" over recent judicial desegregation rulings than he could remember them being over any question during his entire career.[115]

This was illustrated by the response of whites in Lamar, South Carolina, to a recent judicial order that reassigned teachers and pupils with immediate effect, in midyear. One reporter recounted how a "mob" of 200 men and women confronted a bus approaching the entrance to Lamar High School: "Men tore at the hood. A woman leaped onto the bus . . . bent into the engine, tearing furiously at the wires, ripping out parts and throwing them over the heads of the mob into the pecan grove." A second bus approached, and "the mob again surged forward, crashing at both buses. . . . Ax handles slammed against windows, bricks and bottles hurtled inside the bus, showering glass on the children." Just before the buses were overturned, the black children inside managed to escape into the school, protected by patrolmen firing tear gas. The schools of Lamar closed for a week. When they reopened, "five of every six whites were missing, having left for private school, school in nearby counties, or for no school at all."[116]

In response to stories such as this, Nixon told Haldeman that "this has become the major cause of the moment."[117] Once it had made the leap from being a secondary to a primary concern, Nixon approached it in an entirely different light. In his view, he had spent too much time during his first year dealing with relatively trivial issues, a tendency that he remembered from the Eisenhower years and was anxious to correct. In March, he told his three top White House advisers—Haldeman, Ehrlichman, and Henry Kissinger— that "what really matters in campaigns, wars or in government is to concentrate on the big battles and win them." Some thought that one had to "fight all the little battles" in order to "lay the ground work for winning the big ones," but he disagreed. What broader purpose, he inquired, had been served by his recent meeting with the minister of mines from Venezuela?

In the area of domestic affairs, he continued, there were only three areas where he wished to "take personal responsibility." The first was economic policy. The second was crime. And the third was school integration. "I must assume the responsibility here," he observed, "because it will be the major issue of controversy for the foreseeable future."[118] Having assumed a responsibility that he had previously shirked, the president was characteristically determined to shape events, rather than simply be borne along by them. And even though he had sympathy for Buchanan's point of view, Nixon confided to Ehrlichman and Haldeman that he found the right-winger "not Presidential."[119] Buchanan had offered him a tantrum rather than a solution.

By contrast, although Nixon tended to view his more liberal advisers with ideological suspicion (Haldeman reported his suspicion that "Garment and Moynihan . . . aren't really on our side"[120]), they did tend to offer him the opportunities for surprising, innovative, wrong-footing domestic leadership that he sought during his early presidency. In his role as party leader, Nixon felt that he had to nurture a more dynamic sort of Republicanism: he told one cabinet meeting that "having been in opposition so long, Republicans are inclined to be against, and we must learn to be for."[121] In his memoirs, he recalled thinking that to shed "our public image as a 'negative' party" and eliminate the Goldwaterite tag of being "reckless and racist," the GOP "needed to leapfrog the Democrats on the Great Society issues and get ahead of them."[122] That is why Richard Nathan was able to interest him in revenue sharing, Moynihan in welfare reform, and William Safire in the notion of a New Federalism. Buchanan, Dent, and Agnew, by contrast, were short on policy ideas.

No one was more adept than Moynihan at appealing to the presidential Nixon. Appalled by the counsel that the president was receiving on civil rights from the Right, he reminded Nixon that the United States was undergoing a profound crisis in race relations: "We can help if we make our good faith clear. The problem is that there are people in the administration who are clearly not of good faith on the fundamental issue of racial equality. *They are tampering with the integrity of the Presidency.*"[123] A couple of months later, Moynihan again praised Nixon's "high road" approach and contrasted it pointedly to the "hysterical demagoguery" of Agnew, which he felt had "surely contributed to the atmosphere that led to the killings at Kent State."[124] And in a third memo, Moynihan urged Nixon not to react with anger to a recent denunciation of his policies from the NAACP, remarking that "the dignity of the Republic requires that the President endure the indignities of its politics."[125]

Nixon responded to this sort of argument. In the case of Agnew, he had independently reached the same conclusion as Moynihan, telling Ehrlich-man that someone else would have to represent the administration on the sensitive issue of busing, since "Agnew can go too far—with [a] McCarthy-ite tinge."[126] He also worried about Dent (whose memos were increasingly disregarded during this period), feeling that he was "too oriented toward a regional approach."[127] As for Buchanan, Nixon felt his speechwriter's "seg-regation forever" line to be "extreme."[128]

Having vetoed the Buchanan approach, Nixon did all he could to bring the South into peaceful compliance. William Safire records him as saying that "this is the perfect example of one of those cases where leadership is not good politics, but you have to do it."[129] And George Shultz reports that Nixon told him the same thing "on many occasions."[130] His approach to leadership was very different from that which Johnson had displayed at the time of Selma. LBJ had emphasized the moral imperative of racial justice, ending his great voting rights address with the promise that "we shall over-come," but Nixon felt that the key to success in 1970 was to steer clear of such appeals, for fear of stoking an even greater backlash against integra-tion. He refused to criticize southerners for their immorality or intransi-gence, and neither did he make any positive remarks about the value of an in-tegrated society. Instead, he emphasized the importance of obedience to the law and the need to save the public school system in the South.

The very fact that Nixon was so out of sympathy with the civil rights movement and the courts paradoxically may have allowed him to play a con-structive role at this moment in history. During the spring and summer of 1970, despite Wallace's imprecations, Nixon's standing among white south-erners remained high. Part of that probably had to do with their support for his foreign policies, including the invasion of Cambodia and a belliger-ent bombing strategy in Vietnam. In addition, although his effort to win a place for Harrold Carswell on the Supreme Court ended in defeat, his angry response to the reverse presumably enhanced his standing with anti-integrationists.[131] When Gallup polled white southerners on their attitudes toward Nixon in July, 68 percent of them indicated approval of the job that he was doing.[132]

Nixon said that he was fully committed to upholding the law and sought to convey the sense that desegregation was now inescapable. In his 8,000-word statement (drafted by Raymond Price but heavily reworked by Nixon), the president emphasized that "we are not backing away. The constitutional mandate will be enforced." He had instructed all government officials to be guided by the principle that "deliberate racial segregation of pupils by official action is unlawful, wherever it exists. In the words of the Supreme Court, it must be eliminated 'root and branch'—and it must be eliminated at once."[133]

These actions alarmed some southern Republicans: Haldeman recorded one meeting at which a group of them took two hours to "bitch about [the] Administration shift to the left." In particular, they complained about Jerris Leonard, who had reportedly spoken of sending 100 federal marshals through the South to ensure compliance.[134] Strom Thurmond told the Senate that "the people of the South and the people of the nation will not support such unreasonable policies."[135] When he met with GOP leaders, however, Nixon defended Leonard and emphasized his own determination "to carry out the law of the land."[136]

In private, though, Nixon was irritated by what he saw as radical, intemperate elements within his civil rights bureaucracy. Jerris Leonard himself was a moderately conservative Republican and a trusted associate of John Mitchell. At the same time, he was committed to civil rights (he was principal author of the Wisconsin open-housing law), and Leon Panetta recalls one HEW-Justice meeting at which Leonard slammed his hand on his desk in frustration at the administration's deference to the South.[137] And CRD, like OCR, attracted people with a passionate personal commitment to civil rights. As Fred Graham of the *New York Times* reported, it was not like the department's tax division, whose bright young lawyers would stay a few years to gain experience and then go into private practice. "These people," he was told, "are here because of their social views."[138]

In the wake of *Alexander v. Holmes*, CRD had strong if discreet support from John Mitchell's deputy, Richard Kleindienst. At one meeting, CRD lawyers distributed lists of noncompliant school districts to U.S. attorneys in the southern states. When that was done, remembers Frank Dunbaugh, "all of the career Justice people were sent out of the room." Subsequently, he learned that Kleindienst had "told all of the U.S. Attorneys that it was the President's wish to get this done and that if any of them had a problem with the program, they should resign immediately." And when CRD and OCR officials met the chairs of noncompliant school districts, they were invited to either (1) submit a plan for voluntary compliance, or (2) "meet with Mr. Dunbaugh . . . to provide him with the names of all of the school board members and school officials to be sued."[139]

Despite his support for this approach, Nixon remained fearful that excessive civil rights ardor at HEW and Justice could imperil his low-key strategy and inflame the forces of massive resistance. He was far from low key in characterizing their activities, referring variously to "eager beavers," "wild young horses," and the "pipsqueak, snot-nosed attitude" that he detected "in the bowels of HEW." After the federal marshals incident, he told Ehrlichman that he would like to "wring Jerry Leonard's neck."[140] The key to keeping the agencies in line was to direct events from the White House, through the Cabinet Committee on Education.

The Cabinet Committee on Education

The central task for the CCE was to foster a spirit of compliance, in part by identifying and encouraging a different type of southern leadership from that represented by Wallace and Kirk. Garment remembers that "many Southerners were looking for a way to meet the deadline dilemma without tearing their communities apart," and the CCE worked to help them. Some encouraging early news came from Greenville, South Carolina, where a midterm desegregation order passed off peacefully owing to the political courage of a biracial group of local leaders: not politicians, for the most part, but rather church leaders, business people, newspaper editors, school board members. Forming a Citizens' Committee, they urged obedience to the Court, holding out the promise that "together we can create superior public schools in Greenville" and "be a model community that leads the region in education, in economic progress, in spirit."[141] Thanks to the attitude of the local newspaper, the citizen group was able to disseminate its message to parents throughout the district, noting inter alia that "parents' positive attitudes can be of the utmost help in the student's adjustment to change."[142] Two weeks before the compliance deadline, more than 3,000 angry white parents from Greenville had led a motorcade to the state capitol and besieged the White House with telegrams. But when the fateful day came, one columnist spoke of a "miracle," the impossible task having been accomplished "with almost dazzling ease."[143]

The emphasis on "superior public schools" was well judged, for the weakness of southern education had been a long-standing matter of concern throughout the region. A number of "education governors" had been elected, including former advocates of massive resistance such as Mills Godwin, whose 1966 crusade to overhaul Virginia's school system reportedly created such a reaction that the Commonwealth's politicians started to "lack . . . the certainty of the mid-1950s that race was the primary issue."[144] In the years that followed, it remained common for politicians to win office by preaching defiance, but the availability of ESEA dollars after 1965, the Supreme Court's resolute insistence on immediate desegregation, and Nixon's commitment to uphold the law all strengthened the possibility of an alternative approach based on notions of a forward-looking and modern South.[145]

Appeals to racial justice were uncommon in community-level campaigns for compliance. The guiding spirit behind the Greenville committee was Brown Mahon, "a conventional Southerner who was uncomfortable with school desegregation" but whose "personal sentiments were overridden by his commitment to public education and obedience to law."[146] In other cases, southerners who were personally comfortable with integration nevertheless recognized that the communities to which they had to appeal were deeply skeptical. A visiting Nixon staffer found South Carolina governor Robert McNair to be "extremely progressive on the race issue," but the only way for him to "sell" compliance was to transcend the race question in some way.[147]

Over the course of the summer, the CCE established seven biracial State Advisory Committees (SACs), not for the purpose of drawing up desegregation plans but rather to facilitate the work of local people undertaking that task. Setting them up was no small task. When Patrick Gray visited Mississippi in June to recruit community leaders, only one of the first six whites whom he contacted said yes. Eventually, he was able to draw up an interracial committee of fifteen, but even these people were "very skeptical."[148] Not one of the whites would serve if there was even the slightest hint that the SAC was pro-desegregation, and the black members were reported to have practically no confidence in the goodwill of their white counterparts. Robert Mardian had a similar experience in Georgia.[149] In Florida and Louisiana, meanwhile, the committee's task was complicated by the hostility and grandstanding of Governors Kirk and McKeithen. It appears that only in Arkansas was it easy to set up an SAC, thanks to the constructive engagement of Governor Winthrop Rockefeller.

Still, the committees were established, and they played a significant role. In South Carolina, the Greenville precedent was helpful: its superintendent, M. T. Andreson, told a meeting of twenty-five upstate mayors that "thousands of volunteers and the news media" had played a decisive role in his city. "At first I didn't think we could do it," he said, "but the community leadership, our administration and our teachers were dedicated to maintaining the public schools and we did it." Another contributor to the seminar predicted that "South Carolina is on the brink of a great industrial expansion. If the state can come through this crisis, we will go forward by leaps."[150]

The CCE recognized the importance of Andreson's point about the news media. Nixon's friend Billy Graham was persuaded to make a number of television "spots" advocating compliance, and they ran throughout the Deep South, Leonard Garment having persuaded station owners to donate free time.[151] Graham recorded six different messages. In a typical one, he started by emphasizing that he was "very proud to be a Southerner" and expressed confidence that his audience would agree to three considerations that made compliance essential:

> First of all, I think that Southerners agree on the tremendous value of their public school system and the danger of damaging it. Secondly, I think Southerners realize that they cannot teach their children respect for law if they themselves defy it. And then thirdly, I think that Southerners realize that their children's education is at stake and that it's far too important for them to permit their fears and frustrations to endanger it.[152]

In addition to distributing these exhortations, SACs coordinated their own publicity drives, tailored to local circumstances. North Carolina public television aired an "appeal for support of public education, based on several themes, such as religion [and] economics." In South Carolina, local business-people were prompted "to write letters carrying the SAC message to their employees." Local newspapers also spread the word. The *Birmingham News* reported that the Alabama SAC was a diverse group, but that its members all shared a belief "in the importance of public education." The paper endorsed that view, arguing that "Alabama can't permit its public school system to collapse in chaos and confusion."[153]

There was no hint of integrationist evangelism in these appeals. Although each committee contained some racial liberals, they were dominated by businesspeople who may well have been outraged by integration personally, and furious at HEW and the courts, but whose anger was outweighed by a mixture of civic-mindedness and hard-headed self-interest, plus the sense that opposition to desegregation was now futile. The consequences of noncompliance seemed stark. White taxpayers would send their children to educationally inferior segregated academies in still larger numbers, sharply dissipating support for financing public education. Noncompliant districts would be vulnerable to losing not only their vital federal funds but even the money that they received from their state.[154] And outside businesses might decline to invest in the region.[155]

As soon as each SAC had been formed, its members visited Washington to meet with the CCE and with the president. Raymond Price's account of the Mississippi meeting illustrates the role that the administration played in ameliorating tensions within them. This committee "included not only blacks and whites but liberals, conservatives, segregationists, integrationists, educators, and industrialists." At the initial White House meeting there was "an atmosphere electric with tension," SAC members clearly being "unsure whether they could trust one another, much less the federal government."[156]

Presiding over this meeting was George Shultz, whom Nixon had come to admire and whose background in labor-management disputes gave him just the attributes that were needed in this fraught environment. Shultz recalls having been initially silent while black and white members of the committee argued about the desirability of desegregation for about two hours. His first intervention came when he asked John Mitchell what the Justice Department's approach was to desegregation. Shultz recalls his response and demeanor: "'I am attorney general, and I will enforce the law,' he growled in his gruff, pipe-smoking way. He offered no value judgments and did not take part in the debate about whether this was good, bad, or indifferent. 'I will enforce the law.' Then he left. No nonsense. Both the blacks and the whites were impressed."[157]

Shultz believes that the effect of this intervention was to move the debate along from "whether" to "how" desegregation was to take place. Over lunch, he sat with the head of the Mississippi Manufacturers' Association and the president of the Biloxi chapter of the NAACP, urging them to take the lead in forging a workable committee from these fractious elements. Both were deeply ambivalent but eventually accepted their assignments, agreeing that "we're probably the only black and white men in the state who can get together on something like this." Their civic-mindedness contrasted notably with the attitude of the Mississippi congressional delegation, all of whose members refused invitations to attend the luncheon. One told a CCE member: "You've been around long enough to know I'm against desegregation, and most of all against eating with niggers."[158]

Some of the initial distrust dissipated, Shultz took his visitors across to the Oval Office, where Nixon spoke to them "with a great sense of conviction and with considerable emotion." According to Shultz, the president's remarks made a decisive difference, leaving members of the delegation "charged up to get their backs into making the school openings and subsequent operations of the schools go forward as smoothly and constructively as possible."[159]

The Outcome

With the start of the 1970 school year came what journalist Tom Wicker has characterized as "a spectacular advance in desegregation."[160] James T. Patterson, a cautious historian of the legacy of the *Brown* decision, concludes that the shift since 1968 was "extraordinary and dramatic."[161] This is not to say that the transition to unitary systems was trouble free: how could it be, given the extraordinary complexity and sensitivity of the task, one whose seeming hopelessness had led the Johnson administration to postpone the implementation deadline every year after 1966. There were some boycotts and instances of violence, and there was troubling evidence of black principals losing their jobs, of school districts providing public resources to private academies, of "integrated" schools operating a system of segregated classrooms. But those who had predicted mass resistance and a bloodbath, such as Buchanan and Agnew, were proved wrong.

This comes across in contemporary news coverage. Garment and Shultz had feared that the media would accentuate the negative, but instead they focused on success stories. As one Washington reporter noted, "it is almost axiomatic in journalism that serenity is not news; but today the news is that hundreds of white students entered two previously all black schools for the first time without a hitch." In Augusta, Georgia, there was strong hostility to new cross-town busing arrangements on opening day, but the school board reported normal attendance on the second day, disappointing the Save our Schools Committee, which "had hoped to force repeal of integration with mass absenteeism." In Alabama, Governor Brewer was surprised by how few whites abandoned the public schools.[162]

To judge from the reactions of national liberals and civil rights leaders, though, one would have thought that the Nixon administration's desegregation strategy had been a charade and a failure. Reacting to the 8,000-word statement that Nixon issued on March 24, John Brademas concluded that "Nixon has gravely abdicated leadership for achieving integrated schools" and was "determined to pursue his Southern strategy at all costs," and Bayard Rustin espied "just one more attempt to woo the Wallace vote."[163] When the IRS ruling that denied tax exemption to segregated academies was announced, Senator Walter Mondale (D-Minn.) angrily dismissed it as a "hoax."[164] Meeting for its annual convention in July, the NAACP announced that "we cannot too strongly condemn the Nixon administration for failing to correct blatant forms of segregation in Southern schools." And it was at this same meeting that Bishop Stephen G. Spottswood famously charged that Nixon led the first openly antiblack administration since that of Woodrow Wilson.[165]

The invective continued into the new school year. Martin Luther King's former lieutenant, the Reverend Andrew Young, accused Nixon of an "attempt to divide people, based on color of skin."[166] The head of the Civil Rights Commission, Rev. Theodore Hesburgh, condemned "a "major breakdown" in enforcement.[167] The National Education Association decried a "lack of commitment" to desegregation at the White House.[168] And in October, the NAACP launched a lawsuit against the Department of Health, Education, and Welfare for its failure to enforce Title VI. Attorney Joseph L. Rauh, explaining this move, said that "I don't think the Nixon administration is making any effort."[169]

Why did the Nixon administration not receive more credit for its role in the desegregation of southern schools? In part, Nixon's political enemies hated and distrusted him so much that they could not bring themselves to give him any credit. During the spring and summer of 1970, they had more reasons for hatred and distrust than ever: the nation was enduring a period of intense instability following the administration's invasion of Cambodia and the tragedies at Kent State and Jackson State universities. In such circumstances, it is not surprising that they were disinclined to view his actions in other areas with a generous eye.

Also, longtime crusaders for civil rights conceived of their struggle in fundamentally moral terms: the perpetrators of racial discrimination were sinful and must be forced to acknowledge the fundamental human rights of those whom they had oppressed. By contrast, Nixon very rarely characterized his task in moral terms and had no appetite for *forcing* the South to do anything. Sensing Nixon's lack of moral intensity, civil rights advocates were understandably suspicious, especially in view of the political gestures that he had made to the white South.

But in retrospect it seems likely that Nixon's emphasis on carrying out the law—on obeying the Constitution, rather than on carrying out a moral obligation—was precisely what was needed to bring about the peaceful desegregation of the South. There were strong forces of racial division, hatred, and fear throughout the often black-majority districts that retained dual systems, and state politicians were wont either to keep their heads down in this atmosphere or to foment resistance. To accomplish desegregation in this environment the federal government surely *had* to win a certain level of trust among southern whites and had to stimulate grassroots, compliance-oriented local leadership. How else could unitary systems be achieved and sustained?[170]

What gave force to Nixon's strategy, of course, was the uncompromising insistence of the courts on desegregation now and the prior determination that HEW had displayed in enforcing Title VI. Left to his own devices, this is not an area where Nixon would have provided leadership. Even when he was playing a decisive role, Nixon was positively anxious to avoid credit: that would antagonize white southerners and weaken his political standing. In a sense, then, Nixon's critics were right to say that desegregation happened despite rather than because of Nixon. But it was precisely his lack of emotional engagement, and precisely his antienforcement thrusts of 1969, that enabled him to play a constructive role in 1970. The scholarship of those who emphasize the southern strategizing Nixon is not so much wrong—it captures one side of the man—as it is unsophisticated and incomplete. Nixon and his enemies needed one another in order to get the job done.

For 9/29

6

Education Reform in the Nixon Administration

THE CASE OF BILINGUAL EDUCATION

As OCR's role in southern school desegregation diminished, its future became uncertain. It was possible that the southern strategy might make the White House receptive to an increased enforcement operation in the North: Nixon was sympathetic to the argument that the federal government had picked on the South while hypocritically ignoring segregation in other parts of the country.[1] But Nixon also had a northern strategy, based on appeals to urban ethnics, and was strongly opposed to forced busing, which was a prerequisite for achieving integration in urban districts with high levels of residential segregation. Strong enforcement action by OCR in the North could easily leave the agency as exposed politically as had its previous activities.

What few could have anticipated was the enormous expansion in OCR's budget and responsibilities that occurred between 1970 and 1977, years during which its staff tripled, and appropriations grew sixfold.[2] In part, that did reflect its growing involvement in desegregation cases in the North (more as a result of judicial activity rather than White House pressure). But more striking was the series of entirely new responsibilities that it acquired during the Nixon-Ford years. Even as the CCE was coordinating Nixon's 1970 desegregation strategy from the White House, and even as Leon Panetta faced dismissal, OCR was laying the foundations for a bold new enforcement effort on behalf of "language-minority" children, that is, those with limited

OCR growth

(ESL)

English proficiency (LEP). And by 1975, Congress had given the agency three additional, burdensome responsibilities, each time using Title VI as a template. First, in 1972, it approved Title IX of the 1972 education amendments, which barred gender discrimination in educational institutions receiving federal funds. The following year, it adopted section 504 of the Rehabilitation Amendments, which forbade discrimination against Americans with disabilities. Then, in 1975, Congress passed the Age Discrimination Act, which applied the same form of words to the elderly.

In the first case, bilingual education, bureaucratic entrepreneurship at OCR was backed up by the courts and further facilitated by the desire of Republicans as well as Democrats to woo an expanding Mexican American electorate. The story begins in the unhappy final phase of the Johnson presidency, when Congress enacted the Bilingual Education Act.

The Origins of Federal Bilingual Education Policy

The principal author of the measure was Senator Ralph Yarborough, a Texas liberal who had been elected in the triumphantly Democratic years of 1958 and 1964, but who now faced an uphill battle for a third term, in much less propitious political circumstances. To have any chance of success, he would need strong support from Mexican Americans, and he viewed bilingual education in the context of that strategy. Less cynically, it was an attempt to do something about the poor performance of Spanish-speaking schoolchildren. In Yarborough's state, 80 percent of Spanish-speaking children had to repeat first grade, and there were twelve times as many Mexican Americans in first as in twelfth grade (the overall ratio for Texans was three to one). Since 1918, Texas schools had taught LEP children exclusively in English; indeed, it was illegal to teach them in any other language. When introduced, this "immersion" policy represented enlightened, Progressive pedagogy, but by the 1960s educators and Mexican American leaders were increasingly convinced that it was heavily implicated in the disastrous underperformance of Hispanic children in school. Some also worried that "English only" taught Mexican American children to think that there was something second-rate about their own culture.[3]

Although experiments in bilingual education had been launched under two titles of ESEA (I and III), Yarborough believed that it had done little to remedy these problems. His bill, which became Title VII of ESEA, was intended to put that right. The legislative language yields few clues regarding what its architects meant by bilingual education: troubled by "a unique and perplexing educational situation," they relied on local educational agencies to "develop forward-looking approaches." In essence, they proposed that non–English speakers be taught in their own language until they were fluent in English. Children who understood their lessons would feel less alienated from school and society, learn more, and stay in school till graduation.[4]

There was little controversial about this measure, and witnesses before Senator Yarborough's special committee were warmly supportive. The only dispute of note concerned whether the program should be restricted to Spanish speakers, as Yarborough preferred, or opened to other language minorities, as was successfully urged by Maine's Democratic senator, Edmund Muskie. The bill passed easily, but the Johnson administration was hostile. The feeling at OE was that the new program was redundant, since bilingual programs were already permissible under ESEA. Also, John Gardner did not think that a compensatory education measure should be couched in terms of civil rights.[5] Finally, it could be that Johnson was personally opposed to bilingual instruction. When he was a teacher at a Mexican school in Cotulla, Texas, in the 1930s, the English-only approach had been at its height, and LBJ—for all the warm sympathy that he felt toward his charges—had applied corporal punishment to any pupil who spoke Spanish.[6]

Although he signed the Bilingual Education Act, Johnson refused to recommend any appropriation for the current fiscal year and proposed a meager $5 million for FY 1969. Yarborough denounced this as "tokenism" and "an empty gesture" that would "be effectively dashing to the ground all the hopes we have raised."[7] If Lyndon Johnson was hostile, how would bilingual education fare under a Republican administration?

Bilingual Education and the Nixon Administration

Fiscally, Title VII was and remained a small program: $7.5 million was appropriated in 1969, rising to just $35 million in 1974. Still, unlike Johnson, Nixon did support it. That did not reflect any particular enthusiasm for the objectives of the program: to the contrary, he told education aides in 1970 that he was "against the law to teach Spanish in elementary schools."[8] Rather, it reflected his wider attempt to build a new Republican majority and his belief that a well-crafted reform program might win over certain elements of the New Deal Democratic coalition: organized labor, middle-class blacks, Catholics, and Latinos.[9] Even as his administration drifted to the right after the summer of 1970, he remained keen to associate the White House with measures that might boost his prospects for winning Latino votes.[10]

Nixon, like many GOP strategists, believed that his party had a realistic chance of winning over traditionally Democratic Spanish-speaking

Americans. In his own part of southern California, Mexican Americans had been taken for granted by the Democrats and accorded little political power. Partly because of that, the Republicans had performed quite well among this group in 1966, and Governor Ronald Reagan had courted it thereafter (for example, by backing a state bilingual education bill in 1967).[11] Another source of Republican competitiveness, some believed, was the conservative social values of Mexican Americans, whose Catholicism, strong sense of family, and antiabortion sentiments all fit the profile of the new Republican majority that Nixon was hoping to build. Nixon told colleagues that growing up in Whittier he had enjoyed "very close ties" with Mexican Americans, who were "family oriented, law abiding people."[12]

Initially, though, the new administration struggled to convert its warm words into substantive action. Early complaints by Latinos about lack of consultation and lack of senior appointments were echoed by southwestern Republicans, such as Senators John Tower of Texas and Barry Goldwater of Arizona, and second-term congressman George H. W. Bush of Texas.[13] By July 1969, members of California's GOP delegation in the House were reportedly "disturbed and dissatisfied with the understanding and treatment of Latin-Americans by the Administration," contrasting Nixon's performance with the "good rapport" that Governor Reagan enjoyed with the same community.[14]

Meeting Latino concerns required action on four fronts: appointments, the campaign pledge to convene a White House conference on the problems of Spanish speakers, the reorientation of existing federal programs so that they better served Latinos, and the development of new programs to address Latino concerns. On all four, it was easier to promise action than to deliver. In the case of appointments, the administration concluded that most prominent Mexican Americans were either Democrats or radicals, resistant to GOP overtures or likely to cause embarrassment.[15] Martin Castillo, chosen to head the Cabinet Committee on Opportunities for Spanish-Speakers (CCOSS), was sacked after less than two years on grounds of ineffectiveness and partisan championing of the Democratic cause.[16] (To the administration's acute discomfort, it took eight months to find his successor.) With the firing of the Small Business Administration's head, Hilary Sandoval, the administration's highest-ranking Latino official as it approached the end of its third year was Phillip Sanchez, assistant director of the Office of Economic Opportunity, not a high-profile position at a time when the agency was being wound down.[17]

As for the White House conference for Spanish speakers, that was a campaign pledge that Nixon soon had cause to regret.[18] Castillo thought it to have been unwise, given that a similar venture convened by Johnson in El Paso, Texas, in 1967 had backfired, providing a forum for militants and exposing the limits of government action.[19] And Nixon became generally wary of such gatherings following a disastrous White House conference on malnutrition, during which delegates had reportedly "concentrated more on attacking Richard Nixon than on attacking hunger," to the president's fury.[20] When staffers proposed a similar event dedicated to national goals for the 1970s, Nixon exploded to Ehrlichman and Haldeman: "What in the devil is this? Are we going to have another hunger fiasco?"[21] Not surprisingly, the date for the Mexican American conference kept being put back, and in the end it was abandoned, the administration instead convening a series of low-profile regional meetings as a face-saving gesture.[22]

The effort to reorient and coordinate existing programs affecting Latinos was complicated by the lamentable performance of the CCOSS. Castillo had told the White House that its establishment gave the administration "a rare historic opportunity" to reaffirm its commitment to Latinos and a particularly welcome one given "all of the problems we have been facing in preparation for a White House Conference."[23] But here again the story was one of ineptness; the committee failed to convene during Castillo's eighteen-month tenure, despite a congressional requirement that its members get together every six months. During the long post-Castillo hiatus, the clamor of protest from legislators and activists, as well as from within the administration, reached a climax: one Labor Department figure noted that the committee's "credibility with the Spanish Speaking community is virtually non-existent."[24] In spring 1971 Robert Finch sought advice about whether to abolish the committee.[25]

Finch was one of two senior White House staffers deputed by Nixon to clear up the mess, the other being Leonard Garment.[26] Angered by the dismal failure of his administration's early efforts to build Latino support but characteristically protective of Finch, a "very tough" Nixon reportedly "ripped into" Garment, complaining that "nothing was happening."[27] Meanwhile, H. R. Haldeman was presumably expressing the president's views (he rarely revealed his own policy preferences) when he complained that Garment had become too preoccupied with programs for blacks, even though in political terms they had proved a waste of time.[28] Garment, uneasily aware that his liberalism made him ideologically suspect—Haldeman liked to disparage him as "Lenny Government"—wrote a contrite memorandum to the president, acknowledging "a really unfortunate story of misfires, inaction and bad luck" and agreeing that "you are rightly disturbed by it."[29]

Given this catalog of missteps, the Nixon administration might have abandoned its quest for Latino support, but with the 1972 election fast approaching the effort still seemed rich in political promise. Finch told the president that he considered Spanish speakers to be "the greatest potential new source of votes" and vouchsafed his determination to spearhead a "newly reenergized Administration effort" on their behalf.[30] Campaign strategists were equally enthusiastic, telling John Mitchell that "all Spanish-speaking Americans share certain characteristics—a strong family structure, deep ties to the Church, a generally hard-line position on the social issue—which makes them open to an appeal from us." The outlook was bright since "the Democratic Party is under suspicion for favoring politically potent blacks at the expense of the needs of the Spanish-speaking people."[31] Charles Colson, emerging as a powerful force within the White House, anticipated "very significant movement" and argued that "we should do everything possible to encourage it."[32]

Nixon's continuing enthusiasm was evident when he addressed the CCOSS in the second half of 1971. He suggested that Spanish-speaking Americans had not received attention because they had not raised hell, as one increasingly had to do to be heard. Suggesting to the new chair of the committee, Henry Ramirez, that "you need a lobby," he emphasized: "I don't want this Administration to be one that only responds to those who tear up the place and pound fists." Nixon ordered Finch and Ramirez to get moving and cabinet members in general to "get off their duffs."[33]

Of particular concern by then was the administration's continuing difficulty in identifying issues and programs with resonance in the Spanish-speaking community. One campaign strategist was struck by the "considerable animosity among Americans of Mexican descent toward Blacks" and stressed that the president must show that his initiatives on their behalf "are not warmed over black programs."[34] To exploit his opportunity, Nixon sought to demonstrate his awareness that "minority" was not synonymous with "black" and his determination to address the distinctive problems of Spanish-speaking Americans.[35] But what were those problems? To what extent could Spanish-speaking Americans be treated as homogeneous, given the apparent differences of experience and circumstance among Mexican Americans, Puerto Ricans, and Cuban Americans? In what sense, and to what degree, were Spanish-speaking Americans a discriminated-against mi-

is this a Civil Rights issue?

nority? Should the federal agencies that protected the civil rights of African Americans also address the problems of Latinos? If their problems were simply variations on those that had confronted other language minorities, did they warrant special treatment? What about Latinos who were already fluent in English? Were new programs needed, or should the emphasis be on ensuring that Latinos received equal treatment in existing programs?

The answers to those questions were far from self-evident, and the difficulty of answering them lent significant political appeal to a program that was as unambiguously geared to the interests of Latinos as was bilingual education. As the 1972 election drew ever closer, it remained almost the only substantive federal program directed specifically at Spanish-speaking Americans. When Nixon asked Finch about overall efforts on their behalf, the latter had to concede that bilingual education "thus far" represented "the major part of the program."[36] Consequently, it assumed greater political importance than its modest appropriations might suggest. For White House *the proof that Reps cared* strategists and southwestern Republicans in Congress, it symbolized the GOP's claim to care about Spanish speakers.[37] When the Campaign to Reelect the President (CREEP) undertook an investigation of Latino opinion, it found widespread support for bilingual education. Accordingly, a CREEP staffer expressed satisfaction when a bilingual brochure produced by OE gave "prominent attention to the Administration's role."[38]

For all the difficulties and embarrassments, efforts to secure Latino support paid off. In the 1972 presidential election, Richard Nixon won one-third of the Latino vote, more than doubling the level of support that he had received from that group in 1968.[39]

Bilingual Education and HEW

The Nixon White House, then, was interested primarily in the politics and symbolism of Title VII rather than in its educational effectiveness. The president's interest helped ensure that the program would survive, despite the unpopularity of HEW at the White House, despite the Office of Management and Budget's support for eliminating it as costly and ineffective, and despite the administration's general dislike of categorical programs. When Nixon proposed a general education revenue-sharing package in 1972 (the Better Schools Act), he initially proposed to absorb every title of the ESEA. But the decision was reconsidered just before election time. Partly because of the CREEP survey and the entreaties of GOP legislators with big Latino constituencies, bilingual education was kept intact.[40]

Within HEW, however, support for Title VII extended beyond the modest hope that it should survive: Secretary Finch announced at the outset of his tenure that the "prompt, massive upgrading of bilingual education" was "one of the major imperatives now confronting HEW."[41] Finch's instinctive liberalism and his desire to promote the president's interest were in this case doubtless reinforced by his senatorial ambitions. His prediction that 1968 would be "the last election that will be won by the un-black, the un-poor and the un-young" will be recalled from Chapter 5. For Californians such as Finch, Undersecretary Jack Veneman, and Leon Panetta, that meant paying attention not just to blacks but also to the nation's second-largest minority, which was, of course, the *largest* minority in their own state.[42]

Support for the substantive expansion of bilingual education was also strong among some of their subordinates, but the picture was complicated by enervating disputes between rival agencies at HEW. The standard account of the program's early political history, by Susan Gilbert Schneider, concludes that intramural rivalries among a bewildering array of agencies resulted in lack of leadership and clear direction. That was certainly the dominant impression on Capitol Hill, where bureaucratic inertia at HEW and White House hostility were blamed for Title VII's small scale.[43] But such contemporary criticisms were somewhat off the mark. The White House was far from hostile to Title VII, as has been seen. And the charge of inertia at HEW becomes harder to sustain if one brings OCR into the picture. In reality, it was the decisive actor, contributing far more than the Nixon White House, or for that matter Congress, to the tremendous expansion of special provision for language minorities that occurred during the 1970s.

Genesis of the OCR Memo on Language-Minority Rights

During Panetta's final months at OCR (he was dismissed in February of 1970, some six months after he had submitted his undated letter of resignation to Finch), he strove to rebuild his reputation at the White House and to restore morale at an agency that badly needed a fresh outlet for its crusading, activist energies. It was within this context that the problems of language minorities came to the fore. Panetta recalls a late 1969 meeting with Latino leaders in San Francisco, some of them familiar faces from his time on Senator Kuchel's staff. They complained that Spanish-speaking youngsters "were being assigned to classes for the mentally retarded because they could not speak English" and "were dropping out of school at an alarming rate." In his memoir, Panetta describes this as "one of the most intense lobbying sessions I had been through in Kuchel's office or any place."[44] He promised to investigate the matter further, but a proposed directive ordering school districts with substantial language-minority populations to cease their discriminatory practices had not emerged from the HEW bureaucracy by the time of his dismissal.[45] Shortly thereafter, however, the issue acquired further momentum when the California activists won an important legal victory in *Diana v. State Board of Education.* The state's school districts were ordered to reexamine in their native languages all non-English-speaking children who had been classified as mentally retarded on the basis of English-language tests.[46]

Mexican Americans, so long invisible on the national political stage, were becoming more effective. Southwesterners in both political parties were now competing vigorously for the Latino vote, the national parties were also taking an interest, and Latino activists were learning how to use the judicial system and lobby the bureaucracy. A landmark in this process was the founding in 1968 of the Mexican American Legal Defense and Educational Fund (MALDEF), an organization modeled on the National Association for the Advancement of Colored People–Legal Defense Fund (NAACP-LDF), which hoped to win for its constituency the constitutional and statutory protection that the older organization had secured for African Americans. Given the growing Latino militancy at this time (evidenced by César Chávez's migrant labor protests, school walkouts by Mexican American children, the Black Power–influenced La Raza Unida movement, and a spate of riots in Los Angeles in 1970 that attracted nationwide coverage), it is tempting to regard bilingual education as a reaction to the radicalization and politicization of that constituency.[47]

One can take this argument only so far, however: policymakers seem often to have sensed in these stirrings a latent political opportunity, rather than a threat. Indeed, in the early years of MALDEF (soon the most politically important Latino advocacy group) and of the bilingual education program, federal policymakers and foundation executives sometimes seemed to be creating, rather than responding to, constituency demand. We have already heard a frustrated President Nixon lecturing the head of his Latino cabinet committee, "Henry, you need a lobby." In response to that same conviction the Ford Foundation had brought MALDEF into the world, responding not to Latino pressure, but precisely to the absence of such pressure. A couple of years earlier, the foundation—long interested in the problem of poverty and possibly anxious not to be left behind amid the burgeoning rights consciousness of the 1960s—had set up the National Office for the Rights of the Indigent. When that body presented the foundation with shocking evidence of Mexican American poverty and isolation, Ford officials moved swiftly, persuading NAACP-LDF lawyers, government officials, and Mexican American leaders to put together a proposal for an organization to fight for this voiceless minority through the courts. With a $2.2 million donation, MALDEF came into being the following year.[48]

Once MALDEF was up and running, its sponsor continued to take a close interest in its affairs, as when, in a bid to give it a higher national profile, the foundation threatened to withdraw support unless the organization moved its headquarters from San Antonio to a less provincial city. Parts of the federal government also provided crucial support and advice. The Office of Economic Opportunity supplied Volunteers in Service to America (VISTA) attorneys, helping MALDEF to bring its early lawsuits.[49] The Justice Department's Civil Rights Division urged the fledgling organization to be more of a nuisance, noting that "the more complaints one makes the great[er] the opportunity for redress."[50] And HEW officials prodded MALDEF to apply for the "many program resources that could be channeled directly to community organizations."[51]

In this context, and despite Panetta's recollections of his San Francisco meeting, it might be misleading to argue that the OCR's growing interest in Latino affairs was a response to constituency pressure. There was undoubtedly some of that, and the presence in the agency of at least one highly placed Mexican American ensured that such pressure would be felt.[52] Nevertheless, the available evidence (which is limited because the OCR has never released its textual records to the National Archives) suggests that the agency acted largely on its own initiative when, on May 25, 1970, it issued the regulations on language rights that Panetta had had drafted some four months previously.

By this time, J. Stanley Pottinger had succeeded Panetta at OCR, and under his leadership the agency's interest in Mexican Americans became public. Like Panetta, Pottinger was a thirty-year-old California-based lawyer and a liberal Republican. Unlike Panetta, though, he had backed Nixon in 1968, a fact that was duly reported in press coverage of his appointment.[53] If his predecessor had struggled to win the approbation of the Kennedy-Johnson staffers at OCR and failed comprehensively to win the trust of the White House, then Pottinger's political task on assuming office was scarcely less formidable. Ehrlichman remembers that Nixon—who had become obsessed by Panetta's insubordination—viewed the appointment with the utmost seriousness, toying with the idea of approaching future Central Intelligence Agency director William Casey and insisting on someone "strong and tough."[54] On appointment, Pottinger was reputedly told that he must clear with the White House all statements that "in any remote way might be interpreted as hostile to the South."[55] To restless subordinates, infuriated by recent events, the new director must have appeared to be little more than a Nixon stooge, sent in to sort out the left-wingers.

Pottinger, having come to Washington from HEW's regional office in San Francisco, would have known about the California language controversy. Arriving in his new job and finding Panetta's draft memo on the rights of language minorities in his in-tray, he may well have welcomed a serendipitous opportunity to display his activist sympathies to skeptics at OCR while simultaneously ingratiating himself with his superiors at the White House.[56] Certainly, few other issues or causes would have held out much promise of achieving both objectives.

It appears that Pottinger *did* succeed in winning the approbation of the White House (this probably owed more to his tactful approach to the desegregation question than to the May 25 memo). When Elliot Richardson, Finch's replacement at HEW, took a call from John Ehrlichman in July 1970, he ended their conversation by anxiously inquiring: "I hope you people think as well of Pottinger as I do." Ehrlichman's response was reassuring: "We do—we are very high on him."[57]

The Pottinger Memo on Language-Minority Rights

The crucial new OCR regulations were directed at "School Districts with More Than Five Percent National Origin–Minority Group Children." The category encompassed a thousand school districts and an estimated 3.7 million children. The regulatory purpose was to combat "common practices which have the effect of denying equality of educational opportunity to Spanish-surnamed pupils," in breach of Title VI of the 1964 Civil Rights Act. Aiming to "clarify" HEW policy on discrimination in "federally assisted programs," Pottinger issued a key edict: "Where inability to speak and understand the English language excludes national origin–minority group children from effective participation in the educational program offered by a school district, the district must take affirmative steps to rectify the language deficiency in order to open its instructional program to these students." Pottinger also ruled that children must not be placed in remedial classes simply on the basis of language skills and that "any ability grouping or tracking system" connected with language deficiency "must be designed to meet . . . language skill needs as soon as possible and must not operate as an educational dead-end or permanent track." Finally, school districts must keep parents who did not speak good English informed of school activities, a task that might require notification "in a language other than English."[58]

Although these regulations were purportedly rooted in the requirements of Title VI of the Civil Rights Act, this claim was tenuous. Nothing in the legislative history of the 1964 debate suggests that supporters of the Civil Rights Act anticipated so broad a construction; indeed, they were at pains to emphasize the limited scope of the new regulatory regime and took a particularly limited view of the national-origins clause.[59] It is hard to argue that they expected it to be invoked on account of a program's failure to discriminate between groups, the basis for the 1970 memo. Finally, as John David Skrentny has observed, it is not logical to say that members of a language minority are discriminated against on the basis of national origin, when other members of that minority are fluent in English and fully able to participate in the public schooling system.[60]

Still, since 1964 the courts had been adopting new definitions of discrimination that paid more attention to the *effects* of a policy and less to its *intent*. In his *Jefferson County* decision, for example, Judge Wisdom had found unconstitutional ostensibly nondiscriminatory "freedom of choice" plans that had the effect of perpetuating segregation. And following the Supreme Court's subsequent ruling in the *Green* case, school boards now had an "affirmative duty to take whatever steps might be necessary to convert to a unitary system," that is one "without a 'white' school and a 'Negro' school, but just schools." The area of employment policy provides a second example of this intellectual shift away from classical nondiscrimination. In 1971, the Supreme Court ruled that ostensibly nonracial selection practices that had a "disparate impact" on minorities were unconstitutional, unless they could be shown to be essential to the job.[61] The discovery that the Civil Rights Act entitled language minorities to special educational provision was similarly underpinned by a "disparate impact" rationale: equal treatment produced unequal educational results and was therefore not good enough.

Nevertheless, even in this context, Pottinger's 1970 memo remains arresting. Just as in the case of the 1966 desegregation guidelines, HEW administrators were setting the pace for the judges and not simply responding to their rulings. In a way, this was an even bolder example. In the previous case, Harold Howe had at least been able to claim that the guidelines were broadly in line with the trend in federal jurisprudence (the *Briggs* dictum having been weakened, though not overturned, by two of Wisdom's earlier decisions). In this case there was not even the hint of a constitutional mandate, so OCR's expansive new regulations had to rest entirely on a highly debatable construction of Title VI.

Enforcing the New Language Rights

OCR's insistence that school districts "take affirmative steps to rectify . . . language deficiency" might have rested on somewhat shaky foundations, but having been published in the *Federal Register*, the new regulations possessed the full force of law. On paper they extended federal influence on local schooling in unprecedented ways, making districts with high concentrations of national-origin minorities vulnerable to cutoffs of federal aid, the sanction that had just been downgraded in conflicts about school desegregation. And although the May 1970 memorandum made no specific reference to bilingual education, it was the most obvious remedy, required as a matter of course in subsequent administrative and judicial rulings when school districts were found to have violated the civil rights of language minorities.

The extent of federal intrusion that conscientious implementation of the regulations would require became clear when OCR drafted enforcement guidelines at the end of 1970. They specified that a district could assign language-minority children to special education classes (the basis for the *Diana* controversy in California) only if it set up an advisory committee with a "majority composed of persons from each disadvantaged minority group." This body, the regulations continued, must have the "authority to disapprove and permanently halt any . . . pre-assignment testing or student assignment." Grudgingly conceding that a school district might play some role in selecting the members of the committee, OCR nonetheless required that the nominees come from community organizations "composed of persons at least 50% of whom are members of the minority group."[62]

Such requirements illustrate the marked suspicion with which the federal agency viewed the nation's school districts, and this attitude was still more evident when Elliot Richardson gave testimony before Senator Mondale's investigation into equality of educational opportunity. Asked what the government expected of school districts, he indicated that OCR would require "total institutional reposturing (including culturally sensitizing teachers, instructional materials and educational approaches) in order to incorporate, affirmatively recognize and value the cultural environment of ethnic minority children so that the development of positive self-concept can be accelerated."[63] In other words, not only was HEW in favor of bilingual education, it also supported the more radical of the two rationales most often advanced for it: cultural maintenance, rather than academic progress.

We have seen that many Mexican American children in the Southwest experienced severe educational difficulties and the circumstances surrounding the *Diana* suit suggest the crass insensitivity in some school districts' response to the problems of non–English speakers. There is also plenty of evidence that in parts of the Southwest (notably Texas), the problems were compounded by outright discrimination, albeit not to the degree experienced historically by African Americans. So it is not surprising that OCR should have viewed the school districts charged with implementing the Pottinger memorandum with a certain distrust.[64]

Still, one might have anticipated a somewhat less abrasive approach by the federal agency. First, the recent ending of massive resistance to school desegregation in the South had demonstrated the value of establishing a cooperative relationship with local authorities. Second, OCR was targeting educational practices that the federal government had previously held to be unobjectionable. Third, school districts outside the segregated South were still accustomed to considerable political autonomy, had traditionally been treated with great deference by Washington bureaucrats, and were unlikely to respond well to such intense federal micromanagement.

Finally, these instructions were not accompanied by new federal money. At OE, the Pottinger memorandum generated some anxiety about funding: school districts, unaccustomed to federal orders, might expect the feds to foot the bill, yet in the new fiscal climate of the 1970s, the money simply was not there.[65] From the perspective of OCR, however, that objection was moot. When civil rights were involved, questions of funding were immaterial: the school district simply had to find the resources to meet the fundamental human rights of those against whom it had discriminated.

In retrospect, these new regulations were an early example of the "unfunded mandates" that would generate such political unrest later in the 1970s.[66] To federal officials whose desire to sustain the reformist momentum of the Great Society was threatened by budgetary belt tightening they were highly attractive, but at the state and local level—and in the private sector, also much affected by the new politics of regulation—they created real difficulty. School districts, for example, were losing unprecedented numbers of bond votes, a portent of the taxpayer rebellion that was to culminate in 1978 in the passage of Proposition 13 in California.[67] Struggling to meet even their existing responsibilities, they were now expected to shoulder the substantial additional burden of instituting bilingual education (think of the hiring, resource, and retraining implications of having to teach each subject in more than one language).

The disdain with which OCR treated the nation's school districts contrasts markedly with its elaborate deference to minority-rights activists. The senior staffer charged with drawing up detailed enforcement instructions for the Pottinger memorandum was Martin Gerry, the twenty-six-year-old lawyer who had also drafted the original regulations. Gerry was a liberal Republican with a long-standing commitment to civil rights; as an undergraduate student, he had participated in Freedom Summer in Mississippi. Like Panetta, who was his friend, he did not approach the rights of language minorities in legalistic terms. Instead, he approached the subject as a passionate believer in minority rights who felt that "if in fact kids are suffering from discrimination . . . , then there has to be a remedy to correct that." Interviewed about his role some three decades later, he remembered "very little discussion with either Leon or Stan [Pottinger] about the basic assumptions which were that simply exposing kids to instruction that they couldn't benefit from was discriminatory."[68]

Despite his friendship with Panetta, Gerry had strong credentials with the White House because he had previously worked for the Nixon Mudge law firm in New York. On joining the administration, he had received a personal welcome from the president, and he remained in contact with such trusted party regulars as Rogers Morton and Pat Gray.[69] But those establishment connections did not diminish his ardor for civil rights. Unveiling the enforcement criteria for the May 1970 memo, Gerry emphasized that they had been drawn up in consultation with "outstanding Mexican-American and Puerto Rican educators, psychologists, and community and civil rights leaders." A panel created to advise noncompliant districts, he revealed, comprised "75 Mexican American, Puerto Rican, and Native American educators, psychologists, and community leaders." As for the future, Gerry indicated that HEW would "continue to place primary reliance on the policy developmental capabilities" of those individuals.[70]

Why did Gerry and Richardson attach so much importance to the sensitivities of the minority constituencies and so little to those of the affected school districts? (In contrast, Orfield reports that "civil rights groups had remarkably little involvement" in shaping the original Title VI regulations in the mid-1960s.[71]) A number of explanations are possible. In part, the OCR was simply consulting the people who knew most about the problems of language minorities and about possible remedies. But on the same basis it could be argued that school districts and local politicians knew most about the politics and economics of local schooling. An alternative explanation might focus on the fact OCR was a civil rights, rather than an education, agency. As Rabkin has observed, "the civil rights perspective seems to preclude the weighing of countervailing claims."[72] In this connection, OCR choices about consultation reflected predispositions that had emerged during the often frustrating battle with segregated school systems in the South. School districts were seen as disreputable bastions of prejudice and obstruction, civil rights groups as allies in a morally unassailable crusade for justice.

The preoccupation with rights and redress had one other consequence: it made OCR less concerned about social policy outcomes. (Wilbur Cohen felt this to be true of civil rights activists in general, charging in one interview that "they are much more interested in the 'enforcement of the Civil Rights Act', even if it deteriorates the quality of education, than improving the quality of education."[73]) Officials in some other parts of HEW were sometimes troubled by the absence of any evidence that bilingual schooling was educationally beneficial, but such concerns were less likely to worry the civil rights agency. When Martin Gerry was asked about the likely policy effectiveness of bilingual education, the OCR man laconically acknowledged that "there aren't any federal studies worth a damn." In his view, education research tended to have limited value; his approach had been fueled more by the conviction that English-only teaching told children that there was "something wrong with their language and their culture."[74]

Superficially, OCR's deference to the activists fits the "capture" model, according to which the new civil rights agencies came to be controlled not by the parties being regulated (such as school boards), as had been the economic regulators of the past, but by client groups (such as MALDEF) passionately committed to regulation.[75] Certainly, there is evidence of a highly cooperative relationship between agency and clientele, even if credibility within the civil rights fraternity dictated that MALDEF accentuate the negative.[76] For one thing, there developed significant two-way traffic in employment between MALDEF and the federal government.[77] For another, the two parties were careful to coordinate their activities: OCR let MALDEF see its files on particular Title VI cases, kept it informed on prospects for reaching settlements, encouraged the civil rights group to pursue lawsuits where those prospects seemed dim, and urged it to hold off where the portents were more encouraging.[78]

Whether this relationship amounts to "capture" is unclear. Clearly, OCR officials were extravagantly eager to please their new Latino constituency and commensurately indifferent to the claims of its principal adversary, namely the school districts. At an ideological or intellectual level, that amounts to a form of capture that came naturally to a civil rights agency. If, however, capture requires an agency to buckle in the face of political pressures it is powerless to resist, then it does not apply to the case of bilingual education. If anything, federal agencies and departments (along with MALDEF's paymasters at the Ford Foundation) were initially exercised by the new organization's *weakness* and looking for ways to build its reputation and influence. Having done so, they perhaps got more than they had bargained for and—as with the War on Poverty a few years earlier—struggled to meet the expectations of those whom they had helped mobilize. But initially, OCR enjoyed considerable autonomy.

The OCR was captured more by its own regulations than by any exogenous force. They proved impossible to enforce comprehensively, for all sorts of reasons: limited resources at both OCR and Justice (in terms of personnel, funding, and time); competing responsibilities (those new mandates to attack discrimination on the grounds of gender, age, and disability); a protracted enforcement process and the self-defeating nature of cutoffs; the difficulty of proving discrimination against language minorities outside the South. Almost four years on, only 4 percent of the school districts covered by the Pottinger memorandum had been reviewed.[79] In about half of those cases, the OCR had established noncompliance and come to an agreement with the district, but a critical report by the U.S. Commission on Civil Rights highlighted other instances where districts simply "refused to negotiate or submit plans."[80] Only once had HEW undertaken an "enforcement proceeding," the prelude to cutting off funds.[81] Such was MALDEF disappointment at what it took to be HEW foot-dragging that in the mid-1970s it joined other civil rights groups in suing HEW for failing to uphold Title VI of the Civil Rights Act.[82]

Bilingual Education Advances through the Courts

By then, litigation had already laid the foundations for the massive expansion in bilingual education provision that was to occur during the second half of the 1970s. The initiative was taken in part by civil rights groups such as MALDEF and the Puerto Rican Legal Defense and Educational Fund (PRLDEF; founded in 1972), who argued that the right of language minorities to be taught in their own language was protected not simply by Title VI but by the U.S. Constitution.[83] Starting in 1970, they gained important help from government lawyers. First, at a time when MALDEF was struggling to find the resources and expertise to bring its early cases, the federal government helped out, providing volunteer lawyers courtesy of the VISTA program. Second, the Justice Department filed suit in late 1970 against the state of Texas, charging discrimination against Mexican Americans as well as blacks and demanding bilingual education as part of the remedy. Third, also in 1970, OEO-funded San Francisco antipoverty lawyers joined forces with a group of Chinese American parents to bring the case *Lau v. Nichols*, arguing that the city school board was depriving their children of an education by failing to offer bilingual instruction.[84]

The Texas case was settled on appeal in July 1971, when the U.S. Court of Appeals for the Fifth Circuit ruled that the state's desegregation plan must take account of the unique circumstances of Latino children with limited English proficiency, in order to fulfill the requirements of the Fourteenth Amendment. And toward the end of the year, a lower federal court judge, the splendidly named William Justice, ordered the state to provide bilingual education. More than that, he ordered a form of bilingual instruction that would celebrate cultural diversity, rather than simply permitting the absorption of Mexican Americans into Anglo society.[85]

A much more important ruling came at the beginning of 1974, when the Supreme Court handed down its decision in the *Lau* case. The lower court judges had been unpersuaded by the constitutional argument advanced by Lau's OEO lawyers: ignoring the disparate impact concept, the judges observed that Chinese American children received just the same form of education as all other San Francisco children, and hence there was no discrimination. The Justice Department joined the case at the appeals stage, stressing the constitutional case as part of its broader effort to establish Spanish-speaking Americans as a discrete ethnoracial minority, entitled to the same kind of constitutional protection accorded to blacks.[86]

When that did not work, the lawyers appealed to the Supreme Court, which agreed to hear the case and listened to oral arguments in October 1973. Edward Steinman, the antipoverty lawyer in charge of putting Lau's case, continued to stress the constitutional argument. The Justice Department also put that case, in the person of no less a devotee of strict construction than Robert Bork, who had recently left the Yale law faculty to take up the position of solicitor general. Incongruously, the man who had once opposed the 1964 Civil Rights Act as unconstitutional now found himself rejecting the "narrow and mechanical" argument

> that the school district's sole obligation under the equal protection
> clause is to provide for all its students the same facilities and curriculum

even when this would consign non–English speakers to educational failure.

He elaborated:

> Respondents' decision to deny petitioners any assistance in learning the language of instruction in the schools excludes them from the educational program because of a national origin–related characteristic, just as effectively as would a policy of barring them from the school house. This unequal treatment . . . is a constitutionally impermissible act of *de jure* discrimination, from which petitioners are entitled to relief.[87]

By this time, however, the Justice Department was placing greater emphasis on the *statutory* basis for language-minority rights.[88] That was probably a response to the Supreme Court's recent ruling in the *Rodriguez* case, which had indicated a growing unwillingness on the part of the majority of justices to endorse bold constructions of the equal protection clause. Also, there may have been some concern that the authority of the 1970 memo—already diminished by spotty enforcement and compliance—would be further undermined if the likely negative ruling on the constitutional claim were not accompanied by an endorsement of the federal government's statutory claim.

If that was the government's thinking, the strategy worked well. Even though it dismissed the constitutional claim, the Supreme Court unanimously upheld OCR's regulations, giving them new force and paving the way for the dramatic expansion in bilingual provision that followed.[89] All three branches of the federal government played a role in that development, and the cumulative result of their activities during the mid-1970s was what Gary Orfield has described as "an explosion of bilingual education, often directly in response to a federal requirement." The place to start, again, is with the federal bureaucracy. HEW exploited its new regulatory authority, Orfield notes, "by spelling out detailed requirements for testing non-English-speaking children and automatically placing them in programs of bilingual-bicultural education."[90] These requirements, the 1975 Lau Remedies, did not formally require bilingual education, but they did require districts making different provision for language minorities to show that their response would be at least as effective in meeting the educational needs of LEP children. In practice, neither the courts nor HEW was prepared to endorse the obvious alternative, namely intensive English instruction, which they considered unresponsive to the minority's educational needs and civil rights.[91]

The Politics of Bilingual Education after Lau

Like earlier HEW desegregation guidelines, the Lau Remedies were not published in the *Federal Register* and therefore lacked full legal weight. They were distributed to all school districts possessing high concentrations of language-minority children, however, and for confused superintendents and school board members who wondered what *Lau* might mean for them, they offered early guidance.[92] Despite being overstretched on other fronts, following the range of new responsibilities that Congress had thrust upon it since 1970, OCR made a determined effort at strong compliance. In January 1975 it ordered 333 districts in twenty-six states to explain what compliance measures they would have taken by the start of the next school year. And when those districts submitted a plan based on intensive English instruction, OCR would reject it, and insist on bilingual education instead.[93]

It was not simply the confusion of local officials that gave force to the Lau Remedies. Money was also a consideration. True, the cost of implementing bilingual education was often high: New York City, even as it teetered on the edge of bankruptcy, developed a program that envisioned the hiring of 1,700 new bilingual teachers, and a recent survey suggested a national need for 70,000 additional teachers. But the potential cost of noncompliance was also high. Although there was little talk now of established federal funding being cut off, OCR did make clear that it would defer new spending where a district was found not to have made satisfactory arrangements for implementing *Lau*. The Seattle school district, for example, was denied funds under the Emergency School Aid Act when it failed to come up with a bilingual instruction program for the forty or so language minorities within its public school system. In cases such as this, OCR threatened protracted enforcement proceedings, with new funding becoming available when they were satisfactorily resolved. Faced with that prospect, most districts were minded to cooperate. One midwestern OCR official proudly told the *American School Board Journal* that "we have a plan or damn near a plan in every district in the region."[94]

The strong enforcement effort continued through the Carter years.[95] By 1980, OCR had undertaken 600 *Lau* reviews and negotiated 359 plans. In addition to the question of funding, districts agreeing to bilingual education were influenced by the broader momentum of the program. In particular, two federal judicial decisions handed down within a year of *Lau* went

Momentum

beyond what the Supreme Court had seemed to require, yet were unchallenged. In *Serna v. Portales*, the judge ruled that bilingual education was the only appropriate remedy for the discrimination that Mexican Americans in New Mexico had experienced. And at the other end of the country, 200,000 Puerto Rican children in New York City were found to be entitled to bilingual instruction. In that case, *Aspira v. New York*, the New York City Board of Education had been disputing PRLDEF's claim since 1972, arguing that—to the extent that an entitlement *might* exist—the federal government should be a party to the suit, on the grounds that it should be responsible for funding the settlement. After *Lau*, though, the board rapidly signed on to a consent decree.[96]

Congress also made a contribution to the momentum in 1974, when it enacted the Equal Educational Opportunities Act. The main purpose of the legislation was to restrict busing, but a little-noticed amendment required every "education agency to take appropriate action to overcome language barriers that impede equal participation by its students in its instructional programs." This gave the May 1970 memorandum a considerably more solid statutory basis than it had previously possessed. On the face of it, it also extended its remit to districts that did not receive federal education funds and to those with very small concentrations of LEP children.[97]

Courts struggled to know how to interpret this language, in part because they had so little legislative history to work with.[98] Still, the cumulative impact of these administrative, judicial, and legislative actions was a great expansion in bilingual education. To the extent that ambiguity remained, moreover, concerning the extent of the right to bilingual schooling, it was lessened by a series of state laws that mandated such provision. Massachusetts had passed such a law as far back as 1971, but it was in the aftermath of *Lau* that they became common.[99] By 1976, most states with high concentrations of Spanish-speaking children had some such law on the books, including Illinois, Texas, Michigan, New Jersey, Colorado, and California. (In some cases, the new laws superseded statutes passed only a few years previously, in the aftermath of Title VII, that had repealed English-only laws and *permitted* bilingual instruction. Such was the momentum of bilingual education in the 1970s.) In addition to the factors already mentioned, the new laws were influenced by the activities of an increasingly effective lobby of bilingual education teachers.[100] In some cases, too, state legislators were influenced by the feeling that manageable statutory mandates might forestall more far-reaching judicial requirements.

Unmentioned in this account is the most conspicuous legislative contri-

Lobbying teachers

bution to the politics of bilingual education during the mid-1970s, namely the renewal of the Bilingual Education Act in 1974. Historians of bilingual education have rightly presented this as a consequential moment in the development of the program.[101] Its contribution to the expansion of bilingual provision was slight, however, in comparison to the actions of the courts and the federal bureaucracy: the act's provisions remained voluntary, and appropriations remained low. Its main contribution was to focus political attention on the divisive debate about the purpose of bilingual education: was it to ease the transition of LEP children to English-language instruction, or was it to encourage ethnoracial pride? Key legislative sponsors led by Senators Edward Kennedy (D-Mass.) and Alan Cranston (D-Calif.) successfully pushed the "cultural maintenance" approach. In retrospect, though, their victory looks to have been a pyrrhic one that helped to stimulate the strong backlash against the Title VII program and the *Lau* decision that developed later in the decade and strengthened during the Reagan years.[102]

Also contributing to that backlash was the argument that bilingual instruction was not educationally effective and that its main function was as "the Hispanic equivalent of affirmative action, creating jobs for thousands of Spanish teachers."[103] In the conservative political environment of the 1980s, these charges combined with the argument about cultural separatism to weaken support for bilingual education, not least within the Mexican American community, and to strengthen the English-only movement. This process culminated, in the following decade, in the passage of Proposition 227 in California, which barred bilingual instruction entirely in favor of intensive English instruction. And in 2002, as part of the No Child Left Behind Act, the Bilingual Education Act was repealed, yielding to a new block grant program that encouraged school districts to employ innovative new English language–based techniques to overcome the problems of language minorities. HEW's Office of Bilingual Education became the Office of English Language Acquisition.[104] *Shift back*

Conclusion

Despite that trajectory, the circumstances surrounding the expansion of bilingual education remain instructive, illuminating some important broader themes in American political development after 1968, including some that often elude historians.[105] First, it suggests that it is not enough to say that Great Society liberalism collapsed in the 1960s and yielded during the 1970s to a strong rightward political impulse. That impulse existed, to be sure, but it cannot be taken for granted that the political system yielded to it. On the contrary, the 1970s, every bit as much as the 1960s, need to be considered as a reform decade.

To some extent, we already saw that in Chapter 5, where the final collapse of massive resistance came not under LBJ, but during the second year of the Nixon presidency. In that case, at the heart of the explanation was a set of legacies from the Johnson years that segregationists were powerless to roll back: the effects of the HEW Guidelines, the *Green* decision, and the strong civil rights mentality of career officials at OCR, CRD, and even the IRS. Nixon's role was also decisive, but it was this inheritance that persuaded him to take the lead in coaxing the Deep South to comply with *Alexander v. Holmes* in 1970.

The case of bilingual education is different. Here, we see not just aftershocks of the Great Society, but the development of a new brand of reform politics, with its locus not in the White House, but in a congeries of unelected political actors: federal bureaucrats, judges, interest groups, foundation executives. If one concentrates solely on the actions of legislators and presidents, then the story of bilingual education supports the traditional account of 1960s liberalism. In this reading of events, the passage of the Bilingual Education Act illustrates the decline of liberalism from the zenith of 1964–1965: a small, largely symbolic initiative, resisted by an embattled White House on fiscal grounds, deployed by its sponsor as a way of distancing himself from a now discredited regime. During the Nixon years the program staggered along because of a rather cynical, bipartisan quest for Latino votes, but Nixon held appropriations down, in a deteriorating budgetary climate, and in that context it was certainly not plausible to view this as a serious federal reform initiative. In 1974, one could continue, the legislative renewal of Title VII prompted another round of tokenism: as one of a number of gestures to the decade's ephemeral ethnic pride movement, Congress gave it a new emphasis on "cultural maintenance." But with the conservative movement burgeoning, that gambit turned the Bilingual Education Act from being an uncontentious exercise in tokenism into a divisive symbol of the "culture wars," paving the way for the long decline of the program after 1980.

If one brings the unelected actors into the picture, then the story looks rather different. Whereas in the case of school desegregation, every activist move by a federal administrator or judge seemed to generate headlines and outraged speeches in Congress, with bilingual education one is struck by the *lack* of attention. The promulgation of the May 1970 memo received no media coverage, the activities of MALDEF went largely unreported, and even the *Lau* decision earned only a single sentence in the *New York Times*. Yet these events contributed far more to the expansion of bilingual education than did anything happening on Capitol Hill. The two most important legislative contributions, indeed, only reinforce the sense that this process came about through a series of almost invisible steps: when Title VI was passed in 1964, no one anticipated that it might be used on behalf of the rights of language minorities, and when the Equal Educational Opportunities Act of 1974 was amended to strengthen the statutory basis for the 1970 memorandum, the provision drew no congressional attention at all.

To understand the vigor of the reform impulse of the 1970s, then, it is not enough to study elections, presidents, and political rhetoric. Instead, one must also pay attention to the entrepreneurial activities of activists and federal officials who rarely if ever made the headlines, or for that matter even the index, of the *New York Times*. In the case of bilingual education, what one finds is creative OCR bureaucrats bending Title VI of the Civil Rights Act to assert a right to bilingual schooling, Latino activists and government lawyers advancing the same proposition before the courts, federal judges endorsing their arguments, and Supreme Court justices providing sufficient support to trigger a massive expansion in bilingual provision in the late 1970s.

Considering these mutually reinforcing actions, two patterns warrant particular attention. The first is that shift in the locus of reform, from the world of electoral politics to that of bureaucratic and judicial discretion. The second is the extraordinary weakening of American federalism that occurred during the late 1960s and early 1970s. The case of bilingual education illustrates this second process particularly vividly. In 1967, before this process gained its full momentum, legislative supporters of Title VII were already impatient with subnational actors but acknowledged that any federal bilingual education program would perforce be purely voluntary. In 1970, OCR found a way of getting around that problem by discovering that the Civil Rights Act required school districts to make special provision for non-English-speaking children. By 1971, it was contending that such a right also existed under the U.S. Constitution. Two years later, Robert Bork, of all people, was defending that proposition before the U.S. Supreme Court. In the congressional debate over renewal of the Bilingual Education Act in 1973–1974, liberal legislators were boldly dismissive of the states, where earlier they had been grudgingly respectful. And the following year, OCR interpreted *Lau* in a way that forced school districts that left to their own devices would have done nothing to adopt often far-reaching bilingual programs.[106]

Although liberals went farther than conservatives in embracing a forceful federal approach, the extent to which people such as Robert Bork and William Rehnquist were prepared to endorse mandatory bilingual education during the mid-1970s is arresting. Part of the explanation is doubtless political: conservative Republicans as well as liberal Democrats wanted Latino votes. But there is more to it than that. As Martha Derthick has observed, "the tenacity and violence of southern resistance to changes in race relations gave federalism a very bad name."[107] Although in the case of school desegregation, the scale of the resistance led Nixon to adopt a strategy that emphasized voluntary compliance, the more general consequence was to legitimize projections of federal coercive power during the 1970s that would have been unthinkable back in 1964, especially where a question of civil rights was at stake. Chapter 7 considers the case of education to the handicapped, which would result in a much more decisive and enduring change in the federal role in the nation's school districts.

Transforming Special Education

THE GENESIS OF THE EDUCATION FOR

ALL HANDICAPPED CHILDREN ACT

The Education for All Handicapped Children Act of 1975 (PL 94-142) was a far-reaching civil rights measure that entitled all children with disabilities to a "free, appropriate public education" and transformed special education provision in the United States.[1] It was not the first important civil rights measure for the disabled: that distinction goes to the Rehabilitation Amendments of 1973, which had contained a strong antidiscrimination provision modeled on Title VI.[2] But in the annals of federal education policy 94-142 was unique, for it was the first law in this area that told the states what to do. In its prescriptiveness, in the degree to which it departed from the hallowed tradition of local control of schooling, 94-142 established an important precedent for the No Child Left Behind Act.

The impact of the law on educational provision for children with disabilities has been dramatic. Experts disagree about the precise nature of the benefits that they have derived from this increased provision, but it is obvious that they receive much greater funding, attention, and understanding than during earlier times.[3] During the first decade after its enactment, the number of special education teachers increased from 179,000 to 275,000, despite declining school enrollments.[4] During its first quarter century, the number of children with disabilities enrolled in public schools increased from 3.7 million to 6.3 million. That was 13.3 percent of total enrollments, compared to 8.3 percent.[5] Also expanding dramatically was litigation arising from disagreements over how to interpret the rights secured by the act: at a time when education-related lawsuits in general were declining in frequency, the volume of special education suits more than doubled.[6]

It is not surprising that these difficulties arose, given the complexity and ambiguity of the questions that 94-142 raised. What constituted an "appropriate" education? Could periodic catheterization or tracheotomies be regarded as falling within a school's "educational" responsibilities? How should the act's requirement that students with disabilities be educated in the "least restrictive setting" possible be interpreted? Under what circumstances could a disruptive child with disabilities be suspended from school? Was the school following the agreed Individualized Education Program (IEP), and were all the elaborate procedural regulations pertaining to its development and implementation being observed? The potential for disputes and uncertainty was vast and created a lucrative new area of private law, even before Congress encouraged the development still further in 1986 by allowing special education attorneys to be paid from the proceeds of legal settlements.[7]

How did such a measure come about? In part, any answer to that question must focus on endogenous factors such as the way in which new knowledge challenged old ideas about "ineducability." But the wider political environment was also important, including a minority rights revolution that, having originated in the African American freedom struggle, subsequently expanded to include such diverse constituencies as women, Latinos, consumers, homosexuals, the aged, and now the disabled. Also relevant was a series of changes in American politics: the mobilization of the constituencies already mentioned into pressure groups; institutional change in Congress (the weakening of party, the proliferation of subcommittees); divided government; and, finally, the Warren court's revolution in jurisprudence.

Here, the main focus will be on three institutional issues.[8] First, the passage of 94-142 needs to be seen in the context of Congress's growing centrality to reform politics during the early 1970s, as Democrats reacted against the perceived unfriendliness of the Nixon-Ford White House to "progressive" social policies. Like consumer protection, environmental legislation, Title IX, and the Occupational Safety and Health Act, this is a measure that had much stronger roots on Capitol Hill than in the White House. Second, the legislative initiative for 94-142 came from unelected actors operating behind the scenes: there were plenty of legislators who were keenly interested in disability issues and who vied with one another for attention, but the act had its origins not in their activities but in connections between congressional staffers and lobbyists. That was not unusual, but rather is typical of the way that Congress operates. What *is* distinctive is the greater access that recent institutional changes in Congress had given to previously weak groups such as the disabled. Before 1972 the Council for Exceptional Children (CEC) had to compete with all sorts of other groups and issues for the attention of the Senate Labor and Public Welfare Committee's education subcommittee. After that year, its director of federal relations could go to the new subcommittee on the handicapped, chaired by Jennings Randolph.

The third institutional factor is less obvious, but arguably still more important. It concerns the role of the courts. In 1971–1972, the federal courts handed down three rulings that helped to establish the idea that children with disabilities had a constitutional right to an education. Without *Wyatt v. Stickney*, *PARC v. Commonwealth of Pennsylvania*, and *Mills v. Board of Education*, it is inconceivable that Congress would have even considered a law that entitled all handicapped children to a "free, appropriate public education" (FAPE) and stipulated due process standards that schools must meet in devising each child's IEP. Those statutory rights to due process, an FAPE, and an IEP were all derived from the courts, and in terms of 94-142's remarkable departure from traditional patterns of American federalism, it is those judicial rulings that represent the point of departure. Once they had been handed down, states across the nation rapidly started incorporating their logic into statute law, meaning that subnational versions of 94-142 were already in effect across the country by 1975.

That meant that when the federal law came about, it did not *seem* to be such a radical departure. Also, it promised fiscal relief at a time when special education costs were mounting precipitously. When 94-142 was making its slow way through Congress between 1973 and 1975, educators were told that the federal government would furnish 75 percent of the additional cost of educating handicapped children. The final version was less generous, but legislators still held out the promise that federal funding would amount to 40 percent of those additional costs by 1982. (In the event, by the second year of the Reagan presidency, Washington was contributing just 10 percent.[9])

The great irony of all this is that the judicial rulings that set this ball rolling turned out to be evanescent.[10] Once the Supreme Court had handed down its key 1973 ruling in the case of *San Antonio I.S.D. v. Rodriguez*, the federal courts became less bold in their interpretation of the Fourteenth

Amendment, and the constitutional foundations of *PARC* and *Mills* looked suspect. By 1975, however, 94-142 was on the books, and its language and assumptions were strikingly legalistic, with "a focus on the individual as the bearer of rights, the use of legal concepts and mode of reasoning, and the employment of legal techniques such as written agreements and court-like procedures to enforce and protect rights."[11] During the next three decades, the federal courts remained central to the contentious politics of special education, but 94-142 rather than the constitution provided the basis for the litigation.

Before the Revolution: Lobbying Congress, 1950–1970

A prerequisite for 94-142 was the emergence of new attitudes toward mental retardation during the years after World War II.[12] During the first half of the twentieth century, such attitudes—both popular and professional—had been characterized by fatalism. In the scientific terminology of the time, states tended to make educational provision for "high-functioning morons," but there seemed little or no point in trying to educate those identified by IQ tests as being "cretins" or "idiots": congenitally ineducable and not even "trainable" (the term used for children who could be taught to be at least somewhat independent and perhaps to hold down an unskilled job), they were destined to be mere charges on society. Society's main obligation, it seemed, was to keep such unfortunates from becoming public nuisances when they got older (by committing crimes or by having children). Many quite mildly retarded children (and a scandalously high number who had simply been mislabeled as such) were committed to institutions for the "feeble-minded," and the mission of those institutions was overwhelmingly custodial rather than habilitative. None of these responses to retardation appeared cruel: rather, they seemed realistic, based on science, and in the interests of society, "retardate," and family.

These beliefs persisted well into the 1960s and beyond but were increasingly challenged by less fatalistic attitudes. The potential of children with developmental disabilities, some experts now thought, was determined by their learning environment. Institutionalization remained the norm—indeed the numbers peaked in 1961—but policymakers placed greater emphasis on training and education. Meanwhile, school systems started to take a greater interest in the educational needs of their "exceptional children," states passed new laws that required them to do so, and advocacy groups, politicians, and bureaucrats started to worry about the chronic shortage of special education teachers and classroom facilities. Lawrence Derthick, commissioner of education under Eisenhower, told Congress in 1957 that "not more than one in four" retarded children "has the opportunity for suitable education at present" and that there were only twenty-eight full-time special instructors nationwide training teachers of the mentally retarded. Something had to be done, not least because "under the right conditions of education and training, a vast majority of these children can become good adult workers, and, therefore, good citizens."[13]

These developments are relevant to 94-142 in three ways. First, a law entitling all handicapped children to a free, appropriate public education would not have come about had it not been for the conviction that even severely retarded children were capable of benefiting from schooling. Second, it became clear as early as during the Eisenhower administration that *national* action was a prerequisite for progress: it was not realistic to expect the forty-eight states to undertake individually the tasks of researching how retarded children learn and training special education teachers. The Cooperative Research Act, enacted in 1954 but first funded in 1957, started to address the first problem.[14] The Mental Retardation Act of 1958 addressed the second. At a time when the topic of federal aid to education in general was highly controversial, the 1958 act was uncontentious. Legislators considering these measures were establishing what was to become a striking pattern in the congressional politics of disability: this was not an issue that significantly divided the parties or separated liberals from conservatives, for the idea that handicapped Americans deserve federal help seemed self-evident. Nearly all the key measures enacted after that time would attract consensual support.[15]

Third, among the groups whose leaders testified with Derthick on behalf of the Mental Retardation Act were the National Association for Retarded Children (NARC) and the Council for Exceptional Children. Both were new to national politics, and each was to become closely associated with the issue of education for handicapped children and to play a significant part in promoting a larger federal role. CEC, an international organization of special education professionals, had been founded in 1922, but its involvement in national politics dated from the decision to open a small Washington office in the headquarters of the NEA (with which it was affiliated) in 1950. NARC, founded in Minneapolis in 1950, grew out of a cluster of local associations formed in the previous few years by parents of mentally handicapped children. In 1954 it too was able to set up a national office, with the donated proceeds of a best-selling book that the wife of Hollywood cowboy

Roy Rogers had written about their deceased daughter, who had been born with Down syndrome (a "mongoloid idiot," in contemporary parlance).[16]

The gains that this involvement in national politics yielded look rather small, viewed from the perspective of the 1970s: some funding for academic research, help with the construction of new facilities, modest support for teacher training, seed money for states wishing to overhaul their administrative arrangements for special education, the establishment of a Bureau for the Education of the Handicapped (BEH) in the U.S. Office of Education. In none of the federal disability legislation from 1950 through 1970 (see the following list) was there any suggestion that children with disabilities had rights, and the states were not *required* to take any action at all:

- 1954 Cooperative Research Act (PL 83-531)
- 1958 Mental Retardation Act (85-926)
- 1963 Mental Retardation Facilities Act (88-164)
- 1965 Federal Assistance to State Schools for the Handicapped (89-313)
- 1966 Elementary and Secondary Education Amendments (89-750)
- 1968 Handicapped Children's Early Education Assistance Act (90-538)
- 1970 Education of the Handicapped Act (91-230)

Cumulatively, however, these measures had the effect of greatly expand- ing federal spending on the education of the handicapped: from $2 million in 1959 to $15.4 million in 1964, $53.4 million in 1968, and $99.5 million in 1970.[17] More important, they had the intended catalytic effect on training programs and the states. Between 1962 and 1972, the number of special education teachers employed by the states increased from 20,000 to 162,000.[18] During the fifteen years following the 1957 hearings, the number of colleges and universities offering training in special education increased from 40 to more than 300.[19] And state and local spending on special education trebled between 1966 and 1972.[20] In the early 1950s, it had been estimated that only 15 percent of handicapped children were receiving specialized educational assistance. By the early 1970s, the proportion had quadrupled. The director of special education in Vermont, testifying before Congress in 1973, expressed wonderment that a federal grant of just $200,000 had triggered "a whole new approach" and a 40 percent increase in state funding.[21]

The 1966 amendments to ESEA added a new title for the handicapped to ESEA, Title VI. As well as distributing additional funds to the states, it established the BEH, giving advocates for the handicapped a much stronger voice in HEW than they had hitherto enjoyed. Fearing that BEH would be *too* clientele oriented, Johnson had opposed its creation, but it won influential backing on the Hill for precisely the same reason, especially from John Fogarty and Hugh Carey in the House of Representatives and from Jack Forsythe, of the Labor and Public Welfare Committee staff, in the Senate.[22]

Advocates for exceptional children were pleased with the progress that they made through their efforts on Capitol Hill during the 1960s. Elizabeth Boggs of NARC and Bill Geer, executive director of CEC, became familiar and influential figures within this specialized policymaking world.[23] Each year, Geer would meet congressional staffers and executive officials in a hotel on Capitol Hill to plan strategy, and their record in achieving the incremental objectives that they hatched at those meetings was quite good.[24] Geer and Boggs—although passionate about the cause of improving educational provision for children with disabilities—were also habituated to this rather cozy world, and when a new generation with a more activist temperament emerged within the disability community at the end of the 1960s, the difference in approach was marked.

Representative of the new breed was Frederick Weintraub, who was appointed assistant executive director of CEC in 1968 at the age of twenty-eight, with the principal task of modernizing its federal relations operation. Revering Geer, who was his mentor, and greatly admiring Boggs as well, he nonetheless had a different mentality, shaped by having come of political age amid the fervid rights-conscious atmosphere of the 1960s and shaped too by personal encounters with the grievous wrongs that the education system routinely wrought on children with disabilities. Two years earlier, while a doctoral student in special education at Teachers College, he had been on the staff of a commission that Mayor John Lindsay of New York City appointed to look into educational provision for the retarded. Weintraub's particular task was to investigate conditions at the Willowbrook School on Staten Island, and he was horrified by what he found. He reported, for example, that HEW-funded research being undertaken at the school into possible cures for hepatitis entailed infecting residents with the disease. Mayor Lindsay was aghast, but this mood reportedly abated when he learned that responsibility for administering the facility lay with Governor Nelson Rockefeller up in Albany, rather than with himself. Weintraub, though, remained aghast: when he went to Washington to work for CEC, he was eager to promote fundamental changes in the way the United States treated its handicapped children.

Council for Exceptional Children

For the new political leadership of CEC, therefore, and for younger elements within NARC and other disability organizations, the political successes of the 1950s and 1960s seemed insufficient: they were less struck by what had been achieved than by the enormous amount that still had to be done. As the 1970s began, HEW estimated that only about half of the nation's 6 million handicapped children were receiving the education that they needed: one million were at home, and 2 million were in regular classes where they received no special provision.[25] As the number of special education teachers rocketed, so did estimates of how many more were needed: nearly 140,000 according to John Brademas (D-Ind.), chair of the House subcommittee on special education and someone whose sensitive political antennae quickly responded to the new mood within the disability community.[26] CEC statistics revealed disturbing variation in provision between even quite similar states: Connecticut spent 8.41 percent of its education budget on special education, Massachusetts just 3.28 percent. Some of the poorer states continued to spend only a tiny proportion of their already small education budgets on the handicapped: the figure for Alabama was 2.49 percent, for Mississippi it was 1.63 percent, for Arkansas a paltry 1.05 percent. The proportion of handicapped children served by the state varied, it seemed, from 81 percent in Washington state to 8 percent in North Dakota. These figures were problematic, but that substantial variation existed could hardly be doubted and was hard to defend.[27]

But as political success, generational change, and rapidly developing perspectives on the educability of the disabled were breeding greater ambition, prospects for winning new funding from sympathetic but hard-pressed legislators seemed increasingly bleak. At the federal level, a growing gap was opening up between authorizations and appropriations: in 1966, it was only $200,000, but by 1973 it had reached $353 million.[28] At the state and local level it was unclear that the impressive gains being registered in special education spending by 1973 could be sustained, given a fiscal crunch that was at least as serious as the one in Washington. Although political strategists at CEC retained their customary interest in legislative politics, they were also on the lookout for new ways to expand the educational rights of children with disabilities.

From Legislation to Litigation

The notion that disabled children possessed rights was not entirely new.[29] But until the 1950s it was more common to conceive of the handicapped— and especially those who were mentally retarded or had severe physical disabilities—as unfortunate victims of fate who deserved compassion and good works but could not be expected to wield "rights" in any meaningful way.[30] The activities of the Easter Seal campaign and March of Dimes fund drives exhibited some of that mentality, and so even did NARC in its early days.[31] By this time, however, a more recognizably modern version of rights for the disabled was also beginning to emerge, rooted in broader societal notions of universal human rights and in more sophisticated understandings of various handicapping conditions. "The retarded have a potential contribution to make [to] the world in which they live," declared Commissioner Derthick in 1957. "They are citizens, too, with the right to an opportunity to work and fulfill their role in our democracy."[32]

That theme suffused the 1962 report of John F. Kennedy's presidential commission on mental retardation.[33] Included in its eight principal recommendations was a plea for "an enlightened attitude on the part of the law and the courts" toward the retarded: the United States needed "*a new legal, as well as social, concept of the retarded*, including protection of their civil rights."[34] Members of the commission's task force on law saw the judicial role not in terms of securing broad rights, but rather in terms of individual disputes having to do with guardianship, sterilization, marriage, adoption, and custodial care. Even then, they declared: "We would minimize intervention by the law insofar as possible. The courts should be regarded as a residual resource, if not a last recourse."[35]

They may have been influenced by the poor track record of courts in this area; their best-known intervention in the realm of the rights of the retarded up to this point had been the 1919 ruling *Beattie v. State Board of Education*, in which the Wisconsin supreme court had validated the exclusion from school of a child with cerebral palsy on the grounds that his "condition" produced a "depressing and nauseating effect on the teachers and school children and that he required an undue portion of the teacher's time."[36] More likely, it simply did not occur to task force members that the kinds of class action suit that had only previously been filed in the contexts of black civil rights and First Amendment freedoms might be applied to this case.

Absent the counsel of a group such as the NAACP Legal Defense Fund or the American Civil Liberties Union (ACLU), there was no reason why NARC parents would have thought of themselves as representatives of a "discrete and insular minority" possessing rights under the Fourteenth Amendment. Even within the legal profession, the idea that federal judges could force state legislatures to spend money—the overwhelming prerequisite for *effecting* as opposed to merely *proclaiming* the rights of the handicapped—

was novel. Other federal impositions on the states—in the areas of desegregation, criminal due process, reapportionment, privacy, and prayer in schools—had not generally resulted in legislators having to appropriate major additional funds. Indeed, the lawyer who would represent the Pennsylvania Association for Retarded Children (PARC) in its litigation with the Commonwealth of Pennsylvania, Thomas K. Gilhool, had, while a third year law student at Yale in 1964, helped pen a letter to the *New York Times* containing the then seemingly self-evident observation that "the courts cannot, after all, order a city council or a state legislature to allocate more money for schools."[37] Lacking that power, state disability groups such as PARC — like parents and like their national body—seemed best advised to pursue the nonconfrontational, coalition-building approach.

Enter the Lawyers

Left to themselves, then, it is not at all clear that the disability groups would have taken the route of litigation. Certainly, there is no reason to think that they would have been drawn to the kind of constitutional claim that underpinned *Wyatt, PARC,* and *Mills.* The decisive role in tutoring CEC and NARC regarding the possibilities of litigation, and in framing the cases, was played by a new breed of public interest lawyer.[38] In the first two cases, the judicial process utterly transformed the initial complaint, resulting in much more far-reaching rulings than could have been anticipated by the plaintiffs. As for the third case, it was *instigated* by the lawyers, with the role of the ostensible plaintiffs purely nominal. Given these circumstances, the political milieu, educational experiences, and career choices of the lawyers bear examination. They were Charles Halpern and Bruce Ennis in the case of *Wyatt v. Stickney;* Thomas Gilhool, in the case of *PARC v. Commonwealth of Pennsylvania;* and Halpern, Patricia Wald, and Stanley Herr in the case of *Mills v. Board of Education.*

The place to start is the early 1960s, with the black civil rights movement and the avalanche of seminal decisions handed down by the Warren Court, not just on racial questions but on all manner of other contentious issues in national life. For young Americans stirred by the emergent spirit of change, restlessness, idealism, and rebellion and wishing to change society for the better, law school must have seemed an attractive option. If in the not so distant past the courts had the reputation for being conservative, now the world of the law seemed rich with promise. Significantly, all of the lawyers listed above bar one (Ennis, who went to Columbia) chose to go to Yale, with its progressive reputation for "legal realism" stretching back to the New Deal era. Gilhool and Halpern were both editors of the *Yale Law Journal*, and Gilhool was a prominent civil rights organizer in the Freedom Summer of 1964, in Mississippi. What might have stirred their activism at Yale was less their professors, and the courses that they took, and more one another, the school's historic reputation, and the wider atmosphere of civil rights and Vietnam-related ferment and protest that permeated New Haven, like other college towns, during the 1960s.[39]

But on graduating, how could these young lawyers best use their talents? Two traditional outlets were private law firms that allowed their associates to engage in pro bono work (such as Arnold and Porter, in the District of Columbia) and government service (the Justice Department's Civil Rights Division was an obvious choice). During the 1960s, however, antipoverty law emerged as a third option. In 1962, the Ford Foundation started funding free law clinics in poor neighborhoods, the genesis of the 1964 War on Poverty's neighborhood legal services program. With foundation and then government money, neighborhood legal services expanded rapidly. By the early 1970s, 130 law schools were reportedly teaching antipoverty law (an unheard-of specialty at the start of the decade), and many were starting "clinical" programs that allowed students to gain direct exposure to this and other public interest activities.[40] Growing numbers of law students began to contemplate career paths other than the traditional one of entering private practice. In 1969, only 31 percent of Yale Law School graduates joined a private practice, and not one of the *Harvard Law Review*'s thirty-nine editors would admit to an intention to take the traditional path.[41]

But if providing legal aid to the poor clearly had considerable appeal, it also had two shortcomings, besides inadequate remuneration. The caseload for poverty lawyers was often overwhelming, something that diminished the capacity of its practitioners to do a good job or achieve broad social change. And the work, if important, was often unstimulating: divorces, custody cases, job dismissals, helping tenants in battles with landlords. Amid the environment of the late 1960s and early 1970s, with the Great Society losing its momentum in the realm of electoral politics, the idea of keeping the flame of reform aloft by bringing test cases and class-action suits became ever more attractive.[42] In 1967, the OEO decided to alter its emphasis from meeting the individual needs of the poor to finding cases that would allow the agency to test broad constitutional principles, and in 1970 this approach had its first big success, with the Supreme Court's ruling in the welfare case of *Goldberg v. Kelly.*[43]

At the same time, the scope for what was coming loosely to be termed as "public interest law" was becoming much more broadly conceived in a second sense, from the poor to the disadvantaged or disenfranchised. The public interest law groups that sprouted around the turn of the 1970s were, for the most part, not concerned solely or even primarily with the poor but rather possessed an eclectic and entrepreneurial approach to seeking a better world.[44] Two program officers for the Ford Foundation—whose centrality to this whole enterprise would be hard to overstate—conveyed this mentality well in a 1972 overview of the kinds of public interest law firm that they liked to promote. They had a preference for "cases that involve new principles":

> Thus, the Center for Law and Social Policy recently has shifted its
> emphasis from the more familiar kinds of environmental protection
> cases, in which it has had success, to urban issues. Where a private firm
> would seek to capitalize on an early lead and pre-eminence, the center
> is leaving the field to others in order to employ its well-developed skills
> elsewhere. This is not a response to traditional client demand, but to a
> problem in which a perceived social need is the client.[45]

As that suggests, the preoccupation with effecting broad social change entailed a much less client-oriented approach than one would associate with either a traditional private sector lawyer or, for that matter, the initial breed of poverty lawyer.

The three key disability cases provide a good illustration of this mentality in action. The first, *Wyatt v. Stickney*, established a constitutional right to habilitative treatment for involuntarily committed mental patients. The second, *PARC*, identified a right to education for all mentally retarded children. And the third, *Mills*, extended that right to all children with disabilities: physical and behavioral as well as mental. What is most important about these cases is their cumulative effect. Individually, they had limited reach (in terms of geography, constituency, and doctrine). Cumulatively, they imparted legal momentum to the idea that the Fourteenth Amendment entitled children with disabilities to an education, even though not one of the cases was heard by a federal court of appeals, let alone the Supreme Court. The three cases also lent broader political impetus to the cause of educational rights for the handicapped. Taken together, they had the effect of embedding in the minds of legislators and state attorneys general the idea that the rights that they were codifying already existed under the constitution.

Wyatt v. Stickney

In *Wyatt v. Stickney*, handed down in March 1971, Judge Frank Johnson of Alabama determined that involuntarily committed mental patients have a due process right to "adequate treatment."[46] The case's primary importance is in the development of mental health provision rather than mental retardation, but it also enumerates a number of the key rights that would later find statutory form in 94-142: the right to "adequacy" in treatment, with all its ambiguity; the idea that cost could not be considered an adequate reason for failing to achieve that standard; the insistence that the patient be treated in the least restrictive environment possible; the emphasis on due process; and the requirement that an individualized plan be prepared for each patient.[47]

The process by which Johnson arrived at his landmark ruling illustrates a broader theme of these disability cases: despite the costs that they entailed for the defendant, the legal proceedings were not rancorous or adversarial. To the contrary, as a CEC official remarked in an overview of early disability litigation, in more than one case "named defendants have spent days preparing defenses for the suit, and nights assisting the plaintiffs to prepare their arguments."[48] When the New York Department of Mental Hygiene was sued by Willowbrook School parents, in 1972, its head promised the prosecuting attorney that he would offer "as defenseless a defense as possible."[49] Similarly, *Wyatt*, *PARC*, and *Mills* were each to some extent products of collusion between prosecution and defense. This is not to suggest that there was anything improper or sinister in their relationship, but rather that defendants shared their critics' desire for institutional reform and additional resources, cared about those for whom they were responsible, and recognized that they had more to gain from defeat than from victory.

The Alabama case provides a vivid illustration of a second broad point about the drive to define new rights for the handicapped. It did not originate with bottom-up civil rights protest or with rights claims by representatives of the disabled. Instead, it originated with lawyers, assisted by federal judges keen to extend the jurisprudential revolution that the Warren Court had wrought. For the most part, these lawyer-reformers were not disability specialists and represented no particular constituency. Rather, they were entrepreneurs, looking for ways of advancing through the courts a reform impulse that seemed stalled on other fronts. In this case, the key figures helping Johnson were Charles R. Halpern of the Washington-based Center for Law and Social Policy (CLASP), and Bruce J. Ennis of the New York Civil Liberties Union (NYCLU). The legal process transformed the case into a test of principles quite different from those that had motivated the plaintiffs to file suit.

Wyatt v. Stickney originated as an employment grievance suit by staff at the Bryce Hospital for the mentally ill. Having been dismissed by the Alabama commissioner of mental health, Stonewall Stickney, following budgetary cutbacks, they alleged wrongful dismissal and breach of contract, and—for obscure reasons—their lawyer brought the case before the federal court rather than the state court.[50] Johnson summarily dismissed their contractual claim on grounds of jurisdiction but was intrigued by a passing reference to the deleterious effect that the firings would have on patients. Could it be, the famed civil rights judge wondered, that the U.S. Constitution entitled these patients to a certain level of care? Johnson instructed the plaintiff's lawyer, George Dean, to go away to research the question and convened hearings in January at which Stickney was asked to defend not the dismissals, but rather Alabama's overall arrangements for confined mental patients.[51]

The defense was not inclined to put up much of a fight, for Stickney and his predecessors had been trying to procure new resources from the state for years, and he viewed conditions at Bryce as being entirely inadequate, albeit better than at other facilities for which he was responsible, such as the Partlow school for the mentally retarded. Right at the outset of the hearing, he "conceded" the existence of a constitutional right to adequate treatment.[52] Had he confronted stronger opposition from the defense, perhaps Judge Johnson might have shrunk from establishing such a bold precedent, for in handing down the only previous decision relating to a right to treatment, the 1966 *Rouse* opinion, Judge David Bazelon had adverted only glancingly to the "considerable constitutional problems" presented by custodial care; ultimately, he had rested his case on statutory grounds.[53] Johnson, by contrast, baldly asserted that mental patients "unquestionably have a constitutional right to . . . treatment," cited *Rouse*, and left it at that.[54] The case, he explained the following year, was "clear beyond cavil."[55]

In handing down his decision, Judge Johnson recognized that determining what level of treatment was constitutionally "adequate" would be a formidable task. Giving the defense six months to come up with "a treatment program so as to give each of the treatable patients committed to the Bryce facility a realistic opportunity to be cured or to improve his or her mental condition," he appointed a "panel of experts . . . to determine what objective and subjective hospital standards will be required to furnish adequate treatment."[56] He also broadened the case to include the mentally retarded residents of Partlow, on the grounds that they enjoyed the same rights as the mentally ill and that conditions at Partlow were far worse than those at Bryce.

Among those enlisted in this investigation were the Justice Department's Civil Rights Division and HEW, both of which accepted Johnson's request that they join the suit as amici; the Federal Bureau of Investigations, which helped with the continuing effort to establish what went on at Bryce; and the new U.S. attorney for Montgomery, Nixon appointee Ira DeMent. DeMent's encounters with Bryce and Partlow made him an impassioned advocate of reform, and even before Johnson had handed down the first of his two decisions, DeMent was corresponding with him about whether the United States might intervene in *Stickney v. Wyatt*, either as a party or as amicus curiae. Having discussed the matter with Jerris Leonard, DeMent recommended that Johnson write to the CRD chief requesting government participation. "As a tactical matter," he suggested, "you may even wish to constructively criticize the Government for not having taken action in this matter heretofore."[57] Lawyer George Dean later remarked that "we got more out of the Nixon Justice Department than you can imagine."[58]

Also joining the case at this point at Johnson's request were the two public interest lawyers, Halpern and Ennis. Halpern was the director of CLASP, which had been founded in 1969 with foundation money and with help from former Supreme Court justice Arthur J. Goldberg.[59] Prior to that, Halpern had clerked for a member of the influential District of Columbia circuit court of appeals and had worked for Arnold and Porter. CLASP was a small outfit—with only five full-time lawyers, it relied heavily on clinical law interns from Yale and other schools—but nonetheless made an immediate impact, especially in the areas of consumer protection and environmental law.[60] By the early 1970s, those causes had plenty of champions, and CLASP was looking for new issues. It was in this context that Halpern went to Alabama to help out with the Bryce Hospital case.

Ennis was a graduate of the University of Chicago Law School, where he was a member of the *Law Review*. Following a federal clerkship, he entered the world of corporate law, but in 1970 he decided to apply for a job directing a new mental health litigation project for the NYCLU. Prior to that he had had no particular interest in the rights of mental patients, but in 1970 such "ignorance was little barrier—no one in 1970 knew what mental health law was or what the rights of the mentally ill might be."[61] Certainly, no one at the ACLU would have been familiar with these issues: its overwhelming focus during the past half-century had been on First Amendment cases.[62]

Ennis got the job and became the first lawyer in the country working full-time on mental health rights. His early reading converted him to Thomas Szasz's view that mental illness is a "myth" and made him a strong advocate of deinstitutionalization. A believer in the idea that institutions such as Bryce should be closed down rather than reformed, he had some qualms about getting involved in *Wyatt v. Stickney*, but he overcame those doubts on the grounds that Alabama could not afford expensive reforms and would be forced to close its institutions.[63] So he joined Charles Halpern in Alabama.

Their shared experience led Ennis and Halpern to create the Mental Health Law Project in 1972 (now the Bazelon Center for Mental Health Law) and also gave Ennis the idea of bringing federal suit against the state of New York to protest conditions at the Willowbrook School.[64] Subsequently, he became director of the ACLU and one of the nation's most prominent First Amendment lawyers.[65] In the immediate case, the first task for Dean, Halpern, and Ennis was to persuade Judge Johnson that the mentally retarded residents of Partlow had a constitutional right to "habilitation" similar to the right to "treatment" already discovered in the case of Bryce; the second was to persuade him to stipulate stringent minimum standards for both institutions. In both instances, they were successful.[66]

PARC v. Commonwealth of Pennsylvania

The second case originated as a complaint by PARC about facilities at the Pennhurst institution for the mentally retarded in Altoona. Years of negotiations with state officials had failed to resolve long-standing grievances that centered on overcrowding, neglect, squalor, cruelty, and understaffing. The chair of PARC's committee on residential care was Dennis Haggerty, a Philadelphia lawyer whose severely brain-damaged son, Boomer, had been a resident of Pennhurst for seven months in the mid-1960s.[67] Haggerty had removed Boomer when he learned that his son had lost the top of his ear not in a shower accident, as Haggerty had been informed, but rather when a fellow resident being taught barbering had made a mistake.[68] Following an investigation into the institution that he commissioned in 1968, Haggerty urged delegates attending PARC's annual convention to contemplate legal action against the Commonwealth of Pennsylvania, perhaps with a view to having the institution closed down.

That would not be easy. For one thing, PARC was in part funded by the commonwealth. For another, many association members were involved in running special schools that also received state money. In addition, the membership was internally divided regarding the appropriate care of men-

tally retarded children: the more radical element believed in deinstitutionalization, another faction favored community-based care, and the old guard
continued to believe that residential institutions offered the best approach.
Finally, PARC members with a child at Pennhurst or a similar institution
had to balance distress at its manifest failings with the desirability of maintaining good relations with its staff.[69] Haggerty recalls that the initial response of PARC convention goers to his presentation was "timid," but the
mood changed when he dimmed the lights and displayed a photograph showing the body of a boy who had died at Pennhurst nine months previously.

> The official cause of death was pneumonia. The death was never
> reported to the boy's mother. . . . The boy had been stored in a
> medical facility for experimentation and on ice when it was found by
> your investigator. Photographs were taken at the morgue after the
> body was discovered that indicated the presence of burns on the boy's
> body which had been preserved by the freezing process. A follow-up
> on the investigation indicated that the boy's friend stated, "Johnnie
> died in a fire." The PARC Board, after the lights were turned on,
> voted unanimously to accept the recommendation that suit against
> Pennsylvania was appropriate.[70]

Having won PARC's permission to seek counsel, Haggerty sought out
fellow Philadelphia lawyer, Thomas Gilhool. Gilhool had a mentally retarded brother, giving him an intensely personal stake in the rights of the
disabled.[71] Having graduated from Yale, he had spent a year studying at the
London School of Economics and had worked on Eugene McCarthy's 1968
presidential campaign, prior to finding a job with the OEO's legal services
program. When Haggerty approached him, he had moved on to a Philadelphia law firm and was engaged in a significant amount of "public interest"
litigation, winning cases having to do with welfare rights, public housing,
and civil rights. Aided by fellow McCarthy veterans, he was also seeking
election to the Philadelphia City Council.[72]

Gilhool's mandate was to provide PARC with ideas for how legal action
might be used to end the abuses at Pennhurst. Considering the options, he
sought out Fred Weintraub, whom Haggerty had already been in touch with
by phone. Weintraub recalls that Gilhool used to come down to Washington
on the bus in the evening and that they would spend the night strategizing in
a twenty-four-hour diner. Also involved in the early strategizing, in a necessarily covert fashion, was Bill Ohrtman, director of special education in
Pennsylvania, active member of CEC, and someone who was keen that the

lawsuit should go ahead and succeed. Weintraub acted as a conduit between Ohrtman and Gilhool.[73]

The PARC resolution had made no reference to the rather abstract consideration of educational rights, centering instead on the immediate health and welfare abuses and on the possible need to have Pennhurst closed. That said, PARC's president had made it clear that he was keen to promote broader change, telling delegates: "We have a hunting license to innovate. It's up to us!" Following Haggerty's presentation, delegates approved the following "Bill of Rights for Pennsylvania's Retarded Citizens":

> Every retarded person, no matter how handicapped he is, is first of all in possession of human, legal and social rights. As much as possible, retarded persons, whether institutionalized or not, should be treated like other ordinary persons of their age are treated in the community. Every effort should be made to "normalize" the retarded person, to emphasize his similarity to normal persons and to diminish his deviant aspects.[74]

Gilhool suggested five possible lines of attack, the fourth of which was a federal lawsuit based on the claim that residents enjoyed a constitutional right to an education that was being denied them on the spurious grounds that they were uneducable.[75] The particular attraction of that option to a public interest lawyer lay in the facts that it would make the Pennhurst suit a test case for broader principles and that the case would be heard before a federal rather than a state court. Also, the possible existence of a constitutional right to an education was receiving growing attention within the legal community.[76] In a more narrow sense, it was one way to get Pennhurst closed, on the grounds that its residents should be transferred to the regular public school system or to community-based facilities.[77]

PARC went ahead with a suit based on the constitutional right to an education and persuaded the chief justice for the eastern district of Pennsylvania, Thomas Masterson, that there was a serious constitutional issue at stake. Then, however, events took a turn that made a ruling about unconstitutionality unnecessary. Following preliminary hearings at which expert witnesses declared all retarded children "capable of achieving some degree of self-care," the Commonwealth (i.e., Ohrtman) dropped its defense, and the parties' lawyers drew up a consent agreement. The state agreed to conduct a census of all retarded children, in a bid to uncover the many thousands whose special educational needs were being neglected; agreed, too, that all of these children were entitled to a free, appropriate public education in as normal a setting as was possible, but with whatever special assistance they required;

and consented finally to a detailed process that must be followed in identifying and implementing each individual's needs. The degree to which this agreement anticipated 94-142 is striking. So, too, is the complete absence of any reference in the decree to the institution whose appalling conditions had prompted PARC to go to court.[78]

All Judge Masterson had to do in his October 1971 opinion was to ratify the agreement, which he duly did.[79] Half a year later, in a second opinion designed to show why the case fell within federal jurisdiction, he explained: "We are convinced that the plaintiffs have established a colorable claim under the Due Process Clause."[80] As R. Shep Melnick has argued, that was rather an "oblique" way to establish new rights.[81] But elected politicians at both state and federal levels behaved as if the constitutional case established had been entirely clear-cut. Why did they do so? Most obviously, three and a half months later, Judge Joseph Waddy of the District of Columbia federal district court had handed down his decision in *Mills v. Board of Education*, embedding and extending Masterson's rather precarious constitutional principle.

Mills v. Board of Education

The plaintiffs in this case were seven children who had been excluded from District of Columbia public schools because of behavioral problems or alleged retardation and for whom no alternative educational arrangements had been made. Judge Waddy ruled that the federal constitution, as well as District of Columbia statutes, entitled "each child of school age" to "a free and suitable publicly-supported education regardless of the degree of the child's mental, physical or emotional disability or impairment."[82] In essence, he was extending to all handicapped children the educational rights that *PARC* had posited in the case of the mentally retarded.

As in *Wyatt* and *PARC*, the defendants did not mount much of a defense: they accepted the facts as laid out by plaintiffs' lawyers and endorsed their constitutional complaint.[83] Their only defense, in fact, was that which Stonewall Stickney had advanced in the Alabama case: the legislature (in this case, Congress) had not furnished the necessary resources. Waddy, like Frank Johnson, responded that this was no excuse for depriving the plaintiffs of their constitutional rights, citing the Supreme Court's recent ruling to that effect in *Goldberg v. Kelly*.[84] Also like Johnson, Waddy took a very fragile constitutional precedent (in this case Judge Masterson's reference to a "colorable" claim) and presented it as having the appearance of established law. As with Johnson's bold construction of the *Rouse* decision, he did not explain the constitutional basis for this claim in any detail. Rather, the case was presented as being uncontestable, something made possible by the fact that (again) no one was contesting it in the courtroom.[85]

Mills v. Board of Education provides a particularly good illustration of the role played by public interest lawyers in promoting the educational rights of the handicapped. This was, David Kirp concludes, "a lawyers' venture" from beginning to end. Although many parents were angry about the often capricious way in which their children had been denied an education, "there existed in Washington no broad-based parents' group historically committed to and able to follow through on the issue."[86] The initiative came instead from three public interest law groups. The first was CLASP. The second was the Harvard Center for Law and Education (HCLE), education arm of the War on Poverty's legal services program and publisher of the clearinghouse journal, *Inequality in Education*.[87] The third was the National Legal Aid and Defenders Association (NLADA), an organization that dated back to the Progressive Era and that provided pro bono assistance to indigents.[88]

CEC was also closely involved in bringing the *Mills* case to trial: although its name did not appear on any of the lawsuits, litigation had now become central to its political strategy. Serendipitously, just as NLADA's National Law Office was considering how best to challenge the District's arrangements for special education, CEC was in Washington holding its annual meeting. NLADA's Stanley Herr, a Yale Law School graduate who would go on to a distinguished career in special education law at the University of Maryland, worked closely with Fred Weintraub and Alan Abeson of CEC to plan the case.[89] In particular, the three of them thought hard about how best to make the case that all children with disabilities are educable; although the idea was gaining momentum, it was far from settled, *PARC* notwithstanding. They hired a legal secretary, and she took depositions from special education professionals who were in town for the CEC conference.[90] Weintraub recalls that they were carefully coached and their depositions entirely scripted. Still, their evidence helped convey the impression that the educability of all children was an established fact.[91]

From Litigation to Legislation: The Road to 94-142

Activists for the rights of the disabled took great heart from the outcomes in these three cases but remained nervous. In public, Fred Weintraub and Alan Abeson strove to create the impression that the constitutional rights proclaimed in *PARC* and *Mills* were securely established: that was the message of articles that they published in *Phi Delta Kappan* and the *Syracuse Law Review*.[92] In private, they were less certain, apprehensive that they might lose a case, anxious that none of those that had been won should go to appeal.[93] Much would depend on the judge and on the quality of the lawyer putting the case. Those doubts notwithstanding, the public campaign was tremendously successful, contributing to the ever-greater salience of the issue of education for the handicapped in state politics. Indeed, a poll of governors undertaken in 1974 by the Education Commission of the States revealed that education provision for the handicapped had become one of their two biggest political priorities.[94]

By the time that 94-142 was enacted the following year, the rights that it extended were already incorporated into state laws across the country, with nearly all of these laws having been passed since 1970.[95] Litigation was not the only factor; the new laws were also grounded in the longer-term forces (new research, a growing mobilization of parents and professionals, increasing federal interest). By the mid-1970s, litigation additionally needs to be seen as part of a broader responsiveness to the problems of the handicapped that centered on such matters as employment rights, transportation, access to public buildings, and disability benefits. But to Weintraub and Abeson, writing in 1974, it seemed that the most immediate stimulus for this "quiet revolution" had been lawsuits.[96] By the time that the governors were polled, thirty-six right-to-education lawsuits had been filed, and the Supreme Court's opinion in *Rodriguez* did nothing to slow the momentum.[97] Not a single case had been lost.[98]

By this time, moreover, education rights for the handicapped had become a popular cause, hard to oppose without appearing callous.[99] As the programs were implemented, they had the potential to become more contentious. But in the short term, the big problem was finding the money.[100] Accordingly, when Congress embarked on Education for All Handicapped Children Act hearings in 1973, what caught the eye was not the federal mandates or the potential for bureaucratic excess but rather the sense that this was an idea whose time had come, that it built logically on what was happening at the state level and in the courts, and that it promised very significant fiscal relief in the form of 75 percent of the excess cost of educating exceptional children. As Harrison Williams (D-N.J.)—chairman of the Senate Labor and Public Welfare Committee and principal sponsor of the measure—explained at the outset of the 1975 hearings: "I do believe that we can assure States of both the maintenance of a certain level of funding as well as . . . assist[ing] them in meeting their constitutional responsibility to assure all handicapped children a free, appropriate, public education."[101]

Still, these judicial and state legislative actions during the early 1970s did not make congressional passage of something like 94-142 inevitable. On the contrary, one might wonder why it was necessary to pass a civil rights measure when the rights in question had already been mandated through the courts and by the states. Surely what was most needed from Washington was not mandates, but money? Why was it not enough simply to increase appropriations under existing legislation, such as the Education for the Handicapped Act of 1970 (PL 91-230), which was up for renewal in 1973?

We already have a big part of the answer: disability lobbyists feared that they would lose a court case and that the entire constitutional argument would unravel. They felt the need to press for federal civil rights legislation while the legal momentum was still on their side. At the point when S 6 and HR 70 (the Senate and House versions of what became 94-142) were introduced in 1973, the Maryland Association for Retarded Citizens had just won a big victory in the state courts, the legal momentum was great, and the possibility existed of building a distinctly eclectic, not to mention incongruous, coalition in favor of the measure. Weintraub thought in terms of a trinity of interests: disability rights campaigners enthusiastic about the new civil rights approach; state legislators and governors, who desperately needed federal funds to implement existing and imminent mandates; and school administrators, "driven crazy" by the uncertainty that all the lawsuits had created regarding the nature of their legal obligations and pleading: "just tell us what the law is."[102]

Even to the extent that those obligations could be clarified through unambiguous state legislation, the suspicion existed that the states would not fulfill their obligations unless they were put under considerable pressure. In part that suspicion arose out of the more general climate. By the early 1970s, even so redoubtable a conservative as John Byrnes (R-Wis.), ranking member of the House Ways and Means Committee, could be heard to exclaim: "Hell, we can't trust the states. We can't depend upon them to carry out the philosophy of our program." By this time, Melnick observes, "states' rights was becoming a policy without a constituency."[103]

In the case of disability policy, such suspicions were entirely understandable: many states had had statutes on the books for years, but they had not been enforced. John Brademas, chair of the select education subcommittee in the House and one of the principal authors of 94-142, was strongly critical of the record of the states in this area. But so too was Albert Quie, now ranking Republican on the Education and Labor Committee, whose interest in the education of the handicapped went back to the mid-1950s.[104] In general, he favored general aid over categorical aid and was suspicious of excessive federal direction. But in the case of aid to the handicapped, he thought strong national standards and categorical grants were the only way to ensure action at the state level. Despite a justified suspicion that the federal government would insist on the mandates without supplying the necessary funds, he worked closely with Brademas to secure House passage of HR 70.

Also relevant in explaining the civil rights orientation of the bill might be the tight fiscal climate of the mid-1970s. In a time of recession, high inflation, and ballooning budget deficits, legislators wishing to do something more for the disabled simply did not have the option of pumping billions of dollars into state special education coffers. True, draft versions of S.6 promised a 75 percent contribution to the "excess costs" of the states, but that was entirely unrealistic. In the version that President Ford signed in November 1975, the federal share was a paltry 5 percent, albeit with assurances of better things to come (10 percent in fiscal year 1979, 20 percent in 1980, 30 percent in 1981, and 40 percent in 1982).[105] Without the civil rights mandates, this would have been an almost pointless measure, embarrassingly incommensurate with the grand ambitions of its legislative sponsors.

The Congressional Environment

Those ambitions and calculations have to be considered in their institutional context. Congress in the early 1970s was in an activist mood, members of its Democratic majority (and a significant number of Republicans, especially in the Senate) feeling that they would have to pick up the torch of reform that—in their view—had been discarded by the Nixon administration. This mentality was particularly strong among their young staff members. Nik Edes, who was an aide to Senator Harrison Williams (D-N.J.)—chair of the Senate Labor and Public Welfare Committee and primary sponsor of S 6—recalls their attitude:

> I'll tell you the frame of mind we all had. We had lived for three years under Richard Nixon, and under being told no, no, no, no, no by an executive branch which was totally unresponsive to the programs of the sixties, and to the things that were still felt important during that time of the seventies by a vast majority of the Congress. . . . We were angry at the Nixon administration, and we wanted to do everything we could to do as much as we could to help people. Whether it be disabled people, minorities, poor people, you name it. Even the middle class. . . .
>
> It was an important thread running through everything that was done at those times. It was: I'll get those sons of bitches, they don't want

to show any positive inclination toward doing things at all, then we're going to really stick it to them. And in the process, help people.[106]

It is not surprising that this mentality should have particularly influenced disability policymaking, where the tradition of Congressional leadership long predated Nixon and had a bipartisan cast. With the exception of the 1963 mental retardation bill, none of the important disability legislation of the past decade had emanated from the White House. As Quie observed in 1969, "regardless of administration, it . . . falls to the Congress to initiate, advocate, and develop legislation for this field."[107]

A second feature of the changes sweeping Capitol Hill was the proliferation of subcommittees, as junior and liberal members of Congress sought to promote sundry reform causes, and their own careers, by wresting power away from the conservative Dixiecrats who chaired most key committees.[108] In the case of education for the handicapped, the staff of Brademas's subcommittee—Jack Duncan on the majority side, Martin LaVor for the minority—developed a close interest in handicapped issues as well as good working relations with the key interest groups and with each other.[109] But it was in the Senate that the institutional changes of the 1970s had the greatest impact on the politics of education for the handicapped.[110] The Labor and Public Welfare Committee established a subcommittee on the handicapped in 1973, the year that S 6 made its debut. Previously, handicapped issues had been considered in the context of general education bills and had often struggled for visibility, but now they had the attention of a second specialist subcommittee, again with full-time, knowledgeable, and committed staff. That greatly improved the access of disability lobbyists to Congress and increased the number of legislators who took an educated interest in handicapped issues. Its chairman, Jennings Randolph, broadened his long-standing interest in the problems of the blind, and Alan Cranston (D-Calif.), Robert Stafford (R-Vt.), and Jacob Javits (R-N.Y.) all became ardent champions of disability issues.

What really caught the eye of insiders, though, was the combustible staff politics surrounding the subcommittee's operations. It appears that the impetus behind S.6 in the Senate came from two members of Senator Williams's staff, Lisa Walker and Nik Edes. They apparently assumed that their boss would chair the new body, meaning that they would become its principal staff members and important players in the world of disability politics. As a matter of Senate courtesy, however, Williams offered the chairmanship to his senior colleague, Jennings Randolph. To the surprise and perturbation of the two staff members, who knew that he was kept busy by his role as chairman of the Public Works Committee, Randolph said yes.[111] Worse still, he appointed Patria Winalski Forsythe, a formidable figure in Washington disability politics, as his chief aide.[112] Given how busy Randolph was, she was certain to run the subcommittee. And since she and Lisa Walker did not get along, their common interest in disability issues made them rivals rather than—as one might anticipate—allies. When Walker persuaded Senator Williams to become principal sponsor of 94-142, Forsythe got Randolph to put his name to a rival measure, S 896, motivated at least in part by a desire to stymie her staff rival's measure. (It seems that Randolph was oblivious to the contretemps and that he and Williams remained on good terms throughout.)

Unelected political actors were central to the passage of S.6.[113] That was neither unusual nor new. What was new was the *extent* of staff power in the recently decentralized and democratized Congress. Harrison Williams may have been chief sponsor of S 6, but it is clear that his role in the story was minor. By contrast, that of his aide, Lisa Walker, was central. Despite Jennings Randolph's seniority and considerable reputation, Patria Forsythe similarly was the key player in the subcommittee. And in the House, although Brademas did whatever he could to advance HR 70, it was Jack Duncan who had more to do with the content and philosophy of the measure. Looking back on his two decades in Congress, Albert Quie—blessed throughout that career with outstanding staff—nevertheless regretted the degree to which elected legislators had lost control of the legislative process since the 1950s.[114] Although it would be misleading to suggest that legislators were marginal to 94-142, the story of its passage is at least consistent with Quie's point.

The first bill bearing the title Education for All Handicapped Children Act was introduced to the Senate by Harrison Williams in May 1972. It had very little in common with the version that President Ford would sign some three years later, for it did not propose new civil rights for the handicapped.[115] Rather, it was a money bill, envisioning a 75 percent federal contribution to the additional cost of educating handicapped children. Neither Weintraub nor Lisa Walker (Weintraub's closest ally in the legislative fight) thought that it would pass; rather, at a time when the crisis in school finance was generating talk of a much greater federal contribution, they simply wanted to ensure that the financing of special education was part of that discussion.[116]

By 1973, when Williams introduced a new version of the bill, the *Mills* decision had been handed down, as had an important state court decision in Maryland, and other lawsuits were in progress around the country. Now, it was a civil rights measure, as well as a money bill, with much of its key language derived directly from the recent court cases. Judicial momentum and state legislative activity greatly enhanced its prospects for passage, but it still faced a number of obstacles, not least divisions among supporters of educational rights for the disabled. Perhaps the most potent threat came from Patria Forsythe's rival proposal, S 896, which proposed to meet the immediate financial needs of the states by simply expanding federal financial aid under the 1970 Education for the Handicapped Act.

Weintraub could not oppose a measure that increased funding by $600 million per year, but neither did he wish to support a bill that would break apart the eclectic coalition that he was trying to assemble for S 6. If states could have money without mandates via S 896, why would they support S 6? Weintraub was immensely relieved when Randolph was persuaded to amend S 896 so that it provided only a one-time, one-year injection of funds, giving states the immediate fiscal relief that they needed but ensuring that they would remain interested in the longer term fix offered by S 6. When Randolph presented revised S 896 to an almost empty Senate floor, it existed only on a yellow legal pad. Asked by one colleague about a particular clause in the bill, Randolph reportedly growled: "Just vote for it."[117]

Other obstacles remained. For one thing, disability and education groups wanted different things out of the bill. School boards and municipal officials wanted federal funding to pass straight through to school districts, whereas state educators felt that they should have discretion over distribution. Although disability advocates believed strongly in the "least restrictive setting" provision, NEA and AFT worried about the additional pressures such mainstreaming might create for already hard-pressed teachers. Another difference centered on whether "specific learning disabilities" should be included in the bill's list of handicapping conditions.

In picking their way through these thorny questions, Weintraub and Walker were assisted by Edwin W. Martin, director of BEH.[118] The Nixon White House had no particular interest in disability issues, but that very disinterest created an opportunity for Martin, who was an energetic and politically adept advocate for the handicapped.[119] As a congressional aide in 1966, Martin had played a role in creating BEH, prior to becoming a career official at the new agency the following year, with particular responsibility for congressional liaison. During the Nixon administration he was awarded the top job at the bureau, despite being—by his own admission—"a McGovern-ite, or worse." Evidently he managed to avoid coming to the attention of Fred Malek, the White House aide who had been charged with rooting out disloyalty at HEW. Making the most of his anonymity and exploiting his connections on the Hill and with disability groups, Martin made an entrepreneurial contribution to the growing effort to move the education of the handicapped up the political agenda. The most visible manifestation of this contribution came when he was interviewed by Barbara Walters on the *Today* show in 1970.[120] It helped too that the commissioner of education, Sidney Marland, felt a keen sympathy for the handicapped, accepting Martin's suggestion that a 1980 target date be set for ensuring that all handicapped children received the education that they needed.[121] Normally, though, the BEH moved by stealth, under the radar of American politics.[122]

S 6 picked up considerable momentum during 1973. Hearings that the full Senate committee held at Walker's suggestion in New Jersey, South Carolina, New York, and California helped here, as did her proselytizing letters to governors, encouraging them to take pride in a measure that— she insisted—was modeled on their own statute. The next year, though, it seemed to come to a "juddering halt." Weintraub blames Watergate, thinking that it took congressional attention away from substantive business as the drama of Nixon's fall from grace gathered pace.[123] Whatever the explanation, the momentum picked up again in 1975, with Brademas providing crucial leadership in the House, where he was now majority whip. Following some important changes in conference (including that massive decline in the federal contribution), the bill was approved almost without opposition.

The final act of the long drama came in November 1975 when President Ford signed PL 94-142. That was not predictable, despite the lopsided congressional majorities and the lack of effective, organized opposition from interest groups that had reason to view the bill with anxiety. HEW secretary David Mathews recommended a veto, despite a strong personal sympathy for the disabled that dated from his encounters with the Wyatt case while president of the University of Alabama (earlier, he had had vacation work at the Bryce asylum).[124] He was worried by its prescriptiveness. Meanwhile, OMB was worried by the question of funding: less by the immediate price tag, which was now small, and more by the staged percentage increases that were built into the bill. The White House asked Edwin Martin to prepare a veto message. Unsurprisingly, he refused, but he helpfully offered to write a message for the signing ceremony instead.[125] Unpopular, facing an uphill battle for reelection, and possessing too a strong sympathy for the handicapped, Ford decided to sign the measure. Had he not done so, many old Republican friends in Congress would have been very unhappy with him: they did not want to be put in to the position of having to vote on the override. That said, Ford's statement sounded more like a veto message than a ringing endorsement: he warned that S 6 promised much more than it could deliver and that it reached too far into the affairs of the states.

Conclusion

As in the previous two chapters, the case of education for the handicapped sees the cause of liberal reform accelerating rather than decelerating after 1968. This time, again, the Nixon administration played some role, if a less prominent one than in the cases of bilingual education and school desegregation. But, unlike in those two instances, the White House was completely absent from the story: instead the leading actors were low-profile individuals such as Edwin Martin of BEH and U.S. Attorney Ira DeMent.

Neither does 94-142 owe much to some mass mobilization of the disabled in favor of their civil rights: such a movement was only just beginning to emerge when S 6 was introduced to Congress. Instead, the central event in explaining 94-142 is the shift in the principal locus of disability politics from legislatures to courts that occurred at the beginning of the 1970s. That shift might well not have taken place had it not been for the emergence of a new breed of lawyer-reformer for whom this was just one of many progressive causes that could be advanced through the courts in an otherwise adverse political environment. In the fourth and final civil rights case considered in this book, which has to do with school finance arrangements, lawyers would be if anything even more central.

8

Compensatory Education through the Courts

THE POLITICS OF SCHOOL FINANCE

For congressional supporters of compensatory education, the years after 1968 were dispiriting, punctuated by negative evaluations of Title I and Head Start and by broader doubts about the capacity of schools to equalize life chances. The big programs of the Johnson years endured, and in political terms one could even say that they flourished. But in comparison to earlier years, confidence in their compensatory potential was lacking. The popularity of Title I owed more to constituency politics, and to the modest fiscal relief that the program provided to hard-pressed school districts, than to its efficacy in tackling the roots of poverty. If one's point of comparison is the bright expectations that had surrounded ESEA at the time of its enactment, then the reform impulse of the 1960s had palpably waned.

If the focus shifts from Congress to the courts, however, a new brand of reform politics on behalf of the poor comes into view, and far from waning as Lyndon Johnson's presidency drew to an unhappy close, it was just beginning to stir. Very different in objective and political character, this brand easily matched Great Society liberalism circa 1965 in terms of ambition, excitement, and zeal. And in terms of the challenge that it posed to the tradition of local control, it was of a different order of magnitude altogether. At its heart was the claim that states violated the equal protection rights of the poor when—as was the case in forty-nine of the fifty states—education resources varied according to the wealth of the school district.[1] Were this claim to be upheld, the result would be a very substantial redistribution of education resources from rich districts to poor districts.

This equalization campaign acquired considerable momentum during the early 1970s, just as legal efforts to mandate bilingual education and better education for the handicapped were also reaching their peak. The big breakthrough came in the summer of 1971, when the California Supreme Court endorsed the principle of "fiscal neutrality," the idea that resources must not vary according to district wealth, in the case of *Serrano v. Priest*.[2] For some observers, the case appeared to be equivalent to *Brown* in terms of its significance for American education.[3] This time, however, there was to be no moment of crowning glory comparable to *Lau*, in the case of bilingual education, or 94-142, in the case of education for the handicapped. Instead, supporters of school finance reform suffered a bitter reverse in 1973, when the U.S. Supreme Court handed down its decision in a Texas case, *San Antonio Independent School District v. Rodriguez*.[4] Writing for a bare 5–4 majority, Justice Lewis Powell ruled that there was no constitutional right to a fiscally neutral system of school finance.

Pondering the broader meaning of this ruling, two journalists for the *Washington Post* reported the "widely believed" sense that the long "chapter in the quest for equality" that had begun with the *Brown* decision nearly two decades earlier was drawing to a close.[5] In terms of the Supreme Court's approach to interpreting the Fourteenth Amendment, history has tended to confirm that judgment.[6] In terms of the broader politics of school finance, however, the impact of *Rodriguez* is less cut-and-dried. Justice Powell's ruling may have brought a definitive end to efforts to secure change through the *federal* courts, but the judicialization of school finance politics if anything intensified after 1973, with the locus of reform energies reverting to the state system. That litigation would transform school finance arrangements across the nation.[7] In that sense, the story of *Rodriguez* illuminates not just the rise and fall of the liberal impulse but also some enduring institutional changes in American democracy. The historical significance of those changes becomes clearer if one thinks about the pre-*Rodriguez* era, when school finance arrangements were a matter for legislatures rather than courts.

The Old Politics of School Finance

When school finance reformers started to look to the courts, in the late 1960s, the largest source of revenue for elementary and secondary education in most states was the local property tax.[8] That created big inequalities because of the uneven distribution of personal and commercial property throughout a state. Taxpayers in a district rich in property could tax themselves very lightly and still generate much higher revenue per child than a poor district, even if inhabitants of that poorer district levied a substantially higher rate of taxation. In Los Angeles County, for example, the wealthy taxpayers of Beverley Hills taxed their property at a rate of 2.38 percent in order to spend $1,231.72 per pupil. In working-class Baldwin Park, meanwhile, a school tax of 5.48 percent resulted in per pupil spending of only $577.49.[9] That was an extreme example, but the basic problem recurred throughout the nation, resulting in substantial interdistrict disparities in spending within the same state.[10]

This problem was not new; rather, it was as old as the system of universal public education itself. Efforts to remedy it also went back a long way, at least to the very early years of the twentieth century. Then, states had sought to ensure a minimum level of education provision in all districts through flat grants to school districts and through so-called foundation programs, which established a notion of minimal provision and used state funds to ensure that every district reached that level. The equalizing effects of such programs were modest at best, but the barriers to more comprehensive reform were formidable. Even many reformers were loath to contemplate centralization of funding within the state, feeling that school districts were more likely than states to pioneer imaginative new educational approaches and that they should be encouraged to raise as much money for schools as their taxpayers would bear. They also recognized that the local property tax system had real advantages, not just as a guarantor of local control but in terms of predictability of revenue.

But it was raw political considerations that did most to explain the persistence of inequitable arrangements. Political reality dictated that any "equalization" program provide at least some funds even to the most affluent districts. That meant that school finance reform was expensive, entailing new ad valorem or income taxes, an unappetizing prospect to tax-averse state legislators. Also, there was little if any organized pressure for reform from those who stood to benefit from reform, while the laborious analyses produced by education economists were scarcely calculated to appeal to the political imagination.

For all the political ferment of the Great Society era, those factors were as salient in 1968 as they had been half a century earlier. True, there was plenty of evidence of mounting and widespread popular dissatisfaction with the schools tax, as taxpayers across the nation rejected new bond issues and property tax levies in record numbers. But this dissatisfaction emanated less from the poor than from general antitax sentiment, especially among elderly property owners on fixed incomes (not a group that was particularly enthusiastic about funding schools). State politicians generally conceived of equity in terms of the plight of the elderly property owners rather than the plight of the poor.[11]

Beneath the surface, though, a new approach to reform was stirring by the end of the 1960s. Just as in the case of education for the handicapped, the principal locus of school finance reform politics was on the point of shifting from the unyielding, majoritarian world of legislative politics to the potentially more propitious terrain of Warren Era judicial politics. The first visible portent came in February 1968, when the Detroit school board sued the state of Michigan for more money, on equal protection grounds. By the end of the year, additional suits had been brought in Illinois, Virginia, Texas, and California.

These suits were unprecedented. Where did they come from? As with disability politics and bilingual education, part of the momentum came from a nexus of antipoverty lawyers, civil rights activists, and foundation executives. But there are differences too, at least of emphasis. In particular, academics played a larger role in this case: it was they who debated legal strategies, documented the discriminatory effects of the existing system, and posited more egalitarian arrangements. By contrast, the role of the ostensible beneficiaries of reform—children, parents, and educators in poor school districts—was insubstantial. To a still greater degree than in the cases of bilingual education and education for the handicapped, then, this was distinctly a top-down movement. Another difference was the limited role played by elected political actors. True, President Nixon and members of Congress observed the drama as it made its way through the courts, commented upon it, and initiated investigations of the school finance problem. But they had almost no impact on the flow of events.

The evolution of the legal strategy during the three and a half years that culminated in the *Serrano* decision had three stages. First came a clutch of retrospectively naive suits aimed at forcing states to meet the full educational "needs" of poor schoolchildren. Those cases received short shrift from judges who found the concept of need to be "nebulous" and "nonjusticiable."[12] In their wake came a second approach that one might term the "kitchen sink" technique. These cases (comprising *Serrano* and *Rodriguez* in their original iterations) retained need as one standard but added a whole set of additional claims based on race, geography, poverty, and tax equity, on the theory that judges might find at least one of those claims appealing. That approach too was unsuccessful. Third came an approach that focused narrowly on the question of "fiscal equality," expressed in the following negative proposition: "The quality of public education may not be a function of wealth, other than the wealth of the state as a whole."[13] "Proposition I," as it was styled by its authors, finally gave the cause of school finance reform some desperately needed legal momentum. Indeed, all of the victories of 1971 and 1972 were based on the idea that the Fourteenth Amendment's equal protection clause forbade discrimination on the basis of school district wealth, rather than on notions of need, or race, or strict equality.

The Road to *Serrano*

The first scholar to explore the possibility that existing school finance arrangements might be overturned in the courts was Arthur Wise, then a graduate student in education at the University of Chicago.[14] In a short 1965 paper he noted that recent Supreme Court opinions on race, reapportionment, and the rights of criminal suspects had left discrimination on the basis of geography and wealth constitutionally suspect and suggested that school finance systems across the United States discriminated on both grounds.[15] Two years later, he elaborated on that argument in his doctoral dissertation, which was published almost immediately as *Rich Schools, Poor Schools*.[16] At a University of Chicago conference organized around his thesis, one of Wise's mentors, the distinguished constitutional lawyer Philip Kurland, predicted that the courts would find his argument attractive, observing that "few of the Court's recent opinions are so rich in precedent as this one would be."[17]

A few months later, the Detroit school board brought a federal school finance suit against the state of Michigan, perhaps inspired in part by Wise's work.[18] The novelty of the suit earned it national publicity and inspired copycat actions in Illinois and Virginia, brought in those cases by poverty lawyers rather than school boards.[19] But whereas Wise's favored remedy was a rough equalization in per pupil expenditures, these three suits were each based on the claim that states were constitutionally obliged to meet the educational "needs" of all children. Judges found that approach to be worryingly imprecise, wondering how they were to know what constituted a constitutionally acceptable level of provision. Accordingly, the Detroit suit never came to trial, and the other two complaints were dismissed by three-judge federal district courts.[20] Unwisely, plaintiffs' lawyers in the Illinois and Virginia cases appealed to the Supreme Court, whereupon the lower court decisions were affirmed without comment or debate.[21]

By then, a second approach had been launched, in California. Its intellectual inspiration came from Harold "Hal" Horowitz, a law professor at the University of California, Los Angeles (UCLA) who had been writing about the Fourteenth Amendment since the 1940s. As well as being a distinguished scholar, Horowitz had worked in the HEW general counsel's office under Kennedy and Johnson, helping to draft Title VI of the Civil Rights Act and serving on Sargent Shriver's antipoverty task force.[22] Being in Washington during those heady years of reform had turned him from scholar to scholar-activist, and when he returned to Los Angeles toward the end of the Johnson years, he and his wife became closely involved in the work of the OEO-funded Western Center for Law and Poverty (WCLP), which was housed near the Watts ghetto.[23] Among the courses that he now taught was one, Law, the Lawyer, and Social Reform, that all UCLA law students were required to take.[24]

Horowitz's interest in school finance arose out of his involvement in the black civil rights movement during his time in Washington. First, he got involved in the important legal case of *Hobson v. Hansen*, which centered on racial discrimination *within* the District of Columbia's single school district. Then, he was asked by the U.S. Civil Rights Commission to investigate whether the Fourteenth Amendment might be used to attack racially discriminatory spending patterns *between* districts.[25] In each case, the result was a law review article that went beyond race, reflecting Horowitz's broader scholarly interest in the scope of the Fourteenth Amendment.[26] In the second article, Horowitz and his coauthor concluded that "it should be held violative of the equal protection clause for a state . . . to maintain a pattern of internal territorial boundary lines which results in substantial inequalities in educational opportunity from district to district."[27]

Horowitz became personally involved in school finance litigation when he was approached by Sidney M. Wolinsky, a volunteer at WCLP. A 1961 Yale Law School graduate, Wolinsky had long nourished a desire to help the poor and sought a career that advanced that ambition. He considered Legal Aid, the most obvious route, to be "very limited, very frustrating and not very intellectually challenging," however, and went to work for a Beverly Hills law firm.[28] That position soon palled, not surprisingly, whereas the world of antipoverty law simultaneously became more enticing, with class-action lawsuits becoming more common and the OEO establishing neighborhood law centers around the country. Ready to move on, Wolinsky started teaching a Politics and Civil Rights course at the University of Southern California and volunteering for WCLP. It was in this context that he read Horowitz's law review piece and sensed an opportunity to make a difference to the lives of the poor.

The director of WCLP at this time was Derrick Bell. Bell had served with the air force in Korea, prior to joining the Eisenhower administration's Justice Department, in its Civil Rights Division. Resigning that position in protest at a bar on NAACP membership, he had then been recruited by Thurgood Marshall to be an attorney for the Legal Defense Fund. In 1962, he made the *New York Times* and the *Washington Post* when he was imprisoned for refusing to leave a Mississippi railroad waiting room that was reserved for whites. Most recently he had been deputy director of the newly established Office for Civil Rights at HEW.[29]

Bell felt that WCLP was struggling to find its raison d'être. "The center had a lot of money," he later recalled, but was struggling to transcend the old legal services paradigm, "doing a lot of divorces, the kind of things that wear you down." He felt that "we had to show the law could be used in a dramatic way to change people's lives. We had to generate some excitement."[30] Fired by the same ambition, Wolinsky asked Horowitz if anyone had ever considered bringing litigation to test his thesis. Horowitz explained that some suits were underway, but that they were being poorly managed, whereupon Wolinsky suggested that they try to assemble a better case on the West Coast. Horowitz liked that idea, and shortly thereafter WCLP found a plaintiff, John Serrano, a Los Angeles psychiatric social worker. Serrano's son had recently transferred from a poor high school in the East Los Angeles barrio out to a middle-class school in the suburbs. Angry that this had been necessary, Serrano wondered what could be done. When Bell met him at a cocktail party and suggested that he put his name to the putative school finance lawsuit, Serrano readily assented, although he initially felt it was "a pretty hopeless court complaint."[31] As Serrano later recalled, "That's all I had to do with the case. After that it was the lawyers' case."[32]

Wanting to shield the issue from the U.S. Supreme Court until a solid body of precedents had been established, Horowitz and Wolinsky elected to file a state suit. Their complaint contained as many as nine discrete arguments, reflecting Wolinsky's belief that such a document should not be "lean and clean" but rather "should be loaded up with a number of alternative theories," giving the court "a wide variety of options."[33] Among the grounds for complaint were discrimination on the basis of geography, race, poverty, and district wealth. The lawyers went to enormous trouble in putting together their case, going through twenty drafts of the complaint and digging out large quantities of information about the discriminatory effects of the California system of school finance. Such a suit would normally have been very expensive to bring, but in this case WCLP interns helped with the research, Horowitz provided high-powered intellectual analysis free of charge, and Wolinsky took the case pro bono, causing raised eyebrows among fellow partners at the Beverly Hills law firm, who dismissed the case as "crazy."

This was a more professional suit than its three predecessors, but it suffered the same fate, at least initially. First it was dismissed by a Los Angeles county judge, and then Wolinsky lost the appeal, on the grounds that the case was too similar to the failed Illinois suit.[34] Judges across the country, in state and federal courts alike, had now determined school finance arrangements to be fundamentally "non-justiciable," a matter for legislators. The last throw of the dice in the *Serrano* case was an appeal to the state Supreme Court. Recognizing what a hole they were in, Wolinsky and Horowitz belatedly abandoned the "kitchen sink" approach and elected to frame their final appeal quite differently, as a test of the theories of John E. Coons, a professor at the Boalt School of Law at Berkeley. With that decision, the two-year litigation struggle entered a new and more promising phase.

Private Wealth and Public Education

Up to a point, Coons fit the stereotype of the lawyer-activist.[35] At Northwestern University, where he had taught prior to moving to Berkeley, he had been on the board of the Illinois ACLU, participated in civil rights protests at Selma, and written a report on racial discrimination in Chicago for the Commission on Civil Rights. It was in preparing that report that he had first learned of the great disparities in per-pupil spending between Illinois school districts. Finding those differences to be repugnant and irrational, he wondered whether they might also be constitutionally problematic.[36] In 1965, with financial help from the Russell Sage Foundation, he and two talented graduate students, William H. Clune and Stephen Sugarman, began work on the project that five years later would yield a landmark book called *Private Wealth and Public Education*.

They evidently approached the distinctly unexciting literature of education economics with remarkable energy and zest. Coons told one journalist: "All I remember is the three of us pacing around patios and living rooms listening to the endless disquisitions of wild schemes accompanied by endless disposition of beer." On one occasion, making a pot of coffee at Coons's house, Clune was so engrossed in a manuscript that he failed to notice that the pot handle was alight until Coons's wife dashed down the stairs to rescue both him and it.[37] Unsurprisingly, the book that resulted from these sessions started with a passionate moral statement: the authors expressed "outrage" at the prevailing variation in per-pupil expenditures and declared discrimination against poor school districts to be not just wrong, but "grossly offensive."[38]

Still, in comparison to the work that other activist legal scholars were producing during the late 1960s and early 1970s, *Private Wealth and Public Education* was not a strident book. Indeed, in two respects it stands out for its caution. First, its authors had assumed since the early days of their project that judges would need a lot of persuading to enter this particular "political thicket." By contrast, lawyers whose sensibilities had been more centrally shaped by the black civil rights struggle sometimes assumed that, where an issue of fundamental injustice was at stake, the cause of moral righteousness must ultimately prevail in the courts.[39]

The second respect in which Coons, Clune, and Sugarman parted company with their colleagues concerned their attitude to local control. Involvement in the struggle for black civil rights tended to make lawyer-activists impatient with, or inattentive to, questions of local control or popular opinion. When they approached questions of poverty, they demanded the same kind of strongly egalitarian remedy that the courts had endorsed in the context of race. To the extent that they made this sort of analogy between race and other forms of inequality, it seemed improper to make justice contingent on local control, or tradition.[40] David Kirp, the young director of the Harvard Center for Law and Education, argued that the state was "constitutionally obliged . . . to provide effective equality to all" and that it must ensure "an equal chance of an equal educational outcome." In his view, "the pertinent question for the court is whether everyone has an equal share of the goods, measured according to need." He conceded that "the cost of such an effort, seriously undertaken, will be immense." But Kirp assured his readers that "the result [will be] well worth the cost."[41]

In the light of these views, what stands out in the work of Coons, Clune, and Sugarman is less their activism than their circumspection; their egalitarian instincts coexisted with an admiration for local control. Coons was a practicing Catholic, a product of the Minnesota parochial school system, and had a distinctively Catholic approach to thinking about social justice, grounded in the notion of "subsidiarity," the idea that all functions should be discharged at the most local practicable level.[42] During his research, he also developed a fundamental skepticism about the capacities of professional educators.[43] Reflecting both of those two dispositions, a prefatory reference to the "grossly offensive" discrimination embedded in the current system of school finance is immediately followed by the more heterodox observation that "we find equally offensive the current efforts to use the Constitution as a battering ram for uniformity."[44]

Their attitude was also shaped by a more practical consideration: they suspected that the Supreme Court would be reluctant to take on the school finance question. They were less confident than Wise that easy analogies could be drawn between the Warren Court's jurisprudence in other areas—such as race, reapportionment, voting rights, and criminal law—and the area of school finance. After all, there was no reference in the U.S. Constitution or Bill of Rights to education. True, the Constitution had been a very adaptable instrument during the previous decade and a half, with the Supreme Court regularly marching boldly into new territory in other areas. But it had not done so in the area of school finance. On the contrary, it had declined to get involved, twice affirming lower court rulings that education spending was a matter for legislators, not judges.

In *Private Wealth and Public Education*, Coons and his students frankly acknowledged that the sort of model of "fiscal equality" they had in mind would require a judicial leap, relying less on any clear precedent than on a congeries of jurisprudential, societal, and education trends that might cumulatively persuade the Supreme Court to act.[45] Yet in the late 1960s, the general context was not encouraging. For one thing, the educational benefits of equalization were by no means obvious, given the findings of the Coleman Report and negative early evaluations of Title I. Also, education remained the quintessential local function, a tradition so engrained that—save in the context of race—it had easily survived the massive growth of state and then federal power during the previous forty years, including the advent of federal aid to education. A ruling of the kind that Arthur Wise and others had in mind would overturn the way that every state bar one funded its schools, transforming American federalism still more than the reapportionment decisions of the early 1960s. Even if the benefits to the poor were clearcut, such a ruling would be contentious, greatly adding to the intense controversy already swirling around the role of the courts in American politics.

How could one of the swing justices—a Byron White, or a Potter Stewart—be persuaded that he should grasp this thorny nettle? Coons, Clune, and Sugarman felt they would need to be persuaded that judicial intervention was compatible with local control and would preserve legislative discretion. That was the primary purpose of *Private Wealth and Public Education*, whose intended audience is evident as early as the dedication page:

whimsically, they chose to dedicate it to the "Nine Old Friends of the Children."[46] To try to win over these "friends," they developed Proposition I: "The quality of public education may not be a function of wealth, other than the wealth of the state as a whole."[47]

What would it mean, in practical terms, if the Supreme Court were to adopt this standard? The simplest way for a state to comply would be complete centralization of funding within a state. That, though, would mean the end of local control. Anxious to show that this was not the necessary outcome of their proposition, Coons and his coauthors unveiled a mechanism that they termed "district power equalizing." At its heart was the idea that districts would be free to levy whatever rate of taxation they pleased, but each rate would only be allowed to generate a certain level of revenue. If, because of a district's poverty, the chosen rate of taxation produced less than that level of revenue, the state would make up the difference. If a district's wealth enabled it to generate revenue in excess of that level, then the surplus would be "recaptured" by the state.

District power equalizing, the authors claimed, was both equitable and compatible with local control. In terms of equity, taxpayers would be rewarded or penalized on the basis of their tax effort, rather than because of the wealth of their neighbors. As for preserving local control and minimizing judicial meddling, it did not require judges to require particular levels of spending, it neither forbade nor mandated different levels of spending for particular groups, and it permitted differences in spending between districts, so long as they were not occasioned by differences in fiscal capacity.[48] State legislators, far from being placed in a straitjacket, would be liberated from the political constraints that had hitherto forced them to distribute resources inequitably. Now, they could experiment with all manner of imaginative remedies. "Considering the multitude of potential compromises," Coons, Clune, and Sugarman concluded, "it is clear that the Supreme Court has the capacity to touch off an explosion of creativity in the structure of education. It is an opportunity that in importance can be compared only to the first flowering of public education in the nineteenth century."[49]

It is superficially surprising that *Private Wealth and Public Education* should have become the "bible" of the school finance reform movement, very soon after its publication in the spring of 1970. Its authors were promoting an unfashionably decentralizing approach and seemed to some to focus more on taxpayer equity rather than on the rights of individual children. That might be politically shrewd, given the rate at which angry taxpayers were defeating bond issues and tax levies. But what would it mean for education? And why should a child lose out on a decent education, simply because his neighbors chose to spend their money on yachts or foreign holidays instead? Was that any less capricious than the existing system?[50]

In part, the impact of the book was a measure of its sheer intellectual firepower. As Kirp and Mark Yudof noted in a review that was simultaneously skeptical and admiring, this was a book that made all previous approaches to the subject "appear almost primitive by comparison."[51] Above all, however, *Private Wealth* came out at a time when approaches more congenial to poverty lawyers, civil rights activists, and big city school systems had all failed. Advocates of those approaches remained keener than ever to topple the existing regime and presumably felt that they could reenter the debate and head off "district power equalizing," vouchers, or other unwelcome reform proposals when legislatures started to debate new solutions. Whatever the theoretical possibilities, it was perhaps hard for them to conceive that a reformed system might deliver less to the poor than the current regime.

Serrano v. Priest: A Victory at Last

When Sidney Wolinsky appeared before the California Supreme Court with John Coons in the spring of 1971, the radical antipoverty lawyer had become a single-minded advocate of Proposition I.[52] The strategy worked. When the California Supreme Court handed down its decision in August, by a margin of 6–1, Judge Raymond Sullivan endorsed Proposition I without qualification. In the most-cited passage of what was to become a much-cited opinion, the court observed that "affluent districts can have their cake and eat it too: they can provide a high quality education for their children while paying lower taxes. Poor districts, by contrast, have no cake at all."[53]

This victory was not purely a result of the quality of superior tactics. The context also mattered. California was already giving serious consideration to reforms that would move the school finance system some way toward the "fiscal neutrality" standard, and the proposal had won the endorsement of the state's influential legislative analyst, A. Alan Post, a Sacramento civil servant whose analytical skill and impartiality were respected by the Reagan administration and by the California chief justice, Donald Wright, who was a Reagan appointee. At first, Wright had doubts about taking the case, but Post persuaded him that legislatively practicable solutions existed, in the event that the lower court decision were reversed.[54]

Also relevant was the character of the California Supreme Court. In a wide-ranging overview of its activities, *Wall Street Journal* reporter Joann Lublin observed that it had "won a reputation as perhaps the most innovative of the state judiciaries, setting precedents in areas of criminal justice, civil liberties, racial integration and consumer protection that heavily influence other states and the federal bench." An admiring Stanford law professor and anti–death penalty activist, Anthony Amsterdam, noted that "the California Supreme Court is to the courts what UCLA is to basketball." Less impressed, the Los Angeles police chief complained that its members "aren't lawyers. They're legislative sociologists."[55] When Coons emphasized the essential conservatism of the case that he was presenting, one of the judges leaned forward from the bench and provided reassurance: "Don't worry, Mr. Coons: We are not shrinking violets."[56]

Once the California Supreme Court had spoken, federal and state judges across the nation swiftly followed its lead. Previously, the cause of school finance reform through the courts had had no momentum whatsoever. Within a month of *Serrano* being handed down, though, dozens of lawsuits had been brought, all modeled on the Coons approach. When the Lawyers' Committee for Civil Rights Under Law (LCCR) convened a conference of litigants, hundreds of lawyers, foundation executives, and civil rights and antipoverty activists showed up. A few weeks later, Coons and an LCCR representative were invited to appear before Walter Mondale's Senate select committee on equality of educational opportunity. It was now that journalists began to draw analogies between *Serrano* and *Brown.*

The Nixon administration shared the view that *Serrano* was a landmark ruling. More than that, it applauded the court's opinion. Sidney Marland, the education commissioner, thought it a "very fundamental breakthrough in the concept of state educational system," and Elliot Richardson praised the decision as "the American ideal of labor rewarded."[57] Meeting with school officials toward the end of September, Nixon remarked that the outcome of the case had been "a shocker, in a way" but nevertheless a "good thing." "The real problem," he went on, was "to find a method for financing education that will enable us to sell the people on support for education," particularly the "retired person on [a] fixed income." In that context, *Serrano* could be regarded as valuable "shock treatment," analogous to the current turmoil in the international monetary system. He hoped that the "California decision may shock us into seeking a better way."[58]

Still, the mood at the post-*Serrano* conference in Washington was not euphoric. Leading reform lawyers worried that the very momentum of their cause might land the issue in the Supreme Court sooner than was desirable. It was encouraging that the new suits were generally copied from the California complaint and that judges in five cases had upheld those complaints by the beginning of 1972.[59] But the precedents needed to be more solid, and there had to be more evidence of states moving toward practicable alternative mechanisms that passed both judicial scrutiny and the test of majoritarian politics, before Coons and Wolinsky could be confident of success before the Burger Court. Washington lawyer John Silard, perhaps influenced by his role in the decidedly precipitate Virginia suit, warned of "the real danger of an over-zealous, overoptimistic dash to the court with a lawyer who hasn't really seen the problem of the remedy or the result, or really even seen the connection between the legal theory and the remedy."[60]

The school finance reform movement was becoming difficult to control. Even if all plaintiffs' lawyers took *Private Wealth* as their bible, were they equipped to defend its complex argument? Stephen Sugarman worried that "when lawyers say they are going to win a *Serrano*-type case," they often "don't know what it is they are going to win." The head of the LCCR's new school finance project, Sarah Carey, felt that "a number of these [suits] are very precipitous and there's some question as to whether they are very well put together." Other lawyers at the meeting noted, presumably with a mixture of regret and pride, that "you can't control lawyers." One remarked that "we are stiff-necked people," urging "let's not delude ourselves that people are going to step in line and file the right suits in the right places alleging the right things."[61]

Three months later, both expectations and anxieties came to a climax when a federal district court in Texas upheld a *Serrano*-based complaint in the case of *Rodriguez v. San Antonio ISD*, and the state appealed to the Supreme Court.

Rodriguez v. San Antonio

Rodriguez had not originally been conceived as a test of Proposition I; it started out being primarily about race. The plaintiffs were Mexican American parents from the San Antonio barrio who had formed a neighborhood action group to protest the insensitivity of their white superintendent toward the educational needs of their children. They had managed to force his resignation, but this had not made much difference to the schools. At the suggestion of a local Latino leader, they visited a San Antonio civil rights attorney, Arthur Gochman, who suggested to them that the basic problem was money and that they should consider a lawsuit. When an application to MALDEF for financial support was turned down, this affluent and committed lawyer decided to finance the suit out of his own pocket. According to Demetrio Rodriguez, the lead plaintiff in the case, Gochman invested as much as $10,000 of his own resources.[62]

The federal court initially withheld judgment, accepting the state's assurance that school finance reform was to be considered by the legislature when it next met. When that session ended, however, no action had been taken, and the case went back to court. By now, *Serrano* had been handed down, Gochman was receiving help from some of the nation's leading school finance experts, and Rodriguez's case—based on Proposition I—looked a lot stronger than before. Still, the state sensed no danger. Rather than wrestle with the arguments of John Coons, the assistant attorney general based his case on the claim that the suit was inspired by socialistic doctrine and foreigners.[63] Unimpressed by this line of reasoning and affronted that the state seemed unwilling to take the case seriously, the three-judge panel unanimously endorsed the constitutional claims of the plaintiffs.[64] The state appealed the decision to the Supreme Court.

A Court Divided: The Burger Court and *Rodriguez*

A decade on, when Coons was asked by an interviewer whether *Rodriguez* had come too soon or too late, he replied: "Both." It came too soon for reasons already discussed. It came too late in the sense that the composition of the Supreme Court in 1972 was less propitious than a few years earlier. Contemplating that agonizingly tight 5–4 decision, he noted that "there is not much doubt how Earl Warren, Arthur Goldberg, and Abe Fortas would have voted."[65]

Certainly, Nixon's four appointees were more conservative than the Warren Era justices whom they replaced.[66] Still, the early years of the Burger Court can hardly be said to have had a consistently conservative cast: these were the years when a woman's right to an abortion was established, the death penalty struck down, and racial balance mandated in desegregating school districts and when employment discrimination started to be construed in terms of impact rather than intent.[67] *Rodriguez* too could easily have gone the other way; reading the available private papers of the justices, it becomes abundantly clear that they found this to be an exceptionally hard one to decide.[68] The Court first discussed the case in conference in early June 1972. In the initial vote, two of the three bellwether justices, Lewis Powell and Potter Stewart, were inclined to reverse the federal court's decision, whereas the other, Byron White, felt that it should be affirmed. That meant an initial 5–4 vote for reversal.

Based on that vote, Burger provisionally assigned the case to Powell, who was the Court's acknowledged expert on education in view of his nine years on the Virginia board of education and a similar span as chairman of the Richmond school board. Initially, Powell saw the case as straightforward, thinking that the district court's opinion had been very poorly constructed. He was particularly offended by the argument that the Texas system lacked any rational basis.[69] Also, he assumed that affirming the lower court ruling would result in centralization, a prospect that he abhorred.[70] In addition, he questioned the premise that poor children necessarily lived in property-poor districts.[71] Finally, he doubted the assumption that spending more money on poor children would automatically result in their getting a better education.[72] Each of these views was strongly reinforced by two powerful briefs that supporters of reversal submitted early on in the Supreme Court's deliberations.[73] Accordingly, Powell asked his senior law clerk, Larry Hammond, to try his hand at drafting a reversal.

By the time that oral arguments came around, however, three months later, Powell was approaching the case with less confidence. That reflected the influence of Hammond, who (like most clerks) tended to think that *Rodriguez* should be affirmed.[74] Instead of composing a draft opinion, he sent Powell a learned forty-four page memorandum, laying out the pros and cons and explaining why he thought them so evenly matched. Responding to arguments that Powell had found appealing in the Texas brief, Hammond argued that there was nothing in the lower court decision that led inexorably to centralization, that affirmance need not result in a deluge of further litigation, and that Coons and his colleagues were not mere "activist scholars" (Powell had used that phrase in his first memo on the case).[75] He felt that Powell (who confessed to not understanding "power-equalizing") should try to find time to read *Private Wealth*: "A reading of their book demonstrates that their thesis is not hare-brained, nor is it shallow. You will undoubtedly dispute many of their conclusions but it would still be helpful to see the case presented in its best light."

Powell, a thorough and intellectually rigorous justice, encouraged his clerks to challenge his thinking.[76] Impressed by Hammond's lengthy and objective memo, he responded with a stream of appreciative notes that showed him to be reconsidering the case. The first, which ran to sixteen pages, started as follows:

Your bench memo of 10/2/72 has absorbed my interest and thought for most of the day (Saturday, Oct. 7). May I say at the outset—without reservation—that your memo is thoughtful and penetrating in its analysis, well organized and exceptionally well expressed. However we finally come out in this vastly important case, your thinking will have made a significant contribution to my thinking and ultimate judgment. After reading the briefs with some care, my initial tentative reaction—as you know—was that the factual assumptions and conclusions of the district court were probably erroneous. Your memorandum has assisted me in a more thoughtful reexamination.[77]

Powell was particularly impressed by his clerk's suggestion that the constitution might be construed as embodying a "fundamental interest" in education, on the grounds that other constitutional rights (especially under the First Amendment) were meaningless for the uneducated.[78] Powell was not necessarily convinced by that argument. How was education different from, say, housing or welfare? What might constitute a constitutionally acceptable minimum level of education? Nevertheless, the argument appealed to him as an educator, and he asked Hammond to give it some more thought. He was less persuaded by the argument that local control could survive affirmance. But, again, he wanted to hear the evidence. Five days before oral arguments were to be heard, he summed up his position: "I would like to find a reasoned and principled position that avoided destroying the usefulness of local control of the schools, and which also minimizes the wide gaps which now exist as a result of primary reliance on local funding."[79]

Oral Arguments

At oral argument, the state of Texas was represented not by its hapless assistant attorney general, but by Charles Alan Wright, professor of law at the University of Texas. Wright was a far more formidable advocate; indeed, it is doubtful that the state could have made a better choice. The author of a classic constitutional law casebook, Wright possessed not simply an encyclopedic knowledge of the Constitution but an exceptional mind, together with considerable energy and charisma.[80] The following year, his presidency in peril, Richard Nixon would select Wright to be his personal lawyer. As that example suggests, he was not just able but also very well connected, a major figure in the world of American law. Among his acquaintances were most members of the current Supreme Court: he had got to know both of the "Minnesota Twins" (Warren Burger and Harold Blackmun) as a junior law professor at the University of Minnesota, maintained an extensive correspondence with William Brennan, had a warm and mutually appreciative relationship with Powell, and was particularly close to Potter Stewart.[81]

Wright was an experienced and highly successful practitioner before the Supreme Court bar, having appeared before it on ten previous occasions, eight of them since 1968.[82] Reflecting on this record, a law school colleague could not "think of anyone, except perhaps the Solicitor General, who would have argued [such] a string of important cases as Charlie did in such a compact period." He had only lost three of them, and his most recent appearance, just two days earlier, had gone so well that it would result in the Court's vacating a $145 million antitrust judgment against his client, Howard Hughes.[83]

Meanwhile, Demetrio Rodriguez was still being represented by Arthur Gochman, the San Antonio attorney whose financial support had helped to get the suit off the ground and without whose commitment it would never have reached the Supreme Court. Doubtless he was a talented as well as a committed lawyer, but some leading figures in the national movement for school finance reform viewed the prospect of his appearance with anxiety, regarding him as an essentially provincial figure, clearly out of his depth. During the federal court hearing, one of them had reportedly had a "ghastly" time "trying to keep Gochman on the rails."[84]

Stephen Browning of LCCR worried that a stronger legal context needed to be established before Proposition I was tested in the Supreme Court and tried to persuade Gochman to ask it to hold the case in abeyance, but Gochman insisted that it go forward. Then, Browning and his colleagues implored him to step aside in favor of an attorney with greater experience, but Gochman again resisted, even though—as Coons later exclaimed—"we could have had Archie Cox!"[85] James Kelly, a program officer at the Ford Foundation who specialized in school finance, says that Gochman had never even seen the outside of the Supreme Court building, prior to arriving in the nation's capital to argue the *Rodriguez* case, and recalls that "the entire civil rights intelligentsia of Washington, D.C." spent a week trying to prepare him for what lay ahead. According to this account, the cramming session did not go well: Kelly remembers one agitated participant having stormed out of the room at one point, declaring: "Holy shit."[86]

Reading the transcript of the oral argument, it is painfully evident that Wright and Gochman were poorly matched. In terms of style, Wright comes across as composed, urbane, seemingly enjoying his second appearance before the court that week. He made his points with economy and force, and according to Coons, who was sitting in the courtroom, his performance was "fabulous."[87] By contrast, Gochman appears to have been ill at ease and out of his depth, hopping about from point to point, losing the thread, contradicting himself, and giving convoluted and prolix answers to questions. (The previous week's cramming session had probably been counterproductive.) It seems that he was a less commanding figure than the dapper Wright in other ways, too: in his sparse notes, Harry Blackmun dismissed Gochman as "smaller, balding."[88]

Wright both began and ended with references to *Private Wealth and Public Education*. Acknowledging the sophistication of its argument, Wright concentrated on the criticisms that were being leveled at Proposition I and "district power equalizing" by *advocates* of reform.[89] If the experts were in such disagreement regarding the system that should replace the current regime, was it wise for the Supreme Court to leap into this thicket? Was it not a legislative matter, and one that required further research?

That was a telling point, but not the one that had the greatest impact on Wright's audience, to judge from the notes that the justices made as they were listening and from their subsequent remarks in conference. Still more wounding was his claim that both Proposition I and "power equalizing" might be unconstitutional. If there was a "fundamental interest" in education, as reformers claimed, how could the amount of money spent on schooling be made contingent on the willingness of taxpayers to support schooling? Surely the only constitutional alternative to the current regime would be not "power equalizing" but statewide uniformity? In *that* case, though, some poor children (those in cities, those with special needs) would lose out, because per-pupil school spending on them exceeded the state average. Accordingly, was this case not more about taxpayer relief than education? Thinking more broadly, what would centralization mean for the future of federalism? If education were centralized on the grounds that it was a "fundamental interest" and that no other remedy passed constitutional muster, could not the same be said of housing, or welfare, or health, or sanitation services?

Coons and his colleagues had addressed some of these questions in their book, but it is unlikely that any of the justices other than Powell had read *Private Wealth*. For them, everything would depend on the quality of Gochman's response. In the face of Wright's "fabulous" performance, even Archibald Cox might have struggled to counter some of Wright's arguments. Certainly, it is not surprising that the inexperienced Gochman failed to do so. Adding to his discomfort, justices who had allowed Wright to present substantial portions of his prepared statement without interruption peppered Gochman with questions almost from the outset. First they asked him whether it was really the case that poor children necessarily lived in property-poor districts. Gochman replied in the affirmative. Then they asked him about the "slippery slope" argument: if education were to be declared a "fundamental" constitutional interest, could not the same claim be made on behalf of other services? Gochman's answers were garbled. Finally, they quizzed him at length about "district power-equalizing" and Proposition I, wondering how he could support an approach that might result in spending on the education of the poor going down rather than up. Gochman responded by saying that he could not imagine such a contingency, given the ghastliness of the existing system. Then he added that he did not necessarily endorse power equalizing and commended alternative reform agendas that were then being considered by the state legislature.

At that point, Gochman's thirty minutes were up, before he had even addressed any of Wright's points in a systematic way. The experienced Wright, however, still had some time left, having reserved six minutes for rebuttal. Presumably feeling that Gochman had all but rebutted himself, he did not devote much time to responding to his opponent's arguments. Instead, he lavished praise on Coons and applauded the "devotion and ability with which Mr. Gochman has persevered in this case." In his view, "these people have opened the eyes of the whole country to a very serious problem."[90] Then came the sting in the tail. "Everyone in this courtroom would agree that what we want is better education for all children and especially for poor children." It was not clear whether the remedies proffered by Gochman and Coons would, however, "lead to better education or only more education, whether they would relieve poor children or only children who happen to live in poor school districts," and "whether the remedy that has been offered here is . . . of no benefit to children but only . . . to taxpayers."[91]

Deciding *Rodriguez*

Five days later, the justices met in conference. By now, Lewis Powell's doubts about the case were resolved: he delivered a crisp statement of the case for reversal, restating many of the points that Wright had made in oral argument.[92] Warren Burger, Harry Blackmun, and William Rehnquist each indicated that they also supported reversal of the district court ruling. William Brennan, William Douglas, Byron White, and Thurgood Marshall, meanwhile, still felt that it should be affirmed.[93] That left the outcome in the hands of Potter Stewart. On balance, he was inclined to join Powell, not least because the talk at oral arguments had been more about poor school districts than poor people, but he told colleagues that he was "not at rest."[94] Powell and Marshall (to whom Douglas had assigned the task of making the case for affirmance) proceeded to compete for Stewart's allegiance. Marshall sent a clerk away to produce a lengthy draft opinion that was specifically designed to address the Ohioan's concerns.[95] Meanwhile, Powell shared an early draft opinion with Stewart, before circulation to the conference, and modified it in response to his suggestions.[96] Shortly after that, Marshall circulated his draft opinion, which was widely admired, even by Powell. But it failed to persuade Stewart; following another round of alterations, he signed on to Powell's opinion, providing him with the decisive fifth vote.[97] The effort to secure school finance reform through the federal courts was at an end.

Explaining *Rodriguez*

Why did school finance reform fare less well in the federal courts than bilingual education and education for the handicapped? In the case of disability rights, one big difference was that Fred Weintraub and his colleagues were able to shield the issue from the Supreme Court. Had *PARC* or *Mills v. Board of Education* been appealed to the Supreme Court, it is not obvious that they would have been upheld; just like Coons, Weintraub felt that the constitutional case was vulnerable. But, through a mixture of skill and good fortune, the test never happened. Instead, the cause of education rights for the handicapped flourished in the lower courts and in state legislatures, to such an extent that when Congress enacted 94-142, it seemed to be simply encoding rights that had already been secured. Coons and his colleagues, by contrast, were unable to keep the question of school finance reform away from the Supreme Court, not least because the issue had such tremendous momentum in the aftermath of *Serrano* and was quite beyond their power to control.

In part, *Mills* and *PARC* were not appealed to the Supreme Court because the state and district officials being sued felt a warm sympathy for the objectives of the suits. Quite apart from that, an ambitious politician such as Governor Milton Shapp of Pennsylvania did not want to be put in the position of having to defend the ghastly conditions at the Pennhurst state school. By contrast, although the effects of unjust consequences of school finance arrangements were not hard to document, they were scarcely as vivid, while the cause of local control retained some appeal. And although this cause was fought on behalf of the poor, the claim was not unproblematic: equalization could result in reduced spending in the ghetto, and in a "power-equalized" system, taxpayer relief might trump better schools.

Another distinguishing feature of the school finance case was the lack of a clear constituency. Although bilingual education and education of the disabled started out as top-down reform projects, at least there were clear, articulate constituencies that could be mobilized around these respective causes: bilingual teachers and language minorities in the one case, special education teachers and the parents of handicapped children in the other. Each cause developed a network with roots and passion. By contrast, the school finance reform network had passion but not roots. Teachers and school districts were not centrally involved, for the most part, and neither were the poor. To a much greater degree than in the other instances, this was a lawyers' cause.

Bilingual education *did* reach the Supreme Court, but with a different outcome. In *Lau v. Nichols* the Court was able to avoid a constitutional rationale because of the existence of a statutory route. Despite the incongruous advocacy of Solicitor General Robert Bork, the case would probably not have gone the same way had it hinged decisively on equal protection grounds. Although the Burger Court was more willing than is sometimes acknowledged to strike out bold new constitutional ground, its Fourteenth Amendment jurisprudence was comparatively circumspect, and *Lau* illustrates that fact as well as *Rodriguez*.

Finally, the broader implications of *San Antonio v. Rodriguez* for federal-state relations were enormous. Coons, Clune, and Sugarman strove hard to alleviate the Burger Court's concerns on this score, by emphasizing that Proposition 1 and local control were entirely compatible. But it did not work: Concerns about the wider implications of *Rodriguez* heavily influenced the votes of Justices Powell, Stewart, and Blackmun.[98] Each feared that affirmance would establish a precedent with unpredictable but far-reaching consequences for federalism. In his opinion, Lewis Powell argued: "It would be difficult to imagine a case having a greater potential impact on our federal system than the one now before us, in which we are urged to abrogate systems of financing public education presently in existence in virtually every State."[99]

In the light of all this, it is less striking that *Rodriguez* failed than that it came so excruciatingly close to success. For all that the exogenous factors summarized above contributed to the outcome, one must not lose sight of the role played by sheer happenstance. After all, had the state of Texas still been represented by the cavalier assistant attorney general who had so mishandled the case in its earlier stages, or had Demetrio Rodriguez been represented by Archibald Cox or John Coons, the outcome could possibly have been different, despite all of these formidable barriers to success.

The Legacy of *Rodriguez*

What is the enduring significance of *Rodriguez?* To some scholars, it marks the point at which the jurisprudential revolution of the Warren Era reached its limits.[100] *Rodriguez* should not be conceived solely in these terms, however, for it is equally valid to see the litigation of 1968–1973 as the first critical stage in a three-part reform process with enduring consequences. The second stage, triggered by Justice Powell's opinion, was a series of lawsuits in the state courts, aimed at securing the same objective of "fiscal equality" that had been at stake in *Serrano* and *Rodriguez*. The third stage, which began at the end of the 1980s and continued into the twenty-first century, featured lawsuits demanding educational "adequacy" for all children. By 2005, school finance litigation had been filed in all but six states.

Experts disagree about the cumulative effect of all these lawsuits. The fact that there have been so many, over such an extended period of time, and that some suits have dragged on for many years, tells us something about the limits of state courts as instruments of reform, suggesting that this is a story of frustration as well as achievement.[101] Still, a majority of the suits have been won by the plaintiffs, including two-thirds of those filed after 1989. This story does not fit easily into an "end of reform" account of post-1968 politics.

That is especially the case if one places the recent history of school finance litigation in a broader historical context. Before 1968, school finance litigation had been unknown. Despite long-standing concerns about the injustices associated with the existing regime and the difficulty of undertaking comprehensive reform through the legislature, it seemed axiomatic that this was the only available avenue. The Supreme Court did little to encourage the idea that education might be a fundamental right under the Constitution. To the contrary, having hinted at the possibility in *Brown*, the Warren Court maintained a conspicuous silence on the question, despite its adventurous activism in other areas.[102]

By 2002, however, a leading proponent of school finance reform could write that "the emerging *constitutional* concept of adequacy is a prudent judgment concerning the basic educational opportunities that a child will need to take his or her place as a functioning adult in contemporary society."[103]

What made that claim seem not just plausible but "prudent" was the shift from federal to state litigation. At a certain level, it makes obvious sense to see such a shift as being symptomatic of the declining national momentum of the spirit of reform during the 1970s. In the case of school finance, however, the shift may have been helpful. Looking back on *Rodriguez* from the perspective of the mid-1990s, one legal scholar concluded that the early litigants had "lost sight of the most plausible textual basis for arguments addressing issues of adequacy—the state constitutions' education clauses."[104] Whereas the federal constitution says nothing about education, every state constitution includes the right to a "thorough and efficient education," or some equivalent language.[105] Political scientist Douglas Reed sees in the willingness of state courts to take on this issue an important extension of the egalitarian thrust of the Warren Era.[106]

The cycle of litigation that began in 1989 presented a striking contrast to that of the late 1960s and early 1970s. During that earlier period, an initial effort to force legislators to meet the educational "needs" of children yielded to an emphasis on "fiscal neutrality," in response to the strong feeling of judges that need was too "nebulous." Yet the post-1989 suits were based, for the most part, on notions of "educational adequacy" that bore an obvious resemblance to those early, failed claims. In 1971, it was the shift from "need" to "fiscal equality" that gave the movement for school finance reform some desperately needed momentum; in 1989, it was the reverse shift that lay at the heart of its improved success rate.

How is this to be explained? Part of the answer may be that education researchers had developed better ways of measuring adequacy.[107] More important, though, was the emergence after the mid-1980s of a national "standards" movement rooted in the idea that the American education system was failing not just the educationally disadvantaged, but the nation as a whole. Numerous states passed laws establishing minimally accepted educational standards, and with those goals came ideas about what level of provision might be needed in order for the standard to be attained. This gave judges the rule of thumb that they had previously lacked. Ideas of need that seemed far-fetched when adumbrated by the Detroit school board in 1968 now appeared practicable. In that sense too, the debate about school finance reform in the early twenty-first century had progressed in ways that would have appeared improbable in earlier times.

Education Politics in the
Carter-Reagan Years

Teacher Power

CARTER, NEA, AND THE CREATION OF

THE DEPARTMENT OF EDUCATION

Presidents left little imprint on education policymaking after 1965. In part, that reflected White House inattention: education was not a principal concern for the Nixon-Ford presidency, and even Johnson—an education president if ever there was one—could not give the subject very much of his time after 1965. But even when presidents did try to assert themselves, they were conspicuously unsuccessful: Johnson was unable to prevent Congress from adding three clientele-oriented titles to ESEA between 1966 and 1968, Nixon's block grant proposals got nowhere, and efforts by Nixon and Ford to rein in education spending were largely unsuccessful. In those cases, Capitol Hill was the principal locus of education policymaking, with interest groups enjoying striking influence on legislators. In the context of civil rights policymaking, meanwhile, it was two other institutional actors who came to the fore: the federal bureaucracy and the judiciary. Again, White House influence on policymaking was relatively slight, save for Nixon's role in desegregating southern schools. It was all a big change from 1965, when ESEA had been conceived within the Johnson White House and forced through Congress very nearly as proposed.

During the late 1970s, there was one important deviation from this norm: The establishment of a Department of Education (ED) in 1979 was the clearest illustration of presidential leadership in education policy since 1965. Congress was not especially enthusiastic about the idea, many Democrats were opposed, and without President Jimmy Carter's strong backing, the department would not have come into being. The story of how ED came into being also illustrates, however, a further *erosion* of presidential authority: Carter would not have fought for the bill, and most likely would not even have endorsed it, had it not been for the unprecedented influence that the National Education Association enjoyed within his White House. In earlier years, education client groups had come to enjoy great influence within the Congress, the judiciary, and the federal bureaucracy. Now, it seemed, the most important single such group had gained considerable influence with the White House too, despite Carter's emphatic aversion to lobby politics.

NEA's influence owed much to the confluence of two historical streams flowing out of the tumultuous 1960s: the transformation of the NEA from professional association to teacher union and the changes in the Democratic Party's presidential nomination process following the Fraser-McGovern commission.

NEA: From Professional Association to Teacher Union

Back in 1965, NEA was already politically influential and had been for years. Its headquarters were located in the nation's capital, just a few blocks north of the White House, at a time when that was unusual for education organizations. Also, it had a permanent lobbying staff in Washington and in the field, at a time when that too was uncommon, and had ties to paid staff in every state capital. In addition, it had a membership approaching one million, a budget many times larger than that of any other education group, and—not surprisingly, given all this—good ties to key legislators and the Office of Education. But, for all that, it was not as influential as it liked to claim and nowhere near as influential as it would subsequently become. NDEA and ESEA had in a real sense been defeats for NEA, which strongly preferred general aid to categorical assistance.

Leaders of the old-style NEA went to elaborate lengths to project a bipartisan and even above-the-battle image. NEA was not a union, but rather a "professional association," representing not just teachers but the wider education community and the nation's children. A substantial portion of its budget went to statistics gathering and educational research, and its monthly magazine, *NEA Journal*, often featured articles about teaching methods or new technology. When controversial issues were engaged, they normally appeared in the regular "Opinions Differ" column, with two contrasting perspectives being presented side-by-side. The *Journal's* coverage of the Johnson versus Goldwater contest had not even hinted at any partisan preference. Instead, its editor merely reproduced both party platforms and candidate statements, in the hope that this "should help readers make their choice on November 3."[1]

NEA members in 1965 did not engage in anything so sordid as collective bargaining. Rather, they pursued their objectives through "professional negotiation." And when negotiations broke down, the NEA did not endorse strike action. Instead, it employed "professional sanctions." At the association's annual meeting, presidential addresses were long on patriotic rhetoric and Cold War competition and regularly featured paeans to the glorious privilege and responsibility of teaching young minds. Politicians were invited to speak at these gatherings, but their remarks revealed that they understood this to be a nonpolitical, or at least a bipartisan, occasion. As recently as 1956, an internal poll had suggested that only 23 percent of teachers felt that they should get involved in politics.[2]

In part, this reflected the broader character of American politics in the age of the Cold War consensus. It also owed much to the way that the NEA was constituted. First, it contained administrators as well as teachers: the American Association of School Administrators, another member of the "Big Six" education groups, was in fact a constituent element of NEA. Second, it had a federal structure, and many of its strongest state and local chapters were in rural and conservative parts of the country.[3] Third, the federal role in elementary and secondary education was small, efforts to expand that role continually ran aground, and most of the NEA's important political business was conducted in state capitals, rather than Washington. Fourth, the Washington staff was dominated by administrators rather than teachers, and the long-standing executive director, William Carr, was a British-born, Canadian-raised conservative. He cherished the association's professional status and its research focus and was committed to preserving its traditional character. In that ambition, he was not unduly disturbed by the coming and going of successive NEA presidents, who held office for only a year and tended to regard the position as being primarily honorific.[4]

During the 1960s, though, the NEA leadership increasingly came under challenge from reform-minded elements, leaving Carr embattled. Many teachers (growing proportions of them married, and male) objected to low pay and poor working conditions that belied all the pious talk at headquarters about professionalism. Black teachers and white allies demanded that the NEA's seventeen all-white state affiliates be disaffiliated or forced to integrate. And in urban areas where NEA was under strong pressure from the rival American Federation of Teachers, labor-oriented chapters urged greater militancy and abandonment of the polite fictions of "professional negotiation" and "sanctions." There, and in places where administrators were unsympathetic and money for schools hard to raise, teachers increasingly rejected the notion that they and their principals and superintendents were united by some mystical higher calling.

Confronted with all of these strains, and in the wider context of tumult and dissension that marked the later 1960s, the old NEA collapsed.[5] In 1965, two state affiliates energized by successful strike action formed Political Action Committees (PACs), sparking a debate about whether the national association should follow suit. The following year, segregated affiliates were instructed to integrate or leave the association. This proved to be an agonizing process that was not completed until 1974, but the NEA's election of its first black president, Elizabeth Koontz, in 1967 highlighted how much the association had already changed. That same year, Carr stepped down, after fifteen years at the helm, and was replaced by his protégé, Samuel Lambert, a moderate who nevertheless recognized the need to respond more forcefully to the changes sweeping through the organization.[6] By this time, teachers were entirely dominant within the association, collective bargaining was the norm, strike action was commonplace, and the NEA's transformation into a labor union was already greatly advanced. (The administrators formally disaffiliated in 1970.)

A further threshold was crossed during the early years of the Nixon presidency, perceived within NEA as "antieducation." Association presidents during this era, especially George Fischer and Donald Morrison, excoriated Nixon in the most inflammatory terms. According to Stanley McFarland, whose team of NEA lobbyists continued to build cross-party alliances on the Hill, Fischer was a "bull in a china closet," a man with "an ego that wouldn't stop."[7] As for Morrison, when Nixon introduced a wage-price freeze that resulted in a delay to teacher pay raises, he characterized it as "probably the grossest violation of rights since we put the Japanese-Americans in concentration camps during World War-II."[8]

By this time, the association was taking an interest in all manner of issues that had no direct connection to education: it opposed the Haynsworth and Carswell nominations, for example, and also the bombing of Cambodia.[9] By 1971, President Morrison seemed intoxicated by visions of teacher power, declaring that "teachers' potential influence in political matters staggers the imagination. The time is right."[10]

The logical culmination of all these events and trends came in 1972–1973. First, in 1972, the NEA formed a Political Action Committee. Although the membership decided not to make a formal endorsement in that year's presidential election, the leadership made its preferences clear when its immediate past president, Don Morrison, its current president, Catharine Barrett, and its president-elect, Helen Wise, formed a group called "Educators for McGovern."[11] NEA-PAC did get heavily involved in the year's congressional elections, playing a decisive role in the reelection of Senator Claiborne Pell (D-R.I.), chair of the Labor and Public Welfare Committee's education subcommittee.[12] The editors of *NEA Journal* reveled in this triumph for "teacher power." Then, in 1973, Sam Lambert was forced to resign as executive director and was replaced by Terry Herndon, a thirty-three-year-old militant labor activist from Michigan who had previously headed the NEA's Department of Collective Bargaining.

Under Herndon's leadership, the NEA's transformation into a labor union with broad left-leaning political interests and enormous political clout was completed. Still opposed to affiliating with the AFL-CIO, it instead made common cause with a number of other, expanding white-collar unions, forming the Coalition of American Public Employees.[13] NEA president John Ryor grandly declared: "We must become the foremost political power in the nation."[14] One important manifestation of that ambition was an announcement that NEA intended to endorse a presidential candidate in 1976.[15]

Carter and NEA in 1976

Of all the candidates for the Democratic nomination—the other leading contenders were Senators Henry "Scoop" Jackson (Wash.) and Birch Bayh (Ind.) and Congressman Morris Udall (Ariz.)—it was Carter who recognized the potential value to his candidacy of NEA's announcement. Perhaps that reflected his superior grasp of a related, but broader, development in American politics: the transformation of the Democratic Party's presidential nomination process. Until recently, the delegates who chose the nominee had been selected by state and local party establishments that were dominated by party regulars: machine bosses, elected officials, labor leaders. In some states, delegates were obliged by the outcome of a primary election to support a particular candidate, but the most common forum for making this decision was a closed-party caucus. In combination with a number of other practices, this meant that the candidate with the broadest appeal in primary elections would not necessarily prevail at the national convention.[16] That was why Hubert Humphrey had been nominated in 1968, despite not having even entered those contests.

Still, Humphrey's nomination proved to be the last hurrah for the old Democratic politics, for the outrage that it provoked among the New Politics activists who had flocked to the primary campaigns of Robert F. Kennedy and Eugene McCarthy forced the party to create a Commission on Party Structure and Delegate Selection, or the Fraser-McGovern Commission. Based on its recommendations, the party adopted new procedures, insisting on primaries or open conventions, requiring delegates to commit themselves to a particular candidate, and establishing quotas for three constituencies: women, African Americans, and young people. The result was to open up the process to the activist and often narrowly focused New Politics constituencies that had first come to the fore in 1968 and to greatly diminish the authority of the party regulars. Following the McGovern debacle of 1972, some of these rules were modified, but the key to winning the nomination continued to lie in appealing to particularist, activist constituencies: among them were environmentalists, feminists, consumer advocates, public sector unions—and teachers.

It was this imperative that made Jimmy Carter's nomination possible. Under the old rules, so obscure a candidate could surely not have overcome someone like Jackson or Humphrey (another contender), with their deep roots in the party. In 1976, however, initial obscurity turned out to be one of Carter's greatest assets: lacking standing within the national party and largely unknown outside of Georgia, he had no alternative but to tend to the party's new grassroots. So when NEA announced its intention to make an endorsement in 1976 and invited prospective candidates to meet with its leadership, Carter responded with alacrity, joining a gathering of the union's state leaders in Las Vegas in the fall of 1974. He was the only presidential aspirant to take up the invitation.

Herndon recalls having had to "really twist arms" to get any delegates to attend the breakfast that he had organized for Carter. And Stanley McFarland remembers that even the head of the Georgia affiliate was reluctant to attend, feeling that Carter had not been a good friend of the Georgia Education Association during his term as governor.[17] (Another problem, he adds, was finding a grocery store in Las Vegas that sold grits.) But if that suggests an inauspicious start to the relationship, an important seed had been planted. In conversation with Carter, McFarland and Herndon were each impressed by his intelligence and drive, and when Carter got in touch again a year later, they knew who he was.

The occasion for that second interaction was the run-up to the crucial Iowa caucus. Speaking to a group of teachers in Waterloo, Iowa, Carter formally declared his support for one of NEA's core objectives, establishing a cabinet-level Department of Education.[18] That was an important gesture, but it was not enough to secure the NEA's backing. Cannily, the national body decided to defer to the state associations during the primaries: if NEA delegates were committed to more than one candidate, that increased the likelihood that the association would play an influential role at the convention, should the nomination remain undecided. Neither did Carter's announcement win over the Iowa teachers: they preferred their fellow midwesterner, Birch Bayh. Still, as in Las Vegas, Carter did not give up on the NEA. On the contrary, he called Executive Secretary Herndon at home. Explaining that he was anticipating victory in Iowa, Carter told Herndon that he knew that its teachers were committed to Bayh and hoped that they would not resent his likely success over the Indianan, since he was keen to maintain a good relationship with educators.[19]

Carter duly won the Iowa caucus, went on to win the New Hampshire primary, and became an improbable front-runner. By the time delegates met in New York City in July, he had sewed up the nomination. Of those 3,000 delegates, 172 were affiliated to the NEA, a testament to the tactical acumen of its state affiliates and national leadership during the primary season.[20] No other labor organization came close to this figure. Indeed, only one *state*, California, supplied more delegates than did the NEA. The choice of Walter Mondale as Jimmy Carter's running mate probably owed something to the NEA's influence too: he was a strong supporter of the association, and his brother, Mort, was president of the Minnesota Education Association. According to Herndon, when Mondale learned that his name was being mentioned as a possible running mate, he asked NEA to effect an introduction to Carter, who had not yet spoken to him and whom he had never met.[21] Certainly, in his witty address to the association the following year, the vice president would make clear his sense of obligation:

> It's a delight to be with John Ryor again who I understand is the first President of the NEA ever to be re-elected. The President and I would like to see you John shortly in the White House to see how it's done. I've always considered John a person of extraordinary judgment and

thoughtfulness; but when he led that delegation of the labor coalition presidents to see Jimmy Carter in New York last July and urged that he pick me as Carter's running mate, I realized that Ryor was a man of true vision.[22]

Already influential at the convention, the NEA's importance to the Carter campaign increased during the summer and fall of 1976, as his one-time 30-point lead over Gerald Ford evaporated. It is not just that the union poured $400,000 into the Democratic campaign, or that teachers voted in unusually large numbers (85 percent of NEA members went to the polls, according to one account, making a decisive difference to the outcome in Ohio, Pennsylvania, and Florida).[23] Also important was the grassroots organizing capability of NEA, with members in almost every political precinct in the nation and an average of 4,000 members in each congressional district. In his speech to NEA the following year, Mondale reminisced that "you didn't just endorse us, you worked for our ticket. I never stopped at a single campaign stop at any time in that campaign where there wasn't a good turnout of NEA participants working to elect Mr. Carter the President. We want to live up to the trust you showed us last November."[24]

After the Election

Following Carter's tight victory over Ford, John Ryor exulted that "teachers in 1976 earned an 'A' in Advanced Politics." Carter's campaign manager, Hamilton Jordan, acknowledged that "the massive support from teachers was crucial to our winning this election. All over the nation, we turned to the NEA for assistance. We asked for their help, and they delivered." President-elect Carter called Ryor immediately after the election to thank him for his staunch support.[25]

But the warm afterglow of victory soon faded, yielding to a mood of mounting anxiety at NEA regarding the extent of its influence on the Carter White House, which seemed to be much less than Ryor had anticipated. Carter's desire to draw a strict distinction between campaigning and governing was part of the explanation. The new president had a pronounced distaste for what he took to be the seedy and self-serving world of lobby politics and had campaigned as a nonpolitician who would clean out the Augean stables of Washington. Quite apart from that, *any* president has no choice but to place the demands of particular interest groups in the context of overall budgetary and policy priorities. Jimmy Carter reflected on this responsibility in his presidential memoir, *Keeping Faith:*

When the interests of powerful lobbyists were at stake, a majority of the members [of Congress] yielded to a combination of political threats and the blandishments of heavy campaign contributions.

Members of Congress, buffeted from all sides, are much more vulnerable to these groups than is the President. One branch of government must stand fast on a particular issue to prevent the triumph of self-interest at the expense of the public. . . . When Congress and the Presidency succumb to the same pressures and bad legislation is passed, the damage to our nation can be very serious.[26]

Elsewhere in his memoir, the moralistic Carter took pride in having battled legislators on pork-barrel projects, noting that an unwise early compromise on a matter of principle had stiffened his resolve in subsequent encounters with Congress. He remarked that even though "oil producers, *teachers*, lumber companies, veterans, and other groups" certainly had the right to organize in pursuit of sectional interests, "ultimately, public officials have to decide what action to take for the public good."[27]

1977: A Waiting Game

On the campaign trail, Carter could endorse the creation of a federal Department of Education without feeling that he was compromising his principles. True, he generally opposed the proliferation of executive agencies and had promised to cut their number from 1,900 to 200. But concentrating education programs that were currently administered by some twenty different agencies into one new department could be seen as an act of consolidation.[28] During the transition, however, and during the early part of Carter's presidency, the administrative advantages of such a move became less obvious. A transition task force came out against the idea, on the grounds that a second-tier ED secretary would be an ineffective advocate: "It was better to have a fraction of the HEW Secretary's time than a second-rank Secretary of Education."[29] That was also the dominant feeling within the Office of Management and Budget. Its head, Bert Lance, to whom Carter was close, opposed the new department. So too did members of Lance's Presidential Reorganization Program (PRP), which was responsible for designing an overall plan for reshaping the federal government.[30] The most vociferous opponent, though, was Joseph Califano, whom Carter had appointed as secretary of HEW. He continued to believe, as he had during the Johnson administration, that the president should have fewer people reporting to him rather than more, and he felt that an NEA-captured department would lack credibility.[31]

On the other hand, some of Carter's most influential advisers—chief of staff Hamilton Jordan, press secretary Jody Powell—were less interested in policy substance than in narrowly political considerations.[32] Jordan, Vice President Mondale, and Les Francis (a former NEA official who worked in the congressional liaison office) strongly favored an early restatement of the campaign promise to create a Department of Education.

Despite their pressure, however, Carter took his time. By March, Terry Herndon was so concerned that he sent the president a letter in which he complained that he and his colleagues were "becoming increasingly anxious regarding our plight" and requested a personal meeting. "Your promise for a Cabinet-level Department of Education," he charged, "appears to be of no consequence to your appointees. Many fears and anxieties would be quelled if you would reaffirm this promise and make a specific announcement regarding schedules and assignments for its fulfillment."[33] When the meeting that Herndon had requested took place a month later, however, the outcome was disappointing. Far from "reaffirming his promise," Carter equivocated. Califano, who was also there, recalls his satisfaction as the president "hedged," going no further than to pledge to "work on it and study it." He continues:

> As I sat there, I sensed that Carter, whatever he had felt during the
> campaign, had serious doubts whether the separate department was
> a good idea. McFarland's face revealed the same intuition. He sensed
> the danger to NEA's cherished goal; his cheeks flushed, he started
> to speak, but then remained silent. Carter read what I had seen
> in McFarland's face and said that he would have Mondale, the
> administration's strongest proponent for a separate department,
> and me review the situation.[34]

Things got worse. Not surprisingly, Mondale and Califano could not agree on a solution.[35] Instead, they recommended a six-month review by OMB. NEA initially saw that as a step forward, thinking that the OMB study group would be studying the question of "how" to implement the campaign pledge. But when McFarland and two government relations colleagues met with its members, they learned that the question was still "whether" it was a good idea. An in-house NEA history of the broader ED struggle by Gail Bramblett, one of those colleagues, captures the occasion:

> Stan McFarland, Ros Baker, and Gail Bramblett, representing the NEA
> in the meeting[,] were suddenly confronted with a group whose attitude

appeared to range from questionable neutrality to outright opposition to the concept of a Department of Education. Needless to say, we were dumbfounded. After about five minutes of questions and answers on "why there should be a Department of Education," Stan's disgust became obvious. He finally intercepted the "philosophical discusser" with the flat pronouncement: "The issue of whether there should be or there should not be a Department of Education is not before us now. That was decided—in 1976—and by the final authority [of] President Jimmy Carter. We're here to discuss when, how and what shape it will be."[36]

Patricia Gwaltney, head of the PRP's human resources operation, was reportedly so upset by the tone of this meeting that "she did not return NEA's phone calls for the next month-and-a-half."[37] Six months earlier, NEA had helped to elect a president. Now, it seemed, it could not even make contact with middle-ranking officials in the Office of Management and Budget. Part of the problem was that when Domestic Policy Staff (DPS) officials totted up all the pledges that had been made during the 1976 campaign, they arrived at a total of 200 distinct and sometimes contradictory promises. Clearly, those could not all be redeemed at once, if ever.[38] And education was not a priority issue for the new administration: in comparison to arms control, international human rights, economic recession, and the energy crisis, it lacked urgency.[39] Neither was it a priority matter on the Hill: bills to create a Department of Education had been introduced every year since the early 1960s, but such was the lack of interest in them that not one had even been considered in committee. In these circumstances, Carter decided according to Jordan—that "major commitments made during the campaign deserve a close review from the different perspective of the Presidency in light of changing circumstances and better information."[40] A White House aide confirmed that decision to the *Washington Post* in mid-1977: "The President is dealing with a clean slate. He will make a decision based on merit . . . not on the needs of separate constituent groups."[41]

Although that claim was a little suspect, stated so boldly, it makes sense that even interest groups whose support had been vital to the Carter campaign might struggle to have commensurate influence during the early months of his presidency. At this stage, the administration was comparatively popular, the White House emphasis was on charting out a broad agenda for the next four years that bore Carter's distinctive stamp, and pressing outside events clamored for presidential attention. Meanwhile, a

White House whose members had little knowledge of Washington politics struggled to learn its complex ways. In that environment, and with renomination and reelection worries not immediately pressing, niggling campaign promises having to do with secondary issues had comparatively little political salience.

Still, by November 1977 Carter had made a private decision to renew his support for an Education Department, a couple of months later he would make that decision public, and in April 1978 administration officials testified before the Senate in support of Senator Abraham Ribicoff's ED bill. One reason was that OMB had overcome its skepticism about the concept of a Department of Education. That probably owed something to the internal dynamic of an intensive, six-month reorganization investigation. As Radin and Hawley put it, "after all, reorganizers want to reorganize."[42] It is likely too that Hamilton Jordan put personal pressure on them to move the question on from "whether" to "how."[43] Whatever the explanation, when they presented their findings to Carter in November, their top preference, among three possibilities, was for a new "Department of Education and Human Development." Their second preference was for Califano's recommendation: a department based on a defense-type model, with undersecretaries for each of HEW's three core functions. Their least favorite option was for a narrow Department of Education, to be created simply by taking the "E" out of HEW.

The administration's change of heart was also influenced by the fact that Senator Abraham Ribicoff had by this time commenced hearings on a bill to create a Department of Education.[44] This move, carefully coordinated with NEA, was intended to force the administration to end its procrastination, and it had the desired effect. Bert Carp, Stuart Eizenstat's deputy on the Domestic Policy Staff and a close ally of NEA, feared that "the chances are excellent that we will wind up politically with the worst of all worlds— open alienation of the NEA and a major hassle with the Congress next year." Eizenstat concurred, noting that he was "very concerned with alienating NEA."[45] The most important move was that Hamilton Jordan warned Carter about the possibility that Congress would pass the Ribicoff bill before the president had gotten around to endorsing it:

> If we opposed the establishment of a separate department and had
> Congress create such an entity over our objection, we would be in an
> impossible situation politically. *It would be difficult to veto a bill that was*
> *compatible with a campaign promise and embarrassing to sign a bill which had*

created, over our objection, a department we had promised in the campaign. In terms of Congressional outlook, I think that you have to assume that a bill creating a separate Department of Education would have very few opponents.[46]

The resignation of Bert Lance in September following allegations of improper financial dealings may also have played a role in resolving the debate within the administration about ED. His successor at OMB, James McIntyre, was less interested than Lance in the management side of the job and a much less substantial figure, in terms of his influence with the president. To judge from the rather limited memo traffic in the Carter library, he was inclined, like Jordan, to think of education reorganization through an exclusively political lens.

When members of the ED reorganization team met with Carter in November to brief him on their three options, he went with their first preference, indicating that he wanted "the broadest possible Department of Education we can get." Quite what that meant was unclear: the OMB took it to mean a broad education and human development department, but when Carter left the room, Eizenstat stood up and asserted that political feasibility dictated a narrow department, on the grounds that veterans, civil rights groups, nutrition advocates, Head Start partisans, and Indians would all be likely to oppose a broad one, making passage impossible.[47] That alarmed the reorganization team, for whom this was the least satisfactory of the three options that they had outlined. But a few months later, when McIntyre and Eizenstat sent Carter recommendations for a relatively narrow department, the president overruled them, instructing his OMB chief to testify to Ribicoff on behalf of a substantially broader measure, one that could be defended on its merits and not merely on grounds of political expediency.[48] NEA had finally secured White House backing for an ED bill, but Carter seemed to have managed to hold on to his principles too. Whether or not so broad a bill could be passed was another matter.[49]

The ED Fight in 1978: Teacher Power and Its Limits

Although the administration endorsed Ribicoff's broad bill in April 1978, it was nearly eighteen months before Congress approved the measure, by which time it had become much narrower in scope. Initially, Ribicoff's bill had made good progress, negotiating some tricky parliamentary hurdles and passing the Senate by the impressive margin of 71–22. In the House, however, it ran into difficulty, and 1978 ended without its having come to a vote.

Much the same pattern unfolded in 1979, at first, but the outcome was different: in the House, the ED bill squeaked through the Government Affairs Committee by 20 votes to 19, and it prevailed on the floor by the agonizingly close margin of 210–206.

The story of how the Department of Education came about, and why its legislative journey was so difficult, sheds light on both the extent and the limits of NEA power.[50] Eventual passage was indisputably a testament to the new political power of the union, following the dramatic changes that it had undergone during the previous decade. In particular, the creation of NEA-PAC and the decision to endorse Jimmy Carter had transformed its influence. In 1972, when the PAC was created, it contributed to the campaigns of 32 congressional candidates. Four years later, the figure had climbed to 300, of whom more than 80 percent had been successful, and by 1978 it had reached 350.[51] A majority of representatives in the 96th Congress had received the endorsement of the NEA. As for the Carter endorsement, it was clear by 1979 that the NEA's investment had paid off handsomely. During the summer of 1979—when the prospects of the ED bill looked indifferent—President Carter personally lobbied as many as a dozen members of congress, impressing on them that this was one of the administration's highest priorities.

The NEA devoted an extraordinary amount of time and effort to the struggle for the ED bill, which had become a vital symbolic test of its political power.[52] Gail Bramblett, who was deeply involved in the legislative effort, emphasized the scale of the operation in the helpful in-house history that she prepared in 1980. NEA, she revealed, helped Ribicoff staffers to craft the initial bill, dictated the timing of the first set of hearings, advised the committee on which witnesses it should call, mobilized other interest groups, found cosponsors, organized grassroots pressure on key legislators, negotiated amendments, held "how to" training sessions for inexperienced lobbyists, debated parliamentary strategy with committee staffers, conducted vote counts, funded an advertising blitz in the press, and advised the White House on which legislators needed calls from Carter and Mondale.[53] In 1978, three NEA government relations lobbyists worked full-time on the ED bill. In 1979, as many as half a dozen did so.

Without this effort the ED bill would have sunk without trace, as so many similar proposals had in the past. Even with NEA's backing, the proposal ran into severe difficulties, especially in the House of Representatives. Part of the problem was that the bill did not go to Carl Perkins's Education and

Labor Committee, with which NEA had close ties, but instead to the Government Affairs Committee, which it knew much less well. The chairman was Jack Brooks of Texas, who had little enthusiasm for the ED bill and required White House pressure before he would even commence hearings. Some of the Democrats on the committee, moreover, had ties to groups that were hostile to the bill or to NEA: the American Federation of Teachers, the AFL-CIO, the U.S. Catholic Conference (the opposition of these groups is discussed further below). Ben Rosenthal of New York and Leo Ryan of California, two of those Democrats, made common cause with conservative Republicans on the committee, led by John Erlenborn (Ill.), in a bid to prevent the ED bill from reaching the floor. Stanley McFarland tried to persuade Brooks to expedite matters, but found him "hard to reach" and adamant that he was going to run his committee his own way.[54] According to one account, the chairman greatly resented pressure from lobbyists, exploding to NEA officials on one occasion that "your teachers are crawling all over us."[55]

The Texan's outburst suggests an additional reason why the ED bill fell short in 1978. Despite Carter's intervention with chairman Brooks earlier in the session, the overall strategy for passing the bill was being directed overwhelmingly from NEA headquarters. Such was its dominance, and so muted was the role of the White House, that the measure was being tagged an "NEA bill." The impression gained ground that nobody else much wanted it. Superficially, that might not seem too much of a problem, given that a majority of members of the House had received money from the NEA. Still, that very fact might have made them sensitive to the allegation of good government groups (such as John Gardner's Common Cause) that their votes were for sale to the highest bidder.[56] Post-Watergate, that sort of charge might be especially wounding, especially to members of the big Democratic freshman class of 1974, many of whom had come to Washington, a bit like Carter would two years later, pledged to stamp out corrupt political practices.[57]

Anxiety about interest group influence was also strong within the House Democratic leadership, whose members associated NEA power with the decline in their own political authority that had taken place during the 1970s. As early as 1969, Speaker John McCormack and Majority Leader Carl Albert had worried about the growing impact of education interest groups, fearing that the activities of the full-funding coalition posed a threat to institutional comity and to the authority of the Appropriations Committee. Since that time, the power attached to a leadership position had deteriorated markedly, following the institutional changes of the Watergate years. In the aftermath of those changes, Speaker "Tip" O'Neill, Majority Leader Jim Wright (D-Tex.), and Majority Whip John Brademas strove to keep intact such authority as they had retained.

To judge from anecdotal evidence, they regarded the NEA with some suspicion and at times with outright animosity. Speaker O'Neill in particular had an uneasy relationship with the union: this Boston-Irish, New Deal Democrat was reluctant to acknowledge that "NEA was an up-and-coming political force in American labor," one that deserved his respect. NEA government relations staff struggled to establish a good relationship with him in 1978. That became a problem when the ED bill was eventually reported out of committee near the end of the session and needed strong backing from the Speaker and the majority leader if it was to make it onto the House calendar. As for the third-ranking Democrat, when NEA lobbyists attempted to apply political pressure to Brademas, he was reportedly furious, buttonholing McFarland and demanding that he "pull your people off me."[58]

NEA officials recognized that if the ED bill were to pass, it needed to surmount the damaging perception that only NEA wanted it and only NEA was fighting for it. The obvious solution was for the union to try to take a less conspicuous lobbying role, but that was easier said than done, for it was not at all clear to McFarland and his colleagues who else could be entrusted with the task. Within the Carter administration, there was no Larry O'Brien or Wilbur Cohen to pick up the slack. On the contrary, Carter's congressional liaison team, headed by the hapless Frank Moore, had a poor reputation, and the more savvy Capitol Hill operatives at HEW were almost entirely disengaged from the ED fight because of Joe Califano's intense hostility to the bill.[59]

The other obvious strategy was to reach out to other education groups. NEA made some moves in this direction, as when it set up a Citizens Committee for a Cabinet Department of Education, under the titular leadership of Grace Baisinger, of the National PTA.[60] Such efforts had a slightly perfunctory character during 1978, however. That is not surprising, given the way that NEA dwarfed all other education groups. No other such group maintained a PAC, or endorsed candidates for public office, or maintained a Washington government relations staff of twenty, or took positions on the Equal Rights Amendment, the Strategic Arms Limitation Talks (SALT), and the Panama Canal treaty.[61] At meetings of the "Big Six" education groups during the Carter years, McFarland recalls occasionally startling his colleagues by producing some confidential administration document that he had been able to procure, courtesy of NEA's unique access to the White House.[62]

Even though other education lobby groups too had beefed up their operations on the Hill during the past decade or so, they remained puny by comparison. NEA lobbyists came to view their colleagues in the other organizations if not with disdain, then at least with a certain skepticism about their capacity to add much to the kind of political operation that the new-look NEA was now able to mount. Only when they had failed to force a vote on the ED bill during the frenetic final days of the 1978 congressional session did NEA fully appreciate that it needed to reevaluate its political strategy.

Gail Bramblett recalls a postmortem by NEA officers in November that may have been the turning point. Again, the first response was to think that they needed to try harder: to spend more NEA staff-hours on the operation, spend more time working with the staff and members of the House Government Operations Committee, mobilize a better grassroots operation. But, she adds, having covered all of those points, "finally the NEA slowly came to the recognition that we could not do it alone."[63] Perhaps they were influenced not just by recent legislative history but also by the appearance just that month of a damaging article in *Reader's Digest*. Entitled "The NEA: A Washington Lobby Run Rampant," it conjured up the image of an incipient "permanent Potomac power elite" and presented the association's "drive for power" as "a classic study of how special-interest politics can overwhelm the public interest."[64]

That sort of press was alarming not just to NEA, but to other educators who supported the idea of a Department of Education but had felt sidelined during the recent legislative effort. Ultimately, it was their initiative that gave NEA a way of acting on its still halting embrace of coalition politics. Just about the time that NEA was holding its postmortem, a conference of chief state education officials was taking place in Scottsdale, Arizona. It was attended not just by state education officials but also by congressional staff and officials from HEW and OMB. Meeting in informal conclave at the hotel pool to discuss the fate of the ED bill, they pondered the *Reader's Digest* piece and concluded "that's the problem."[65] The obvious solution, they concluded, was to convert the paper coalition of the past year into a more genuine operation, headed by an association other than NEA, and they deputed two of their number to undertake the delicate task of feeling out the haughty teachers' union. The first was Allan Cohen, Washington lobbyist for the Illinois state superintendent of education. The second was Don White, who performed the same role for the state of California.[66]

When Cohen and White went to see NEA to discuss forming a substantive Ad Hoc Committee for a Cabinet Secretary of Education, in place of the previous year's paper group, the teachers' union remained hesitant. Although NEA recognized the need to defuse the charge that this was just an "NEA bill," it "was not about to give up basic control of the issue."[67] Still, its leadership endorsed the proposal, and the ad hoc group met for its first meeting in Reston, Virginia, in the outer suburbs of Washington, D.C. (This location was chosen with some care, on the grounds that "downtown D.C." was "regarded as NEA territory."[68]) At that meeting, forty groups were represented, including NEA.[69] By the time it met for its third meeting, that number had swelled to 100, the venue was the White House, and the host was Vice President Mondale, who emphasized the priority that the administration attached to the ED bill: "It's a sign of the importance I attach to this effort that I just came through a rain storm to be with you. I can't think of any meeting I would rather attend or any objective of our administration that the President and I place at a higher priority."[70]

From Policy to Politics: Carter and the ED Bill in 1979

If one measures that claim against the administration's record during the twelve months since the ED bill had first been submitted, it seems suspect: only rarely had the White House demonstrated much concern for its passage, and plenty of other issues had manifestly had a greater priority.[71] Right at the end of the year, administration officials did work closely with Congress and NEA in a vain effort to secure a House vote, but for the most part they were relatively low-level OMB and White House personnel. The only high-ranking administration official who appears to have been consistently engaged in the battle at this stage was Califano, and he was on the other side.[72] At the end of the 1978 session, when Carter did get personally involved, his intervention may have helped to sink the bill: he did not include it among his priorities for the frantic closing days before adjournment, and when a reporter asked him how high a priority the White House attached to the ED bill, he surmised that "it is unlikely that the bill will pass this year." Some supporters of the bill felt betrayed, considering that this removed any incentive that O'Neill might have had to bring the bill up during the last week of the session.[73]

This lack of priority was not surprising, given the other issues that were clamoring for Carter's attention during 1978. They included, at home, a sluggish economy and an energy crisis, and abroad, the two great diplomatic triumphs of the Carter administration: the Camp David negotiations and the ratification of the Panama Canal treaty. If anything, other business was still more pressing the following year, for the White House was locked in a whole series of intensely difficult political battles on the Hill, including the effort to ratify the SALT-II treaty, the bailout of the Chrysler corporation, tussles over a parsimonious budget, and the struggle for national health care. Despite that, however, in 1979 passage of the ED bill became one of the White House's top priorities, one that by the late summer was involving both Carter and Mondale in intensive, personal lobbying. According to one account, only the fight for the Panama Canal treaty involved a stronger presidential effort.[74] Califano believes that no other issue within his purview received such close attention from the president.[75] And Radin and Hawley observe that "the ED initiative held the administration captive, usurping invaluable and irreplaceable White House resources while other issues of national and international importance were also in need of presidential attention."[76]

The explanation lies in the growing political vulnerability of the Carter presidency. Just as the NEA's influence on Carter had reached its previous peak during the 1976 campaign, when the candidate had needed its endorsement and votes, and then plummeted as campaigning gave way to governing, it came to a second peak during the summer and fall of 1979, when the 1980 campaign was increasingly coming to the fore.[77] Talk was rife that Edward Kennedy—lion of the left, and the president's most forceful Democratic critic—would fight Carter for the Democratic nomination, and Carter's ability to fend off that putative challenge was not clear, given his sagging poll numbers and Kennedy's obvious ideological appeal to the activists who dominated the NEA representative assembly.[78]

In that environment, the administration's interest in the substantive content of the ED bill yielded almost completely to the political imperative of passing a bill, *any* bill. That meant avoiding controversial transfers that were unpopular with particular constituencies: infant nutrition, Indian education, Head Start, and the National Endowments for the Arts and the Humanities were all excluded. (The only major transfer from outside the existing education division now would be the Department of Defense overseas schools program.) Whereas the previous year's proposal had been for a relatively broad department, one that comported with Carter's concern for administrative efficiency, the Education Department that he was now prepared to endorse consisted of little more than the current Education Division.[79] It looked, in other words, very much like the proposal that OMB had criticized as the least desirable approach to reorganization.

In the new political environment, the administration capitulated to a whole series of clientele demands that were uncongenial on administrative grounds. Willis Hawley observed this change with dismay from his perch at OMB. In 1978, policy analysts at the agency had pored over every suggested congressional amendment to the Ribicoff bill, pondering the implications for administrative efficiency. The following year, though, "the original team of education analysts were [sic] superseded by political advocates. . . . No further analysis would take place. All resources would be devoted to negotiating and compromising."[80] The predictable result was a proliferation of clientele-oriented offices and assistant secretaryships: the bill was amended to include assistant secretaries for postsecondary education, nonpublic education, civil rights, and elementary and secondary education, each with its own office. The administration blithely approved each demand. Hispanics also won an Office for Bilingual Education, and "museum interests were assured that their $13 million program would have a direct reporting line to the Secretary."[81]

Besides the administration's strong support, the other new ingredient in the 1979 ED battle was the work of the 100-member coalition of lobby groups, headed by Allan Cohen. Bramblett, who chaired the coalition's "legislative group," acknowledges the tremendous help that she received from her colleagues, who were drawn from the Chief State School Officers, the National PTA, the National School Boards Association, the Secondary School Principals, the Council for Exceptional Children, and the American Educational Research Association. "These individuals," she notes, "ultimately carried the bulk of the work for the Coalition," discharging their tasks "efficiently and effectively." Naturally, NEA continued to play a vital leadership role, but Bramblett makes it clear that it was a genuine team effort.[82] Strongly recalling the full-funding coalition of a few years earlier, one of its key tactics was to mobilize grassroots support. When Brooks's committee met to consider the 1979 version of the ED bill, and during the subsequent floor debate too, members encountered hundreds of educators wearing red, white, and blue buttons that bore the slogan: "A DEPARTMENT OF EDUCATION/YES!"[83]

Despite all this, the fight remained exceptionally tough, in some ways more difficult than the previous year. During the 1978 midterm elections, Republicans had made significant gains in the House. And as the scope of the bill became narrower, press criticism broadened: the *Washington Post*, *New York Times*, and *Wall Street Journal* all condemned what they continued to portray as a cynical payoff to the NEA. The narrowness of the bill to some degree vitiated the beneficial impression created by the activities of the Ad Hoc Committee. While it had been possible to argue that the previous year's relatively broad bill would create a department able to resist client pressures, this case was harder to make now. And how could it be argued that a department consisting of little more than the current HEW education division would make a big administrative difference?

Conservative enemies of the bill worried that the advent of an NEA-controlled Education Department would increase the likelihood of a big expansion in the federal role in elementary and secondary education. That was why House conservatives such as John Erlenborn, Robert Walker (R-Pa.), and Dan Quayle (R-Ind.) opposed the measure. Still, in comparison with earlier years, and certainly in comparison to 1965, the "federal control" argument lacked salience and was not the principal factor that complicated passage of the bill. So accepted had the federal role in education become during the 1970s that senators as conservative as Jake Garn (R-Utah), Strom Thurmond (R-S.C.), and Thad Cochran (R-Miss.) were prepared to vote for the new department.[84]

Much more salient were battles over "turf." The Children's Defense Fund opposed the breakup of HEW because it feared that it might leave Head Start politically exposed. Black groups worried about responsibility for civil rights enforcement's being divided between two departments, charging that this would lead to a less effective effort. Higher education groups thought that a narrow Education Department would be controlled by elementary and secondary education. Catholics feared that an Education Department would be inattentive to the private school sector. And the AFL-CIO felt that the broader labor–social welfare coalition would be weakened by the breakup of HEW. But the strongest and best-organized opposition came from the AFT, whose widely respected leader, Albert Shanker, reportedly "roared" when he heard the White House justify the ED bill in terms of "improved efficiency," thinking that the only beneficiary would be his union's arch rival, the NEA.[85]

Although each of these groups had its own particular reason for being worried about the prospect of an Education Department, they all shared the natural hesitation that interest groups feel when existing institutional arrangements, and carefully nurtured bureaucratic contacts, are under threat. In this case, such hesitation was even evident where those institutional arrangements had previously been regarded as unsatisfactory. Black groups and members of the Congressional Black Caucus, for example, were generally worried about the breakup of HEW, even though the NAACP had been engaged in litigation against its Office for Civil Rights throughout the entire decade.[86] Similarly, the Indian groups that opposed the transfer of Indian education to the new department had been highly critical of the Bureau of Indian Affairs in the past. As one Indian lobbyist remarked: "They may be bastards, but they're *our* bastards."[87]

Despite all the talk in 1978 and 1979 about "teacher power," and the immense political clout of the new-look NEA, these reactions reveal that its power was not quite so great as its enemies believed. To prevail on the ED bill, it had to overcome resistance from vested interests and the normal inertia of a lumbering, fragmented government. All its political opponents had to do was defend the status quo, a much easier task. In these circumstances, and given the difficulty of defending the 1979 bill on administrative grounds, it is highly unlikely that the measure could have succeeded had the Carter White House, led by Mondale, not strained every sinew to force it through.[88]

Final Passage: The Impact of Presidential Leadership and Party Loyalty

Uncertainty about the outcome remained intense right up to the final House vote on the conference bill in September. The ED bill nearly failed in Brooks's committee, passing by 20 votes to 19 when Carter interceded personally with Rep. Elliott Levitas, a fellow Georgian.[89] Then it barely emerged from a sharply divided Rules Committee. Its chairman, Richard Bolling (D-Mo.), opposed the measure but ultimately responded to the argument that "his first loyalty was to the Speaker and the Democratic President." During his committee's executive sessions, members associated with AFT and the Catholic Conference initially looked to have the upper hand, but Bolling managed to stall the decisive vote by calling a series of recesses, until sufficient pro-ED colleagues had arrived.[90]

The subsequent floor debates—on the House bill in June and July and on the conference bill in September—were also extremely tense, with White House head counters predicting a narrow defeat right up until the vote. The more the White House got involved, the more it became a partisan fight. One consequence of that was that Republicans who had previously supported the bill were under increasing pressure to give the president a bloody nose. Bramblett recalls the frenetic atmosphere and near desperation that accompanied the final White House effort "to put us over the top."

> Anyone at the White House who had any contact with the Hill was
> required to make calls. Meetings were scheduled for the president with

members of Congress. Commitments were exchanged. Tickets to see the Pope or to ride on Air Force I were given away. When asked what they had had to promise certain members to get their votes, the White House lobbyist replied: "Don't ask because you really don't want to know!"[91]

In contrast to the previous year, when O'Neill and Wright had refused to force the ED bill onto the calendar, this time the House leadership played an important role in keeping it alive. That may have owed something to NEA's determined efforts to improve its standing with the Speaker.[92] More important now that it was becoming more of a straight party battle, O'Neill's strong instinct was to fight for a Democratic president, even Jimmy Carter. Although enemies as diverse as Dan Quayle and David Obey dragged the floor debate out over a period of six weeks, aggravating dissension within liberal ranks and delaying consideration of other business, O'Neill, Wright, and Brademas refused to pull the bill from the calendar.[93]

Eventually, the bill passed, by a four-vote margin, just before the summer recess. When Congress reconvened, it considered the conference bill. With the Democratic leadership nervous about the outcome, O'Neill made one of his rare floor speeches, imploring colleagues to vote with the president. During the vote itself, meanwhile, Wright, Brademas, the regional whips, and Jack Brooks worked intensively to cajole doubters to vote yea. That resulted in a 215–201 win for the administration, a desperately needed victory following a series of demoralizing defeats on other bills. A beaming President Carter celebrated "a significant milestone in my effort to make the federal government more effective. We will now have a single cabinet department which can provide the coherence and sense of direction needed to manage U.S. dollars."[94]

NEA Cashes Its Chips

The very next day, the National Education Association endorsed President Carter's bid for the Democratic presidential nomination.[95] With Kennedy's putative challenge gaining considerable momentum, Terry Herndon was worried about its likely appeal to NEA members. Doubtless in different circumstances, he too would have felt that appeal, given that his policy preferences on issues other than education were well to the left of those of Jimmy Carter. But with the ED bill passed, NEA officers were in no doubt as to whom they should favor, and this early response helped to head off the prospect of an "NEA for Kennedy" movement.[96]

Political scientist Byron Shafer observes that "the NEA went on to mobilize all its resources behind the Carter campaign—in truth, to *become* that campaign in locality after locality." It put fifty staff members and $500,000 into the nomination campaign alone, and at the 1980 Democratic convention, NEA power reached new heights, with the 311 NEA delegates (out of a total of 3,331) constituting by far the largest Carter bloc.[97] Democratic senator Daniel Patrick Moynihan—who had opposed the ED bill—quipped that the Carter campaign had become "a wholly-owned subsidiary of the NEA."[98] In eight states, NEA had more than a fifth of the total delegation. It was also strongly represented on the Platform Committee. (The convention went on to endorse a big increase in education spending.)[99]

Obviously, the NEA had become a major force in Democratic Party politics. Quite what that meant for its future prospects, however, was less obvious, and the lessons that the ED fight offered were mixed. It was apparent that NEA-PAC had made NEA a truly formidable group in Congress and that the 1976 presidential endorsement had given it unprecedented influence on the Carter White House, after a slow start. Still, it was also the case that NEA's perceived power in Congress was something of a problem, in terms of its image, and that it still needed friends in order to get its way. As for the White House, the lessons were again mixed. The NEA had only been able to realize its investment in Carter in full in the summer of 1979, when the president was weak, when a tough renomination fight loomed, and when governing had started to yield to the distinctive political exigencies of campaigning.

It was also unclear how much substantive difference the creation of a cabinet-level Department of Education would make to the federal politics of education. During the debate over its creation, opinions on that point had been sharply divided. Supporters of the idea argued that it would lead to greater efficiency and coordination and that a seat at the cabinet table would give advocates the kind of influence on presidential policy that they had hitherto lacked.[100] Opponents, by contrast, argued that a weak NEA-controlled Education Department would be a less effective advocate for education than a strong HEW secretary.[101] A third possibility was that simply taking the "E" out of HEW would make no difference. According to Wilbur Cohen, who opposed the new department, what mattered was not the administrative setup but rather whether a president cared about education. If he did care, then the structure of HEW was no obstacle, as witness his experience with LBJ. And if he did not care, simply having a Department of Education would not change that fact.[102]

One person to whom having a Department of Education certainly made a difference was Ronald Reagan. In contrast to congressional conservatives such as Senator Thurmond who had supported the idea, he believed that it was a dangerous development and pledged to dismantle it, as part of a broader effort to return responsibility for the schools back to the states. The Reagan presidency promised to present a major test both of the power of the new-look NEA and of the power of a seemingly fragile new federal department to resist the conservative counterrevolution. More than that, it was a test for the entire edifice of federal responsibility that had been constructed since 1965.

Education and the Reagan Revolution

During the 1970s, Ronald Reagan was a vocal critic of the expanding federal role in education. In his weekly syndicated radio addresses, he set himself apart from many other conservatives by the extent to which he continued to resist this process. Among the issues that he covered in these talks were prayer in schools and private education—which he supported—and bilingual education, sex education, progressive teaching methods, and the NEA—all of which he criticized. Highlighting all the advances in human knowledge that had been made by Americans in the past quarter-century, he asserted that

> it doesn't take a genius to figure out that the men and women responsible for those advances got their education in the old-fashioned system the educationists are so determined to scrap. . . .
>
> Are we to believe those who harnessed the atom, took us to the Moon, gave us the miracles of computers, electronics, jet travel, an end to so many crippling and death-dealing diseases did all of this in spite of their education? Someone in those old-fashioned schools so despised by today's elitists must have done something right.[1]

While other conservatives made pragmatic adjustments to the new federal role, Reagan continued to advocate a return to the 1950s, insisting that

American education had been in much better shape before Washington got involved. Surely, he suggested, it was no coincidence that Scholastic Aptitude Test scores had declined as the federal role had increased.[2] And, by implication, was the key to reversing that pattern not to restore the old ways that had served the nation so well in the past?

When Congress created a Department of Education, Reagan espied a new threat to local control and educational standards, telling his listeners that "it means, of course, federal regulation of our schools under the domination of the National Education Association, which is in truth a great and powerful union." He went on to inquire: "Is the government that administers the postal service and Amtrak—to say nothing of energy—qualified to educate our children?" His broadcast ended with the claim that, in time, "a national Department of Education would extend its power to cover independent parochial schools. Indeed part of its dream is incorporation of such schools in the public system."[3] On the campaign trail, a year later, he expanded on this theme, telling students at California's Claremont Men's College that "it is naïve to think that [ED] is anything but a first step toward federalizing education in this land" and introducing "a system of Federal licensing of all educational institutions in this land."[4] It is not surprising that the Republican Party's platform in 1980 included a commitment to abolish the new department before it had an opportunity to implement this furtive, unacknowledged agenda.

Following Reagan's victory over President Carter, he designated Edwin Meese to head his transition team, charged with staffing the new administration and with converting the president-elect's campaign promises into substantive policies. Meese, James A. Baker, and Michael Deaver went on to constitute the "troika" that choreographed the Reagan presidency during its first term. Like Deaver, Meese was one of that band of immensely loyal California Reaganites who had been with Reagan throughout his political career, believed deeply in his greatness, and accompanied him to Washington when he became president. During the gubernatorial years, Meese had first been legal affairs secretary and then chief of staff, and the governor had developed a warm appreciation both for his loyalty and for the skill with which Meese translated Reagan's core ideas about government into words and policy.[5] According to Lou Cannon's standard account of Reagan's presidency, Meese had nourished hopes of being chief of staff, but that job went to the politically shrewd Baker instead; Meese became counselor to the president, with the responsibility for overseeing policy development. (Deaver became Baker's deputy, with the president's public image being his particular responsibility while Baker handled the politics.)

During the transition, Meese established a large number of policy task forces, including one on education, chaired by Lorelei Kinder, a California GOP activist who had been national political coordinator for the Reagan-Bush campaign.[6] Kinder notes that she was not an education "policy wonk"; rather, she was a private citizen who shared the president's views on the subject and felt that no issue mattered more to the future of the Republic.[7] Other members included Thomas Sowell, a conservative, black economist; Nathan Glazer, a leading neoconservative intellectual and strong critic of the Great Society; James Koerner, author of *The Miseducation of American Teachers*; Onalee McGraw, an education specialist at the Heritage Foundation; Edith Green, the iconoclastic Democrat whose stinging critique of the education-industrial complex was encountered in previous chapters; Gary Jones, a vice president at the American Enterprise Institute (AEI) and research director of the Reagan for President campaign; and Chester Finn, a former graduate student of Daniel Patrick Moynihan who had worked for his mentor on education policy both in the Nixon administration and on the Hill and who had become an articulate critic of the federal role.

This was a conservative group, very different in character from equivalent bodies in the past. Its composition and recommendations present an instructive contrast, for example, with those of Nixon's education task force, which had been chaired by Alan Pifer of the Carnegie Corporation and composed exclusively of familiar establishmentarians, including LBJ's first education commissioner, Francis Keppel, and a number of other veterans of the 1964 Gardner task force. In 1980, the think tank members came not from Carnegie or the Ford Foundation, but from such conservative bastions as the AEI, the Hoover Institution (where Sowell was based), and the Heritage Foundation. There were no former superintendents or commissioners, such as Sidney Marland or James Allen. In their place were strong critics of the education establishment, such as Green, Kinder, and Koerner.

The composition of the Reagan transition group emphasized the extent to which Reaganauts such as Meese and Hoover Institution economist Martin Anderson were keen to break with what they regarded as having been the muddled statism of the Nixon era.[8] (Anderson had served in the Nixon administration, and Meese was a veteran of Governor Reagan's tussles with its Department of Health, Education, and Welfare.[9]) True to that mission, the Kinder group urged a sharply reduced federal role in education, to be achieved through reduced funding, program consolidation, administrative reform, and deregulation. (By contrast, Pifer's body had recommended a "dramatic" increase in federal funding to Nixon, and someone had leaked its confidential report to the press to ensure that this finding was not ignored.)[10]

Kinder's group set out a blueprint for reducing the federal presence in the nation's schools but said little about the issue that Meese and some other movement conservatives considered to be most important, namely the abolition of the Department of Education. That reflected disagreements within the task force. Charles Radcliffe, the veteran Republican staffer on the House Education and Labor Committee who served as a consultant to the transition group, felt that it would be a waste of energy and political capital to focus on abolishing ED, seeing this as a symbolic issue and thinking that program content was both more important and easier to fix. That was also the view of Green and Finn. Thomas Sowell, though, was an antistatist purist and a nonpolitician, and he attached great significance to symbols: feeling that the task of cleaning out the Augean stable could not be undertaken in a half-hearted manner, he worried that the pragmatic approach would simply preserve the status quo.

Meese shared Sowell's approach. According to Nancy Reagan—fiercely protective of her husband and always worried that the Reaganauts might get him into political trouble—Meese was "by far the most ideological member of the troika, a jump-off-the-cliff-with-the-flag-flying conservative. Some people are so rigid in their beliefs that they'd rather lose than win a partial victory, and I always felt that Meese was one of them."[11] Meese's first postelection public intervention into the politics of education certainly suggested that he was impatient to make a start on rolling back the leviathan state and keen to start with the issue that Radcliffe wanted to put on the backburner. In early January, Meese made his animus to ED clear in an indiscreet speech to the U.S. Chamber of Commerce: "The Department of Education was just a ridiculous bureaucratic joke. They took functions that were already in existence in other portions of the government, slapped them together, put in a secretary and a bunch of assistants who were almost dedicated to the objectives of a particular special interest group, and then sent them out to do mischief on the children of America." To Meese, there was an obvious need to "pull that operation apart." He believed that this was "not going to be that hard," for "I would say that there is a great deal of sympathy for that kind of action in Congress."[12]

Ronald Reagan's perspective was rather different. On the merits, he doubtless shared Meese's views, but on the politics they parted company. Whereas

Meese's long-term aspiration was apparently to remove the federal government altogether from elementary and secondary education, Reagan's early public references to the topic included an acknowledgment that Washington did have *some* legitimate role to play.[13] And when reporters asked him and his press chief, James Brady, about the status of the pledge to abolish the department, each equivocated.[14] Reagan's conservatism, although fully as deep as that of Meese, was modified by a strong streak of pragmatism; both as a governor and as a president, he derived strong satisfaction from establishing good working relationships across party lines. In the case of education, it is not at all clear that he genuinely felt there to be areas where the federal role was beneficial or sufficiently beneficial to outweigh the costs. More likely, he assumed that there were areas where the federal role was so entrenched that there was no point in even trying to roll back the tide: he would not win, he would make enemies, and all this in a cause that did not loom large in his overall agenda.

Even though Reagan had strong views about education, this was not a high-priority issue. According to Reagan's top pollster, Richard Wirthlin, the president-elect's three biggest preoccupations were "the Soviets, the economy, [and] federalism." In comparison to those issues, education policy per se was a distinctly low priority: Cannon ranks it, together with health policy, as a "backburner" issue that rarely commanded the president's attention.[15] Where it *did* command his attention, he viewed it through the lens of broader concerns: the state of the economy in 1981, the desire to restore federalism in 1982, and electoral exigencies in 1983–1984.

It was the first of these three concerns that yielded the Reagan administration's main achievement in education policy, the Educational Consolidation and Improvement Act of 1981 (ECIA). In early 1981, all other domestic objectives were subordinated to the central task of responding to alarming and worsening economic conditions: inflation stood at 12 percent, interest rates had reached a staggering 21.5 percent, unemployment was approaching double figures, and the budget deficit was ballooning way beyond the outgoing Carter administration's projections. In an interview with *U.S. News and World Report*, President-elect Reagan referred to a "grave deterioration" in the economy, insisted that "we cannot any longer engage in business as usual," and urged "a combination program of reducing the tax rates and attacking government spending. The budget is out of control."[16]

If these circumstances were genuinely alarming, then they were also propitious, inasmuch as they enhanced prospects for effecting budgetary and fiscal changes that Reaganites already supported for ideological reasons.

Seizing the moment, and exploiting his abundant political capital, Reagan hammered home his central message: only by cutting taxes, government spending, and red tape could the promise of the American dream be rekindled. Specifically, he demanded 10 percent reductions in income tax in each of the next three years and cuts of $130 billion in nondefense spending. When the administration released its Economic Recovery Program in March, those expenditure reductions included a proposal to slash education spending by no less than 25 percent, a figure that was to be achieved by folding forty-four elementary and secondary education programs into two block grants and greatly reducing funding. Title I, aid to the handicapped, and bilingual education all faced the ax.[17]

The program was bold in its conception, much more so than the education block grant proposals that Nixon and Ford had half-heartedly floated back in the early and mid-1970s. Like the Kinder task force, it served to emphasize the differences between this administration and its Republican predecessors. That said, the proposal owed less to the distinctive ideas of Reaganite education specialists than it did to the passion that the new budget director, David Stockman, brought to the broader task of making a "frontal attack on the welfare state."[18] Stockman, aged just thirty-four, was a fierce ideologue who had traveled a long way from his Marxist youth while preserving his disdain for muddle-headed centrism. Following the election, Jack Kemp and other disciples of "supply-side" economics had told the president-elect that this combative, intellectual, egotistical, hard-driving Michigan congressman would be the ideal person to force the Reagan Revolution through the administration and Congress.[19]

Accepting the job, Stockman conceived of his task in extraordinarily personal terms. Disdainful of Meese and his transition effort, doubting that Reagan cared as much about spending as he did about taxes, and assuming that even Reaganite cabinet heads would resist any serious effort to cut spending in their own departments, he felt that it was overwhelmingly *his* responsibility to put the $130 billion program together. Some might have viewed that prospect with trepidation, but not Stockman, who glimpsed a once-in-a-lifetime opportunity to free America from the clutches of the leviathan state. To judge from his vivid memoir, Stockman was not inclined to think about cuts in terms of what was politically realistic. Rather, he viewed that kind of calculation with contempt and made his decisions on the basis of principle, the main principle being that "the vast Great Society–spawned system of federal categorical aid for nearly every imaginable purpose from rodent control to special education for gifted children was nonsense."[20]

As Stockman and his admiring acolytes at OMB went about their task, they soon realized that they needed still greater cuts than they had imagined if they were to balance the budget by 1984, which was the administration's target. Again, Stockman was not discomfited, detecting "another, unexpected opportunity to force the logic of my Grand Doctrine deeper and more comprehensively into the initial economic program of the Reagan Administration." He records that "the morale at OMB was fantastic. We were ripping through the stuff. Today the Energy Department, tomorrow Education, the day after, the world! There was a feeling of 'it can be done.' "[21] With Reagan riding high in the polls, liberalism on the ropes, and the economy creaking, unhappy departmental heads were "browbeaten . . . into accepting the cuts." In the case of education, department secretary Terrel Bell managed to salvage bilingual education funding, but in general—Stockman says—OMB "shackled" Bell, imposing "a sweeping retrenchment."[22] According to Chester Finn, a well-informed observer of Washington education politics, OMB's strategy was "to eliminate all funding for education programs as quickly as possible."[23]

The New Politics of Education

One only has to think back to the budget battles of the Nixon-Ford years to see that, back then, a plan that cut education spending by 25 percent would have been dead on arrival. Back then, the challenge for successive OMB directors had been to control the growth of politically popular education programs and to counter the influence of the full-funding coalition. Now, however, that world suddenly seemed to exist in the past, because Reagan took office at one of those moments, rare in American politics, when radical change seems possible. As well as electing Reagan in 1980, with a massive margin in the electoral college, the American people had elected a GOP Senate, for the first time in more than a quarter century. The margin of control was not great, 53–47, but there were as many as 12 new GOP senators, most of them more conservative than the people whom they replaced. Some big liberal names had been defeated: George McGovern, Frank Church, Birch Bayh, Gaylord Nelson, Warren Magnuson, Jacob Javits. As for the House, the Democrats remained in control, but Reagan's long coattails had produced 33 Republican gains, leaving conservatives in a better political position there than they had enjoyed since the early 1950s.

During the first half of 1981, economic difficulties continued to multiply while Ronald Reagan's popularity burgeoned, especially after an assassination attempt in late March. Legislators voting on Stockman's economic plan found that issues were being framed not in terms of the merits and costs of each proposal, but rather in terms of whether they were "with Ronald Reagan or against him." That affected Democrats as well as Republicans, whether they represented blue-collar districts in the Midwest or Republican-leaning districts in the South. In such an environment, the fact that Democrats retained control of the House of Representatives had less political salience than would otherwise have been the case. Speaker Tip O'Neill, an old pro, understood this well and recognized the futility of a purely obstructionist response to the Reagan agenda: "The Congress goes with the will of the people, and the will of the people is to go along with the President. I know when to fight and when not to fight."[24]

Meanwhile, public support for public education was at a low ebb, lending at least surface plausibility to the proposed 25 percent cut. *Education Week* reported that "the public seems less willing than in past years to invest any more money in public education." According to one poll, only 30 percent of Americans favored higher taxes for this purpose. (Even in 1969, when the taxpayer rebellion against school bond issues was growing, the figure had been 45 percent.[25]) Another revealed that only 29 percent of Americans believed that a federal Department of Education was necessary. And a third, taken in 1982, recorded the belief of a clear majority of Americans that the federal government had too much influence on the nation's schools.[26]

Despite Reagan's sense that federal aid in some form was here to stay, to others it seemed possible that practically all of the big federal education initiatives of the past decade and a half might be in peril: ESEA, bilingual education, Title IX, the right of handicapped children to a "free, appropriate public education." Even the two most popular programs were under attack: Stockman, in his pomp, spoke blithely of eliminating Head Start, and the perennial presidential challenge to impact aid—always rolled back in the past—now had far greater strength than before.

Educators and their lobbyists were alarmed. In some quarters, the tone was one of rebuke: the education journal *Phi Delta Kappan* argued that NEA had put all its eggs in Carter's basket and wondered whether the education community in general would now have to suffer the consequences.[27] Terry Herndon did not accept that criticism, but he shared *Phi Delta Kappan*'s alarm at the prospect of a Reagan presidency. Presenting the 1980 election as a wake-up call to "a too comfortable community of school supporters who assumed a perpetual political commitment to public education," he warned that "our contemporary right-wing political phenomenon constitutes a conspiracy to significantly injure or destroy public education as we have known it."[28]

Applying the Knife: The Omnibus Budget Reconciliation Act of 1981

Still, serious obstacles to education cuts remained. For one thing, Republicans, including some quite conservative Republicans, had supported programs such as impact aid, bilingual education, education for the handicapped, vocational education, and Title I. For another, it was unlikely that governors—irrespective of party affiliation or ideology—would respond warmly to initiatives that forced them to contemplate spending cuts or tax hikes at the state level. Finally, even if a moderate-conservative coalition had the numerical advantage in the House, its members could not be said to dominate the key committees. There was some prospect that Stockman's education cuts would emerge unscathed from the Senate Labor and Human Resources Committee, whose ideological character had been transformed by the addition of five newly elected Republicans, staunch conservatives all. But the House Education and Labor Committee was still led by the wily and obdurate Carl Perkins, who regarded the preservation of the Great Society as his life's work and who had notched up an impressive record of success, beginning with the defeat of the Quie amendment in 1967 (the year that he took over the committee from Adam Clayton Powell) and continuing through the Nixon-Ford years, when he had done as much as anyone to prevent significant program consolidation.

In a deft political move, the administration used "reconciliation"—a hitherto obscure provision of the 1974 Congressional Budget Act—to circumvent Perkins and other Great Society–minded committee chairmen. Acting on the suggestion of Senator Pete Domenici (R-N.M.), Stockman consolidated more than $40 billion in FY 1982 cuts into a single bill, the Omnibus Budget Reconciliation Act (OBRA). The plan was to put that consolidated package to a vote on the floor of each house of Congress right at the beginning of the budget debate, along with "reconciliation" instructions that mandated each authorizing committee to stay within prescribed spending limits. Finally, the budget committee in each house would submit a single, aggregated measure to the floor, under a rule that prohibited amendments.

Overall, the strategy worked very well, and the administration secured passage through Congress of $36 billion in expenditure cuts, prevailing in the Democratic-controlled House by five votes. It was the biggest legislative success that the administration would ever enjoy, appreciated at the time as a dramatic moment that symbolized just how much the 1980 elections had transformed the political landscape. Still, that five-vote margin suggests how close the administration came to defeat in the House, and the particular journey of Stockman's education package through Congress illustrates the continuing popularity of education programs in Congress, even in 1981. The final bill was very different from Stockman's original proposal: education spending was reduced by 10 percent, rather than 25 percent, and only twenty-nine categorical programs were consolidated, rather than forty-four. Moreover, those consolidated programs were very small: their total authorizations amounted to only $400 million. Title I, vocational education, and aid to the handicapped all survived, as indeed did every other significant categorical program.[29]

This compromise measure was deeply unpalatable to Stockman, but conservatives in Congress felt the same way about *his* proposal. Take, for example, John Ashbrook, ranking Republican on the House Education and Labor Committee. This ten-term congressman from Ohio was best known for having stood against Nixon during the 1972 GOP primaries on the grounds that the president had betrayed his conservative supporters. But when Ronald Reagan called him to ask for his support now, Ashbrook—an old friend and ally—explained that he could not oblige and requested that Stockman familiarize himself with the congressional politics of education.

Had anyone at OMB contacted Ashbrook in advance about the education package (he was bemused and offended by their failure to do so), he would have told them about his experience in the previous Congress, when he had sought to push through a comprehensive block grant proposal and had won scarcely any support. Having developed close ties to educators in his home state, he knew how outraged they would be by Stockman's plan and recognized that budgetary proposals derived mainly from ideological principles were more likely to obstruct conservative goals than to facilitate their attainment. More than that, as he reflected upon its programmatic implications, he concluded that it went too far. Every other Republican on the committee felt the same way: not one of them supported the administration's bill, although John Erlenborn did agree to introduce it in committee as a matter of courtesy.

With Carl Perkins in control, even strong GOP support for the OMB bill would not have been enough during the committee stage. Although Perkins was constrained by the April budget resolution to find billions of dollars in cuts in education, health, labor, and antipoverty programs, he found a way around the problem via a tactic known in Congress as the "Washington Monument strategy" (a committee proposing cuts to National Park Service funding for the monument could be confident that the funds would be restored on the floor).[30] Other committee chairs followed suit, meaning that the version of OBRA that the House Budget Committee approved in June, while formally in line with the earlier budget resolution, stood very little chance of being enacted.

The only way that OBRA could now pass was as a substitute offered on the floor of the House, one that preserved the overall figure but distributed the pain in more politically acceptable ways. It was as they went about the delicate task of assembling this substitute that the dispute between OMB and Congress over education cuts became acute. From the vantage point of Capitol Hill, the key question was tactical: at what point would education cuts become so unpopular that the House would throw out the whole Reagan budget? For Stockman, however, that was the wrong approach altogether. When House minority leader Bob Michel told the press that "I'm not hung up on saying we've got to have everything we want," Stockman felt that he had adopted "a disastrous attitude." For him, it was axiomatic that the administration had to get *everything* that it had asked for, and he regarded Republicans who took a different view as "saboteurs."[31] For Charles Radcliffe, by contrast, it seemed that Stockman and his crew were "jackasses" and "ideologues," with no understanding at all of how popular federal education spending was on the Hill or how well equipped supporters of Title I and aid to the handicapped were to derail a budget that eliminated their programs, even in 1981.

OMB struggled hard to preserve its proposed cuts in something resembling their original form but was forced by implacable Republican opposition to yield. One crucial moment came when William Goodling (R-Pa.), a respected member of the Education and Labor Committee and former school superintendent, confronted Stockman off the House floor the morning before the critical vote on Gramm-Latta (the administration's floor substitute). He vowed to take "ten Republicans with me" in opposing it if Stockman did not abandon his insistence on putting the school lunch and child nutrition programs into the block grant. Stockman evidently regarded that as a credible threat, for he backed down, possibly saving OBRA from defeat in the process.[32] By the time that Gramm-Latta came up for a vote, the OMB education package had been entirely withdrawn. In its place, Ashbrook proposed the Education Consolidation and Improvement Act, which

Radcliffe had drawn up for him some eighteen months previously, following the failure of his 1979 block grant scheme. It made important changes to Title I, achieved modest program consolidation, and won the unanimous backing of Republicans on the Education and Labor Committee.

According to Radcliffe, Title I supporters and lobbyists for the handicapped were so relieved when they learned that their programs had survived that they largely refrained from trying to lobby against ECIA on the House floor. Before, they had felt that the sky was falling and that all their past accomplishments were in danger. Now, for all that 10 percent cuts were still deeply unwelcome, they had the feeling that they had dodged a bullet. That was also the reaction of Harold Howe, Francis Keppel, and Sidney Marland, all former commissioners of education who importuned Radcliffe during the days before ECIA replaced the Stockman cuts. With luck, the lost funds could be restored in future years, when political conditions would surely be more propitious than in 1981.

For Stockman, laws like ECIA symbolized the likelihood that OBRA would represent not the first step along the road to dismantling the welfare state, as he had hoped, but rather the limits to Congress's willingness to cut spending.[33] That turned out to be an accurate assessment. Many legislators felt that they had made considerable sacrifices in supporting OBRA, and when the administration attempted a second round of savings later in 1981, even conservative members of Congress like Richard Cheney (R-Wyo.) and Trent Lott (R-Miss.) refused to go along.

ECIA dimmed prospects for further education cuts in another way. For Radcliffe, its principal architect, the most important component of the legislation was not Chapter 2 (the consolidation title) but Chapter 1, which reformed the ESEA compensatory education program that Stockman had hoped to eliminate, Title I.[34] In putting Chapter 1 together, Radcliffe and Ashbrook consulted widely with recipients of Title I funding, such as big city school chiefs, and developed ideas for how to fix some of its more administratively burdensome aspects, aspects that tended to undermine the political standing of this otherwise popular program.[35] Title I/Chapter 1 was probably politically stronger now than it had been before.

For all that he was a strong conservative, Radcliffe took satisfaction in that fact, and not just because of pride of authorship, or because he resented OMB's challenge to the congressional role, or because ECIA as altered had facilitated the passage of OBRA, which he strongly supported. In addition, confronted with the possibility that ESEA might unravel, his instinct was to fix the program instead. As with so many other conservatives on the Hill, he had come to accept the basic principle that the federal government had a legitimate role to play in helping school districts meet their responsibilities, especially in meeting the needs of disadvantaged children.

The next test for the Reagan Revolution came a few months later, in the fall of 1981, when the White House focus shifted to what had been the highest-profile education policy pledge of the 1980 campaign, namely the promise to dismantle the Department of Education.

The Department of Education under Siege

For some of the movement conservatives who came to Washington with President Reagan, abolishing ED should have been the number one priority. (One urged Congress to "move rapidly to abolish this giant octopus thrust upon the nation against its wishes."[36]) Passionate admirers of Reagan, they saw in his election a historic opportunity to reverse the inexorable rise of the state and were eager to participate in this noble quest. Meese had the challenge of finding positions for them within the federal government, so that they could act as the president's praetorian guard. A number of them ended up with senior positions in the Education Department. Robert Billings, a Baptist minister and formerly the executive director of Jerry Falwell's Moral Majority, was chosen to head ED's network of regional offices. Daniel Oliver, former editor of William F. Buckley's *National Review,* assumed the important position of general counsel.[37] And a number of Heritage Foundation people found positions too.[38]

Perhaps the strongest bastion of movement conservatism was the National Institute of Education, founded by Nixon a decade earlier, but seen by Reaganauts such as Martin Anderson as a particularly objectionable manifestation of federal intervention. (Reminded of NIE's provenance, Anderson reputedly joked to Meese: "I always knew they impeached Nixon for the wrong reason."[39]) Ed Curran, a member of Meese's staff who had previously been headmaster of the National Cathedral School in Washington, was chosen to lead NIE, and his deputy was Lawrence Uzzell, another strong conservative with a passionate aversion to the education bureaucracy.[40]

Also at NIE was Robert Sweet (he would direct the agency for a while, following Curran's departure in 1982). His road to ED provides a useful glimpse into the personal inspiration that so many antistatist conservatives drew from Reagan during the 1960s and 1970s. A New Hampshire textbook salesman in his forties, Sweet believed that educational standards had deteriorated sharply since his days as a science teacher during the early 1960s and attributed this development to the spread of "progressive" teaching methods, as purveyed in the books that he sold for Holt, Rinehart, and Winston. He felt that federal agencies such as NIE and the National Science Foundation, and legislation such as NDEA and ESEA, had played a decisive role in promulgating these "progressive" ideas. Meanwhile, service on his local school board during the mid-1970s had exposed Sweet to other, newer aspects of the federal role in education, such as PL 94-142. Until Reagan came to New Hampshire, during the early stages of his 1976 presidential bid, Sweet had not been sure how this seemingly inexorable tide might be rolled back. When he heard Reagan speak, however, he felt inspired: here was a man who believed in local control and who had the charisma and self-belief to get things done. Already active in GOP politics at the state level, Sweet worked strongly for Reagan's election four years later, and in 1981 he secured the position in NIE that he anticipated would allow him to work for the department's abolition.

Some movement conservatives anticipated that abolishing the department would be rather straightforward. That is not simply because they were politically naive, although it is true that many of them had comparatively little experience of Washington politics. Rather, their view was widely held in 1981. One education correspondent felt that "the department doesn't have enough supporters left to make for a real fight" following the 1980 elections, and there was "no reason to think Congress won't endorse the demotion."[41] Education Secretary Terrel Bell shared that view, assuming that Reagan's campaign promise would be carried out in some form.[42] ED career employees were demoralized, telling reporters variously that "it's awfully hard to gear yourself up for something that's already dead" and that "it's like working in a garbage dump—no offence to garbage men." According to a staff newsletter, "Morale in ED is lower than low. On a good day, the atmosphere is dehumanized and dispirited."[43]

With the benefit of hindsight, the belief that ED would be easy to dismantle is surprising. It is rarely easy for presidents to persuade Congress to disturb established clientele relationships.[44] True, ED had been hard to create, had not been in existence for long enough to put down deep roots, and was imperiled by the vigor of the Reagan Revolution during the early months of 1981. But it was not obvious that Democrats who had opposed the creation of ED (mostly labor Democrats and big city Catholics, deeply antagonistic to Reaganism) would want to hand the president this victory. Prospects for abolition were certainly not enhanced when Reagan appointed Bell to head the department. He had been acting commissioner of education under Nixon and full commissioner under Ford and was a moderate Republican with a strong belief in an active federal role. His tenacious opposition to proposed OMB cuts during the Ford presidency had earned him the moniker "bantam rooster" (it also referred to his diminutive stature). Just like previous GOP-appointed commissioners such as James Allen and Sidney Marland, he was a member in good standing of the education establishment. Since leaving federal service in 1977, his most prominent public role had been to testify in support of a Department of Education.[45]

The education community was delighted by the appointment. Terry Herndon pronounced him a good man, and NEA and AASA gave the nomination their enthusiastic blessing.[46] Senator Claiborne Pell of Rhode Island, ranking Democrat on the education subcommittee, told Bell that "I really cannot overstate my joy that you are the nominee."[47] Conservatives were less complimentary: one complained that Bell was "for everything Reagan says he's against."[48] The editors of *Human Events* (among Reagan's biggest champions) were "dumbfounded," digging out a whole series of incriminating comments by Bell, such as this one from 1976:

> I came [to Washington] feeling that education was almost exclusively a state responsibility. My view has shifted to where I feel that education is vital to what this country is trying to accomplish, and it is the prime instrument for attaining our ideals. Congress and the federal statutes can no longer defer to the states and say, "you take the lead." The federal government must guarantee certain rights and in doing so it should specify the ends of education and provide the financial support to meet those ends.[49]

On the face of it, the appointment was inexplicable. It took Bell by surprise, even though he had been approached by the Reagan campaign at the time of the Republican convention and asked for policy ideas.[50] Most likely, the administration did not take this appointment very seriously, precisely because the department was expected to be dead at some point during the next four years. As Sweet explains, it seemed like a "throwaway" position.[51] Why would anyone want to take a job whose primary responsibility was to make himself unemployed? Reflecting that difficulty, the appointment dragged out: when all of the other twelve departmental cabinet positions had been filled, ED still remained vacant. With a number of people having turned the position down and with inauguration just a week away, the administration asked Bell if he would take the job. He said yes, and assured Reagan that he would help him to honor his campaign commitments.[52]

In retrospect, the selection was misguided; Meese and his appointments chief Pendleton James failed to see how it would complicate the task of abolishing ED. They seem to have seen no danger signals when Bell, in his first meeting with the president-elect, insisted that the task of designing options for reorganization be undertaken by him, rather than by movement conservatives at the White House such as Kenneth Cribb or Robert Carleson. This was a costly error, suggestive already of the way in which Bell would run rings around the Reaganauts during his four years in charge of ED.

During the early months of the administration, however, it seemed to some conservatives that Reagan might have made a good choice after all. That too was a tribute to Bell's political skill. A number of his early moves were designed to disarm his conservative critics, and they worked well. Conservatives were delighted, for example, when Bell withdrew the Lau Remedies, the far-reaching bilingual education regulations that Carter had promulgated the previous fall as part of an effort to win Latino support. In truth, Congress had already acted to deprive those regulations of much force, but at a symbolic level Bell's move was highly effective. Another popular move was his announcement that he intended to slash four assistant secretaryships and as many as thirty-five deputy assistantships.[53] These seemed promising beginnings, indicating that Bell really did want to shrink ED down to size. In some interviews and speeches, too, he came across as a conservative and a strong believer in states' rights. In March, he told the National Conference of State Legislatures that the administration's "mission . . . is simply to get the federal government off the backs of the people and the governing bodies of this country," and a couple of weeks later he declared himself "proud to be a part of . . . the historic effort by President Reagan to put education back where it belongs—at the state and local levels."[54] In Cabinet meetings, according to Meese, Bell came across as "an enthusiastic, almost sycophantic, booster for the President."[55]

Conservatives were delighted. *Human Events*, "dumbfounded" by Bell's appointment in January, was strongly in his corner just four weeks later. In a story headed "New Education Chief Proves a Surprise," the journal commented approvingly on his early decisions, observing that they "must have had NEA leaders reeling."[56] Five months later, it was even more enthusiastic, noting admiringly that the secretary was flouting a "basic rule of survival" for an agency head, "criticizing his 'constituency' and making a lot of waves." It went on: "It will be interesting to see how this Don Quixote of sorts fares in his attempts to shape up a bureaucracy grown too big, too fast. The education establishment can be expected to fight him at every turn, but it may have met its match."[57]

In reality, Bell was telling diverse constituencies what he thought they wanted to hear. While conservative-leaning audiences were learning of his strong support for tuition tax credits for private schools and of his sternly traditional views about discipline and pedagogy, he managed to stay on the right side of Democrats in Congress too.[58] Occasionally, news would leak out of Bell's tussles with Stockman over the budget. (When the periodical *Education Week* was launched, in the fall of 1981, it soon started to benefit from strategic leaks of this kind, including the full text of two letters complaining about cuts that Bell had written to the OMB director.[59]) Appearing before Congress, he made no effort to hide his disquiet at the cuts and strongly defended the Title I program, helpfully highlighting recent evidence that it was working even as the administration was trying to dissolve it into a block grant.[60] According to his friend and chief of staff, Elam Hertzler, he had a clever way of including in his testimony ammunition that could be used to attack the administration line that he was ostensibly defending ("Now, critics of my approach are going to argue . . .").[61]

When Bell joked before education audiences that "it's nice to be among friends, even if they are not your own," they understood that he really remained one of them, after all.[62] After one such session in which Bell had defended the administration's education program, William Ford, a Democrat from Michigan, slapped him on the back, remarking "Great performance, Mr. Secretary." Asked about this remark by a reporter, Ford explained that "He's not the enemy, he's the messenger" and expressed his confidence that "Bell tried to hold the line [on spending] as much as he could."[63]

As for the project to abolish ED, it moved slowly. Because the White House was preoccupied with the economic recovery package, Bell was initially under no great pressure to move. Absent such pressure, he "commissioned astoundingly complex and lengthy studies of where to put the programs after his department went down the tubes."[64] Every time that Elam Hertzler told colleagues on an interagency reorganization task force that these studies were not yet ready, conservatives in OMB and other agencies became more suspicious.[65] Still, by August 1981 the task force had completed its work, and at a superficial level, its report was calculated to appeal to conservatives like Anderson and Meese. In terms of tone, it featured multiple references to James Madison, the Tenth Amendment, and the baneful influences of the teacher unions and the courts. As for substance, it appeared to endorse an organizational solution that had initially been floated by Meese, namely that ED be replaced by a National Education Foundation, similar in character to the National Science Foundation (in other words, a grant-awarding body with a much-reduced policymaking role and limited access to the president). *Newsweek* surmised that Bell wanted Reagan to "reverse a 25-year trend by expelling Washington from the nation's schools."[66] And a reporter for the *Wall Street Journal* thought that Bell, "a Reagan loyalist," had shown himself to be "more than willing to scotch his department and many of its programs."[67]

But White House Reaganauts saw through the conservative veneer without difficulty. From their perspective, the task force had proposed a purely cosmetic change. Most of the key functions performed by ED, Meese and Anderson noted, would continue to be undertaken by the putative foundation (its budget would still be more than $10 billion, compared to the present level of $12 billion), making the analogy to the National Science Foundation meaningless. What they wanted, by contrast, was the dispersal of all programs to other agencies in the short term and their elimination in the longer term. Dissatisfied, Meese established a second task force, designed to present the president with a wider range of options.[68] During the fall of 1981, it struggled to overcome sharp internal disagreements: Anderson and Meese insisted that only the complete dismantling of ED would be consistent with President Reagan's campaign promises, whereas Bell argued that this idea was both undesirable on the merits and impossible to sell politically.[69]

The Reagan Revolution Loses Momentum

This disagreement unfolded in a rapidly deteriorating political environment for the Reagan administration. Earlier in the year, economic difficulties had helped to fuel the Reagan Revolution. By the late summer, however, they were having the opposite effect: with the economy worsening sharply, and projections for the budget deficit continuing to soar, the administration's budgetary priorities—cuts in social programs, massive increases in defense—came under strong attack. After a hesitant start, Speaker O'Neill had found his stride and was using the "fairness issue" against Reagan: OBRA and the tax bill, he argued, had favored the rich and soaked the poor. It appeared that the strategy was beginning to work. The president's popularity was starting to dip: it fell from 68 percent to 51 percent during the second half of 1981. And as it dipped, Republicans who had previously wanted to bask in his reflected glory began to keep their distance, with one eye on the 1982 midterm elections.[70]

Conservatives such as Meese, Anderson, and speechwriter Lyn Nofziger lost influence at this time, as a newly vulnerable Reagan increasingly listened to political moderates (such as James Baker, Richard Darman, and Vice

President George Bush) and to advisers who were concerned less about policy than with his personal standing in the country (Nancy Reagan, Michael Deaver). Disheartened, both Anderson and Nofziger left the administration, and another strong conservative, National Security Council head Richard Allen, was forced out. *Human Events,* with characteristic lack of restraint, detected not just an unwelcome trend but "one of the most bizarre reversals in the history of our politics." The administration, its editorial warned, was "close to being captured by 'moderate' Republicans who opposed [Reagan's] presidential aspirations." [71]

The internal debate over ED unfolded in a way consistent with this version of events. Meese and Anderson, who had dismissed the Bell foundation proposal in August, had to endorse it in December. (According to Bell, Meese put a brave face on the matter, presented this recommendation as "an interim measure until we could phase out all federal spending for education." [72]) By this time, however, the debate had changed. Now, the key question was not so much what form the ED proposal would take. Rather, it was whether any effort to abolish the department could succeed. Initial soundings taken by the administration on Capitol Hill were not encouraging.

In part, the administration was a victim of its earlier success. If ECIA had not been all that Reagan had asked for, and if the repeal of the Lau Remedies had been largely a symbolic act, these measures had nevertheless done much to diminish any sense that ED was some kind of out-of-control bureaucratic monster, inexorably encroaching on the rights of the states. Certainly, it was no longer plausible to argue that the department was in the pocket of the NEA. To the extent that congressional support for abolishing ED was actuated by fears of federal control and hostility to NEA, it was likely to have been diminished rather than fueled by Reagan's early record.

It was politically unhelpful that Reagan presented the move not just as an administrative reform but as part of a concerted effort to further reduce the federal role in education. In a poorly received September 24 television address, Reagan claimed that "There's only one way to shrink the size and cost of big government, and that is by eliminating agencies that are not needed and are getting in the way of a solution." [73] From one point of view, that formulation made eminent good sense: what was the point of abolishing an agency, if the policies were unchanged? In strategic terms, however, the twinning of reorganization with cuts was problematic. To the extent that the abolition of ED was presented as a vehicle for further cuts, legislators were unlikely to be supportive. And some education lobbyists who had opposed the creation of the department in 1979 now opposed its abolition on the grounds that, as Albert Shanker put it, "this Administration wants to get rid of the federal role in education."[74] In response, Meese sought to "calm fears that the Reagan administration does not believe in the importance of education."[75] But the charges persisted.

The administration's new political weakness became further apparent when a group of twenty-one GOP freshmen—part of a cohort whose previous lockstep support for the president had earned them the sobriquet "Reagan's Robots"—formed the Coalition Against Reductions in Education (CARE) and declared the president's plans "unacceptable."[76] As for the abolition of ED, when Reagan asked Senator Thad Cochran of Mississippi what he thought about the ED reorganization question, this loyal ally's response was blunt:

> I voted for a cabinet-level Department of Education because I saw a dire need for a centralized emphasis on the dissemination of information and assistance to our schools, rather than the fragmented system of programs available to them before its creation. That need still exists, and is perhaps even more urgent. . . . Frankly, I am not inclined to support any measure that would risk undermining the support we need for our educational system. . . . The expanding opportunities for a quality education for every American child have been a remarkable aspect of the growth and development of our nation. Succeeding generations have benefited from this national emphasis on education. Any proposal affecting education must reflect its overwhelming importance to our nation's future.[77]

Another ally who was troubled by the proposal to abolish ED was Samuel Hayakawa, formerly a professor of semantics, now a GOP senator from Reagan's home state. He had known Reagan since 1968, when the governor had appointed him acting president of the San Francisco State College, at a time when the campus was wracked with violent antiwar protests. He supported eliminating ED in principle but was unenthusiastic about the timing, warning of "strong congressional opposition" from Republicans facing difficult reelection fights. Program transfers, he told Bell, "might send the wrong signals to our constituents. They could easily misinterpret this to mean that the Federal government does not take education seriously." If that impression continued to gain ground, it could be "politically threatening" to the administration's broader agenda.[78]

This was good advice, but hard to take, given the need to show readers of *Human Events* and other strong conservatives that Reagan had *not* been captured by moderates, appearances to the contrary. So the proposal to turn ED into a foundation was included in the 1983 budget bill, along with sharp programmatic cuts, and Bell was dispatched to Congress to extol its virtues.[79] The first person whom he called on was Senate majority leader Howard Baker. Since Baker had close ties to educators in his home state of Tennessee and was a strong supporter of education appropriations, Bell knew that he might take some persuading. Sure enough, Baker stated categorically that "we can't abolish the Department of Education. We just went through a big fight a couple of years ago to establish it." When Bell tried to counter that argument, Baker smiled, acknowledged that the secretary had "made a good pitch" and "done your part," but added "I don't think you really believe it." Baker said that he would use all of his power to oppose abolition.

This placed Bell in a difficult position, politically adroit as he was. He would clearly have been personally pleased to learn that the tide was running so strongly against the abolition of ED, but the danger was that he would be blamed for any failure to implement the president's promise, endangering his position in the cabinet just as surely as the abolition of his job. In an effort to demonstrate his commitment, he went to Reagan, explained the problem, and asked the president to call Baker. Reagan did so, but to no avail: he told Bell that he had never seen Baker so determined on any issue.

The next name on Bell's list was William Roth (R-Del.), who had taken Abraham Ribicoff's position as chair of Government Operations, the Senate committee that would consider the ED bill. But he too had supported the creation of the department in 1979.[80] Before Bell had even finished outlining his ideas, Roth interrupted him and "dumped on me and my bill so heavily that I knew it would be futile to ask him to sponsor it." Although he was a strong fiscal conservative, Roth shared Cochran's belief that the federal government had an important role to play in education. Over in the House, it was the same story. When Bell went to see Trent Lott, who was a keen supporter of the Reagan Revolution, "Trent explained to me how many members of his own family had been teachers. He went to some lengths to explain how important education was" and "had no enthusiasm for abolishing the Department of Education." By this time, it was obvious that the ED bill would fail. The administration declined even to send it to Congress.[81]

Still, the effort did yield one important result: education lobby groups rediscovered their cohesion and their morale. Allan Cohen, the Illinois lobbyist who had led an ad hoc coalition to create a Department of Education two years previously, now found himself at the head of another one, this time dedicated to saving ED.[82] And whereas the effectiveness of the earlier group had been somewhat vitiated by the opposition to ED of AFT, the Catholic conference, and the AFL-CIO, this time all three were on the same side as the NEA.

If ECIA had been a partial success for the administration—a significant reform, if one that fell short of expectations—then the attempt to abolish ED ended in complete failure. It would be a mistake to portray this as a major defeat for Reagan, who evidently regarded it as a comparatively small issue and was not inclined to use it as a test of his political authority.[83] Still, for some Reaganauts, it was a devastating reverse, explicable only in terms of Bell's apostasy. *Human Events* argued that the secretary had cunningly sold the foundation plan as a moderate one that would be acceptable to Republicans facing reelection, when in fact its main attribute was its complete unacceptability to "the President's most faithful and longstanding supporters," who were not interested in simply rebranding ED as a "foundation." Absent their support, they asked, how could the administration bill possibly have succeeded?[84]

Rolling Back the Reagan Revolution

The failure of the half-hearted effort to abolish ED marked the point at which the brief and incomplete Reagan Revolution in education started to be rolled back. The main causes of that reverse, like the reasons for the survival of ED, were exogenous. By 1982 the White House had concluded that there was no way of eliminating the federal budget deficit, and by 1984 it appeared that it could continue to balloon without Reagan sustaining significant political damage. That made the task of forcing through unpopular cuts in social programs less urgent than it had been in 1981.

Also, as the 1984 election drew nearer, Michael Deaver, James Baker, and the First Lady continued to worry about the "fairness issue" and distanced the president from policies that might lend it additional salience. Meese apparently continued to hope for the abolition of ED, but even to the ideologues at OMB that now seemed quixotic.[85] When William Bennett was nominated to replace Bell as secretary at the start of Reagan's second term, the Senate made its approval contingent on his pledging that the administration had no intention of renewing the abolitionist quest. He took the pledge.[86]

By then, the position of movement conservatives within ED, never all that strong, had been badly weakened.[87] In 1982, a number of Bell's most determined critics were forced out, chief among them Ed Curran, head of NIE. Without telling Bell, Curran had written a personal letter to Reagan urging him to abolish his agency (this did not require legislative action) and had used a special code supplied to him by the recently departed Lyn Nofziger to ensure that it would reach Reagan's desk.[88] Learning of this ploy, a furious Bell insisted that Curran be dismissed; otherwise, *he* would quit. In different circumstances, Reagan might have welcomed a showdown with Bell, whose honeymoon with the Right was now well behind him, following the failure to abolish ED. Now, however, even Meese reportedly felt that it was Curran who had to go: with the White House trying to defuse the "fairness issue," the last thing that it needed was a public spat with an ex-secretary Bell. Shortly after Curran's departure for a position in Meese's office, movement conservatives suffered a second blow when Bob Sweet, who had sought to continue Curran's work at NIE, was also sacked. (He too found refuge in Meese's office.[89])

The following month, a third recently sacked NIE Reaganaut, senior policy analyst Charlotte Iserbyt, wrote an angry letter to the president, remarking that "the Reagan agenda for education is hardly distinguishable from that of President Carter and the NEA." She asked: "What ever happened to the Reagan Revolution?" charging that

> Reagan appointees, who stood on principle and backed your philosophy to the hilt, have been asked to resign or have voluntarily resigned in disgust over the present policies of the Department of Education. . . .
> How can your revolution take place without principled Reaganaut soldiers[?] The educationist philosophy of the past thirty years . . . proceeds apace, and a strengthening of the very establishment you pledged to reduce . . . continues without a hitch or a peep from the White House. . . . Grassroots citizens, who worked day and night to get you elected, ask me "What is going on?" Since I am loyal to you, all I can say is "I guess the President isn't allowed to know what is really going on. If he were, he would certainly take steps to reverse the present course in the Department of Education."[90]

Movement conservatives could draw little comfort from federal spending patterns. Here too, the fall of 1981 seemed to mark the end of the Reagan Revolution. True, OMB was still trying to cut ED spending, most dramatically in the FY 1983 budget, which called for draconian cuts. But if that was vexing for Bell, his irritation must have been eased by the knowledge that there was no prospect at all that Congress would go along with OMB. The White House recognized that too and did not invest much political capital in the fight. In this new environment, Bell's allies in Congress, together with

TABLE 10.1. ED Requests and Appropriations, FY 1980–1988 (in $billions)

Fiscal Year	Budget Request (current $)	Appropriation (current $)	% Difference Request/Appropriations	Appropriation (real $)
1980	12.3	14.5	17.3	13.9
1981	13.5	14.8	9.3	13.4
1982	12.4	14.8	19.4	12.4
1983	9.9	15.4	55.0	12.5
1984	13.2	15.4	17.1	11.9
1985	15.5	19.1	23.2	14.2
1986	15.9	17.9	15.4	12.6
1987	15.2	19.7	29.4	13.6
1988	14.0	20.3	44.6	13.5

Source: Tables 1 and 2, Deborah Verstegen, "Education Fiscal Policy in the Reagan Administration," *Educational Evaluation and Policy Analysis* 12, no. 4 (Winter 1990): 359, 367.

the education interest groups, slowly regained their self-confidence. That was already clear during 1982 and became progressively more so in the wake of that year's midterm elections, in which the GOP lost twenty-five House seats. This was not a disaster, but it did deprive conservatives of their ideological majority, and it was a major boost for supporters of education spending.[91] In the Senate, the Republicans retained control, but that was in part because moderates facing tough races had resisted the White House's education agenda.[92]

When the 98th Congress convened in January 1983, Reagan's budget was summarily dismissed by the House in favor of a more expansive Democratic version including a substantial rise in education spending. It won approval in the GOP-controlled Senate.[93] It was still not a propitious environment for forging ahead with bold new extensions of the federal role in education. Rather, the story was one of gradual, uneven recovery from the shock of 1981. Inflation-adjusted spending in 1988 was still below the figure for 1980, with concerns about the federal budget deficit acting as a restraining force during Reagan's second term.[94] (See Table 10.1.)

Still, circumstances were more congenial than in 1981 and probably better than education lobbyists could have anticipated back then. It was now possible to chip away at the modest reforms made by ECIA and to reverse the initial round of spending cuts.[95] By July 1983, when *National Journal* assessed education politics on the Hill, the title of the story was "The Education Lobby Reborn."[96] And when *Congressional Quarterly* evaluated Reagan's first term, it concluded that developments in 1984, "halting and cautious" as they were, "did take education programs out of the holding pattern that had stalled virtually all initiatives since the 96th Congress [1979–1980]."[97]

Shortly after Reagan's triumphant reelection in 1984, Stockman's office produced an overview of education politics during the first term. Its tone was decidedly gloomy. OMB detected "growth spurts" in spending on each of the big programs (vocational education, impact aid, Chapter I, aid to the handicapped), all at higher levels than when Reagan had come into office, and after ECIA, "no further program repeals or simplifications occurred." On the contrary, "*every* succeeding reauthorization or 'technical amendment' package has either: (a) restored complexities and limitations, e.g., Chapter 1 and student aid; (b) established a more complex or heavily earmarked program structure, e.g., vocational education; (c) created a deluge of new programs."[98]

Who was to blame for this resumption of politics as usual? The author of the OMB report held Congress primarily responsible but believed that Bell had also played a role:

> The traditional Congressional instinct to create a new little authority for every perceived problem has been reborn with a vengeance. It seems clear that Secretary Bell was willing midwife to the process. No enrolled bill with new authorities was recommended by him for disapproval. . . . Not a single authorization opposed by the Administration has been defeated; no Administration proposal, except Title III endowment funding, has been enacted.[99]

Toward a New Politics of Education: "A Nation at Risk"

The landmark event in education politics during the Reagan presidency came in April 1983, when he presided over the release of an ED report entitled *A Nation at Risk*. At the start of his tenure, Terrel Bell had pushed for a White House commission on U.S. education, but the suggestion was firmly rebuffed, on the grounds that this locus would imply that education was a presidential responsibility, when Reagan was trying to put the opposite case. Bell commissioned a cabinet-level investigation instead, the National Commission on Excellence in Education, but its prospects for making a splash must have seemed dim. Even White House commissions frequently gather dust, rather than stimulating action. How much less likely was it that a cabinet report commissioned by a possibly now-defunct department would have any catalytic impact? Still, Bell hoped that its investigation might help put education in the national spotlight, thereby complicating the task of those who wished to diminish the federal role. Also, the focus on excellence ought to please the Right, which tended to think that the politics of education had been too dominated by considerations of equity since the 1960s and insufficiently concerned with declining academic standards. The Heritage Foundation had recently urged "a blue ribbon panel of distinguished citizens and educators committed to the attainment and improvement of basic academic skills."[100]

The chairman of the commission was David Gardner, president of the University of Utah, and someone whom Bell knew well. Serendipitously (or possibly this was another demonstration of Bell's political deftness), Gardner was also known to the president, for he had been vice chancellor of the University of California at Santa Barbara and then vice president of the whole University of California system, during Reagan's governorship. (That Governor Reagan had admired the firmness that he felt Gardner displayed during those years of campus upheaval was also helpful.[101]) Other members of the eclectic commission included the national teacher of the year, professors from Berkeley and Harvard (the former a Nobel Laureate in Chemistry), the president of Yale University, the school commissioners of Albuquerque and the state of Nebraska, the president of NSBA, a community college president, a big city principal, the retired chairman of Bell Telephone Laboratories, and former Congressman Albert Quie (who had more recently been governor of Minnesota). Although Bell successfully resisted pressure to appoint high-profile conservative intellectuals to the panel, Reagan knew at least five of the commissioners, including Annette Kirk (wife of the revered conservative philosopher, Russell Kirk) and Yvonne Larsen (president of the San Diego school board).[102]

The commission's executive director was Milton Goldberg, a career civil servant at NIE. He helped to organize a series of regional hearings in late 1981 and 1982 on particular themes: Derek Bok, the president of Harvard, hosted a session on provision for gifted and talented students, for example, and the president of Stanford, Donald Kennedy, convened a science and technology discussion. To Goldberg's surprise and pleasure, some of these hearings attracted considerable attention from the local media, from education practitioners, and also from state and local politicians.[103] Partly for that reason, the commissioners evinced uncommon zest for their project: Bruce Boston, a writing consultant who had worked with a number of other education commissions, was impressed that they did not simply leave everything to the staff, which was what normally happened. Even though there were many differences among them, each commissioner seemed to be convinced that "education in this country was in a mess" and that their report must issue a "clarion call" for reform.[104] David Gardner recalls that "the 'chemistry' of the eighteen was remarkably good" and that "caution melted into collegiality and later into friendship."[105]

At the same time, Goldberg's staff struggled to produce a draft report that distilled their rather disparate senses for what constituted the "mess" in American education. Also, Goldberg aide James Harvey, who served as the lead writer, and Bruce Boston, the consultant, were accustomed to what Otis Graham has called "the usual insipidity of government reports on controversial topics."[106] Here, however, Gardner wanted a report that "provoke[d] the public and media to take note." The writing team went through numerous drafts, but he found them "scholarly in tone, jargon-filled, lengthy, and, in my view, of interest to almost no one." At the chairman's suggestion, the commissioners decided to present their report as an "open letter" to the American people. Gardner explains their reasoning: "Were we to do this, the entire character of the report would change: it would be written in plain English, it would be brief, it would be less official and more open, it would be less encumbered by political sensitivities."[107]

Despite that decision, the chairman remained "concerned with the continuing gap between the substance and tone of the drafts being prepared by the staff and what some of us were looking for in the report." Finally, he asked Gerald Holton, professor of physics at Harvard, to produce an entirely fresh draft. To Harvey, accustomed to the dry, measured language of the standard government report, Holton's response seemed "a wild screed," full of inflated talk of a calamitous collapse in educational standards that threatened the nation's global standing. Some of the K-12 educators on the panel, he says, viewed it with concern, as an attack on their profession.[108] Still, Boston acknowledges, it made Harvey and him "more comfortable with using more vivid rhetoric . . . , and with being less 'official' and 'measured.'"

When he read Holton's draft, Gardner "knew we were on our way." In his view, this was "the first real draft of the commission's report." Not only did it use vivid, attention-grabbing language, as befit a "letter to the American people," but also its language "allowed for the diversity of opinions on major issues" that existed among commissioners, while allowing the group to "coalesce." Even so, four members were still minded to produce their own minority reports at this point, and Gardner knew that this would greatly diminish its impact. The last of the four, Glenn Seaborg, signed up only two hours before Goldberg had to mail *A Nation at Risk* to the printer.[109]

Bell maintained a studious public distance from the activities of the commission throughout, wanting to avoid any hint that he was seeking to influence its conclusions. His staff member Mary Jean LeTendre kept him abreast of its progress, however, and he also had regular late-night phone conversations with Gardner.[110] Increasingly hopeful that the commission would produce an attention-grabbing report, he sought the unique publicity that would come with a White House launch. Fortuitously, the politics of education were now being viewed exclusively through an electoral lens at the White House, ahead of what looked likely to be a difficult fight for reelection, and Deaver and Baker were worried by a March 1983 poll suggesting that voters disapproved of Reagan's approach to education by 48 percent to 42 percent. They saw in *A Nation at Risk* an opportunity to demonstrate that the president cared about the state of the nation's schools.[111]

Before endorsing a White House launch, Reagan required reassurance that the report did not call for any new federal spending. When Bell duly provided that assurance, Baker went ahead and arranged a cabinet room reception and presidential address. Shortly thereafter, Reagan received a copy of *A Nation at Risk*. Here is how the report began:

> Our nation is at risk. Our once unchallenged preeminence in commerce, industry, science, and technological innovation is being overtaken by competitors throughout the world. This report is concerned with only one of the many causes and dimensions of the problem, but it is the one that undergirds American prosperity, security, and civility. We report to the American people that while we can take justifiable pride in what our schools and colleges have historically accomplished and contributed to the United States and the well-being of its people, the educational foundations of our society are presently being eroded by a rising tide of mediocrity that threatens our very future as a Nation and a people. What was unimaginable a generation ago has begun to occur—others are matching and surpassing our educational attainments.
>
> If an unfriendly foreign power had attempted to impose on America the mediocre educational performance that exists today, we might well have viewed it as an act of war. As it stands, we have allowed this to happen to ourselves. We have even squandered the gains in student achievement made in the wake of the Sputnik challenge. Moreover, we have dismantled essential support systems which helped make those gains possible. We have, in effect, been committing an act of unthinking, unilateral educational disarmament.[112]

In publicizing this hard-hitting report, White House officials felt that they were reinforcing the core Reaganite argument that federal aid had been heavily implicated in a disastrous deterioration in educational standards. This was a searing indictment of American schooling, and its logical implication seemed to be—at least at first glance—that it was the job of states, school districts, and education schools to turn around the catastrophic decline in educational standards that had purportedly placed the nation's economic future "at risk" during the past two decades.[113] Nevertheless, if that is how *A Nation at Risk* was construed by White House aides, they were being a little naive. How likely was it that the state of American education could be presented as a *national* problem, indeed a threat to the nation's economic and geopolitical security, without also being a *federal* problem?

For Bell, it was a tremendous coup when James Baker's staff persuaded President Reagan to give the *A Nation at Risk* report a White House release, before a large gathering of reporters. The occasion itself did not seem to go well, since Reagan's speech made almost no reference to the report's content, focusing instead on such conservative hot issues as tuition tax credits, prayer in schools, and the continuing need to abolish the Department of Education (topics that had not been mentioned in the report). Bell and the commissioners were astonished, and White House conservatives gleeful.[114]

Their sense of triumph was fleeting, however; press coverage ignored Reagan's speech and concentrated on the text of the report, a tribute to its brevity and its plain, eye-catching English.[115] Such was the coverage that Reagan's reelection staff—having initially envisioned a one-time photo op—decided instead to make education one of the principal issues of the campaign. Reagan, having paid almost no personal attention to education during the first two and a half years of his presidency, now embarked on a nationwide speaking tour, accompanied by Secretary Bell and Executive Director Goldberg, designed to publicize the report. As David Gergen explains, "Our point was to let Reagan ride with the report, rather than have it ride over him."[116]

It worked for Reagan. Whereas a month before the report was issued, voters had disapproved of his approach to education by a margin of 48 percent to 42 percent, by the end of his education tour, they approved, by 51 percent to 42 percent. When a reporter suggested to Deaver that voters might be puzzled by the incongruity of an administration that had tried to slash education spending simultaneously trying to wrap itself in the issue, Reagan's communications chief was unbothered: "You can say what you want," he observed, "but the viewer sees Ronald Reagan out there in a classroom talking to teachers and kids, and what he takes from that is the impression that Ronald Reagan is concerned about education."[117]

By the same token, many educators had been troubled by the language of the *A Nation at Risk* report, which they saw as overly negative and as too critical of them. But as education rose up the political agenda, to a position of prominence that it had not enjoyed since Sputnik, the realization dawned that this was the best thing that had happened to them in a long time. Although the White House succeeded in defusing the education issue ahead of the election, the price—at least from the viewpoint of Reaganauts more committed than Reagan to diminishing the federal role in education—was high. *A Nation at Risk* became one more factor contributing to the erosion of the Reagan Revolution in education. By 1984 the federal policy legacies of the 1960s and 1970s were secure.

But that is not the primary significance of *A Nation at Risk*. What was less clear in 1984, but loomed largest subsequently, in the wake of No Child Left Behind, was the fact that the report helped to stimulate a national conversation about educational excellence that would revolutionize the federal role as surely as had the launch of Sputnik, a third of a century earlier.

CONCLUSION

In a 2004 sequel to his classic account of the 1960s, *America in Our Time*, Godfrey Hodgson argued that "between Richard Nixon's departure from the White House in 1974 and the return of the Republican George W. Bush in 2001, a new conservative consensus was forged," taking the place of the "liberal consensus" that had characterized the post–World War II era. "The crucial change," he believes, was "the discrediting of government" that came about as Americans "rejected the ideals or the methods of the Great Society program."[1] Dan T. Carter, biographer of George Wallace, concurs with that assessment, identifying "streams of racial and economic conservatism" that "joined in the political coalition that reshaped American politics from the 1970s through the mid-1990s."[2]

Since Carter wrote those words, a substantial number of historians have sought to discern the origins of the conservative counterrevolution, each persuaded that it has powerfully shaped the development of recent American politics. Some have explained "the fall of the New Deal Order" substantially in terms of liberal missteps and opportunities forgone.[3] Others have seen coded racial appeals as being central to the GOP's new appeal after 1968.[4] More recently, a third group has emphasized the popular appeal of conservative ideas.[5] Whatever the argument, however, all these authors tend to assume the dominance of the Right in American politics since the 1960s. Steve Fraser and Gary Gerstle, for example, have argued that "the Reagan presidency . . . opened wide the portals of executive and administrative leverage to ideologues of the Right," as "the Counter-Reformation fastened its hold on the levers of power and implemented its social policies."[6] And Lisa McGirr observes that "the Right expanded its influence on the national scene in the late 1960s and 1970s and vaulted to national power with the Reagan landslide of 1980." "Since that time," she goes on, "conservatives in Washington have transformed the relationship between federal and state power, limited the regulatory capacity of the central state, and altered the fundamental structure of the New Deal welfare state."[7]

At the same time, as James T. Patterson has documented in *Restless Giant:*

The United States from Watergate to Bush v. Gore, there is more to the story than this. "Conservative presidents and members of Congress after 1974," he observes, "learned to their dismay that while people might claim to despise government, they also developed ever higher expectations from it." In that environment, he continues, New Deal and Great Society programs survived, and even continued to expand.[8] These expectations, Patterson concludes, were boosted in part by the "rights revolution" of the 1960s. Although it is not hard to identify reactions against—say—affirmative action, gay rights, and welfare during the years since, Patterson is more impressed by the continuing "spread of tolerance and rights-consciousness," concluding that the enduring legacy of the 1960s included "greater civil rights, civil liberties, entitlements, protections, and freedoms" for all manner of groups whose members had been harshly treated during the "Good Old Days" of the 1950s.[9]

A number of historians have agreed with Patterson's point about tolerance and rights-consciousness.[10] Fewer have pursued his other point, about the growth of government in an antigovernment era. The classic source here remains the late Hugh Davis Graham, one of the few historians of recent U.S. politics to have wrestled with the Madisonian structure of American federal democracy in all its formidable complexity and with the profound changes in American governance that came about during the Great Society era. Without denying that the years after 1968 featured a strong political reaction against liberalism, Graham's work on civil rights, immigration policy, and education documents the inventive and determined ways in which activists within and without the government kept the banner of reform aloft during the 1970s and shows that they enjoyed considerable policy success.

Sometimes Graham wrote about presidential leadership and bottom-up social protest (the two approaches to social reform most favored by historians). Often, though, he was concerned with more anonymous political actors, such as the "coalition of mostly white, second-tier civil servants" whose "low-visibility internal debate" shaped affirmative action policy during the 1960s.[11] They produced "such gray contrivances of statutory law and the bureaucratic imagination" as the Department of Labor's Revised Order No. 4, which stated in 1971 that federal contractors should hire ethnoracial minorities and women in numbers proportional to their presence in the general population. With understatement, he observes that Revised Order No. 4 lacks "the graphic and emotional appeal of the murders of civil rights workers in Mississippi or the ghetto riots in Watts and Detroit." But, he goes on, "in the long run of policy continuity and its aggregated impact," these "gray contrivances" were "probably more important."[12]

In his final two books, *The Civil Rights Era* and *Collision Course*, and in a cluster of important articles, Graham probed the aspects of the American political system that allowed these anonymous actors to shape policy, often absent broad public debate, or—in some cases—in the face of public opinion. Some of these aspects—iron triangle relationships, bureaucratic discretion in rule making, the difficulty of eliminating established federal programs—were intrinsic to modern American government. Others—the growth of social regulation, the enhanced role of the federal courts, divided government—were specific to the 1960s and 1970s.

Where there is policy discontinuity between those two decades in Graham's scholarship (and this is a dominant theme of his work), it generally takes the form of a bold advance into new territory, rather than a retreat. In the case of affirmative action, for example, the "soft" hiring targets of the Johnson years yielded to the "hard" quotas of the Minority Set-Aside Program, "nondiscrimination" theory gave way to an "underutilization" model, group rights replaced individual rights, and the minority rights revolution in government policy broadened to encompass groups that had been politically marginal at the time of the Civil Rights Act. In each instance, seeds sown during the Johnson presidency germinated in the Nixon-Ford years and left many of the policies of the high Great Society era looking somewhat modest and traditional. The result, says Graham, was "a paradigm shift in social policy and administration," largely unanticipated by many of its early progenitors but profound in its public policy consequences.

Where did this transformation in civil rights enforcement come from? In part, it was engineered in the White House, and in Congress, and it owed *something* to bottom-up protest. But, he concludes, its basic contours were "determined more in the federal courts and the agencies of the permanent government," and that this could be so illuminates the "fundamental shift in authority and power" that had occurred in American government between 1965 and 1972.[13]

In the case of education, Graham's earlier book *Uncertain Triumph* ends in 1968 and is therefore less concerned with this shift in governance than were his later books and articles. But education politics after 1968 followed a similar trajectory. The federal role in schools became bolder and ever more entrenched between then and 1984, despite a lack of convincing evidence that federal dollars were improving the quality of American education, and despite the fact that there were Republicans in the White House much of the time who were committed to reining in federal spending, and overhauling ESEA.

Why did the federal role in education endure and expand? One must begin by noting that there was *not* a dramatic expansion in federal spending on elementary and secondary education during this period: it remained stuck between 7 and 10 percent of total spending on schools, after the one-time near doubling in the federal share that occurred in 1965–1966. In this sense, what needs to be accounted for in relation to ESEA is not its expansion, but rather its durability. Here, the explanation is straightforward, located in the routine operations of American democracy that make it hard to dismantle any federal program, once that program has acquired a constituency, and once that constituency has learned how to exploit the structure and processes of American government to its advantage. Part of the explanation also has to do with the way that Americans have always tended to idealize education, seeing in public schools an almost magical mechanism for equalizing opportunities between individuals, without greatly redistributing income. That ideal transcends differences between liberals and conservatives and is unlikely ever to be displaced by evidence that schools cannot, in fact, compensate for societal inequality.[14] Accordingly, it is not only their mastery of the labyrinthine procedures and structures of American democracy that helps to explain the political success of education lobbyists during the 1970s. They also managed to frame the defense of Great Society programs in terms of whether one was "proeducation" or "antieducation." Framed thus, there was only one side of the argument to be on, and even conservative Republicans in Congress adjusted to that reality during the Nixon-Ford years.

Rather than spending levels, what stands out in education policy after the 1960s is the increase in federal regulation, especially in the area of civil rights enforcement. The federal effort to desegregate southern schools spawned a number of other regulatory missions, requiring school districts to eliminate discrimination vis-à-vis language minorities and the handicapped and on the basis of gender. The cumulative impact of these interventions was to expand the federal government's role in the nation's school districts and to make it much more assertive in these civil rights contexts, even though in the case of ESEA Washington continued to be deferential to the states. These precedents helped to make the subsequent intrusions of NCLB seem less revolutionary than would otherwise have been the case, especially since George W. Bush explicitly presented that revision to the 1965 law as being about the civil rights of the educationally disadvantaged.[15]

Other than the degree of federal direction, perhaps the most significant feature of this education regulation regime was its comparative detachment from the world of majoritarian politics. The leading actors in federal policymaking by the 1970s were not presidents. Instead, they were, for the most part, unelected political actors: judges, career civil servants, public interest lawyers, congressional subcommittee staffers, interest group lobbyists. There is no suggestion here that their actions were in any way furtive or sinister, but one is struck by the degree to which important measures such as Stanley Pottinger's 1970 memorandum on language rights, or Joseph Waddy's ruling in the *Mills* case, went largely unobserved. Yet, in some respects, measures such as these altered the federal-state relationship in education rather more dramatically than had the Elementary and Secondary Education Act of 1965.

Meanwhile, Richard Nixon, George Wallace, Ronald Reagan, and Jimmy Carter were capitalizing on a burgeoning antigovernmental mood, rooted in anger about the Vietnam War, urban riots, perceived moral decline, rising welfare rolls, stagflation, and a whole raft of contentious liberal judicial rulings (concerning busing, abortion, prayer in schools, capital punishment, pornography, and the rights of criminal suspects). What explains the vitality of education reform in this seemingly adverse climate? Why, indeed, was the federal role in the nation's school districts so much more assertive during the Nixon-Ford years than it had been under Johnson?

Divided government helped in some respects: between 1969 and 1976, Democrats in Congress sought to keep the banner of reform aloft and to protect the Great Society from White House efforts at retrenchment. But in cases such as school finance reform, bilingual schooling, and the education of the handicapped, the most important political momentum came through the courts or through the bureaucracy. Even where Congress was involved, as with PL94-142, the stimulus came from "iron triangle" relationships and from the courts, rather than through the initiative of elected representatives.[16] This is not to say that the reform impulse emerged triumphant on every occasion: in the case of school finance, or busing, the Supreme Court drew back from bold interpretations of the Fourteenth Amendment during the mid-1970s; and in the case of bilingual education, the following decade would bring a sharp counterreaction that unraveled many earlier gains. Edward Berkowitz is right, accordingly, to distinguish between the early 1970s, a period during which the reforming impulse retained striking vigor, and the latter half of the decade, during which the going became harder.[17]

At the same time, it would be going too far to say the late 1970s and

1980s brought easy policy victories for the Right. In the area of school finance, "equity"-based claims won in the state courts during the late 1970s, while "adequacy" suits were chalking up impressive victories by the end of the 1980s. Those suits—both directly and because of the broader conversation about the fairness of traditional arrangements that they stimulated within the states—contributed to a big increase in the state share of total expenditures during the 1970s and early 1980s and diminished reliance on local property taxes (two of the core liberal demands of the *Rodriguez* era).[18] In the case of education for the handicapped, meanwhile, there was no reversal of the momentum. On the contrary, the attitudinal and policy shifts of the early 1970s have been long-lasting, revolutionizing the way that children with disabilities are taught and regarded throughout the United States. As for presidential action, Ronald Reagan's efforts to diminish the federal role in education and abolish the Department of Education were rolled back with comparative ease, much greater ease than had been anticipated during the early months of his administration.

The most important enduring legacy of the 1970s, though, has to do not with any particular policy but with overall conceptions of the federal role in education. The lopsided votes for renewal of ESEA in 1974 and 1978, the almost complete lack of opposition to PL 94-142 in 1975, and the resistance of people such as Thad Cochrane and Trent Lott to the proposed abolition of the Department of Education during the early 1980s all suggested that most conservatives had come to terms with the expansion that had taken place in the federal presence since 1965. In 1965, only 26 percent of House Republicans voted for ESEA. By 1974, that figure had climbed to 74 percent, by 1978 to 90 percent, and by 1988 to 99 percent.[19] Rather than fight the expanded federal role, Republicans increasingly sought a share of the political credit.[20]

From *A Nation at Risk* to No Child Left Behind

As of 1983, however, those Republicans would still not have been prepared to countenance a measure such as the No Child Left Behind Act. Neither would liberals, given how unwelcome many of that measure's provisions were to the teacher unions and to other education lobby groups. If one regards ESEA as having constituted one important stage in the expansion of the federal role in schools, and the civil rights enforcement activities of the Nixon-Ford years as having constituted a second stage, then the national conversation about educational excellence that started in the mid-1980s, following *A Nation at Risk*, marked a third stage.[21]

Between 1965 and the early 1980s, the federal role had centered on questions of equity: on provision for the poor and for discriminated-against minority groups. Now, those concerns became less central, yielding to a preoccupation with the overall quality of American schooling. To some extent, that resembled the post-Sputnik mood of the late 1950s, which had spawned the first big federal intervention in elementary and secondary education, NDEA. This time, though, the stimulus for concern was less the Cold War than issues of economic competitiveness.

Support for an active federal role in education, already strong, became stronger still as it acquired this new dimension, and the conservative charge that misguided Great Society policies had been implicated in a decline in the quality of American schooling did nothing to diminish that support. If anything, the idea that the nation's schools were in crisis lent even more legitimacy to the view that national politicians had an obligation to intervene. In the late 1980s and early 1990s, however, this did not result in any profound shift in federal-state relations: as in earlier times, federal leadership during Reagan's second term and the first Bush presidency took the form of encouraging action at the state level, rather than telling the states what to do.

Governors across the nation responded to this stimulus, seeing the importance of the growing crusade for educational excellence both in terms of the competitiveness of their states and as a good issue in political terms. The annual surveys that the federal Department of Education started to publicize during the second half of the 1980s indicated that these efforts were not bearing much fruit in terms of educational "outputs." That was troubling, but it also presented a political opportunity for George H.W. Bush, who wished to project the image of a "kinder, gentler America" as something of a reaction developed against the perceived harshness of the Reagan years. Bush made education one of his top political issues, most notably with the Charlottesville summit of governors, in 1989.

The fact that this was a summit of governors was significant, and so too was the fact that it took place outside of Washington, D.C., on the grounds of the University of Virginia. As education moved up the political agenda and occupied more presidential time, and as it received greater attention from governors and business leaders too, Congress found that it was rather less central to the debate than in earlier times. That in turn complicated life for education interest groups, skilled defenders of the Great Society regime on the Hill who now had to cope with the enthusiasm of presidents, think tanks, the Business Coalition for Education Reform, and governors for new policy directions.[22]

During the 1990s, under both Bush and his Democratic successor, Bill Clinton (formerly a prominent education governor), talk of educational excellence centered on the need for "accountability" and "standards." States, school districts, and individual schools, according to the emerging orthodoxy, must show that increased spending on schools was resulting in improved performance, and they should be held accountable for any failure to meet goals. Although governors in both parties were participants in this talk about standards and accountability, it worried some movement conservatives, whose keenness to berate teacher unions and "progressive" pedagogic techniques coexisted with a continuing suspicion of federal control and a desire to rein in federal spending.

ESEA retained its compensatory thrust and its categorical character during the 1990s, despite renewed Republican efforts to convert it into a block grant program. That is not to say, however, that it remained unchanged from the 1970s. On the contrary, when it came up for renewal in 1994, just before the midterm elections, it was reformed in important ways that strongly anticipated NCLB. Specifically, new conditions were attached to receipt of Title I funds, requiring states to institute annual testing of elementary school students, to set standards that children were expected to achieve, and to develop curricula that made those standards achievable. Because the Clinton administration did not enforce these requirements, they did not amount in practice to a revolution in the federal role: only one-third of the states came into compliance. But it was significant that legislators had been prepared to endorse such theoretically strong and intrusive measures, a sure sign of the momentum of the education reform movement, the lessening power of the education lobby groups (which opposed most of these provisions), and the diminished force of the local control argument. In retrospect, the 1994 renewal of ESEA looms large in the story of how NCLB came about.

At the end of that year, Republicans succeeded in taking control of Congress for the first time since Eisenhower's first term, and conservatives consolidated their grip on the GOP, especially in the House of Representatives. Amid the giddy excitement of the "Contract with America," Speaker Newt Gingrich spearheaded an ambitious attempt to drive down federal spending on schools and eliminate the Department of Education.[23] Robert Dole also supported these objectives in his 1996 presidential campaign. The GOP presidential platform that year declared that "the federal government has no constitutional authority to be involved in school curricula" and promised that President Dole would "end federal meddling in our schools."[24]

This assault turned out to be not so much ambitious, as foolhardy. Opposed by many Republicans and by prominent business groups, and gleefully exploited by Clinton, this Gingrich Revolution in education came to nothing and contributed to Dole's defeat. Even more than Reagan's efforts during the previous decade, it had the paradoxical consequence of further entrenching the federal role. As Republicans found themselves scrambling again to avoid the "antieducation" tag, they competed with the Clinton administration to claim the credit for *increasing* federal spending. Indeed, Clinton ended his second term trying to pare back GOP-sponsored education appropriations bills that far exceeded his budgetary requests. At the state level too, GOP governors strove to project a moderate, proeducation message, in order to avoid being cast as clones of Gingrich. They included George W. Bush of Texas, who made improving education his top political priority.

Their activities highlighted an important broader aspect of the educational "excellence" movement. Even though it had originated in part from a sense that the federal role had been too narrowly geared to the goal of equality, as a practical matter *any* effort by the federal government to influence the way that schools taught was bound to have a strong equity element, given that this was where Washington had leverage (because Title I and aid to the handicapped were the two biggest federal grant programs to schools). This equity element was strengthened further during the second half of the 1990s by the GOP effort to escape Gingrich's shadow. In Texas, for example, Governor Bush made improving education in inner cities, among Hispanics, and among African-Americans absolutely central to his keynote reform. The way to achieve educational excellence, he argued, was to ensure that no child was left behind. In the immediate aftermath of *A Nation at Risk*, talk of an "achievement gap" had centered on comparisons between the United States and her international competitors. By the mid-1990s, it centered additionally on differences between racial and ethnic groups in the domestic population.[25]

The "no child left behind" formulation worked well for Governor Bush in political terms, and in his 2000 presidential campaign against Vice President Al Gore he made education his number one issue. That was an extraordinary development in the annals of education history, for this had never been one of the biggest issues of a presidential campaign, not even in 1964. It was attributable not so much to the momentum of the reform issue, or to any powerful sense that there was a crisis in the nation's schools, as to the absence of other compelling political issues. The Cold War was gone, terrorism did not yet loom large, the economy was doing well, the federal budget was in surplus, and the candidates did not inspire strong feelings among the electorate.

What had worked for Bush in Texas also worked for him on the national campaign trail, notably during his first debate with Gore, at the University of Massachusetts. According to one account, when it came to education, "Bush soon had Gore on the ropes."[26] That too was a remarkable contingency, for this, like health care and Social Security, was one of those issues where the Democrats invariably had a strong advantage. Naturally, when he was ajudged to have won the election, Bush made education reform his top domestic priority after tax reduction, submitting the No Child Left Behind Act of 2001 to the new 107th Congress as HR 1.

References to vouchers, merit pay, more rigorous teacher certification, and greater state flexibility in using federal dollars ensured that some old-line Democrats would view the measure with considerable suspicion. On the other hand, they saw an opportunity to greatly expand federal funding, liked Bush's strong rhetorical emphasis on "the scandal of illiteracy in high-poverty schools" and "the soft bigotry of low expectations," and appreciated the new president's efforts to reach out to such leading liberal Democrats as Senator Edward Kennedy and Congressman George Miller (D-Calif.).[27]

By September 11, 2001, when terrorist attacks on the World Trade Center and the Pentagon utterly transformed the political environment, versions of NCLB had passed each house of Congress, but a difficult conference lay ahead, with some conservatives *and* liberals queasy about the idea of mandated federal testing and liberals also worried about state flexibility provisions. Still, the backing of Kennedy and Miller and of such strong Republican conservatives as Senator Judd Gregg (N.H.) and Congressman John Boehner (Ohio) helped in conference. Also, in the aftermath of the terrorist attacks and the war in Afghanistan, there was a short-lived mood of bipartisanship in the nation, and President Bush enjoyed exceptionally high popularity ratings. In December, when the conference bill came before Congress, the House endorsed NCLB by 381 votes to 41, and the Senate by 87 to 10.

The Enduring Great Society

It is instructive to think of NCLB in relation to the claims about the trajectory of American politics since the 1960s that were cited at the beginning of the chapter. Take, for example, the observation of one historian that "conservatives in Washington have transformed the relationship between federal and state power" and "limited the regulatory capacity of the central state." It is certainly the case that conservatives helped to transform the federal role in the nation's schools when they voted for NCLB, but they did so by greatly *expanding* "the regulatory capacity of the central state."[28] What would Barry Goldwater or Ronald Reagan have made of a law that required school districts to bring all their children up to a federally approved state standard and threatened to penalize states, districts, and schools that fell short of achievement? What, for that matter, would liberals have made of such a law, back in 1965? As one of the creators of ESEA, Samuel Halperin, observed in 2006, "*None* of the original ESEA creators could have foreseen the incredible intrusiveness of the federal government as now ensconced in NCLB. Only the opponents of ESEA—out of their fears—could project the feds getting into everything!"[29]

It is not enough to conceive of American political history after the Johnson presidency simply in terms of a sustained and largely successful attack on the liberal 1960s. On the contrary, the decline of antistatist conservatism since then may be fully as consequential a development as the travail of the Left. If so, then it may be useful to think of the Great Society, like the New Deal, not just as a set of policies, or a brief liberal moment, but as having bequeathed an era. In the case of education, Americans at the beginning of the twenty-first century were still living in the Great Society era, even if the federal role had expanded in ways that Lyndon Johnson could not possibly have imagined a third of a century earlier.

Revenues (by Source of Funds) and Expenditures for Elementary and Secondary School: Selected Years, 1955–2003

School Year	Revenues (% dist.)			Current Expenditure per Pupil in ADA[1] (2001/02 dollars)
	Federal share	State share	Local Share	
1955–56	4.6	39.5	55.9	1,950
1959–60	4.4	39.1	56.5	2,275
1963–64	4.4	39.3	56.3	2,660
1965–66	7.9	39.1	53.0	3,003
1967–68	8.8	38.5	52.7	3,449
1969–70	8.0	39.9	52.1	3,849
1970–71	8.4	39.1	52.5	4,087
1971–72	8.9	38.3	52.8	4,286
1972–73	8.7	39.7	51.6	4,483
1973–74	8.5	41.4	50.1	4,614
1974–75	9.0	42.0	49.0	4,695
1975–76	8.9	38.3	46.7	4,831
1976–77	8.8	43.2	48.0	4,972
1977–78	9.4	43.0	47.6	5,186
1978–79	9.8	45.6	44.4	5,256
1979–80	9.8	46.8	43.4	5,214
1980–81	9.2	47.4	43.4	5,146
1981–82	7.4	47.6	45.0	5,151
1982–83	7.1	47.9	45.0	5,365
1983–84	6.8	47.8	45.4	5,556
1984–85	6.6	48.9	44.4	5,847
1985–86	6.7	49.4	43.9	6,150
1986–87	6.4	49.7	43.9	6,360
1987–88	6.3	49.5	44.1	6,522
1988–89	6.2	47.8	45.4	6,829
1989–90	6.1	47.1	46.8	6,988
1990–91	6.2	47.2	46.7	6,996
1992–93	7.0	45.8	47.2	6,981

School Year	Revenues (% dist.)			Current Expenditure per Pupil in ADA[1] (2001/02 dollars)
	Federal share	State share	Local Share	
1994–95	6.8	46.8	46.4	7,095
1996–97	6.6	48.0	45.4	7,169
1998–99	7.1	48.7	44.2	7,595
2000–01	7.3	49.7	43.0	8,044
2002–03	8.5	48.7	42.8	n/a

Source: National Center for Education Statistics, *Digest of Education Statistics: 2004,* tables 152 and 162; http://nces.ed.gov (accessed July 24, 2006).

[1]ADA = annual daily attendance.

NOTES

Abbreviations

ACE papers	Papers of the American Council on Education, Hoover Institution, Stanford, California
Blackmun papers	Papers of Harry Blackmun, Manuscript Reading Room, Library of Congress
Bramblett MS	Draft history of the struggle to create a Department of Education, January 8, 1980, 41 pp. (author's collection)
CCE Records	Cabinet Committee on Education Records, Nixon Project
CEC Archives	Council for Exceptional Children Archives, Reston, Virginia
CF	Confidential Files
Cohen papers	Papers of Wilbur J. Cohen, State Historical Society of Wisconsin, Madison
Colson office files	Charles Colson, office files, Nixon Project
Dent office files	Harry Dent, office files, Nixon Project
Ehrlichman office files	John Ehrlichman, office files, Nixon Project
Eizenstat office files	Stuart Eizenstat, office files, JCPL
Finch office files	Robert Finch, office files, Nixon Project
Finch papers	Personal papers of Robert H. Finch, Nixon Library, Yorba Linda, California
Haldeman office files	H.R. Haldeman, office files, Nixon Project
HUCRDP	Howard University Civil Rights Documentation Project, Moorland-Springarn Library, Howard University, Washington, D.C.
JCPL	Jimmy Carter Presidential Library, Atlanta
JFKL	John F. Kennedy Library, Boston
Jordan office files	Hamilton Jordan, office files, JCPL
LCCR transcript	"School Finance Litigation: A Strategy Session," roundtable discussion convened by Lawyers' Committee for Civil Rights Under Law, Washington, D.C., October 15, 1971, reproduced in *Yale Review of Law and Social Action* 2, no.2 (Winter 1971).
LBJL	Lyndon B. Johnson Library, Austin, Texas
LCCR papers	Leadership Council on Civil Rights Papers, Series I, Manuscript Reading Room, Library of Congress

Magnuson papers	Papers of Warren G. Magnuson, University of Washington Library, Seattle
MALDEF papers	Papers of Mexican American Legal Defense and Education Fund, Green Library, Stanford University, Palo Alto, California
Mardian papers	Papers of Robert Mardian, Hoover Institution, Stanford, California
McClure OH	Stewart McClure, Senate Historical Office Oral History Collection, Manuscript Reading Room, Library of Congress
Keppel papers	Francis Keppel Personal Papers, JFKL
Moynihan papers	Papers of Daniel Patrick Moynihan, Manuscript Reading Room, Library of Congress
NARA	National Archives and Records Administration
Nixon Project	Richard Nixon Presidential Project, NARA, College Park, Maryland
OH	oral history
POF	President's Office Files, Nixon Project
Powell papers	Papers of Lewis Powell, Washington and Lee University, Lexington, Virginia
Quie papers	Papers of Albert H. Quie, congressional series, Minnesota State Historical Society, St. Paul
Richardson papers	Papers of Elliot Richardson, Series I, Manuscript Reading Room, Library of Congress
RG	Record Group
WHCF	White House Central Files

Introduction

1. For general overviews of the character of this new system, see Anthony King, ed., *The New American Political System* (Washington, D.C.: American Enterprise Institute, 1978); Richard Harris and Sidney Milkis, *Remaking American Politics* (Boulder, Colo.: Westview Press, 1989); Benjamin Ginsberg and Martin Shefter, *Politics by Other Means: The Declining Importance of Elections in America* (New York: Free Press, 1990); Marc Landy and Martin Levin, eds., *The New Politics of Public Policy* (Baltimore, Md.: Johns Hopkins University Press, 1995); R. Shep Melnick, *Between the Lines: Interpreting Welfare Rights* (Washington, D.C.: Brookings Institution, 1995); Sidney Milkis, *The Presidents and the Parties: The Transformation of the American Political System since the New Deal* (New York: Oxford University Press, 1993); Martha Derthick, "Crossing Thresholds: Federalism in the 1960s," in Derthick, ed., *Keeping the Compound Republic: Essays on American Federalism* (Washington, D.C.: Brookings Institution, 2001), 138–152; Byron Shafer and William Claggett, *The Two Majorities: The Issue Context of Modern American Politics* (Baltimore, Md.: Johns Hopkins University Press, 1995).

2. See, in particular, Hugh Davis Graham, *Uncertain Triumph: Federal Education Policy under Kennedy and Johnson* (Chapel Hill: University of North Carolina Press, 1984), *The Civil Rights Era: Origins and Development of National Policy* (New York: Oxford University Press, 1990), *Collision Course: The Strange Convergence of*

Affirmative Action and Immigration Policy in America (New York: Oxford University Press, 2002), and "Legacies of the 1960s: The American 'Rights Revolution' in an Era of Divided Governance," *Journal of Policy History* 10, no. 3 (1998): 267–288. The first historian to recognize this aspect of post-1968 politics was Otis L. Graham Jr., writing in the immediate shadow of Watergate. See Graham, *Toward a Planned Society: From Roosevelt to Nixon* (New York: Oxford University Press, 1975), 188–263.

3. William C. Berman, *America's Right Turn: From Nixon to Clinton*, 2nd ed. (Baltimore, Md.: Johns Hopkins University Press, 1998); Michael Schaller, *Right Turn: American Life in the Reagan-Bush Era, 1980–1992* (New York: Oxford University Press, 2007); and Godfrey Hodgson, *The World Turned Right Side Up: A History of the Conservative Ascendancy in America* (Boston: Houghton Mifflin, 1996). See also Thomas Edsall, *Chain Reaction: The Impact of Race, Rights, and Taxes on American Politics* (New York: Norton, 1991). The idea that U.S. political history since the 1960s can be understood primarily in these terms also appears commonly in undergraduate textbooks, including such superior examples as Alan Brinkley, *The Unfinished Nation: A Concise History of the American People*, 4th ed. (Boston: McGraw-Hill, 2004), and William H. Chafe, *The Unfinished Journey: America since World War II*, 6th ed. (New York: Oxford University Press, 2007).

4. Dan C. Carter, *From George Wallace to Newt Gingrich: Race in the Conservative Counter-Revolution* (Baton Rouge: Louisiana State University Press, 1996); Michael B. Katz, *The Undeserving Poor: From the War on Poverty to the War on Welfare* (New York: Pantheon, 1989); Jonathan M. Schoenwald, *A Time for Choosing: The Rise of American Conservatism* (New York: Oxford University Press, 2001); and Gareth Davies, *From Opportunity to Entitlement: The Transformation and Decline of Great Society Liberalism* (Lawrence: University Press of Kansas, 1996).

5. The classic bottom-up account of reform politics is Frances Fox Piven and Richard A. Cloward, *Regulating the Poor: The Functions of Public Welfare* (New York: Pantheon, 1971). For a recent example, boldly applied to the case of affirmative action, see Nancy Maclean, *Freedom Is Not Enough: The Opening of the American Workplace* (Cambridge, Mass.: Harvard University Press, 2006), 35–113.

6. A recent book that challenges this idea of a lurch to the right, drawing on the work of Hugh Graham, is James T. Patterson, *Restless Giant: The United States, from Watergate to* Bush v. Gore (New York: Oxford University Press, 2005).

7. Hugh Davis Graham and Gary Fink, eds., *The Carter Presidency: Policy Choices in the Post–New Deal Era* (Lawrence: University of Kansas Press, 1998).

8. Among the topics that would warrant extended treatment in a general history, but which receive little attention here, are the development of the Head Start program and the use of compulsory busing to achieve school desegregation. For good treatments of these respective subjects, see Maris A. Vinovskis, *The Birth of Head Start: Preschool Education Policies in the Kennedy and Johnson Administrations* (Chicago: University of Chicago Press, 2005), and Gary Orfield, *Must We Bus? Segregated Schools and National Policy* (Washington, D.C.: Brookings Institution, 1978). The Johnson years in general receive less attention than the Nixon-Ford period, having received their definitive treatment in Graham, *Uncertain Triumph*.

9. There is an extensive literature on this subject. See, for example, Milbrey McLaughlin, *Evaluation and Reform: The Elementary and Secondary Education Act of 1965* (Cambridge, Mass.: Ballinger, 1975), and Susan Roy Jeffrey, *Education for*

the Children of the Poor: A Study of the Origins and Implementation of the Elementary and Secondary Education Act of 1965 (Columbus: Ohio State University Press, 1976).

Chapter 1. Race, Religion, and Reds

1. The best of them is Hugh Davis Graham, *Uncertain Triumph: Federal Education Policy under Kennedy and Johnson* (Chapel Hill: University of North Carolina Press, 1984). For an invaluable, in-depth examination of the failure of federal aid between 1945 and the early 1960s, see Frank Munger and Richard H. Fenno, *National Politics and Federal Aid to Education* (Syracuse, N.Y.: Syracuse University Press, 1962). Also good on the historical background, but focusing more on the particular circumstances surrounding ESEA in 1965, is Eugene Eidenberg and Roy Morey, *An Act of Congress* (New York: Norton, 1969). Other competent overviews are James L. Sundquist, *Politics and Policy: The Eisenhower, Kennedy, and Johnson Administrations* (Washington, D.C.: Brookings Institution, 1968); Susan Roy Jeffrey, *Education for the Children of the Poor: A Study of the Origins and Implementation of the Elementary and Secondary Education Act of 1965* (Columbus: Ohio State University Press, 1976); and Philip Meranto, *The Politics of Federal Aid to Education* (Syracuse, N.Y.: Syracuse University Press, 1967).

2. Speech to National Meeting of Diocesan Attorneys, February 8, 1965, p. 2. Subsequently, Msgr. Hurley became archbishop of Anchorage. I am grateful to Archbishop Hurley for supplying me with a copy of his speech.

3. See Sundquist, *Politics and Policy*, chapter 5. These defeats are also well treated in Munger and Fenno, *National Politics*, and in Robert Bendiner, *Obstacle Course on Capitol Hill* (New York: McGraw-Hill, 1964).

4. Sometimes it also referred more directly to McCarthyite fears about communist penetration of the American education system. See Diane Ravitch, *The Troubled Crusade: American Education, 1945–1980* (New York: Basic Books, 1983), 81–113.

5. For example, this had happened in social welfare policy, highway construction, taxation, the criminal justice system, free speech, and race relations. In the latter three instances, the federal agent of transformation was the Supreme Court, acting on an expanded doctrine of incorporation. See Henry J. Abraham, *Freedom and the Court: Civil Rights and Liberties in the United States*, 5th ed. (New York: Oxford University Press, 1988).

6. On the financial pressures, see Peter Veillette, "State and Local Efforts to Finance Schools since 1945," *Current History* (June 1972): 293–297.

7. Thomas A. Shannon, *The National School Boards Association: Reflections on the Development of an American Idea* (Alexandria, Va.: National School Boards Association, 1997), 30.

8. The NSBA did not even give testimony on ESEA in 1965. The organization's headquarters were in Evanston, Illinois. It opened a branch office in Washington in 1966.

9. McClure OH, January 28, 1983, interview no. 4, 110–111. McClure was chief clerk to the Labor and Public Welfare Committee.

10. On Halleck's strong antistatism, see William E. Leuchtenburg, *In the Shadow of FDR: From Harry Truman to Ronald Reagan*, rev. and updated ed. (Ithaca, N.Y.:

Cornell University Press, 1983), 55. In 1957, he conspired with Smith to defeat federal aid. See Sundquist, *Politics and Policy*, 172.

11. Remarks at press conferences on March 27, 1957, *Public Papers of the Presidents of the United States: Dwight D. Eisenhower: 1957* (Washington, D.C.: Government Printing Office, 1958), 221–222.

12. Eisenhower made these remarks at a 1959 cabinet meeting. Earlier in the meeting, he had observed that he had been "dragged into supporting" construction aid during his first term. See James C. Duram, "'A Good Growl': The Eisenhower Cabinet's January 16, 1959 Discussion of Federal Aid to Education," *Presidential Studies Quarterly* 8, no. 4 (Fall 1978): 441, 438.

13. Press conference, July 31, 1957, in *Public Papers: Eisenhower: 1957*, 575 (emphasis added). For his earlier expressions of qualified support for construction aid, see his remarks at press conferences on March 27, 1957, ibid., 221–222, and on April 3, 1957, ibid., 243.

14. See Ravitch, *Troubled Crusade*, 43–113. On the origins of progressive education, see David Angus and Jeffrey Mirel, *The Failed Promise of the American High School, 1890–1995* (New York: Teachers College Press, 1999).

15. Charles W. Radcliffe, interview with author, August 5, 2005, Washington, D.C. At this time, Radcliffe worked for Richardson in the OE legislative branch.

16. For an overview of the circumstances surrounding the passage of NDEA, see Barbara Clowse, *Brainpower for the Cold War: The Sputnik Crisis and the National Defense Education Act of 1958* (Westport, Conn.: Greenwood, 1981).

17. McClure OH, interview no.4, 116–117. "I invented that God-awful title: the National Defense Education Act. If there are any words less compatible, really, intellectually, in terms of what is the purpose of education—it's not to defend the country; it's to defend the mind and develop the human spirit, not to build cannons and battleships. It was a horrible title, but it worked. It worked. How could you attack it?" (ibid., 118).

18. The material in this section is taken from Donald White, interview with author, August 6, 2005, Annapolis, Md., and from Bill White to the author, e-mail, containing a message from Donald White, March 2, 2006.

19. Successive administrations were often unenthusiastic about Title III and sought to cut its funding. But White recalls that when the question of its funding came up before the Senate appropriations subcommittee, Cotton would announce "that's mine," and the conversation would move on.

20. The assistant secretary to the Senate Democrats at this time, Bobby Baker, who was from South Carolina, makes a similar observation: "I found those courtly old gentlemen of another era to harbor a great respect for energetic and ambitious young men and to assist and encourage them when they could. They were like surrogate fathers. Had I not been a Southern boy, I firmly believe, my rise in the Senate might not have been half so rapid. Southern staffers were no less clannish. These, too, held powerful positions out of proportion to their numbers." Robert G. Baker, *Wheeling and Dealing: Confessions of a Capitol Hill Operator* (New York: Norton, 1978), 36.

21. Samuel Halperin, interview with author, February 16, 2005, Washington, D.C.; Halperin to author, e-mail, June 29, 2006. Halperin observed the workings of both the Senate Labor and Public Welfare Committee and the House Education and

Labor Committee as an American Political Science Association congressional fellow, before becoming a legislative specialist at HEW in 1961.

22. *Congress and the Nation, 1945–1964* (Washington, D.C.: Congressional Quarterly, 1965), 1200.

23. Remarks at NDEA signing ceremony, February 9, 1958, *Public Papers of the Presidents of the United States: Dwight D. Eisenhower: 1958* (Washington, D.C., 1959), 243.

24. Sundquist, *Politics and Policy*, 187; Graham, *Uncertain Triumph*, 7–8.

25. There is a suspicion that Johnson, as majority leader, engineered the tie vote on the salary amendment that forced Vice President Nixon to take a stand on the measure, by inducing a Democratic supporter of the proposal, J. Allen Frear of Delaware, to abstain. See Sundquist, *Politics and Policy*, 184–185.

26. Ibid., 188.

27. Francis Hurley to author, e-mail, August 3, 2006.

28. Hurley, speech to National Meeting of Diocesan Attorneys, p.1.

29. Initially, O'Neill and Delaney held the general aid bill up in Rules, weakening its momentum. When it finally came up for a vote, O'Neill sided with the administration, but Delaney voted with the conservatives, feeling that a salary bill excluding parochial schools would give public schools an unfair comparative advantage. See Graham, *Uncertain Triumph*, 20–22.

30. For a critical assessment of the Kennedy administration's approach, see ibid., 25.

31. Munger and Fenno, *National Politics*, 18.

32. Graham, *Uncertain Triumph*, xv, 71.

33. Franklin Parker, "Francis Keppel of Harvard; 16th U.S. Commissioner of Education," Office of Education information sheet, 1962, 14. Parker was a colleague from the University of Texas, rather than an Office of Education functionary, and the document conveys Keppel's personality and ideas with brio.

34. Francis Keppel, September 18, 1964, OH for the JFKL, 1.

35. Parker, "Keppel," 1.

36. Ibid., 13.

37. Francis Keppel, April 21, 1969, OH for the LBJL, Austin, 2.

38. Bundy replied: "Mr. President, that's exactly the trouble. You never heard of the fellow." Ibid., 4.

39. Keppel, JFKL OH, 5.

40. Ibid., 7.

41. Keppel, ibid. (emphasis added).

42. Legislative liaison chief Larry O'Brien recounted this in his oral history for the Johnson library: December 29, 1985, interview 2, LBJL, 46, 51; July 24, 1986, interview 11, LBJL, 44. The explanation is probably that race had been the bigger factor, and religion somewhat dormant, during the Eisenhower years. When Powell and the National Association for the Advancement of Colored People (NAACP) were persuaded in 1961 not to press for an antisegregation amendment, that seemed a good portent.

43. The new head of HEW was Anthony Celebrezze, formerly mayor of Cleveland, Ohio, and reputedly appointed by John Kennedy in a bid to boost the senatorial

prospects of his brother, Edward, who was counting on strong support from Italian Americans.

44. Keppel, JFKL OH, 6.

45. Protestant and Orthodox churches were invited to send observer-delegates to the Vatican, and constitutional documents such as *Lumen Gentium* (Light of the Nations) reached out to those "who are honored by the name of Christ, but who do not however profess the Catholic faith in full." See R. F. Trisco and J. A. Komonchek, "Vatican Council II," in *New Catholic Encyclopedia* (Detroit: Thomson/Gale, 2003), 14: 407 418. I am indebted to Samuel Halperin for drawing the impact of Vatican II on U.S. education politics to my attention.

46. Keppel, JFKL OH, 13.

47. For example, there were big rifts within the NEA between a permanent staff that was implacably opposed to any hint of parochial aid and dogmatically wedded to general aid and elements within the membership that favored a more flexible stance. And within NCWC, the spirit of ecumenism encouraged by Vatican II did not prevent more conservative bishops and church officials from viewing the new ways with disfavor. On in-fighting within NEA at this time, see Lloyd A. Garrison (an OE regional representative) to Sterling McMurrin, memo, June 15, 1962, in Commissioner of Education Office Files, Office of Education, RG 12, NARA, box 295. Having just sat in on an NEA convention in Colorado, Garrison detected "much grass-roots concern about the lack of realistic and aggressive leadership at the top in NEA," with Carr's dogmatic opposition to categorical aid one source of dissatisfaction and his timid approach to school desegregation another.

48. Keppel, JFKL OH, 6; Keppel, LBJL OH, 3.

49. Keppel, LBJL OH, 5.

50. Ibid.

51. In the context of this reappraisal of administration strategy at the end of 1962, a number of concepts emerged that would later surface in ESEA, including the focus on the poor and the emphasis on aiding the individual child rather than the school. See, for example, two HEW staff memos, dated October 30, 1962 ("A New Federal Program in Education"), and December 5, 1962 ("Suggested Approach for Administration Education Proposals"), in HEW Budgetary Administration Records, FY 1962–1969, Records of Office of Management and Budget, RG 51, NARA, box 35.

52. They were Edith Green of Oregon, who chaired the higher education subcommittee; Dominick Daniels of New Jersey, whose subcommittee handled aid to the handicapped; and Carl Perkins of Kentucky, who was responsible for elementary and secondary education. They had been treated poorly by Powell's predecessor, the imperious Graham Barden of North Carolina (who only used subcommittees on an ad hoc basis), and appreciated the new chairman's more democratic approach.

53. Graham, *Uncertain Triumph*, 50.

54. Archbishop Francis Hurley, telephone interview with author, May 3, 2006. After what Hurley describes as the "blowout" of 1961, NCWC had little contact with the Kennedy administration, but by now, in late 1963, the relationship had improved.

55. Keppel, LBJL OH, 6.

56. For Halleck's tactics, see the second of two recorded conversations between Johnson and Wayne Morse, December 12, 1963, Tape K63.12.07 PNO 33. All recorded telephone conversations cited throughout the notes were downloaded from the Web site of the Presidential Recording Program, Miller Center of Public Affairs, University of Virginia (www.millercenter.virginia.edu). For LBJ's wider anxiety about GOP efforts to hold up legislation, see his conversation with the Speaker of the House, John McCormack, December 9, 1963, K63.12.05 PNO 22.

57. Telephone conversation with Wayne Morse, December 10, 1963, K63.12.07 PNO 03.

58. Paul Conkin, *Big Daddy from the Pedernales* (Boston: Twayne, 1986), 226. See also Merle Miller, *Lyndon: An Oral Biography* (New York: Ballantine, 1980), 39–44. On the Cotulla experience, see especially Carlos Kevin Blanton, *The Strange Career of Bilingual Education in Texas, 1836–1981* (College Station: Texas A&M Press, 2004), 132–134. Johnson's passion on this subject is confirmed by numerous oral histories. See, for example, Lawrence O'Brien, September 11, 1986, OH, interview no. 14, LBJL, 4–5; Keppel LBJL OH I, 28, OH II (August 17, 1972), 11. Occasionally, Johnson would muse wistfully about the possibility of going back to teaching when he had finished being president. See Lady Bird Johnson, *A White House Diary* (New York: Holt, Rinehart and Winston, 1970), 259–260.

59. See Keppel, JFKL OH, 7. For Keppel's account of LBJ's more emotional commitment to the issue, see his OE OH, 9–10.

60. Lawrence O'Brien, February 11, 1986, OH interview 6, LBJL, 1. On the contrast between Kennedy and Johnson, see also Lawrence O'Brien, December 29, 1985, OH interview 2, 9–12.

61. Keppel, JFKL OH, 10.

62. For a flavor of how other Democrats on the committee felt about Green, see John Brademas, *The Politics of Education: Conflict and Consensus on Capitol Hill* (Norman: University of Oklahoma Press, 1987), 29–34. Not surprisingly, Republicans liked Green. See Radcliffe, interview, August 5, 2005, and Albert H. Quie, interview with author, Minneapolis, Minn., August 11, 2004.

63. Green and the department's top emissary to the Hill, Wilbur Cohen, were not on speaking terms. When President Kennedy floated the possibility of Green's becoming departmental secretary of HEW, Cohen responded with alarm: "I swallowed hard, looked at the President and said Mrs Green was an able and intelligent person." However, "if appointed, she would destroy the morale in the Department of Health, Education, and Welfare." Were she appointed, he would be forced to resign. Fragmentary recollections for a memoir, n.d., Cohen papers, box 278.

64. Keppel, JFKL OH, 10. See also Lawrence O'Brien, September 18, 1995, OH, interview 1, LBJL, 38. Wilbur Cohen, a key figure in the battle for ESEA, is introduced in the next chapter.

65. Charles Radcliffe to author, letter, March 30, 2006.

66. Robert Dallek, *Flawed Giant: Lyndon Johnson and His Times, 1961–1973* (New York: Oxford University Press, 1998), 8.

67. See, generally, Kent Germany and Robert David Johnson, eds., *The Presidential Recordings: Lyndon B. Johnson*, Vols. 1–3 (New York: Norton, 2005). LBJ's successful effort to pass Kennedy's tax cut provides a particularly vivid example (see conversations from January 23 and January 24, 1964, reproduced in vol. 3, 728–772).

I am grateful to Kent Germany for drawing this case study in presidential leadership to my attention.

68. See Wilbur Cohen to Anthony Celebrezze, memo, December 2, 1963, Cohen papers, box 144.

69. Dallek, *Flawed Giant*, 126.

70. For a fuller account, see Guian McKee, "Prelude to Faith-based Initiatives? The Johnson Presidential Recordings and the Debate over Parochial Schools in the War on Poverty," *Miller Center Report* 19, no. 1 (Winter 2003): 21–27.

71. Hurley, telephone interview with author, May 3, 2006. For more on Cardinal Spellman's political activities, see John Cooney, *The American Pope: The Life and Times of Francis Cardinal Spellman* (New York: Time Books, 1984).

72. Telephone conversation, Johnson and Carey, April 8, 1964, WH 6404.04 PNO 20. Msgr. Hurley mentioned a similar, NCWC-commissioned poll: Speech to National Meeting of Diocesan Attorneys, p. 6 (handwritten addition to the text).

73. Telephone conversation, Johnson and O'Brien, April 8, 1964, WH 6404.04 PNO 26.

74. Telephone conversation between Johnson and Rep. Frank Thompson (D-N.J.), May 24, 1964, WH 6405.05 PNO 24 and 25.

75. When Johnson asked his aide, Bill Moyers, "Why do [*sic*] NEA hate to see a Catholic get any aid," Moyers explained that "they believe it will eventually lead to a deterioration in support for public schools, and start draining off funds that they badly need now." Johnson's telephone conversations with Moyers dated May 11, 1964 (WH 6405.04 PNO 18), and May 14, 1964 (WH 6405.07 PNO 6).

76. Not least because they too were angry about proposed base closures: the Watertown Armory and the Boston Navy Yard in the case of O'Neill, the Brooklyn yard in the case of Delaney. See telephone conversation between Johnson and John McCormack, April 28, 1964, WH 6404.14 PNO 22.

77. The material in the next two paragraphs is drawn from Johnson's conversations with O'Brien, May 18, 1964, WH 6405.07 PNO 18, and Shriver, May 13, 1964, WH 6405.05 PNO 15.

78. Trying to bring home to Shriver their strength of feeling, Johnson predicted that "you'd about have a fistfight if you put Bob Poage and Wright Patman in a room with Jim Delaney and Tip O'Neill." (W. R. Poage and Patman were Texas Democratic congressmen with whom Johnson had served in the House between 1937 and 1949.)

79. Johnson reported that Albert had told him: "I've been down the mountains of Oklahoma and it's [i.e., the Catholic issue] already down there [and] it'll defeat me: I can't vote for it."

80. Johnson's conversation with McCormack, Thompson, and O'Hara, May 24, 1964, WH6405.05 PNO 24 and 25. Johnson told the story slightly differently in his autobiography. See Lyndon Johnson, *The Vantage Point: Perspectives on the Presidency, 1963–1969* (New York: Holt, Rinehart, and Winston, 1971), 210. According to one version of the incident, the Baptist minister departed the meeting, telling Moyers: "Give my regards to Dr. Graham." Halperin, interview, February 16, 2005.

81. Telephone conversation between Johnson and Landrum, May 14, 1964, WH6405.07 PNO 3.

82. Bendiner, *Obstacle Course*, 36.

Chapter 2. Making History: The Passage of ESEA

1. Lyndon Johnson, *The Vantage Point: Perspectives on the Presidency, 1963–1969* (New York: Holt, Rinehart and Winston, 1971), 207–208; Douglass Cater, May 8, 1969, OH for LBJL, II, May 8, 1969, 11.

2. The speech was delivered on October 5, 1964. See *Public Papers of the Presidents of the United States: Lyndon B. Johnson, 1963–1964* (Washington, D.C.: Government Printing Office, 1965), 1: 674.

3. For the best account of the task force's activities, see Hugh Davis Graham, *Uncertain Triumph: Federal Education Policy under Kennedy and Johnson* (Chapel Hill: University of North Carolina Press, 1984). Within the administration, there was some feeling that the arguments of the 1950s about a looming crisis had been disproved and that the states had coped quite well with the challenges of the baby boom. See Bureau of the Budget Report, dated June 17, 1964, cited by Graham, *Uncertain Triumph*, 60.

4. He liked to joke that his ecumenical credentials were even stronger than that: his father was Greek Orthodox, and his mother belonged to the Disciples of Christ. All he needed, remarked the single Brademas, was a Jewish bride. See Eugene Eidenberg and Roy Morey, *An Act of Congress: The Legislative Process and the Making of Education Policy* (New York: Norton, 1969), 129.

5. Francis Hurley, telephone interview with author, May 3, 2006.

6. Keppel, July 18, 1968, OH for the OE, copy at LBJL, 10–11; Eidenberg and Morey, *An Act of Congress*, 80–85.

7. The other official was Msgr. O'Neil D'Amour. See Keppel to HEW secretary Anthony Celebrezze, memo, December 2, 1963, in Cohen papers, box 144.

8. Hurley, telephone interview, May 3, 2006.

9. The report, dating from February 1963, was titled *School Programs for the Disadvantaged Children* and is cited by Stephen K. Bailey and Edith K. Mosher, *ESEA:* The Office of Education Administers a Law (Syracuse, N.Y.: Syracuse University Press, 1968), 9.

10. This is from a detailed memo submitted by an unnamed party to the discussions, in Eidenberg and Morey, *An Act of Congress*, 84.

11. Cater, LBJL OH, III, May 26, 1974, 18.

12. This is the view, for example, of Lawrence McAndrews, "A Closer Look: The NCWC and the Elementary and Secondary Education Act," *Records of the American Catholic Historical Society of Philadelphia* 102, no. 1–2 (Spring 1991): 45–65.

13. Edward D. Berkowitz, *Mr. Social Security: The Life of Wilbur J. Cohen* (Lawrence: University Press of Kansas, 1995), 207.

14. Halperin to author, letter, March 30, 2006. See also his 1970 article, "ESEA: Five Years Later," reproduced in Samuel Halperin, *Essays on Federal Education Policy* (Washington, D.C.: Institute for Educational Leadership, 1975), 12–15.

15. There were 107 Catholics in the House, including twenty freshmen. See *Time*, January 15, 1965, 22.

16. Halperin, interview with author, February 16, 2005, Washington, D.C.

17. Keppel, April 21, 1969, LBJL OH, 12, and OE OH, 12. The main legislators consulted were Senator Wayne Morse and Rep. Carl Perkins, chairmen of the education subcommittees. Their education staffers were Charles Lee and Jack Reed, respectively.

18. Larry O'Brien, December 29, 1985, interview 2, LBJL OH, 48, and July 24,

1986, interview 11, LBJL OH, 43. Carey got the idea from the state of Louisiana, which had long provided textbooks and library materials for all schools, public and private.

19. These centers were designed to provide children in both public and non-profit private schools with specialist educational services not being supplied by the school district.

20. Berkowitz, *Mr. Social Security*, 161.

21. Ibid., 166.

22. Larry O'Brien, April 8, 1986, interview 8, LBJL OH, 3–5.

23. Telephone conversation, March 21, 1964, WH 6403.15 PNO 2. All recorded telephone conversations cited throughout notes were downloaded from the Web site of the Presidential Recording Program, Miller Center of Public Affairs, University of Virginia (www.millercenter.virginia.edu).

24. Cater, LBJL OH I, May 8, 1969, 2.

25. Contained in handwritten jottings by Cohen for an unwritten memoir, in Cohen papers, box 278, folder 7.

26. Johnson to Speaker McCormack, May 1, 1964, WH 6405.04 PNO 18.

27. Daniel Patrick Moynihan, letter to author, September 7, 2000. Moynihan, then assistant secretary at the Labor Department, claims to have negotiated this language with Hurley and Keppel. NCWC's role is confirmed by Hurley, speech to National Meeting of Diocesan Attorneys, February 8, 1965, 8.

28. Cater to President, memo, December 26, 1964, referring to Johnson's query. Cater office files, box 13. (Cater had evidently not had much of a Christmas vacation.)

29. The executive director of the CCSSO, Edgar Fuller, was even more intransigent on the subject of parochial aid than NEA's William Carr.

30. For a good account, see Frank Munger and Richard H. Fenno, *National Politics and Federal Aid to Education* (Syracuse, N.Y.: Syracuse University Press, 1962), esp. 34–38.

31. The $2,000 figure was very low (the Office for Economic Opportunity's poverty line for a family of four was $3,000), but the administration did not wish Title I authorizations to exceed $1 billion during the first year. Also, a very low figure increased the proportion of funds that would go to the rural South, increasing ESEA's appeal to legislators who might be uncertain about supporting the bill.

32. In the 1947 case, *Everson v. New Jersey*, the issue at stake was the use of public funds to bus children to parochial schools.

33. For a brief description of Oscar Rose, who was superintendent of the Midway City school district in Oklahoma, see Chapter 3.

34. Keppel, OE OH, 15.

35. McClure OH, 127–128.

36. See Wilbur J. Cohen, May 10, 1969, interview no. 4, LBJL OH, 14. For one HEW reaction to the Dent proposal, see Reginald Conley (Assistant General Counsel, HEW) to Wilbur Cohen, memo, June 4, 1964, Cohen papers, box 147.

37. Keppel, JFKL OH, September 18, 1964, 14–15. According to Hugh Graham, when Title I was presented as an extension of impact aid, "virtually the entire senior bureaucracy of USOE and DHEW and the BOB . . . lost out to Johnson's political instinct." Graham, *Uncertain Triumph*, 76.

38. For example, Francis Hurley saw a draft, and it was modified in response to

his suggestions. Moreover, when Johnson unveiled ESEA, his remarks borrowed directly from a legal memorandum that NCWC's legal department had prepared on the constitutionality of parochial aid. Hurley reported these facts with satisfaction in his speech to National Meeting of Diocesan Attorneys, 9–10.

39. Under the Title I formula, districts such as Westchester County benefited both from being populous and from being located in states with high per capita spending on schools.

40. The most important of them concerned Title II, the library services proposal. In its original wording, the bill had gone beyond the "child-benefit" theory, contemplating direct grants to private schools, so long as they were for secular purposes (book titles would have to be on the public school board's approved list). NCWC must have been disappointed when the subcommittee revised the provision, placing title for all Title II–purchased materials in public education agencies and replacing outright grants to parochial schools with loans. But they went along with the change, as did their political representative on the subcommittee, Hugh Carey.

41. Moynihan to author, letter, September 7, 2000.

42. Hurley's sanguine approach reflected conversations that he had had with Catholic school superintendents. "Less than equal treatment, they agreed, could still provide substantial benefits, especially since federal money would cover only a small portion of educational expenditures. Their message to us was to get them help of some kind." Hurley, like them, hoped that ESEA might "serve as a catalyst for better relations" between the parochial and public school systems. Hurley speech to National Meeting of Diocesan Attorneys, 6, 11.

43. Samuel Halperin to author, e-mail, February 9, 2006. Powell's colleague on Education and Labor, John Brademas, confirms that favorable treatment from the IRS was among the chairman's regular quid pro quos. Brademas, interview with author, July 5, 2006, Oxford, England.

A decade earlier, there had been some suspicion that Powell's surprising support for Eisenhower's reelection had been "in exchange for an administration promise to call off its investigation of the Congressman's tax returns." During the Kennedy administration, Senator John Williams had expressed indignation at the IRS's seeming lack of interest in collecting back taxes from Powell. And in 1964, Larry O'Brien had told LBJ that Powell had "a laundry list a yard long," including demands that the federal government "wipe out the $47,000 indebtedness to 'the' internal revenue" and that it "get that judge to drop any threat of arrest." See James Q. Wilson, "The Flamboyant Mr. Powell," *Commentary* 41, no. 1 (January 1966): 31; Charles V. Hamilton, *Adam Clayton Powell, Jr.: The Political Biography of an American Dilemma* (New York: Atheneum, 1991), 407; telephone conversation between Johnson and O'Brien, May 11, 1964, WH6405.04 PNO 13.

44. According to O'Brien, members of the Rules Committee had initially opposed the bill by as much as 9 votes to 1. O'Brien to Johnson, March 8, 1965, WHCF, subject file LE/FA2, LBJL, box 38.

45. Ibid.

46. Ibid. The committee included Democrats from each of the northern states mentioned here. The only southerners on Education and Labor were Ralph Scott (N.C.) and Sam Gibbons (Fla.).

47. Halperin to author, e-mail, March 2, 2006.

48. O'Brien, who was not in the room, was furious, blaming Halperin for what he saw as an HEW "leak" and wanting to have him sacked. O'Brien was mollified, however, when Hugh Carey drew him quietly to one side and explained what had actually happened. Halperin to author, e-mail, February 9, 2006.

49. Ibid.

50. The next three paragraphs are drawn from a telephone conversation between Johnson and Powell, preceded by an exchange between Powell and Jack Valenti, March 1, 1965, WH 6503.01 PNO 7.

51. Powell reported that these Democrats included Edith Green, James O'Hara, Carlton Sickles (Md.), Ralph Scott, and Sam Gibbons. The identity of the sixth Democrat is not revealed, but it was probably William Hathaway (Maine), who strongly objected to Title II on church-state grounds.

52. According to his biographer, Powell suspected that the federal government tapped his phone. See Hamilton, *Adam Clayton Powell, Jr.*, 416.

53. Powell had disappeared first to Puerto Rico, home of his estranged wife, and then to Bimini, where he vacationed with a female member of his committee staff.

54. William Ayres of Ohio was the ranking Republican on the Education Committee. Johnson was passing on information that had been supplied by NEA officers at a White House meeting earlier the same day.

55. O'Brien to Johnson, memo, March 8, 1965, WHCF, subject file LE/FA2, LBJL, box 38.

56. On Young, see telephone conversation between Johnson and Speaker McCormack, April 28, 1964, WH 6404.14 PNO 22.

57. Telephone conversation with Meany, April 1, 1965, WH6504.01. There is no suggestion in the archival record or in secondary accounts of ESEA to suggest that the outcome of the vote was in doubt, despite its closeness.

58. Charles W. Radcliffe, interview with author, August 5, 2005, Washington, D.C.

59. Eidenberg and Morey, *An Act of Congress*, 130.

60. Without a specific judicial review amendment, this threat did not exist, because of the Court's 1923 decision in *Frothingham v. Mellon*, which denied taxpayers the standing to sue the federal government. On these Catholic fears, see Keppel to Richard Goodwin, memo, December 2, 1964, WHCF Confidential File, LBJL, box 62; and Cater to Johnson, memo, December 19, 1964, WHCF FG 165–4, LBJL, box 245.

61. Valenti to Johnson, memo, March 24, 1965, WHCF LE/FA2, LBJL, box 38. Eidenberg and Morey say that "most of the action was not taking place on the floor itself but rather in the cloak rooms off the floor and in the halls surrounding the House chamber." In these conclaves, lobbyists, especially from organized labor, played a leading role in urging waverers to back the administration bill. *An Act of Congress*, 133. Halperin, interview, February 16, 2005.

62. Halperin to author, e-mail, March 2, 2006. Halperin recalls that "Congressmen sent S.O.S. messages to the galleries, and we responded within minutes to each assault."

63. For a fuller account of the House floor debate, see Dean Kelley and George LaNoue, "The Church-State Settlement in the Federal Aid to Education Act," in

Donald A. Giannella, ed., *Religion and the Public Order: 1965* (Chicago: University of Chicago Press, 1966), 131–150.

64. Telephone conversation between Johnson and Powell, March 27, 1965, WH6503.14 PNO 7.

65. Conversation between Johnson and Meany, April 1, 1965. Johnson was thinking of the 1960 vote, when both House and Senate had approved a bill, but Smith had declined to give a rule to the conference bill. It is not clear, though, how serious the problem was in 1965, for recent changes made it easier than before for the leadership to force a bill out of Rules.

66. In his memoir, Johnson recalled personally lobbying Morse on this matter. *The Vantage Point*, 211.

67. *Wall Street Journal*, March 29, 1965, p. 2.

68. Graham, *Uncertain Triumph*, 78. Halperin believes that Robert Kennedy could have made a lot of trouble for LBJ over ESEA but was biding his time. Halperin, interview, February 16, 2005.

69. Halperin, interview, February 16, 2005.

70. Lee to Morse, memo, April 30, 1965, in Papers of Wayne Morse, University of Oregon, Eugene, Series T, box 39. Lee was preparing remarks for Morse to deliver to a meeting of school superintendents and wanted them to know that his boss's role had been much greater than was obvious from the public record.

71. On White's friendship with Powell, see Samuel Halperin to author, letter, March 30, 2006. Halperin adds that White also had a personal friendship with Jack Forsythe, introducing him to his future wife, Pat Winalski, and hosting their wedding.

72. According to White, "the day before the Elementary and Secondary Education Act was to be reported out of the House Education and Labor Committee, and then enacted into law without change, Adam Clayton Powell . . . told his education staff aide to 'give Don a copy of the draft bill and let him write in what he wants. If he's reasonable, it stays in.'" White to author, e-mail, March 1, 2006.

73. This was PL 89–313. See Chapter 7.

74. Meany telephone conversation, April 1, 1965.

75. Johnson and O'Brien conversation, April 1, 1965, WH 6504.01. This seems to exaggerate the danger posed by the Rules Committee, following the changes in its role that had been agreed upon at the beginning of the 89th Congress, but Halperin observes that "when you are on the firing line you always operate from the assumption that the *worst* possible thing *will happen*." Halperin to author, letter, March 30, 2006.

76. Telephone conversation with Meany, April 1, 1965.

77. Johnson and Moyers were worried by Randolph, a powerful figure in the Senate and currently unhappy about the shape of the Appalachia bill. Moyers hoped that his good rapport with the senator might make a difference: he had managed to secure a job for Randolph's elder son in the Peace Corps three years previously, having initially been turned down, and more recently had secured a part-time job for Randolph's other son at American University. Johnson's telephone conversation with Moyers, April 1, 1965, WH 6504.01.

78. Halperin remembers that lobbyists and legislators who had worked hard for the passage of ESEA were "really resentful" that there was no "big White House

signing ceremony." To appease them, a subsequent event was organized in the East Room of the White House. Halperin to author, letter.

79. Harry McPherson, *A Political Education* (Boston: Little, Brown, 1972), 250.

80. Cited in ibid., 249.

Chapter 3. Putting Down Roots, 1965–1968

1. In particular, sociologist James S. Coleman, in a government-commissioned report issued in June 1966, found to his surprise that spending additional money on schools made little difference to the educational performance of African American children. What mattered more, he found, was the student's nonschool environment. See James S. Coleman et al., *Equality of Educational Opportunity*, 2 vols. (Washington, D.C.: Department of Health, Education, and Welfare, 1966). For subsequent assessments of Coleman's work that largely supported his findings, see Daniel Patrick Moynihan and Frederick Mosteller, eds., *On Equality of Educational Opportunity* (New York: Vintage, 1972), and Christopher Jencks, *Inequality: A Reassessment of the Effect of Family and Schooling in America* (New York: Basic, 1972).

2. *Congressional Quarterly Weekly Report*, January 28, 1966, 275.

3. For the reasons why, see Gareth Davies, *From Opportunity to Entitlement: The Transformation and Decline of Great Society Liberalism* (Lawrence: University Press of Kansas, 1996), 105–108.

4. Reading this chapter, and similar references in chapter 4, Emerson Elliott, who was the Education Budget Examiner at the Bureau of the Budget from 1960 to 1970, commented that "at least in the Budget Bureau there was a different view." He added that "the budget is a political document representing the president's priorities, not an estimate of what will happen and not a document calculated to please members of Congress who have particular interests." To illustrate that Johnson and Budget Director Charles Shultze took the education cuts seriously, he notes that "Shultze, no doubt with presidential prodding, personally learned many of the details of the Impacted Aid Program" and subsequently "displayed his depth of Impact Aid minutiae" at a budget release press conference. Elliott to author, January 20, 2007.

5. Telephone conversation, Johnson and Russell, June 2, 1966, WH6606.01 PNO 5. All recorded telephone conversations cited throughout notes were downloaded from the Web site of the Presidential Recording Program, Miller Center of Public Affairs, University of Virginia (www.millercenter.virginia.edu). Alexandria City and Arlington County, in the prosperous Washington suburbs of northern Virginia, received funds because they were home to large concentrations of federal employees.

6. Charles W. Radcliffe, interview with author, August 5, 2005, Washington, D.C.

7. Huitt to Douglass Cater, memo, December 13, 1965, Cohen papers, box 157. The memo was copied to Secretary Gardner and Undersecretary Cohen. The attached list contained twenty names, together with the names of the members of Congress representing the district in question. For the most part, the districts were home to unusually large military installations, giving the superintendents in question a particularly large stake in the program. Sixteen of the twenty members of Congress listed were Democrats.

8. Alabama would have lost 75 percent of its funds, Fogarty's district would have lost 66 percent, and New York City would have been cut out. For a helpful table

listing each member of Congress and calculating the impact of the proposed cuts on their districts, see *Congressional Quarterly Weekly Report*, March 18, 1966, 622–626.

9. Senate Appropriations Committee, Subcommittee on Labor-HEW, Hearings, *Labor-HEW Appropriation for Fiscal Year 1967*, 89th Cong., 2nd sess., March 2, 1966; *New York Times*, March 3, 1966, 21 (for Cotton quote).

10. House Appropriations Committee, Subcommittee on Labor-HEW, Hearings, *Labor-HEW Appropriation for Fiscal Year 1967*, 89th Cong., 2nd sess., pt. 2, February 8, 1966, 378.

11. See Davies, *From Opportunity to Entitlement*, 105–112.

12. See Mason Drukman, *Wayne Morse: A Political Biography* (Portland: Oregon Historical Society Press, 1997), 367, 391–392; Samuel Halperin, HEW OH, 1968, LBJL,13–14; Roy Millenson (staffer to the committee's Republicans) to author, e-mail, March 22, 2006.

13. Cited by Miller, *Lyndon: An Oral Biography* (New York: Ballantine, 1980), 589.

14. See, in particular, their conversation of January 12, 1965, WH6501.02 PNO 3.

15. Samuel Halperin, interview with author, February 16, 2005, Washington, D.C.; Miller, *Lyndon*, 590.

16. Telephone conversation between Johnson and Morse, July 29, 1966, WH6607.05 PNO 7; Drukman, *Wayne Morse*, 430–432.

17. Halperin, interview, February 16, 2005.

18. Huitt to Henry Hall Wilson, memo, February 10, 1966, in Cohen papers, box 165.

19. F. Robert Smith, "Senator Morse's Advice and Dissent," *New York Times Magazine*, April 17, 1966, p. 25.

20. Senate Committee on Labor and Public Welfare, Subcommittee on Education, Hearings, *Elementary and Secondary Education Act of 1966*, 89th Cong., 2nd Sess., pt. 1, April 1, 1966, 349. For a sample of the attention that Robert Kennedy was gaining in the wake of his break with the administration, see "Student Group Pushes RFK for the Presidency," *Washington Post*, April 3, 1966, p. A4. For a more detailed examination of Kennedy's break with the White House, see Davies, *From Opportunity to Entitlement*, 110–112. See also Jeff Shesol, *Mutual Contempt: Lyndon Johnson, Robert Kennedy, and the Feud that Defined a Decade* (New York: Norton, 1997).

21. McClure OH, interview no. 4, January 28, 1983, 127.

22. Drukman, *Wayne Morse*, 347.

23. Political scientist Norman Thomas, researching for a book on legislative politics, described Lee as Morse's alter ego: "Repeatedly, I was told that Morse's thinking could be ascertained by talking to Lee and that Lee's acceptance of a point at issue would ensure its approval by Morse." Norman C. Thomas, *Education in National Politics* (New York: David McKay, 1975), 133.

24. Drukman, *Wayne Morse*, 381.

25. Cater to Johnson, memo, June 22, 1966, Cater office files, box 15, cited by Graham, *Uncertain Triumph*, 128.

26. See Ralph Huitt to Douglass Cater and Henry Hall Wilson, memo, February 18, 1966, WHCF, FA2, LBJL. Cited by Graham, *Uncertain Triumph*, 123–126. Huitt, a professor at the University of Wisconsin and a leading student of Congress, was an exponent of the new behavioral approach to Hill politics. For a useful

collection of Huitt's scholarly essays (including a piece on Morse), see Ralph K. Huitt, *Working within the System* (Berkeley, Calif.: IGS Press, 1990). I am indebted to Charles O. Jones, Byron E. Shafer, and the late Leon Epstein for acquainting me with Huitt's scholarly contribution.

27. Johnson, still hoping to avoid a tax hike, asked Mills in his "whispering Sam Rayburn way" to tell his colleagues that "without knowing it, they're voting a tax increase" by failing to keep to his budget requests. Telephone conversation, Johnson and Mills, April 27, 1966, WH6604.04 PNO 3.

28. Cater to Johnson, memo, June 22, 1966, cited by Graham, *Uncertain Triumph*, 128.

29. Wilson to Johnson, memo, July 12, 1966, WHCF LE/FA2, LBJL, box 38.

30. See Gareth Davies, "Before Big Government Conservatism," unpublished manuscript.

31. McClure, OH, January 1, 1983, interview no. 3, 77.

32. Telephone conversation between Johnson and Moyers, April 1, 1965, WH 6504.01 PNO 45. This was just after the Selma crisis. For an earlier conversation between Johnson and Hill about Selma, March 8, 1965, see WH6503.04 PNO 1. In that conversation, Hill referred with evident contempt to "that damn little Wallace" but also warned Johnson of the governor's political hold over the people of Alabama: "They get awfully excited down there—*awfully* excited."

33. See Chapter 5.

34. See Wilson to Johnson, memo, July 12, 1966, WHCF LE/FA2, LBJL, box 36; Schultze to Johnson, memo, Schultze to LBJ, July 13, 1966, in Cohen, box 157.

35. Schultze to Johnson, memo, July 13, 1966.

36. Handwritten note, "get Hill in Sat if possible—L," in Cater to Johnson, memo, July 15, 1966, WHCF LE/FA2, box 38, LBJL; *Congressional Quarterly Weekly Report*, July 22, 1966, 1593.

37. Reported in Cater to Johnson, memo, July 16, 1966, Cater files, box 15. The memo, headed "Talking Points with Senator Hill," is reproduced in greater detail in Graham, *Uncertain Triumph*, 128.

38. Meeting with Gardner, Cohen, and Huitt, Morse had asked them: "[In your] professional judgment as educators and administrators—and without any regard whatsoever to budgetary or economic considerations—could a Title I authorization of $1.5–$2.5 billion—a 100–150 percent expansion—be justified in FY 1967 in terms of national educational needs." When they replied "definitely not," Morse invited Cohen to furnish a letter outlining the reasons, for distribution at the markup session. Cohen reproduced these parts of the conversation in Cohen to Morse, letter, July 15, 1966, WHCF LE/FA2, LBJL, box 38.

39. Ibid.

40. Ibid.

41. Cater sought to avoid his president's displeasure by blaming his departmental colleagues, telling Johnson that "it is obvious that HEW does not have enough muscle to do the job." Cater to Johnson, memo, July 15, 1966.

42. Huitt to Cater and Wilson, memo, March 29, 1966, LE/FA2, LBJL, quoted by Graham, *Uncertain Triumph*, 126.

43. Political scientist Richard Fenno reckoned that its members were policy-oriented individualists with a strong instinct for combat, but little inclination to toe

the line and relatively little also of the kind of loyalty to their committee that he encountered elsewhere in the House. See Fenno, *Congressmen in Committees* (Boston: Little, Brown, 1973), 74–79, 85–87.

44. Huitt to Wilson, memo, February 10, 1966.

45. Huitt to Cater and Wilson, memo, March 29, 1966, WHCF LE/FA2, LBJL, box 38. Cited at greater length in Graham, *Uncertain Triumph*, 126.

46. Johnson's conversation with Powell, May 26, 1966, WH66 05.05 PNO 9. The bulk of the conversation is concerned with labor legislation: Johnson interjected the reference to ESEA right at the end.

47. Halperin, HEW OH, 4.

48. Charles V. Hamilton, *Adam Clayton Powell, Jr.: The Political Biography of an American Dilemma* (New York: Atheneum, 1991), 404.

49. Cater to Johnson, memo, July 28, 1996, WHCF LE/FA2, LBJL, box 38.

50. Johnson devoted an enormous amount of time to this quest, both in his public statements and in private meetings and telephone conversations. The recorded telephone conversations for 1966 include a number of urgent entreaties with powerful legislators such as Mills, Mahon, and Senate minority leader Everett Dirksen (R-Ill.). See, for example, his conversations with Dirksen, March 30, 1966, WH6603.09 PNO 13, and with Mahon, August 22, 1966, WH6608.12 PNO 12. In the latter, LBJ declared, "I am just scared to death" of inflation and urged the chairman of the House Appropriations Committee to do more to rein in the big spenders. See also *Congress and the Nation: 1965–1968* (Washington, D.C.: Congressional Quarterly Press, 1969), 129.

51. Johnson's approval rating dropped from 62 percent at the end of 1965 to 46 percent by May 1966 and did not recover during the balance of the year. Davies, *From Opportunity to Entitlement*, 105.

52. See Hugh Davis Graham, *Civil Rights Era: Origins and Development of National Policy* (New York: Oxford University Press, 1990), 255–262.

53. The role of the equivalent Senate committee, which acted after the House, was generally to hear appeals. There was no realistic prospect that the Senate committee would reduce funds approved by Mahon.

54. For this tradition of subcommittee power, see Richard Fenno, *Congressmen in Committees*, 94–97. For the same author's classic extended treatment of the budgetary process, see *The Power of the Purse: Appropriations Politics in Congress* (Boston: Little, Brown, 1966). For an amusing anecdote that illustrates Fogarty's power on the Hill, see Michael Gillette, *Launching the War on Poverty: An Oral History* (New York: Twayne, 1996), 324–327.

55. John W. Gardner, December 20, 1971, OH for the LBJL, 24.

56. Exploiting their deference, Fogarty sometimes behaved as if they worked for him. When he accepted an invitation to give a speech to the American Hockey Coaches Association in 1965, for example, he instructed an OE budget officer to get one of his staff to write it. Four weeks earlier, Fogarty's secretary had asked that same budget officer to prepare a speech for delivery to the National Catholic Education Association, indicating that the chairman "would like this one to be rather outstanding." For a copy of the speech to the hockey coaches and for the letter, Grace W. Beirne to John F. Hughes (the OE official), see Papers of John E. Fogarty,

1965 Speeches Series, Providence College, Providence, R.I., box 14b, folder 8. To judge from the archival record, he made this kind of request fairly regularly.

57. *New York Times*, February 5, 1966, p. 14. Johnson had been a previous recipient. Less than a year later, Fogarty would be dead, following a second attack that took place on the first day of the 90th Congress.

58. Explaining his appearance, Johnson remarked: "I was like the little boy in the mountains who didn't get an invitation to the dance. I just sat down and wrote myself an invitation." *New York Times*, June 14, 1966, p. 44.

59. Telephone conversation with Mills, April 27, 1966.

60. Johnson, telephone conversation with Schultze, September 10, 1966, WH 6609.04 PNO 9.

61. His determination, and the recent change in the attitude of Congress toward spending, were apparent in a phone conversation between Mahon and Johnson on September 19, 1966, WH 6609.09 PNO 10. By this time, Mahon was confident that he could prevent overruns in elementary and secondary education spending.

62. Johnson's overall budgetary request probably fell conveniently between the appetites of Fogarty and his colleagues to massively enlarge the budget and those of Mahon and other conservatives to apply the meat ax.

63. Johnson and Mills, telephone conversation, WH 6611.04 PNO 2. Mills was noncommittal regarding LBJ's contribution to this outcome.

64. See House Committee on Appropriations, *Supplemental Appropriation Bill, 1967*, 89th Cong., 2nd sess., October 14, 1966, H. Rep. 2284, 4. The other "winner" was Defense.

65. The outcome of the midterm elections of 1966 is explored in somewhat greater depth in Davies, *From Opportunity to Entitlement*, 151–154.

66. "GOP State of the Union Address," January 19, 1967, reprinted in *Congressional Quarterly Weekly Report*, January 27, 1967, 131.

67. *Congress and the Nation: 1965–1968*, 121–125, 128–133.

68. Davies, *From Opportunity to Entitlement*, 179.

69. Gardner to Johnson, memo, December 13, 1966, in WHCF FI/FG, LBJL, box 165 (emphasis added).

70. Schultze to Johnson, memo, December 13, 1966, in WHCF FI/FG 165, LBJL, box 28.

71. Gardner to Johnson, memo, December 23, 1966, WHCF FA2, Confidential File, LBJL, box 14.

72. For Lee's call, see Ralph Huitt to Cater, Wilson, and Mike Manatos, memo, January 26, 1967, in Cater office files, box 15, cited by Graham, *Uncertain Triumph*, 147.

73. "A Gadfly to Democrats: Albert Harold Quie," *New York Times*, May 27, 1967, p. 33.

74. "Quie: Congressional Thorn: No. 1 Critic of White House," in *Red Wing (Minn.) Republican Eagle*, July 28, 1967, clipping in Quie papers, box 148. In seeking to characterize Quie, such profiles always made prominent reference to one particular example of youthful exuberance. "One of the more spectacular events of his college career was to fly a Navy trainer across the campus upside down and at third-floor dormitory level. It vibrated pictures and books off the walls, including those of

Quie's future wife, Gretchen, whom he didn't know at the time and who later refused a date with 'that nut.'" See "Rep. Quie Belies 'Crafty Devil' Image," *Washington Post*, May 21, 1967, p. A3.

75. *New York Times*, May 25, 1967, p. 33.

76. See Cater to Johnson, memo, April 26, 1967, in Cater office files, box 16; and Lawrence (Larry) O'Brien, April 22, 1987, interview 14, OH for the LBJL, 21. This was also the editorial line of the *New York Times:* see May 26, 1967, p. 46.

77. An aide, Martin LaVor, recalls being driven to distraction by Quie's fascination with detail: on one occasion, when LaVor was unable to discourse on the more technical aspects of a piece of legislation, Quie insisted on explaining it to him, despite his aide blurting out in frustration: "I don't care." The ascetic Quie, he further recalls, was perplexed by the amount of travel that his colleagues and their staffs liked to undertake, quizzing LaVor about the motivation behind such trips and needing much reassurance before he would travel to Norway on one occasion to pick up a prize. Martin LaVor, interview with author, November 22, 2004, Alexandria, Va. The chief lobbyist for the Council for Exceptional Children, an accomplished and confident witness, recalls that he always approached congressional testimony before Quie with dread, such was the Minnesotan's mastery of and fascination with detail. Frederick Weintraub, telephone interview with author, November 18, 2004.

78. He did so for three reasons: he was unhappy about its distribution formula, which he felt distributed too much money to affluent districts; he doubted the constitutionality of aid to parochial school children; and he shared the then standard Republican qualms about federal intrusion into state affairs. For a typical example of the thorough way in which he approached the issue, see the letter that he wrote to Mrs. Wallace Dunn of Ellendale, Minn., on February 2, 1965. In reply to her brief request for information about federal aid to education, he composed a four-page reply that ended with an apology for its length. It is clear that it was largely his own composition; he seemingly used such letters as a way of sorting out his own thoughts on complex issues of public policy. Quie papers, box 14.

79. Quie to Mrs. Edlo Solum, chairman, Woman's Program in Physical Education, St. Olaf College, letter, March 24, 1966, Quie papers, box 17. St. Olaf was Quie's alma mater.

80. See also Quie to Milton L. Anderson, superintendent of schools for Sacred Heart, Minn., letter, April 18, 1966, Quie papers, box 17.

81. This phrase was coined by Edith Green. See Chapter 4.

82. The National Education Association, National School Boards Association, Council of Chief State School Officers, the American Association of School Administrators, and the Parent-Teachers Association all advocated general aid, as did many school superintendents in big cities.

83. *Wall Street Journal*, April 21, 1967, p. 1. The reporter observed that the war on poverty "would clearly be at the Republicans' mercy" should Quie succeed.

84. *Washington Post*, April 23, 1967, p. A1. Quie later observed that "they thought they were more endangered than I thought they were." See Quie, April 30, 1969, OH for the LBJL, 24.

85. Wilson was from North Carolina. For the high opinion that Johnson and O'Brien had of Wilson, see O'Brien September 11, 1986, interview 14, LBJL OH,

11. Mike Manatos, who headed the Senate liaison operation, had also been in his post since the beginning of the Kennedy administration. It was a strikingly experienced and stable team.

86. According to Samuel Halperin, Cater was generally less involved in education politics by 1967 than he had been in 1965. See Halperin, February 24, 1969, LBJL OH, 11.

87. Ibid., 16.

88. See Chapter 6.

89. Francis Hurley, telephone interview with author, May 3, 2006. Quie had observed this pattern at work in his own district and regarded it as one of the program's real achievements. Quie, interview with author, August 11, 2004, Minneapolis, Minn.

90. Quie, interview, August 11, 2004. (The USCC was the former National Catholic Welfare Conference.)

91. Donohue to Quie, letter, April 17, 1967, in Quie papers, box 21. The letter also refers to the "new climate of cooperation between the public and private school sectors" that had been established since 1965.

92. Jeremiah D. Buckley, executive director, Citizens for Educational Freedom, letter to members, April 20, 1967, copy in Quie papers, box 21.

93. The copy in the Quie papers includes a handwritten note from a staffer that explains "this is a copy of the letter that started all the fuss."

94. Halperin, interview, February 16, 2005.

95. In an interview on September 17, 1969, Huitt referred to Quie as "a splendid, first-rate Republican member of Congress, and a leader in education." See oral history interview conducted by the Howard University Civil Rights Documentation Project (HUCRDP), 5–6. And Quie recalls having had "a great rapport with HEW." Quie, April 30, 1969, LBJL OH, 17.

96. *Congressional Newsletter*, May 15, 1967, in Quie papers, box 148.

97. In response to charges that some states would lose out under his formula, Quie amended his bill again to guarantee that every state would receive at least as much money under his substitute as under ESEA.

98. "Voting Record of Honorable Albert Quie," undated one-page bulletin in Cohen papers, box 160.

99. "A Chronology of Quie Proposal," n.d., Cohen papers, box 160.

100. Johnson, statement delivered at Crossland Vocational Center, Camp Springs, Md., April 27, 1967, copy in Cohen papers, box 160.

101. See *Washington Post*, April 21, 1967, pp. A1, A20. The article also noted that NEA officials were "ill at ease in company with Republicans." The head of its congressional relations team in 1967 was John Lumley. According to Quie, Lumley viewed him as "an enemy who could not be reconstructed." Quie, interview, August 11, 2004.

102. *Washington Outlook on Education*, newsletter of the NEA Division of Federal Relations, May 1, 1967, in Quie papers, box 148.

103. John Brademas alerted the House to the PTA's position on May 3, 1967. See *Congressional Record*, 11655–11656. Rep. John Feighan, a Democrat representing a conservative San Diego district, told colleagues of the NSBA's unanimous opposition on May 15, 1967: ibid., 12658. Cohen's papers include a compilation of state-

ments by the superintendents of New York City, San Diego, and Pittsburgh. See "School Superintendents Speak Out on the Quie Substitute," n.d., Cohen papers, box 160.

104. Hugh Carey, with his close connections to the U.S. Catholic Conference, claimed that passage of the Quie amendment would set off "a holy war that would make the Middle East trouble look like a Sunday school picnic." *Washington Post*, May 23, 1967, p. A4. (The Six Day War began on June 5.)

105. O'Brien to Johnson, telexed memo, May 6, 1967, WHCF FA2, Confidential File, LBJL, box 14.

106. Wilson to Johnson, memo, May 3, 1967, in Wilson office files, LBJL, box 7.

107. Ibid. For more on the enforcement of desegregation guidelines during the Johnson administration, see Chapter 5.

108. Goodell press release, May 11, 1967, in papers of John W. Gardner, LBJL, box 18. In case that initiative proved insufficient, Cohen and Wilson developed a backup plan, namely "some arrangement wherein it would be stated that guidelines will be administered equally in all States of the Union." Cohen also developed an exchange of letters with Rep. Daniel Flood—chair of the HEW appropriations subcommittee, following the death of John Fogarty—designed "to clarify HEW's administration of Title 6." See Wilson to Johnson, memo, May 3, 1967; O'Brien to Johnson, telexed memo, May 6, 1967.

Meanwhile, LBJ held off-the-record meetings with Philip Landrum (D-Ga.), Carl Vinson (D-Ga.), and the entire North Carolina congressional delegation. See O'Brien to Marvin Watson, memo, May 1, 1967, Landrum name file, LBJL. See also Henry Wilson to Marvin Watson, memo, April 12, 1967; note by Johnson, April 15, 1967; and James R. Jones to Henry Wilson, memo, April 22, 1967, all in WHCF HU2–5, LBJL, box 51.

109. She was then infuriated when Perkins told her that he could not support her in public on the grounds that "I'd have a revolution in the committee." She subsequently claimed that "he wanted the amendments to pass, to save the bill. He worked with me in terms of getting Republican support and the necessary Southern support—and the amendments did pass. But on the floor he acted like he really was opposed to them and joined the other liberal Democrats in opposition. I couldn't believe it." Green, LBJL OH, August 23, 1985, ibid., 30. (There is nothing in the archival record to firmly confirm or refute Green's version of events.)

110. See, for example, Drew Pearson and Jack Anderson's account in their Washington Merry-Go-Round column, *Washington Post*, May 31, 1967, p. D11.

111. On civil rights, though, she felt that the Office of Education had enforced Title VI in a clumsy and unjust fashion, paying insufficient attention to the problems faced by southern school districts and ignoring flagrant violations of the law in the North. And even though she supported an expanded federal role in financing education, Green also resented the imperiousness of the "damn bureaucracy" in Washington, feeling "that the people in Oregon were just as smart as the people back there." Green OH, 36–37.

112. They speculated that chairman Powell "knew how to handle the 'gentle lady from Oregon' better than the . . . courtly Kentuckian Carl Perkins." *Washington Post*, May 31, 1967, p. D11.

113. Halperin marginal comments on an earlier draft of this chapter.

114. One bitter Democrat called Green "the drum majorette" leading the GOP-Dixie coalition, and another compared her to Carry Nation. See *Washington Post*, May 23, 1967, p. A4. For Green's earlier investigation into OE, see *New York Times*, December 9, 1966, p. 26.

115. *New York Times*, May 24, 1967, p. 27.

116. August W. Steinhilber, interview with author, Waldorf, Md., August 5, 2005.

117. *Congressional Record*, May 23, 1967, 13582. The administration had previously developed its own version of this amendment, in case its other efforts to woo the South were insufficient (see Note 108).

118. Ibid., 13591.

119. Ibid., 13593.

120. Ibid., 13604. This was Watkins Abbitt (D-Va.).

121. Ibid., 13606.

122. *New York Times*, May 24, 1967, p. 27.

123. Ibid., May 25, 1967, p. 33. It was unusual for the Speaker to intervene like this during a floor debate.

124. *Congress and the Nation: 1965–1968*, 726.

125. This vote was 222 to 194. It calculated state allotments on the basis of one-half of the state average expenditure per pupil or one-half of the national average, whichever was higher.

126. For the roll-call vote, see *Congressional Quarterly Weekly Report*, May 26, 1967, 910–911.

127. See Chapter 6 for bilingual education and Chapter 7 for aid to the handicapped.

128. Wilson to Johnson, memo, May 25, 1967, WHCF LE/FA 2, LBJL, box 39. Johnson responded by placing congratulatory calls to House Speaker John McCormack (D-Mass.), Majority Leader Carl Albert (D-Okla.), Education and Labor Committee chair Carl Perkins, and three colleagues who had shared the job of managing the bill on the floor with Perkins: John Brademas, Jim O'Hara, and Frank Thompson (D-N.J.). See Johnson's handwritten instructions on Wilson's memo.

129. Lawrence O'Brien, April 22, 1987, OH, interview no. 19, LBJL, 22.

130. "Some Observations on the Elementary and Secondary Education Act Fight," May 25, 1967, in Cohen papers, box 160. Although the memo was unsigned, Halperin confirmed to the author that it was he who wrote it.

131. The GOP vote was 121–37 (compared to a 1965 figure of 35–96). For the roll-call vote, see *Congressional Quarterly Weekly Report*, December 22, 1967, 2640–2641.

132. In addition to sources cited in Note 1, see Susan Roy Jeffrey, *Education for the Children of the Poor: A Study of the Origins and Implementation of the Elementary and Secondary Education Act of 1965* (Columbus: Ohio State University Press, 1966), and Milbrey McLaughlin, *Evaluation and Reform: The Elementary and Secondary Education Act of 1965, Title I* (Cambridge, Mass.: Ballinger, 1975).

Chapter 4. How Much? Budget Battles, 1969–1977

1. There were nine bills for these eight years because Nixon vetoed the FY 1973 bill twice, as explained below.

2. See, for example, Phyllis McClure, *Title I of ESEA: Is It Helping Poor Children?* (New York: NAACP, 1969), and Victor Cicarelli et al., *The Impact of Head Start: An Evaluation of the Effects of Head Start on Cognitive and Affective Development* (Athens, Ohio: Westinghouse Learning Corporation, 1969).

3. John W. Gardner had resigned as HEW secretary early in 1968, disillusioned by the budgetary impact of the Vietnam War. For a profile of Finch, see Chapter 5.

4. FY 1969 saw the last surplus until 1998. It resulted from the tax increase that Johnson had belatedly requested from Congress in 1967.

5. House Committee on Education and Labor, *Elementary and Secondary Education Amendments of 1969*, 91st Cong., 1st Sess., March 24, 1969, H. Rep. 91-114, Minority Views, 55.

6. Nixon's decision not to deliver a State of the Union address in 1969 epitomized his broader lack of urgency.

7. House Appropriations Committee, Subcommittee on Labor-HEW, Hearings, *Appropriations for Fiscal Year 1970*, 91st Cong., 1st Sess., pt. 2, March 12, 1969, 29–32. Flood's papers at King's College, Wilkes-Barre, Pa., contain a large volume of correspondence from this period, from educators in his district, urging him to back higher education spending. I am grateful to Judith Tierney for having kindly supplied me with a selection of this correspondence.

8. Ibid., 268.

9. These details were leaked to the *Washington Post*, April 4, 1969, p. A2. For the overall package, see *New York Times*, April 16, 1969, p. 18.

10. This paragraph is drawn from Robert Boyden Lamb, "The Taxpayers' Revolt against Rising School Costs," *Current History* (July 1972): 22–25, 36–37; and *Wall Street Journal*, December 18, 1969, p. 1. Also useful is Robert Bendiner, *The Politics of Schools: A Crisis in Self-Government* (New York: Harper and Row, 1969).

11. Teachers' salaries went up by 128.6 percent between 1952 and 1968 (years during which the consumer price index increased by only 29.4 percent).

12. By 1970, the interest rate on AAA-ranked bonds was 6.50 percent (the 1952 figure had been 1.42 percent).

13. *Wall Street Journal*, December 18, 1969, p. 1.

14. House Appropriations Committee, Subcommittee on Labor-HEW, *Appropriations for Fiscal Year 1970*, pt. 2, April 29, 1969, 656.

15. See, for example, Robert Semple's article in *New York Times*, December 29, 1969, p. 1. In May, for example, the House rejected the five-year renewal of ESEA that had been recommended by the Perkins committee, in favor of the two-year extension favored by the administration. As in 1967, the successful coalition was assembled by Edith Green.

16. The witness was John Morse, appearing on behalf of the American Council for Education. House Appropriations Committee, Subcommittee on Labor-HEW, *Appropriations*, pt. 7, June 2, 1969, 1120.

17. A former Shakespearean actor and a graduate of Harvard Law School, Flood represented the blue-collar coal-mining town of Wilkes-Barre. For his colloquy with Allen, see ibid., pt. 5, May 5, 1969, 8. For an entertaining profile of Flood, see William C. Kashatus III, "Dapper Dan Flood: Pennsylvania's Legendary Congressman," *Pennsylvania Heritage* (Summer 1995): 4–11.

18. Gary Orfield, *Congressional Power: Congress and Social Change* (New York: Harcourt Brace Jovanovich, 1975), 140. Writing to a constituent, Green argued that "the American people ought to have as much concern about it as about the industrial military complex." Green to Mr. D. L. McGregor, letter, February 6, 1970, in Papers of Edith Green, Oregon Historical Society, Portland, box 70-1.

19. This account is based on Stanley McFarland, interview with author, August 19, 2003, Potomac, Md.; August Steinhilber, interview with author, August 4, 2005, Waldorf, Md.; Don White, interview with author, August 6, 2005, Annapolis, Md.; and on Albert Sumberg, "A Brief History of the Committee for Education Funding" (unpublished manuscript, September 1999). I am grateful to Mr. Steinhilber for providing me with a copy of this in-house history. Simmons had just become the leader of the impact aid superintendents, following the sudden death of Oscar Rose.

20. For a prescient article that anticipated this shift of focus, see Samuel Halperin, "Education Legislation in the 90th Congress," *Phi Delta Kappan*, February 1967. Reprinted in Halperin, *Issues on Federal Education Policy* (Washington, D.C.: Institute for Educational Leadership, 1975), 34.

21. Young probably provided the full funding concept. Two months earlier the AFL-CIO executive council had passed a resolution supporting "full and adequate funding of all programs whose goals are the social progress of all Americans." The resolution is reproduced in House Appropriations Committee, Subcommittee on Labor-HEW, *Appropriations for Fiscal Year 1970*, pt. 7, 437–438. It was important that Young be included, says the NEA's McFarland, because labor-oriented legislators would commonly touch base with him before responding to education initiatives. See Stanley McFarland, interview with author, August 3, 2005, Potomac, Md.

22. The changes going on in NEA at this time are treated in greater depth in Chapter 9.

23. The unnamed official is cited in *Congressional Quarterly Weekly Report*, July 18, 1969, 1298.

24. Simmons was associate superintendent of the Detroit school system, which was running desperately short of money. See Chapter 8 for the lawsuit that arose out of its predicament.

25. AASA was an affiliate of NEA, but they were on the brink of separation, the relationship having been ruptured by NEA's growing militancy (see chapter 9).

26. Jack Morse (chief lobbyist of the American Council on Education [ACE]) to Lloyd Elliott (president of George Washington University), letter, May 7, 1971, ACE papers, box 1011.

27. According to Charles Radcliffe, top GOP education staffer on the Education and Labor committee, Edith Green, author of the "education-industrial complex" tag, "despised Don White," and she was not the only powerful legislator who viewed him with suspicion. Robert Michel of Illinois, the ranking Republican on Flood's subcommittee, had recently charged that school officials wasted federal funds on equipment that they did not need: "hardware salesmen put the muscle on," he told colleagues, "and we have stuff sitting in warehouses, down in basements, up in attics, and doing no good." See Radcliffe, interview with author, August 5, 2005, Washington, D.C.; House Appropriations Committee, Subcommittee on Labor-HEW, *Appropriations for Fiscal Year 1970*, pt. 2, 695.

28. Those represented were the Urban Coalition Action Council, the American Personnel and Guidance Association, the National Education Association, the American Library Association, the American Vocational Association, Agudath Israel, the American Federation of Teachers, the Great Cities Research Council, and the impacted area superintendents. House Appropriations Committee, Subcommittee on Labor-HEW, *Appropriations for Fiscal Year 1970*, pt. 2, 1128.

29. See Allen Schick, *Congress and Money: Budgeting, Spending, and Taxing* (Washington, D.C.: Urban Institute, 1980), 32–37, 426–427.

30. See Richard Spohn and Charles McCollum, *The Revenue Committees* (New York: Grossman Publishers, 1975), 250.

31. See Allen Schick, "The Three-Ring Budget Process: The Appropriations, Tax, and Budget Committees in Congress," in Thomas E. Mann and Norman J. Ornstein, eds., *The New Congress* (Washington, D.C.: American Enterprise Institute, 1981), 302–304.

32. *Congressional Record*, June 18, 1969, 16431–16433.

33. *Washington Post*, July 5, 1969, p. A6.

34. Steinhilber, interview, August 4, 2005.

35. Ibid.

36. *Wall Street Journal*, January 20, 1970, p. 19.

37. In this paragraph, I rely heavily on a lucid analysis by staff reporter Norman Miller in ibid., November 1, 1969, p. 16.

38. Charles Saunders, a Nixon appointee in HEW, observed in a 1971 speech before members of Phi Delta Kappa that the acronym SELF was entirely appropriate. See Saunders, "Expanding Options for the Federal Role in Elementary and Secondary Education," October 21, 1971. I am grateful to Mr. Saunders for supplying me with a copy of the speech.

39. *Wall Street Journal*, January, 20, 1970, p. 19.

40. Steinhilber, interview, August 4, 2005.

41. *National Journal*, November 1, 1969, p. 16.

42. In an interview, he recalled: "I went to his office and the first thing he said was 'Here, have one of these Missouri meerschaums,' and he handed me a corn cob pipe and the next thing I knew I was on the Legislative Appropriations Subcommittee." See profile of Joelson by Marjorie Hunter in *New York Times*, May 31, 1969, p. 21.

43. *Congressional Record*, July 29, 1969, 21201.

44. Ibid., 21453.

45. Ibid., 21454.

46. For the roll call, see *Congressional Quarterly Weekly Report*, August 8, 1969, 1472–1473.

47. *New York Times*, July 31, 1969, p. 1.

48. Meeds to Mrs. Earl Hilton, letter, October 28, 1969, Papers of Lloyd Meeds, University of Washington, Seattle, box 182.

49. It read: "Know Ye By These Presents: That ____ served with distinction in the JOELSON AMENDMENT fight of 1969 in the United States House of Representatives by which was added $894.5 million to the budget of the United States Office of Education for fiscal year 1970. It was only through perseverance, diligence, and in-

telligent labor, such as was displayed by the aforementioned person, that a milestone was reached in American education." The certificate was signed by Joelson, Lee, and Perkins. Copy in Papers of Charles S. Joelson, Library of Congress, box 41. See same location for abundant congratulatory correspondence to Joelson.

50. Quie to Robert Michel, letter, August 5, 1969, in Quie papers, box 33.

51. Cohelan was felt by his constituents to be insufficiently vocal in his opposition to the war in Vietnam and lost a 1970 primary challenge.

52. *Congressional Record*, October 28, 1969, 31868.

53. See Rowland Evans and Robert Novak column in *Washington Post*, November 2, 1969, p. A37.

54. The reporter was Robert Semple, whose reporting was admired by Nixon for its fair-mindedness. *New York Times*, December 22, 1969, p. 22.

55. Rowland Evans and Robert Novak, *Nixon in the White House: The Frustration of Power* (New York: Random House, 1971), 103–104. Harlow was also being pestered by presidents, he later reminisced to a reporter from his home state: "I'm there in this room, phones ringing. Over runs a little twinkle-eyed secretary. She says President Johnson is calling. I take the phone. 'Yes, Mr President. Yup. Yup. Yuppity yup. Yes sir.' Then comes the secretary again. 'President Eisenhower is calling.' 'Tell him I'm talking to the president (Johnson) and will call him right back, or if he prefers we can put him on hold.' Believe me, we put him on hold. Now I've got the president (Johnson) on line and the former president (Eisenhower) waiting. In runs Larry Higby and he says, 'Mr. Harlow! Mr. Harlow!' very imperiously. 'The president-elect (Nixon) wants you in his office immediately.' I told him I had a president and a former president on the line, and the president-elect would have to wait his turn." Allan Cromley, "The Adviser Who Had No Peer," *Sunday Oklahoman*, February 22, 1987. I am indebted to Katherine McLemore of the Oklahoma Heritage Society for drawing this article to my attention.

56. Although Nixon liked Harlow and spent a lot of time with him, the Oklahoman seems to have had almost no influence on White House legislative strategy.

57. Also influential in domestic affairs, during the first year, were Arthur Burns and Daniel Patrick Moynihan. They each knew the world of Washington politics well. But they were involved more in long-range strategic planning than in day-to-day politics. Nixon, of course, was extremely familiar with Washington politics, making his inept selections mystifying.

58. Ehrlichman's contempt for Congress and its members resulted in a difficult relationship between the White House and Senator Scott, in particular. One newspaper reporter identified five occasions when Scott had "found himself publicly out of touch with the President," despite the fact that he "works so hard to cultivate the image of a presidential confidante." See Richard Frank, "White House Left Sen. Scott in the Dark," *Philadelphia Sunday Bulletin*, May 18, 1970. Scott sent copies of this article to eight top White House officials, demanding "substantive evidence of support of my leadership" in order to "erase the steady drumbeat of criticism I am receiving." For the article, and his letters, see Papers of Hugh Scott, Small Special Collections Library, University of Virginia, Charlottesville, box 65. For Gerald Ford's dismay at Ehrlichman's attitude, see James Cannon, *Time and Chance: Gerald Ford's Appointment with History* (New York: HarperCollins, 1994), 99. He recalls

that "Ford, who could get along with almost everyone, actively disliked Bob Haldeman and John Ehrlichman. 'They were obnoxious when it came to their dealings with Congress,' Ford said."

59. John Ehrlichman, *Witness to Power: The Nixon Years* (New York: Simon and Schuster, 1982), 195–196. Ziegler was Nixon's press secretary.

60. Haldeman added: "I think Bryce now sees this too, but he sure didn't before." H. R. Haldeman, *Haldeman Diaries: Inside the Nixon White House*, CD-ROM (Santa Monica, Calif.: Sony, 1994), entry for November 21, 1969.

61. See Chester E. Finn, *Education and the Presidency* (Lexington, Mass.: Lexington, 1977).

62. This paragraph is drawn from Haldeman, *Haldeman Diaries*, entries for January 13, 1970, January 21, 1970, and January 26, 1970. See also Evans and Novak, *Frustrations of Power*, 122–124. The televised address is reproduced in *Congressional Quarterly Weekly Report*, January 30, 1970, 299–300.

63. Nixon told Haldeman that "he needs a writer who can put a speech together, so he doesn't have to do all the work." Haldeman, *Haldeman Diaries*, entry for January 26, 1970.

64. Ibid., January 28, 1970. Rather was White House correspondent for CBS News. For his account of the Nixon administration, which is more nuanced than Haldeman would have anticipated, see Rather and Gary Paul Gates, *The Palace Guard* (New York: Harper and Row, 1974).

65. For Flemming and the reaction of higher education, see Jack Morse to Logan Wilson, memo, February 17, 1970, in ACE papers, box 1011. Morse recalled his doubts in a letter to David Cornell, May 5, 1971, ibid.

66. When Stanley McFarland of NEA put the coalition's case to Magnuson's Senate appropriations subcommittee, the chairman snapped: "If we were going to appropriate up to what is authorized, there is no use having the Appropriations Committee." Senate Appropriations Committee, Subcommittee on Labor-HEW, hearings, *Appropriations for Fiscal Year 1970*, 91st Cong., 1st Sess., Pt. 7, December 5, 1969, 1550–1557.

67. Morse to Cornell, letter, May 5, 1971.

68. Steinhilber, interview, August 4, 2005.

69. The CEF was still in existence in 2007.

70. The witness was Peter Muirhead, a senior official at OE. He and Flood knew one another well: Flood called him "Scotty." House Appropriations Committee, Subcommittee on Labor-HEW, hearings, Office of Education, *Appropriations: Fiscal Year 1972*, 92nd Cong., 1st Sess., pt. 1, February 18, 1971, 45. One indication of the CEF's power was that vulnerable parts of the Office of Education/Education Division sought to come under its protective umbrella. Emerson Elliott, deputy director of the National Institute of Education, recalls being "tangentially involved" in such an effort, but "research did not have a good reputation among educators," and they feared "they might be contaminated by . . . association." Elliott to author, letter, January 20, 2007.

71. House Appropriations Committee, Subcommittee on Labor-HEW, hearings, OE, *Appropriations: FY 1972*, 175.

72. Were general aid to come about, they would have to shift their attention back to state capitols. That in turn would further diminish the power of education groups in federal politics.

73. Charles Saunders, who was a deputy commissioner at OE under Nixon, told members of Phi Delta Kappa that "the advocates of the full funding strategy now recognize that this complex array of programs has done little to resolve the problems of the educational system." Yet the "Categorical Camp" was unfazed by this discovery: "Never mind the mounting evidence that much of the Federal money spent was wasted—love that Federal money! Never mind the accompanying red tape; forget about 'accountability': just give us more of the same—lots more." Saunders, "Expanding Options," 3.

74. Some modest consolidation of programs was achieved in the education amendments of 1974, but the reforms had largely been reversed by the end of the decade. On the proliferation of categorical education programs during the 1970s, see Christopher T. Cross, *Political Education: National Policy Comes of Age* (New York: Teachers College Press, 2004), 68–69.

75. See Evans and Novak, *Frustrations of Power*, 127; Haldeman, *Haldeman Diaries*, entries for July 17, 1970, August 5, 1970, and August 7, 1970.

76. Haldeman, *Haldeman Diaries*, entry for August 9, 1970.

77. Ibid., entry for August 9, 1970. For a full analysis, see Robert Mason, *Richard Nixon and the Quest for a New Majority* (Chapel Hill: University of North Carolina Press, 2004).

78. Additionally, many congressional Republicans were reportedly angry with the president for having recently vetoed the popular Hill-Burton hospital construction reauthorization, without consultation. That veto too had been overridden. See Evans and Novak, *Frustrations of Power*, 124–126.

79. This was composed almost equally of education and health spending. By this time, health groups had responded to the success of the education coalition by establishing their own Coalition for Health Funding.

80. For the overall package of measures, see *New York Times*, October 28, 1972, p. 1.

81. Democrats and Republicans alike concluded that the gap was too great to be bridged. In addition, Congress needed to start work on the 1974 budget, and it was impossible for Flood and Magnuson to work on two budgets simultaneously.

82. OMB secretary Caspar Weinberger's claim is reproduced in Louis Fisher, "Impoundment of Funds: Uses and Abuses," *Buffalo Law Review* 141 (1973–1974): 191–192.

83. Congress refused to set an expenditure ceiling in 1972, to deprive Nixon of this argument.

84. Senate Appropriations Committee, Subcommittee on Labor-HEW, *Appropriations for Fiscal Year 1970*, pt. 7, December 4, 1969, 1560. See also various items in Magnuson papers. He told the medical director of the Seattle public school system that even if Congress voted for extra education funds "the President holds the trump cards: through expenditure controls, he can frustrate our intentions, and control the flow of actual spending." Magnuson to Charlotte Bonsmer, letter, September 23, 1969, Magnuson papers, box 262, Series 7.

85. For the distinctiveness of Nixon's approach to impoundment, see Fisher, "Impoundment," 141–200, and "Impoundment of Funds," note, *Harvard Law Review* 86 (1972–1973): 1505–1535.

86. Cited by Louis Fisher, "Impoundment," in Donald C. Bacon, Roger H.

Davidson, and Morton Keller, eds., *The Encyclopedia of the United States Congress* (New York: Simon and Schuster, 1995), 2: 1107.

87. Watergate was part of this, but not the only part. Congress was also worried by Nixon's ideas for overhauling the executive branch, featuring "super-cabinet" secretaries who would belong to the White House staff and not be accountable to the legislature. See *Washington Post*, January 20, 1973, p. 118.

88. As John Morse, director of ACE, observed, there was not much point in trying to "bust the [Nixon] budget," for "it will do little good to appropriate funds that the President is not seeking." Morse to "colleague," letter, April 4, 1973, in ACE papers, box 1011.

89. Steinhilber recalls that he, Ray Peterson (chief lobbyist for CCSSO), and others whose names appeared on the brief each found their tax affairs coming under close scrutiny from the IRS shortly thereafter. Steinhilber, interview, August 4, 2005.

90. *New York Times*, June 9, 1973, p. 16; November 22, 1973, p. 1; *Washington Post*, November 22, 1973, p. A1.

91. For Laird's influence, see *Washington Post*, December 20, 1973, p. A1. Not only was Laird a man of Congress: he had been ranking minority member of the Labor-HEW appropriations subcommittee, in which capacity he had enjoyed friendly relations with both John Fogarty and Daniel Flood.

92. Robert Frase, *Publishers Weekly*, January 21, 1974, 66. Frase was head of the Washington office for the book publishing associations.

93. James T. Patterson, *Grand Expectations: The United States, 1945–1974* (New York: Oxford University Press, 1996), 783.

94. Edward D. Berkowitz, *Something Happened: A Political and Cultural Overview of the Seventies* (New York: Columbia University Press, 2006), 53.

95. U.S. Department of Commerce, *Statistical Abstract of the United States: 1994* (Washington, D.C.: Department of Commerce, 1994), table 504, p. 330.

96. Ibid., table 747, p. 488.

97. Patterson, *Grand Expectations*, 785.

98. Joseph White, "The Functions and Power of the House Appropriations Committee" (Ph.D. diss., University of California at Berkeley, 1989), 107. The staff member is not named. A second change came in 1974, when the subcommittee began to hold its hearings in public, significantly altering their feel and creating a greater temptation for members to play to the gallery. See Schick, *Congress and Money*.

99. See Berkowitz, *Something Happened*, 84–103. These institutional changes are considered further in Chapter 7.

100. *New York Times*, September 11, 1975, p. 68. OE had been detached from the Labor-HEW bill in a bid to ensure that funds were available by the start of the school year.

101. See *Wall Street Journal*, July 28, 1975, p. 3; *Congressional Quarterly Almanac: 1975* (Washington, D.C.: Congressional Quarterly, 1976), 787.

102. *Washington Post*, September 5, 1975, p. A3, and September 10, 1975, p. A1; *New York Times*, September 10, 1975, p. 1.

103. *Congressional Quarterly Almanac: 1976* (Washington, D.C.: Congressional Quarterly, 1977), 795.

104. A. James Reichley, *Conservatives in an Age of Change: The Nixon and Ford Administrations* (Washington, D.C.: Brookings Institution, 1981), 330.

105. They remained formally committed to this increasingly fanciful goal throughout the 1970s. See, for example, John Ryor, "One-third Federal Funding," *Today's Education*: March–April 1977, 6.

106. *Digest of Education Statistics: 2004* (Washington, D.C.: NCES, 2005), tables 163 and 153. Federal expenditure per student increased from $71 in 1969 to $177 in 1977 (the table does not include an inflation-adjusted figure).

Part II. Education and Regulatory Federalism

1. Sec.601, Civil Rights Act of 1964. Title VI is reproduced in full in Stephen C. Halpern, *On the Limits of the Law: The Ironic Legacy of Title VI of the 1964 Civil Rights Act* (Baltimore, Md.: Johns Hopkins University Press, 1995), 338–339.

2. U.S. Commission on Civil Rights, *Southern School Desegregation, 1966–67* (Washington, D.C.: Government Printing Office, 1967), 81.

3. Gary Orfield, *The Reconstruction of Southern Education: The Schools and the 1964 Civil Rights Act* (New York: Wiley-Interscience, 1969), 46.

4. In a fourth case, Title IX of the 1972 education amendments outlawed discrimination on the grounds of gender in any education institution receiving federal funding. I do not discuss Title IX in this book, partly because its effects were felt primarily in the area of higher education but also because it has been so well treated by John David Skrentny, *The Minority Rights Revolution* (Cambridge, Mass.: Harvard University Press, 2002), 230–262. See also Andrew Fishel and Janice Pottker, *National Politics and Sex Discrimination in Education* (Lexington, Mass.: D.C. Heath, 1977), and Timothy Conlan, *The Evolution of a Problematic Partnership: The Feds and Higher Education* (Washington, D.C.: ACIR, 1981).

5. James Q. Wilson, "American Politics, Then and Now," *Commentary* 67, no. 10 (February 1979): 41.

6. Skrentny, *The Minority Rights Revolution*.

7. For regulatory federalism's impact on other policy areas, see, for example, Richard A. Harris and Sidney M. Milkis, *The Politics of Regulatory Change. A Tale of Two Agencies* (New York: Oxford University Press, 1989); R. Shep Melnick, *Regulation and the Courts: The Case of the Clean Air Act* (Washington, D.C.: Brookings Institution, 1983); and Martha Derthick, *Up in Smoke: From Legislation to Litigation in Tobacco Politics* (Washington, D.C.: CQ Press, 2002). (The two cases investigated by Harris and Milkis are the Federal Trade Commission and the Environmental Protection Agency.)

8. Advisory Commission on Intergovernmental Relations, *Regulatory Federalism: Policy, Process, Impact, and Reform* (Washington, D.C.: ACIR, 1984), 1 (emphasis in original).

9. Arthur E. Wise, *Legislated Learning: The Bureaucratization of the American Classroom* (Berkeley: University of California Press, 1979), 2. For a set of essays by educators that vividly illustrate the local impact of the new federal role, see [Samuel Halperin, ed.,] *Federalism at the Crossroads: Improving Educational Policymaking* (Washington, D.C.: Institute for Educational Leadership, 1975).

10. [Timothy Conlan], *Intergovernmentalizing the Classroom: Federal Involvement in Elementary and Secondary Education* (Washington, D.C.; ACIR, 1981), 7.

11. For the broader impact of Title VI in areas other than education, see in particular Hugh Davis Graham, "Since 1964: The Paradox of American Civil Rights Regulation," in Morton Keller and R. Shep Melnick, eds., *Taking Stock: American Government in the Twentieth Century* (New York: Cambridge University Press, 1999), 187–218.

Chapter 5. Ending Massive Resistance: The Federal Government and Southern School Desegregation, 1964–1970

1. This point has been made a number of times. See, for example, Hugh Davis Graham, *The Civil Rights Era: Origins and Development of National Policy* (New York: Oxford University Press, 1990), 82–83; Gary Orfield, *The Reconstruction of Southern Education: The Schools and the 1964 Civil Rights Act* (New York: Wiley-Interscience, 1969), 36, 39–44; and Stephen Halpern, *On the Limits of the Law: The Ironic Legacy of Title VI of the 1964 Civil Rights Act* (Baltimore, Md.: Johns Hopkins University Press, 1995), 32.

2. *Congressional Record*, March 30, 1964, 6543, 6546. Humphrey was quoting from the Supreme Court's ruling in the 1947 case, *Oklahoma v. Civil Service Commission*.

3. Ibid., April 25,1964, 9095; June 4, 1964, 12717.

4. A few weeks earlier, education aid had been deleted from the antipoverty bill because of a church-state flap. See Chapter 1, section headed "Education and the War on Poverty."

5. Halpern stresses the importance of this point in *On the Limits of the Law*, 15–16, 33–41.

6. Orfield, *Reconstruction*, 52.

7. Beryl Radin, *Implementation, Change, and the Federal Bureaucracy: School Desegregation in H.E.W., 1964–1968* (New York: Teachers College Press, 1977), 7.

8. This budget was for providing "technical assistance" to districts undergoing court-ordered desegregation, under Title IV of the Civil Rights Act. Radin, *Implementation*, 59; Orfield, *Reconstruction*, 76.

9. Orfield, *Reconstruction*, 55, 91–92. Keppel was concerned that program administrators at OE had neither the time nor the appetite for this task.

10. David Seeley to deputy commissioner David Sullivan, memo, February 6, 1967, quoted in Radin, *Implementation*, 86.

11. Ibid., 76.

12. Ibid., 102.

13. See Orfield, *Reconstruction*, 117.

14. Harold Howe II, December 12, 1968, oral history interview for HUCRDP, 1.

15. Francis Keppel judged that Celebrezze's "enthusiasm for the Civil Rights Act could be contained in a thimble." Francis Keppel, April 21, 1969, OH for LBJL, 20.

16. Orfield, *Reconstruction*, 146.

17. David Allen, in *Congressional Record*, October 5, 1966, 25353. For a typical complaint about the "arrogance" of the northern law students, see remarks by Senator Spessard Holland (D-Fla.), September 28, 1966, in ibid., 24295–24297. Ralph Huitt, head of congressional relations at HEW, recalls the political difficulty that their activities generated: September 17, 1969, oral history interview for HUCRDP, 11.

18. See Johnson's telephone conversation with his attorney general, Nicholas Katzenbach, April 7, 1966, WH6604.02 PNO 7. All recorded telephone conversations cited throughout notes were downloaded from the Web site of the Presidential Recording Program, Miller Center of Public Affairs, University of Virginia (www.millercenter.virginia.edu). See also Dean J. Kotlowski, *Nixon's Civil Rights Politics, Principle, and Policy* (Cambridge, Mass.: Harvard University Press, 2001), 26–27.

19. For Fogarty's recommendation, see Wilbur Cohen, September 4, 1969, oral history interview for the HUCRDP, 15; and Cohen to Henry Hall Wilson, memo, March 15, 1966, Cohen Papers, box 105.

20. Ibid., 14–15.

21. Leon Panetta with Peter Gall, *Bring Us Together: The Nixon Team and the Civil Rights Retreat* (Philadelphia: Lippincott, 1971), 68.

22. Cohen, Howard University OH, 23.

23. Panetta, *Bring Us Together*, 55, 61.

24. See Lewis Chester, Godfrey Hodgson, and Bruce Page, *An American Melodrama: The Presidential Campaign of 1968* (New York: Dell, 1969), 512–517; Orfield, *Reconstruction*, 346.

25. Arthur M. Schlesinger Jr., *The Imperial Presidency* (Boston: Houghton Mifflin, 1973). Chapter 8 is entitled "The Revolutionary Presidency."

26. Moynihan's handwritten notes on meeting with Nixon, in his journal, March 4, 1970, Moynihan papers, box 227.

27. For an account of his racial attitudes, see Kotlowski, *Nixon's Civil Rights*.

28. In November 1967, Nixon told an interviewer: "I've always thought the country could run itself domestically without a president. All you need is a competent cabinet to run the country at home." Rowland Evans and Robert Novak, *Nixon in the White House: The Frustration of Power* (New York: Random House, 1971), 11.

29. Finch had been a staffer for Nixon during his vice presidency and had run his 1960 and 1962 campaigns.

30. Like Mitchell, Garment was a former law partner at Nixon Mudge. On the circumstances surrounding his appointment, see Leonard Garment, *Crazy Rhythm* (New York: Times Books, 1997), 150–156.

31. Evans and Novak, *Nixon*, 59.

32. On Reagan's attitude to Veneman, see transcribed telephone conversation between Elliot Richardson and John Ehrlichman, March 31, 1971, in Richardson papers, box 129.

33. Panetta, *Bring Us Together*, 63. In his memoirs, Wilkins recalls his pithy reaction: "Fuck you, Finch, I thought." Roger Wilkins, *A Man's Life: An Autobiography* (New York: Touchstone, 1983), 246.

34. On his appointment, Allen explained that his racial views were very similar to those of Harold Howe. Panetta, *Bring Us Together*, 81.

35. Ruby Martin, the black incumbent, declined an offer to stay on.

36. Panetta, *Bring Us Together*, 61, 82.

37. August Steinhilber, interview with author, August 4, 2005, Waldorf, Md.

38. Rufus E. Miles, *The Department of H.E.W.* (New York: Praeger, 1974), 273.

39. See sundry materials in Mardian papers, box 6, folders titled "Thursday Discussion Group (HEW)" and "Vietnam Moratorium, 10/15/69." The material cited here comes from James Farmer to Rep. Elford Cederberg (R-Mich.), letter, Octo-

ber 8 1969; "The Scott Report," *Twin Circle*, August 10, 1969, attached to memo, J. R. Pat Gorman to L. Patrick Gray III, August 8, 1969; FEDS, *The Advocate*, October 1969, 1–4. Adverse publicity in the conservative magazine *Human Events* led HEW to ban FEDS from using federal property for these purposes, but the Thursday Discussion Group then filed a court action appealing the decision and won in the District of Columbia Circuit Court of Appeals. See Mardian to Mr. Fred Wilde (San Jose, Calif.), letter, date illegible (probably October 29, 1969).

40. Dent to Mardian, memo, Mardian papers, box 1.

41. Malek to Haldeman, confidential memo, December 1, 1970, in Papers of Frederic Malek, Hoover Institution, Stanford, Calif., box 6; Malek to John Ehrlichman, memo, December 23, 1970, in ibid., box 7.

42. This choice had been vetoed, but Abert had at least enjoyed the satisfaction of hiring a West Virginia Democrat whose office was reportedly decorated with a poster declaring: "If Hitler was a friend of the Jews, Nixon is a friend of the Blacks."

43. One source of tidbits was Vice President Agnew. See, for example, Agnew to Nixon, confidential memo, May 16, 1969, in President's Office File (POF), box 2.

44. Panetta, *Bring Us Together*, 128.

45. Ibid., 81–82.

46. John Ehrlichman, *Witness to Power: The Nixon Years* (New York: Simon and Schuster, 1982), 226.

47. Fred LaRue, a Mississippi Republican on the White House staff, to Bryce Harlow, memo, February 18, 1969, Confidential Files (CF), HU2-1, Nixon Project, box 35; Dent to Harlow, memo, February 14, 1969, and Dent to Harlow, memo, February 19, 1969, both in Dent office files, box 8; Dent to Harlow, memo, February 20, 1969, in Mardian papers, box 1.

48. H. R. Haldeman, *Haldeman Diaries*, CD-ROM (Santa Monica, Calif.: Sony, 1994), entry for February 21, 1969.

49. Dent to Nixon, memo, April 9, 1969, CF, HU2-1, Nixon Project, box 35.

50. Reported in Alexander Butterfield (deputy assistant to the president) to Robert Finch, memo, March 26, 1969, in WHCF, HU2-1, Nixon Project, box 8.

51. Panetta, *Bring Us Together*, 133.

52. For a vivid example of how this group operated, see Panetta to Finch, memo, July 1, 1969, Finch papers, call number 111.

53. Cited by Panetta, *Bring Us Together*, 133.

54. Ibid., 222.

55. The proportion of African American children attending previously all-white schools had increased from 2.2 percent in 1964 to 16.9 percent in 1966, to 32 percent in 1968. Figures taken from U.S. Commission on Civil Rights, *Twenty Years after Brown* (Washington, D.C.: Commission on Civil Rights, 1977), 48, 50; U.S. Commission on Civil Rights, *School Desegregation, 1966–67* (Washington, D.C.: Commission on Civil Rights, 1967), 6.

56. For a very positive evaluation, see William L. Taylor, *The Passion of My Times: An Advocate's Fifty-Year Journey in the Civil Rights Movement* (New York: Carroll and Graf, 2004), 49–53. (Taylor was staff director of the Civil Rights Commission and helped to craft Title VI.)

57. Panetta to Finch, memo, June 4, 1969, in Finch papers, call number 80.

58. Miles, *The Department of HEW*, 252.

59. OCR statistics, cited in *Race Relations Reporter* 2, no.12 (July 6, 1971): 1.

60. For an attempt at such an assessment, see U.S. Commission on Civil Rights, *Reviewing a Decade of School Desegregation, 1966–75* (Washington, D.C.: Commission on Civil Rights, 1977), 14–19.

61. *Briggs v. Elliott* (E.D. South Carolina, 1955), 132 F.Supp. at 777.

62. John Minor Wisdom, in the *Jefferson County* decision, discussed below, observed that "most judges" did not "know the right questions, much less the right answers." 372 F.2d at 855.

63. Ibid. at 853.

64. See, especially, *Singleton v. Jackson Municipal Separate School District* (5th CCA, 1965), 348 F.2d 729 (known as *Singleton I*), issued following the first set of HEW guidelines, in April 1965.

65. 372 F.2d at 848, 863, 865, 869 (emphasis in original). The decision was handed down on December 29, 1966, and affirmed in March of the following year (380 F.2d 385).

66. He referred to "members of this Court, who for years have gone to bed and waked up with school segregation problems on their minds." 372 F.2d at 858.

67. "We shall not permit the courts to be used to destroy or dilute the effectiveness of the congressional policy expressed in Title VI. There is no bonus for foot-dragging." Ibid., at 859–860.

68. Among those with this opinion was John Doar, head of the Civil Rights Division at Justice. See Orfield, *Reconstruction*, 117, 335–337. St. John Barrett, a career official at CRD, recalls an encounter with Attorney General Nicholas Katzenbach, who "asked me how many additional lawyers I would need to make a major push on school desegregation. I think I said a dozen. The next Monday I was given the names of a dozen lawyers in other divisions who were temporarily reassigned to the Civil Rights Division to work on school cases." Barrett to author, e-mail, November 26, 2006.

69. 391 U.S. at 439 (emphasis in original), 442. The case was decided on May 27, 1968.

70. Panetta to Finch, memo, April 21, 1969, in Finch papers, call number 43–2.

71. *New York Times Magazine*, August 10, 1969, p. 74.

72. Cited in daily news summary prepared for President Nixon, date unclear (probably early September 1969), POF, box 30.

73. *New York Times*, July 9, 1969, p. 1.

74. Ibid., July 10, 1969, p. 1; October 23, 1969, p. 28; Frank Dunbaugh to author, e-mail, October 12, 2006. Civil rights groups had urged Lyndon Johnson's attorney general, Ramsey Clark, to take such action back in 1967, but to no avail. See Minutes of Meeting of the Subcommittee on Education, Leadership Conference on Civil Rights, October 11, 1967, in LCCR papers, box 53.

75. Frank Dunbaugh (head of CRD's Southern Division) to author, e-mail; James Turner (head of its Midwestern Division) to author, e-mail, August 29, 2006.

76. Unless otherwise stated, the material in this paragraph and the next is drawn from Jerris Leonard to author, e-mail, May 16, 2006, and from Jerris Leonard, "A

Catholic Conservative's Experience with Civil Rights in America" (William F. Kelley Lecture, Creighton University, Omaha, Nebraska, April 8, 2000). I am grateful to Mr. Leonard for supplying me with a copy of his lecture.

77. Panetta, *Bring Us Together*, 233. More generally, Panetta and Finch told reporters that the July 3 statement had not modified the HEW guidelines and that OCR was committed to strong enforcement. The White House reaction was to demand Panetta's resignation, but Finch managed to dissuade the White House from forcing the issue until the following February. See Finch to Ehrlichman, memo, October 6, 1969, with handwritten undated resignation letter from Panetta to Finch attached, in Ehrlichman office files, box 23.

78. Finding his state besieged by "Federal bureaucrats, drunk with power," Allen warned that "the public schools in Alabama in the South cannot survive under present policies of HEW and of this administration." *Congressional Record*, September 3, 1969, 24197.

79. Reed to Dent, letter, July 11, 1969, in Dent office files, box 8. See also a letter from the head of the Georgia GOP, Paul Jones, describing the Georgia suit as "a political blunder" that left him "bitterly disappointed": G. Paul Jones to Dent, July 10, 1969, in Ehrlichman office files, box 30.

80. Stennis had recently taken over from Richard Russell as chair of the Armed Services Committee.

81. Panetta, *Bring Us Together*, 265. The source for this newspaper story was reportedly a "source close to the Senator," and Panetta surmises that Stennis was keen that his constituents should know of his actions on their behalf.

82. Finch's letter is reproduced in ibid., 255.

83. Panetta, *Bring Us Together*, 262.

84. Dunbaugh, e-mail, October 12, 2006. He recalls that "one district had a river through it, and the Title IV planners had drawn three attendance areas across the river," even though "only one area had a bridge."

85. Jerris Leonard to author, e-mail, May 9, 2006; *New York Times*, August 27, 1969, p. 1; September 11, 1969, p. 21. Elsewhere in the CRD there was dismay that the federal government should be going to court on the opposite side to the NAACP Legal Defense Fund for the first time. Sixty-five of the division's seventy-four nonsupervisory lawyers issued a letter of protest to Attorney General Mitchell and made sure that news of their action reached the press. See ibid., August 31, 1969, p. E1.

86. *Alexander v. Holmes*, 396 U.S. at 20.

87. See articles from *Atlanta Constitution*, December 16, 1969, and *Washington Post*, December 18, 1969, reproduced in *Congressional Record*, December 19, 1969, 40332.

88. See Harlow to Nixon, memo, February 11, 1970, in POF, box 5.

89. Evans and Novak, *Nixon*, 156.

90. For the "clowns" remark, see Moynihan's notes on a meeting with Nixon and Mitchell, September 18, 1969, Moynihan papers, box 226. The second comment was made to a GOP legislative leadership meeting and is reproduced in Buchanan to Nixon, memo, February 17, 1970, in POF, box 80.

91. Handwritten note to Ehrlichman, appended to Buchanan to Nixon, memo, January 30, 1970, POF, box 5.

92. Ehrlichman meeting notes, January 9, 1970, Ehrlichman office files, box 1.

93. Notes by Daniel Patrick Moynihan on Garment's comments at a staff meeting (presumably of the Urban Affairs Council), September 17, 1969, in Moynihan papers, box 226.

94. See Stephen E. Ambrose, *Nixon: The Triumph of a Politician, 1962–1972* (New York: Touchstone, 1989), 248–249.

95. News summary, week of January 12–18, 1970, POF, box 31.

96. Ehrlichman meeting notes, February 9, 1970, Ehrlichman office files, box 3.

97. Harlow to staff secretary, memo, February 11, 1970, containing notes of a meeting among Nixon, Mitchell, and Harlow, POF, box 80. See also Ehrlichman's notes on a meeting with Nixon and Peter Flanagan, February 9, 1970, in Ehrlichman office files, box 3.

98. Harlow to Nixon, memo, February 11, 1970, POF, box 5, with Nixon's marginal comments appended. Such was the strength of Mitchell's reaction that Harlow—doubtless to his surprise—suggested "it appears more likely that we will get action indicating Administration displeasure and concern from HEW than from Justice."

99. Kirk was the most intemperate. When the courts ordered the integration of the schools of Manatee County, Florida, he used state troopers to prevent federal marshals from enforcing the ruling and reportedly threatened to open fire on the federal agents. He said that if the marshals attempted to serve him with papers, he would have them arrested. "No one is going to touch Claude Jr.," he added. *New York Times*, April 10, 1970, pp. 1, 18.

100. Buchanan to Nixon, memo, January 30, 1970. This memo is not available in the Nixon Project but is reproduced in Garment, *Crazy Rhythm*, 206.

101. A restaurant owner, Maddox was famous for having kept an ax handle behind the counter to deter black patrons. Stephen Tuck, *Beyond Atlanta: The Struggle for Racial Equality in Georgia, 1940–1980* (Athens: University of Georgia Press, 2001), 194.

102. Garment, *Crazy Rhythm*, 207.

103. Pat Buchanan, draft 3, dated February 12, 1970, in Ehrlichman office files, box 30.

104. See Haldeman, *Haldeman Diaries*, entry for February 16, 1970.

105. Ibid., entry for February 17, 1970. In the diary entry for February 16, 1970, Haldeman reported that "P agrees with Buchanan thesis."

106. Agnew *did* still go down to Atlanta, but his speech was a paean to the "new South." Still, the venue at least was calculated to appeal to devotees of an older South—he spoke in front of the confederate memorial at Stone Mountain. See Matthew Lassiter, *The Silent Majority: Suburban Politics in the Sunbelt South* (Princeton, N.J.: Princeton University Press, 2006), 17.

107. The formal head of the CCE was Spiro Agnew, but he "wanted no part of this effort and declined to participate." See George Shultz, "Pages from History: Reflections on Some Experiences with President Richard Nixon" (speech delivered at Nixon Library, January 9, 2003), 5. I am grateful to Dr. Shultz for furnishing me with a copy of these remarks.

108. Garment to author, letter, August 12, 2006.

109. Ehrlichman notes on Nixon meeting with him and Haldeman, March 19,

1970, in Ehrlichman office files, box 3; John Brown to John Ehrlichman, memo, March 3, 1970, Ehrlichman office files, box 30.

110. Dan Carter, *The Politics of Rage: George Wallace, The Origins of the New Conservatism, and the Transformation of American Politics* (New York: Simon and Schuster, 1995), 399.

111. Column by Richard Wilson, *Washington Star*, February 11, 1970, cited in news summary, 1970, with Nixon's annotation, POF, box 31. See also Nixon's marginal comments on news summary, n.d. (but probably January 1970), in ibid. He underlined Wallace's prediction that Nixon would be "a one-term President."

112. Evans and Novak, *Nixon*, 174. Thurmond's former aide, Harry Dent, was keen to stoke Nixon's anxiety about Wallace. See, for example, Dent to Nixon, memo, January 19, 1970, in Ehrlichman office files, box 30.

113. See Ehrlichman's notes on the meeting, August 4, 1970, in Ehrlichman office files, box 4. See also Garment's summary in memo to Nixon, August 5, 1970, POF, box 7.

114. On Nixon's distinct approach to leadership, see Nigel Bowles, *Nixon's Business: Authority and Power in Presidential Politics* (College Station: Texas A&M Press, 2005).

115. Harlow to Staff Secretary, memo, February 21, 1970, reporting February 19 conversation between Nixon and Russell. WHCF, HU2–1, Nixon project, box 9.

116. The reporter was William McIlwain. J. Harvie Wilkinson, *From Brown to Bakke: The Supreme Court and School Integration: 1954–1978* (New York: Oxford University Press, 1981), 122–123. According to one account, the riot was triggered by the inflammatory rhetoric of Rep. Albert Watson (R-S.C.). Gordon Harvey, *A Question of Justice: New South Governors and Education, 1968–1976* (Tuscaloosa: University of Alabama Press, 2002), 14, 122.

117. Haldeman, *Haldeman Diaries*, entry for February 17, 1970. Events in Lamar were covered in Nixon's news summary for March 4, 1970, in POF, box 31.

118. Nixon to Haldeman, Ehrlichman, and Kissinger, memo, March 2, 1970, in Haldeman office files, Nixon Project, box 138.

119. See Ehrlichman notes on a meeting with Nixon and Haldeman, January 9, 1970, Ehrlichman office files, box 3.

120. Haldeman, *Haldeman Diaries*, entry for April 7, 1970.

121. James Keogh, notes on cabinet meeting, November 5, 1969, in POF, box 79.

122. Richard Nixon, *RN: The Memoirs of Richard Nixon* (New York: Grosset and Dunlap, 1978), 267–268. On Nixon's broader penchant for "leapfrogging" the opposition, see William S. Safire, *Before the Fall: An Inside View of the Pre-Watergate White House* (Garden City, N.Y.: Doubleday, 1975), 127.

123. Moynihan to staff secretary, memo, March 5, 1970, WHCF, HU2, Nixon Project, box 2 (emphasis added).

124. Moynihan to Nixon, memo, May 9, 1970, POF, box 6. On May 4, 1970, Ohio National Guardsmen shot dead four students at Kent State University, during one of the many antiwar demonstrations that were taking place on U.S. campuses following the invasion of Cambodia.

125. Moynihan to Nixon, memo, June 30, 1970, in POF, box 6.

126. Ehrlichman's notes of telephone conversation with Nixon, February 12,

1970, Ehrlichman office files, box 3. See also Haldeman, *Haldeman Diaries*, which is full of negative characterizations of Agnew.

127. Nixon to Haldeman, memo, May 25, 1970, Haldeman office files, Nixon Project, box 138; Kotlowski, *Nixon's Civil Rights*, 21.

128. Ehrlichman's notes on Nixon's meeting with him and Haldeman, March 19, 1970, in Ehrlichman office files, box 3.

129. Safire, *Before the Fall*, 305.

130. Shultz to author, letter, June 5, 2006.

131. The Senate, Nixon charged, was not prepared to confirm anyone "who believes as I do in the strict construction of the Constitution." "As long as the Senate is constituted the way it is today," he added, "I will not nominate another Southerner and let him be subjected to the kind of malicious character assassination accorded both Judges Haynsworth and Carswell." *Congress and the Nation: 1969–1972* (Washington, D.C.: Congressional Quarterly Press, 1973), 297.

132. George H. Gallup, ed., *The Gallup Poll: Public Opinion, 1935–1971* (New York: Random House, 1972), vol.3, 2257.

133. Nixon, "Statement about Desegregation of Elementary and Secondary Schools," March 24, 1970, *Public Papers of the Presidents of the United States: Richard M. Nixon—1970* (Washington, D.C.: Government Printing Office, 1971), 304, 305, 314. That speech was followed in short order by a number of measures designed to emphasize the administration's determination: the Justice Department launched fifty-two new desegregation lawsuits, all on the same day; HEW announced three funding cut-offs; and the IRS made its ruling about tax exemptions for private schools.

134. *New York Times*, July 17, 1970, p. 1.

135. Ibid., July 18, 1970, p. 10.

136. Nixon, *RN*, 442–443.

137. For Leonard's prior career, see *New York Times*, January 27, 1969, p. 18. Panetta paraphrases Leonard as follows: "The South . . . the South, I'm so goddamned tired of hearing about the South. When is somebody going to start worrying about the North? That's where the votes are to begin with. Instead, we're fighting over the law in order to give something to a bunch of racists." Panetta, *Bring Us Together*, 111–112.

138. *New York Times*, August 27, 1969, p. 18. For a flavor of the atmosphere at CRD, see chapter 10 of Charles Peters and Taylor Branch, eds., *Blowing the Whistle: Dissent in the Public Interest* (New York: Praeger, 1972), 152–166. The activism at CRD was reportedly so pronounced that Robert Finch sought to defend his embattled OCR chief by contrasting "Panetta's control over his liberal civil rights staff at HEW with Leonard's lack of control over his liberal staff of Justice Department civil rights attorneys." Evans and Novak, *Nixon in the White House*, 158.

139. Dunbaugh to author, e-mail, October 12, 2006.

140. These references were dutifully recorded by Ehrlichman in notes on an August 4, 1970, meeting, Ehrlichman office files, box 4.

141. Garment, *Crazy Rhythm*, 207.

142. Eight-page supplement produced by Citizens' Committee, in *Greenville (South Carolina) News*, February 3, 1970. Copy in CCE Records, carton 5.

143. *Charlotte* (North Carolina) *Observer*, February 18, 1970. Copy in CCE Records, carton 5.

144. Orfield, *Reconstruction*, 234.

145. See Harvey, *Question of Justice*. On this latest version of the New South, see Numan Bartley and Hugh Davis Graham, *Southern Politics and the Second Reconstruction* (Baltimore, Md.: Johns Hopkins University Press, 1975), 136–163.

146. Garment, *Crazy Rhythm*, 215.

147. Robert Mardian, cited in CCE History, CCE Records, carton 4.

148. Gray to CCE, memo, June 15, 1970, in Finch office files, box 3.

149. Mardian to Spiro Agnew, memo, July 6, 1970, in Finch office files, box 4. A prominent Atlantan told Gray that he had "as much chance of succeeding in this endeavor as you would in explaining to your wife that adultery is merely a joyous frolic." Gray to CCE, memo, June 29, 1970, in Finch office files, box 4.

150. *Greenville* (South Carolina) *News*, August 18, 1970, in CCE Records, carton 2.

151. Garment, *Crazy Rhythm*, 215; Mardian to Agnew, memo, September 18, 1970, CCE Records, carton 2.

152. For transcripts of all six broadcasts, see CCE Records, carton 2.

153. *Infoflow*, August 26, 1970; *Birmingham* (Alabama) *News*, August 23, 1970, in CCE Records, carton 2.

154. This fear arose from the *U.S. v. Georgia* suit. In January 1971, a judge "ordered withholding of state funds from districts that do not establish unitary school systems." See *Race Relations Reporter*, no.1, February 1, 1970, p. 1.

155. A Greenville, Mississippi, columnist warned that "companies are finding increasing resistance from key management personnel about coming to Mississippi to live. They are not particularly anxious to put their children in racially imbalanced schools or to have the added expense of sending their children to private academies where the quality of the educational program has not been proven." *Delta Democrat Times*, August 5, 1970, attached to *Infoflow*, August 26, 1970, in CCE Records, carton 2.

156. Raymond Price, *With Nixon* (New York: Viking, 1977), 207.

157. George Shultz, *Turmoil and Triumph: My Years as Secretary of State* (New York: Scribners, 1993), 1046.

158. Price, *With Nixon*, 208. The refusal of the Mississippi congressmen to help was not atypical. Governors McNair and Rockefeller played statesmanlike roles, as did some up-and-coming local figures such as Reuben Askew of Florida and Jimmy Carter of Georgia. But a larger number of southern politicians played no part at all or exploited the racial fears of their voters.

159. Shultz, *Turmoil and Triumph*, 1048.

160. Tom Wicker, *One of Us: Richard Nixon and the American Dream* (New York: Random House, 1991), 504, 487.

161. James T. Patterson, *Brown v. Board of Education: A Civil Rights Milestone and Its Troubled Legacy* (New York: Oxford University Press, 2001), 155.

162. News transcripts from WTOP, August 31, 1970; ABC News, August 27, 1970; NBC News, September 3, 1970; WTTG, August 31, 1970. All in CCE Records, carton 3.

163. *Congressional Record*, April 29, 1970, 13478; *Dallas Tribune*, April 4, 1970, in Leonard Garment office files, Nixon Project, box 81.

164. News report on WETA, August 12, 1970, transcript in CCE Records, carton 3.

165. LCCR papers, box 71; *Time*, July 13, 1970; http://www.time.com (accessed March 14, 2007).

166. ABC News, August 25, 1970, CCE Records, carton 5.

167. *New York Times*, October 13, 1970, p. 1. Hesburgh was speaking to reporters at the conclusion of a six-month investigation by the commission into the state of civil rights enforcement. For its 1,100-page report, see U.S. Commission on Civil Rights, *Federal Civil Rights Enforcement Effort* (Washington, D.C.: U.S. Commission on Civil Rights, October 1970).

168. UPI Teletype, November 13, 1970, in CCE Records, carton 2.

169. UPI Teletype, October 19, 1970, CCE Records, carton 2. This was the *Adams* case, on which see Halpern, *On the Limits of the Law*.

170. In some respects, the gains have *not* been sustained. The proportion of African American children attending white-majority schools in the South reached almost 45 percent during the 1980s but then fell back to 35 percent by 1995. On the other hand, the South since 1970 has been the most integrated region of the country. For a balanced assessment of resegregation, see Patterson, *Brown*, 175–205, 227–235. For an account that emphasizes the problems, see Charles C. Bolton, *The Hardest Deal of All: The Battle over School Integration in Mississippi, 1870–1980* (Jackson: University of Mississippi Press, 2005).

Chapter 6. Education Reform in the Nixon Administration: The Case of Bilingual Education

1. Reflecting this sympathy, when the Voting Rights Act was renewed in 1970, the administration called on Congress to give it a national, and not simply a regional, focus. See Hugh Davis Graham, *The Civil Rights Era: Origins and Development of National Policy* (New York: Oxford University Press, 1990), 346–365. OCR had been increasingly involved in de facto segregation cases since 1967, following that earlier false start in Chicago, mainly in response to pressure from southern members of Congress, but the disestablishment of Jim Crow in the South had remained its overwhelming mission.

2. Jeremy Rabkin, "Office for Civil Rights," in James Q. Wilson, ed., *The Politics of Regulation* (New York: Basic Books, 1980), 338. On the broader expansion in civil rights enforcement spending during the Nixon years, see Graham, *Civil Rights Era*, 448–449.

3. See Carlos Kevin Blanton, *The Strange Career of Bilingual Education in Texas, 1836–1981* (College Station: Texas A&M University Press, 2004).

4. Sec. 701 and Sec. 702, Bilingual Education Act of 1968 (PL 90–247), reproduced in Susan Gilbert Schneider, *Revolution, Reaction, or Reform: The 1974 Bilingual Education Act* (New York: Las Americas, 1976), 172–175.

5. Gardner told Lister Hill that Yarborough's bill "should avoid any restrictions to persons of particular ancestry or ethnic origin," instead being "directed to persons from non-English-speaking backgrounds because that factor—the lan-

guage problem—has educational significance. . . . We believe it is an important principle that the statute should not provide that determinations be based upon consideration of ethnic or national origin (or surname) per se." Quoted in John David Skrentny, *The Minority Rights Revolution* (Cambridge, Mass.: Harvard University Press, 2002), 205.

6. He pinched the ears of the smaller children, while older miscreants were spanked. See Blanton, *Strange Career,* 132–133.

7. Asked about this episode by a historian, Yarborough remembered that "we passed the bill but the Office of Education and the Administration fought it. . . . They held down the funding all the time." Colman Brez Stein, *Sink or Swim: The Politics of Bilingual Education* (New York: Praeger 1986), 31–32.

8. John Ehrlichman, February 2, 1970, handwritten meeting notes, Ehrlichman office files, box 3.

9. For Nixon's bid to create a new Republican majority, see Robert Mason, *Richard Nixon and the Quest for a New Majority* (Chapel Hill: University of North Carolina Press, 2004).

10. On Nixon's early interest in reform, and his turn to the right in 1970, see Gareth Davies, "The Great Society after Johnson: The Case of Bilingual Education," *Journal of American History* 88, no. 4 (March 2002): 1407–1410.

11. In 1970, the principal statewide Latino group, the Mexican American Political Association, refused to support Jesse Unruh's campaign to defeat Governor Reagan. *New York Times,* September 4, 1970, p. 20. (Jesse Unruh was the speaker of the state assembly and an enormously powerful figure in California politics.)

12. Draft minutes of Cabinet Committee Meeting on Spanish Speaking Persons, August 5, 1971, Finch office files, box 16.

13. See WHCF, MC2, Nixon Project, box 2, especially three letters from John Flores of the Hispanic Development and Management Corporation. On the concerns of the GOP legislators, see Bryce Harlow to Charles Wilkinson, memo, October 27, 1969; John Ehrlichman to George Bush, memo, March 30, 1970; and William Timmons to Tod Hullin, memo, April 7, 1970, all in ibid.

14. Rep. Burt Talcott (R-Calif.) to Harry Dent, letter, July 1, 1969, WHCF, FG 145, Nixon Project, box 1.

15. See Brad Patterson to Ehrlichman, draft memo, January 9, 1970, Finch office files, box 16.

16. See Steven Hess to Ehrlichman, memo, September 18, 1969; Bruce Rabb to John Brown and Leonard Garment, memo, August 7, 1969; and Garment to Nixon, February 5, 1971, all in Finch office files, box 22.

17. Phillip Sanchez subsequently became head of OEO. See *New York Times,* February 9, 1971, p. 12; September 8, 1971, p. 21.

18. The speech committing Nixon to the conference is quoted in Garment to Ron Ziegler, memo, August 11, 1970, WHCF, MC2, Nixon Project, box 2.

19. On the El Paso conference, and on the Johnson administration's relationship with Mexican Americans more generally, see Julie Leininger Pycior, *LBJ and Mexican Americans: The Paradox of Power* (Austin: University of Texas Press, 1997).

20. This is according to Rowland Evans and Robert Novak, *Nixon in the White House: The Frustration of Power* (New York: Random House, 1971), 236.

21. Handwritten comment on a December 1969 news summary, POF, box 31.

22. See Charles Wilkinson to Nixon, memo, February 19, 1969, WHCF, MC2, Nixon Project, box 2; Castillo and Henry Quevodo to Hess, memo, August 11, 1969, Finch office files, box 22; Castillo to Garment, memo, December 11, 1969, Finch office files, box 16; Hess to Ehrlichman, memo, September 18, 1969, Finch office files; and Hess to Ehrlichman, H. R. Haldeman, and Herb Klein, memo, July 29, 1969, Finch office files. For HEW's lack of enthusiasm for the conference, see Patricia Hitt to Robert Finch, memo, November 1, 1971, Finch office files, box 21.

23. Castillo to Klein, memo, December 17, 1969, WHCF, FG 145, Nixon Project, box 1.

24. Fred Romero to Finch, memo, n.d. (but May 1971), Finch office files, box 15.

25. See Alexander Butterfield to David Parker, memo, May 28, 1971, ibid.

26. George Grassmuck to Finch, memo, February 25, 1971, ibid., box 22.

27. Haldeman to Finch, memo, February 2, 1971, ibid.

28. H. R. Haldeman, *Haldeman Diaries*, CD-ROM (Santa Monica, Calif.: Sony, 1994), entry for April 7, 1970.

29. Leonard Garment, *Crazy Rhythm* (New York: Times Books, 1997), 152; Garment to Nixon, memo, February 5, 1971, Finch office files, box 22.

30. Finch to Nixon, memo, July 28, 1971, WHCF, FG 145, Nixon Project, box 1.

31. Campaign to Reelect the President to John Mitchell, memo, December 16, 1971, reproduced in Senate Select Committee on Presidential Campaign Activities, *Presidential Campaign Activities of 1972*, pt. 13, 93rd Cong., 1st Sess. November 15, 1973, 5533–5534.

32. Colson to Ehrlichman, memo, December 20, 1971, Colson office files, box 7.

33. For Nixon's comments, see Minutes of Cabinet Committee on Opportunities for Spanish Speakers Meeting, August 5, 1971, Finch office files, box 16.

34. Bill Novelli to Pete Dailey et al., memo, July 25, 1972, Colson office files, box 70.

35. Garment to Ehrlichman, memo, April 20, 1970, Finch office files, box 15.

36. Minutes of CCOSS meeting, August 5, 1971, ibid., box 16.

37. Schneider, *Revolution, Reaction, or Reform*, 101.

38. William Marumoto to Colson and Fred Malek, memo, July 21, 1972, reproduced in Senate Select Committee on Presidential Campaign Activities, *Presidential Campaign Activities*, pt. 13, 5641.

39. Paul Frymer and John David Skrentny, "Coalition-Building and the Politics of Electoral Capture during the Nixon Administration: African Americans, Labor, Latinos," *Studies in American Political Development* 12 (Spring 1998): 159.

40. Schneider, *Revolution, Reaction, or Reform*, 102.

41. Press release, February 12, 1969, OE Records, RG 12, NARA, box 489.

42. Leon Panetta with Peter Gall, *Bring Us Together: The Nixon Team and the Civil Rights Retreat* (Philadelphia: Lippincott, 1971), 10. Panetta records that from the outset Finch was interested in "including blacks and Mexican Americans in leading departmental positions." Ibid., 12.

43. Schneider, *Revolution, Reaction, or Reform*, chapter 6.

44. Panetta, *Bring Us Together*, 335–356.

45. Panetta's draft memo to affected school districts is attached to Leon Panetta to Finch, memo, January 5, 1970, Mardian papers, box 5.

46. On the judicial decree, handed down on February 5, 1970, and the San Antonio case, see Mary Ellen Leary, "Children Who Are Tested in an Alien Language Mentally Retarded?" *New Republic*, May 30, 1970. The article is reprinted in *Congressional Record*, May 26, 1970, 17142.

47. For the Los Angeles riot, which left three people dead, see *New York Times*, August 30, 1970, p. 64; August 31, 1970, p. 32; and September 4, 1970, p. 20. On growing Latino militancy more generally, see Richard Griswold del Castillo and Arnoldo De León, *North to Aztlan: A History of Mexican Americans in the United States* (New York: Twayne, 1996), 125–147; Carlos Muñoz Jr. and Mario Barrera, "La Raza Unida Party and the Chicano Student Movement in California," in F. Chris Garcia, ed., *Latinos and the Political System* (Notre Dame, Ind.: University of Notre Dame Press, 1988), 213–235.

48. See draft proposal to the Ford Foundation, "prepared under the auspices of the NAACP-LDF," August 7, 1967, MALDEF papers, box 1, RG 3.

49. See Cruz Reynoso et al., "La Raza, the Law, and the Law Schools," *Toledo Law Review* 1 (Spring–Summer 1970), 831–837; Joe Ortega to R. Ibanez et al., memo, September 3, 1969, memo, MALDEF papers, box 1, RG 2.

50. See notes of meeting between Los Angeles representatives of MALDEF and Stephen Passek and Sue Coleman of the CRD, February 12, 1970, MALDEF papers, box 24, RG 9.

51. See Gilbert Sanders to Joe Ortega, received February 9, 1970, MALDEF papers, box 28, RG 9.

52. This was Don Morales, whom Panetta describes as his "chief gadfly" on behalf of Mexican Americans. See Panetta, *Bring Us Together*, 335. See Morales's angry complaint to the 1970 presidential commission on campus unrest that Hispanics who graduated from high school became "anglicized and docile and have lost their sense of *la raza.*" *New York Times*, September 13, 1970, p. 84.

53. *New York Times*, March 4, 1970, pp. 1, 29, which also covers the unrest generated at OCR. Panetta's memoir indicates that he had backed Nixon in 1960 and 1962 but could not bring himself to do so in 1968, having found the Republican's campaign "harsh and reactionary." Panetta, *Bring Us Together*, 4.

54. John D. Ehrlichman, *Witness to Power: The Nixon Years* (New York: Simon and Schuster, 1982), 227; Stephen Halpern, *On the Limits of the Law: The Ironic Legacy of Title VI of the 1964 Civil Rights Act* (Baltimore, Md.: Johns Hopkins University Press, 1995), 96.

55. Evans and Novak, *Nixon in the White House*, 145.

56. Absent OCR textual records, one has to rely on circumstantial evidence. Pottinger's appointment came a month after Nixon had signaled his interest in Daniel Patrick Moynihan's recommendation that the administration pay more attention to Latinos (and Native Americans) while adopting a policy of "benign neglect" toward African Americans. See Halpern, *On the Limits of the Law*, 90.

57. Telephone conversation between Richardson and Ehrlichman, July 24, 1970, transcript in Richardson papers, box 127.

58. J. Stanley Pottinger to School Districts with More Than Five Percent National Origin–Minority Group Children, May 25, 1970, copy of original memo in Papers of Shirley Hufstedler, Jimmy Carter Presidential Library, Atlanta, box 15. I

am grateful to the late Hugh Davis Graham for supplying me with a copy of this memo.

59. Jeremy Rabkin, "Office for Civil Rights," in James Q. Wilson, ed., *The Politics of Regulation* (New York: Basic Books, 1980), 326.

60. Skrentny, *Minority Rights Revolution*, 213, 224. A 1977 survey found that fewer than 30 percent of Latino children enrolled in bilingual education programs were deficient in English. See Guadalupe San Miguel, *"Let All of Them Take Heed": Mexican Americans and the Campaign for Educational Equality in Texas, 1910–1981* (Austin: University of Texas Press, 1987), 199.

61. The case was *Griggs v. Duke Power*. See Graham, *Civil Rights Era*, 383–390.

62. Draft OCR paper, December 1, 1970, MALDEF papers, box 156, RG 9.

63. Quoted in U.S. Commission on Civil Rights, *The Federal Civil Rights Enforcement Effort: A Reassessment* (Washington, D.C.: Commission on Civil Rights, 1973), 241.

64. For examples of such discrimination, see Gary Orfield, *Must We Bus? Segregated Schools and National Policy* (Washington, D.C.: Brookings Institution, 1978), 198–229.

65. Skrentny, *Minority Rights Revolution*, 217.

66. For the classic critique, see Edward Koch, "The Mandate Millstone," *Public Interest* 61 (Fall 1980): 42–57.

67. On the politics of school finance during the 1970s, see Chapter 8.

68. Skrentny, *Minority Rights Revolution*, 212, 214.

69. Panetta, *Bring Us Together*, 174–175, 193–194, 274.

70. Martin Gerry, "Cultural Freedom in the Schools: The Right of Mexican-American Children to Succeed," in Alfredo Castaneda et al., *Mexican Americans and Educational Change* (New York: Arno, 1974), 244–253.

71. Gary Orfield, *The Reconstruction of Southern Education* (New York: John Wiley, 1969), 89.

72. Rabkin, "Office for Civil Rights," 317, 331.

73. Cohen, OH for the HUCRDP, 16. He went on to say that "they have their own closed opinion of how to effectuate" civil rights (17).

74. Orfield, *Must We Bus?* 223. On the lack of evidence in favor of bilingual education, see Noel Epstein, *Language, Ethnicity, and the Schools: Policy Alternatives for Bilingual-Bicultural Education* (Washington, D.C.: Institute For Educational Leadership, 1977).

75. On the distinctive dynamics of "client politics," see James Q. Wilson, "The Politics of Regulation," in James Q. Wilson, ed. *The Politics of Regulation* (New York: Basic Books, 1980), 369.

76. The MALDEF papers give a flavor of the public face of the relationship. Hector Garcia, leader of the long-established and moderate G.I. Forum, charged the HEW secretary with "discriminatory practices" against Mexican Americans; a former employee of the OCR's Dallas office working for MALDEF denounced Richardson's protestations of innocence as "the greatest misrepresentation of fact that I have come in contact with in my life"; and the same writer wrote that "the Bureaucracy, and in this instance H.E.W., is Lucifer and Satan in disguise." See Hector Garcia to Elliot Richardson, September 25, 1970; Carlos Vela to Walter Mondale,

letter, October 1, 1970; and Vela to Garcia, December 10, 1970, memo, copied to Mondale and Pottinger; all in MALDEF papers, box 156, RG 9.

77. A later survey noted that "many of its attorneys had government experience prior to coming to MALDEF"; others "continued to speak on behalf of MALDEF from their government positions." See Karen O'Connor and Lee Epstein, "A Legal Voice for the Chicano Community: The Activities of the Mexican American Legal Defense and Educational Fund, 1968–1982," *Social Science Quarterly* 65 (June 1984): 254.

78. See a memo by the associate counsel of MALDEF, Ed Idar, recording a conference with representatives of the OCR regional office in Dallas: file memo, April 2, 1971, MALDEF papers, box 156, RG 9. See also Idar, file memo, February 9, 1971, ibid.

79. In part, the unimpressive numbers were the paradoxical consequence of OCR's effort to make a dramatic impact with its limited resources. The agency decided to investigate just about the most complicated school systems within its remit, those of Boston and New York City. Such choices made it inevitable that the great majority of cases would remain uninvestigated. Civil Rights Commission, *A Better Chance to Learn: Bilingual-Bicultural Education* (Washington, D.C.: CRC, 1975), 176. Neither were its efforts in Boston effective, in part because of the intrinsic difficulty of simultaneously attacking discrimination against language minorities and racial minorities; in part because of staffing difficulties; in part because of the continuing premium that OE attached to good relationships with state educators. See Adam Nelson, *The Elusive Ideal: Equal Educational Opportunity and the Federal Role in Boston's Public Schools, 1950–1985* (Chicago: University of Chicago Press, 2005), chapter 4, esp. 116–119.

80. Commission on Civil Rights, *Federal Civil Rights Enforcement Effort*, 213.

81. Commission on Civil Rights, *Better Chance to Learn*, 178.

82. Halpern, *On the Limits of the Law*, 94.

83. After 1968, the legal defense fund model that the NAACP had pioneered in the 1930s was adopted by other minority groups, including Asian Americans, Native Americans, and women. That process, and the Ford Foundation's role in it, warrants greater scholarly attention than it has received.

84. On the circumstances surrounding the bringing of this suit, see Mark Brilliant, "Desegregation, Bilingual Education, and the Emergence of California's Conflicting Avenues of Civil Rights Redress, 1962–1974," chapter 9 of his forthcoming book, *Civil Rights on America's "Racial Frontier," 1945–1975.*

85. Skrentny, *Minority Rights Revolution*, 220–221. The cases were *U.S. v. Texas* 447 F.2d 441, and 342 F.Supp. 24.

86. Since the 1930s, the courts had classified Mexican Americans as being Caucasian. At the time, that had seemed to be to the advantage of the group, but in the new climate of the minority rights revolution, a discrete ethnoracial identity seemed more likely to bring legal dividends. On this shift, see Steven Wilson, "*Brown* over 'Other White': Mexican Americans' Legal Arguments and Litigation Strategy in School Desegregation Lawsuits," *Law and History Review* 21, no. 2 (Spring 2003): 145–194.

87. Amicus curiae brief, U.S. government, *Lau v. Nichols* (72–6250), 6–7, reprinted in *U.S. Supreme Court—Records and Briefs*, 414 (October Term, 1973), 563–

572. (Pottinger's name also appeared on Robert Bork's amicus brief, the OCR director having recently become head of the Justice Department's Civil Rights Division. He probably played a dominant role in composing the brief.)

88. Herbert Teitelbaum and Richard J. Hiller, "Bilingual Education: The Legal Mandate," *Harvard Educational Review* 47, no. 2 (May 1977): 142.

89. *Lau v. Nichols*, 414 U.S. 563 (1973).

90. Orfield, *Must We Bus?* 219–220.

91. In part this was because it was the traditional remedy, which—it was argued—had not been educationally effective in the past. Also, this was a time when bilingual education was increasingly being presented as being about ethnoracial pride as well as educational achievement. The intensive English approach was clearly inimical to that objective.

92. For their early confusion, see Barbara Dean and Perry A. Zirkel, "The Bilingual Education Mandate: It Says Schools Must 'Do Something,' Must Do It Soon— and Probably Must Find the Money to Get It Done," *American School Board Journal* (July 1976): 29–33.

93. Ibid. On the unacceptability of the English as a Second Language (ESL) approach, see also Craig Kaplowitz, *LULAC: Mexican Americans and National Policy* (Lawrence: University Press of Kansas, 2005), 174–175.

94. "Washington's Message to School Boards: Find a Way to Educate Non English-Speaking Students or Lose Federal Funds," *American School Board Journal* (July 1976): 33–34.

95. Joseph Califano, who was HEW secretary under Carter, believed that "HEW's bilingual program had become captive of the professional Hispanic and other ethnic groups, with their understandably emotional but often exaggerated political rhetoric of biculturalism. As a result, too little attention was paid to teaching children English, and far too many children were kept in bilingual classes long after they acquired the necessary proficiency to be taught in English." Joseph Califano, *Governing America: An Insider's Report from the White House and the Cabinet* (New York: Simon and Schuster, 1981), 313.

96. See Teitelbaum and Hiller, "Bilingual Education," 147, and Estelle Pau-on Lau, "Lau vs Nichols: California's Contribution to Bilingual Education," *Pacific Historian* 24, no. 1 (Spring 1980): 50.

97. Skrentny, *Minority Rights Revolution*, 226.

98. Rosemary Salomone, *Equal Education under Law: Legal Rights and Federal Policy in the Post-Brown Era* (New York: St. Martin's Press, 1986), 101–105.

99. On the passage of the Massachusetts law, see Nelson, *Elusive Ideal*, 103–115.

100. The National Association for Bilingual Education was established in 1975. For the role played by teachers in the growth of bilingual education, see Jennifer Hochschild and Nathan Skovronick, *The American Dream and the Public Schools* (New York: Oxford University Press, 2003), 155.

101. For example, Schneider, *Revolution, Reaction, or Reform?* and Abigail Thernstrom, "E Pluribus Plura—Congress and Bilingual Education," *Public Interest* 60 (Summer 1980): 3–22.

102. On this backlash, see Kaplowitz, *LULAC*, 188–191.

103. Tom Bethell, "Why Johnny Can't Speak English," *Harper's Magazine*, February 1979, 30–33. For a useful account of the role that these arguments played in

diminishing support for bilingual education, see Guadalupe San Miguel, "Conflict and Controversy in the Evolution of Bilingual Education in the United States—An Interpretation," *Social Science Quarterly* 65, no. 2 (June 1984): 505–518. For the educational arguments in favor of bilingual education, see James Crawford, *Bilingual Education: History, Politics, Theory, and Practice*, 2nd ed. (Los Angeles: Bilingual Educational Services, 1995).

104. In fact, Congress—going beyond parody—renamed it the Office of English Language Acquisition, Language Enhancement, and Academic Achievement for Limited-English-Proficient Students, or OELALEAALEPS for short. See James Crawford, "Obituary: The Bilingual Ed Act, 1968–2002," *Rethinking Schools Online* (Summer 2002). Available at www.rethinkingschools.org.

105. A leading student of bilingual education has observed that the decline of the program should not be overstated. Although there is no longer a legal mandate, local programs still exist "and in some areas are flourishing with the spread of dual language immersion (the way bilingual education was designed to work in the experiments of the 1960s)." Carlos Blanton, e-mail to author, November 20, 2006. I am grateful to Professor Blanton for his comments on an earlier draft of this chapter.

106. For Ralph Yarborough's deference to the states in 1967, see Senate Committee on Labor and Public Welfare, Special Subcommittee on Bilingual Education, hearings, *Bilingual Education*, 90th Cong., 1st Sess., May 26, 1967, 235, 268, 479. In 1971, Martin Gerry of OCR claimed that, although the equal protection clause had not yet been applied to minorities besides blacks, "it is implicit in the equal protection guarantee that the same principles enumerated in the *Brown* decision extend to all minority children." See Gerry, "Cultural Freedom in the Schools," 228. See Senate Committee on Labor and Public Welfare, Subcommittee on Education, hearings, *Education Legislation, 1973*, 93 Cong., 1st Sess, October 31, 1973, esp. 2575–2586, 2590–2599.

107. Martha Derthick, "Crossing Thresholds: Federalism in the 1960s," in Martha Derthick, *Keeping the Compound Republic: Essays on Federalism* (Washington, D.C.: Brookings Institution, 2001), 148.

Chapter 7. Transforming Special Education: The Genesis of the Education for All Handicapped Children Act

1. It was subsequently renamed the Individuals with Disabilities Education Act (IDEA).

2. Alternatively, the architectural barriers law of 1968 (PL 90-480) might be a candidate, but it initially lacked a significant enforcement mechanism.

3. The effectiveness of the law in helping children with disabilities lies beyond the scope of the chapter, which focuses on its origins. For a rather critical government report, see President's Commission on Excellence in Special Education, *A New Era: Revitalizing Special Education for Children and Their Families* (Washington, D.C.: Government Printing Office, 2002). For a more evenhanded but early evaluation of the evidence, see Judith D. Singer and John A. Butler, "The Education for All Handicapped Children Act: Schools as Agents of Social Reform," *Harvard Educational Review* 57, no.2 (May 1987): 125–152.

4. R. Shep Melnick, *Between the Lines: Interpreting Welfare Rights* (Washington, D.C.: Brookings Institution, 1995), 136.

5. U.S. Department of Education, *Digest of Education Statistics: 2002* (Washington, D.C.: Government Printing Office, June 2003), 66.

6. Michael Imber and David E. Gayler, "A Statistical Analysis of Trends in Education-Related Litigation since 1960," *Educational Administration Quarterly* 24, no. 1 (February 1988): 70, fig. 10. The National Association of State Directors of Special Education reported that the upward trajectory continued through the 1990s, estimating that the number of special education hearings requested by parents (the prelude to litigation) increased from 4,655 in 1991 to 11,068 in 2000. Cited by Helen Gao, "Special Ed Legal Fights Soaring," *Los Angeles Daily News*, March 15, 2003. I am indebted to Nancy Udell for this reference.

7. On the Handicapped Children's Protection Act, see Perry A. Zirkel, "The Full Employment of Attorneys Act," *Phi Delta Kappan* 69 (October 1987): 165.

8. For a more thorough examination of the relationship between disability rights and the wider rights revolution than is contained in the present chapter, see John David Skrentny, *The Minority Rights Revolution* (Cambridge, Mass.: Harvard University Press, 2002); Richard Scotch, *From Good Will to Civil Rights: Transforming Federal Disability Policy*, 2nd ed. (Philadelphia: Temple University Press, 2001); and Edward D. Berkowitz, *Disabled Policy: America's Programs for the Handicapped* (New York: Cambridge University Press, 1987). For an overview of changing American responses to mental retardation, see James W. Trent Jr., *Inventing the Feeble Mind: A History of Mental Retardation in the United States* (Berkeley: University of California Press, 1994).

9. John C. Pittenger and Peter Kuriloff, "Educating the Handicapped: Reforming a Radical Law," *Public Interest* 66 (Winter 1982): 87.

10. This development is highlighted by Melnick, *Between the Lines*, chapter 7.

11. David Neal and David L. Kirp, "The Allure of Legalization Reconsidered: The Case of Special Education," *Law and Contemporary Problems* 48, no. 1 (1986): 65.

12. New attitudes to and activism by the physically handicapped also played an important role in stimulating new civil rights for Americans with disabilities. In the specific context of education legislation, though, it is the debate about the rights and potential of children with developmental disabilities that has greatest pertinence.

13. Testimony before U.S. Senate Committee on Labor and Public Welfare, hearings, *Mentally Retarded Children*, 85th Cong., 1st Sess. [hereafter referred to as Senate Committee, *Mentally Retarded Children*], April 4, 1957, 5.

14. There was no requirement that grants under the act be directed to this purpose in 1954, but the great majority of grant awards until the early 1960s (by which time other federal funding stream existed) went to disability research.

15. It helped that there were precedents going back to the nineteenth century (Gallaudet University for the deaf, a federal printing service for the blind) and the Progressive Era (vocational rehabilitation).

16. Dale Evans Rogers, *Angel Unaware* (Westwood, N.J.: Revell, 1953). Another celebrity who wrote about her handicapped daughter during this period (having maintained the then customary silence on the subject for three decades) was the Nobel Prize– and Pulitzer Prize–winning novelist Pearl Buck. See Pearl S. Buck, *The Child Who Never Grew* (New York: J. Day, 1950). These works both reflected and did much to promote more enlightened societal attitudes to disability.

17. Figures taken from table 8 in Martin LaVor, "You Want to Change the

System—But Where Do You Begin?" in Frederick J. Weintraub et al., eds., *Public Policy and the Education of Exceptional Children* (Reston, Va.: Council for Exceptional Children, 1976), 276–277.

18. Figures cited by John Brademas in House Select Committee on Education and Labor, Select Subcommittee On Education, hearings, *Education of the Handicapped Act Amendments*, 93rd Cong., 1st Sess. March 9, 1973, 2.

19. Forty was Lawrence Derthick's estimate in 1957, based on course descriptions. See Senate Committee, *Mentally Retarded Children*, 7. But Stephen Kurzman, assistant secretary for legislation at HEW, source of the "more than 300" figure, estimated that "only a handful" of institutions had provided such training in 1960. See his testimony to House Select Committee, *Education of the Handicapped Act Amendments*, 131.

20. Kurzman's testimony in House Select Committee, *Education of the Handicapped Act Amendments*, 132, 139. The figures—$700 million in 1966 and $2,162 million in 1972—refer to the "excess cost" of educating exceptional children compared to "normal" children.

21. Jean Garvin's testimony before Senate Committee on Labor and Public Welfare, Subcommittee On The Handicapped, hearings, *Education for the Handicapped, 1973*, 93rd Cong., 1st Sess., March 20, 1973, 205.

22. For an inside account of the intricate politicking that made the BEH possible, see chapters 1 and 2 of Edwin W. Martin, "A Golden Age for Special Education: Federal Policy 1965–1981," unpublished 2005 memoir. I am grateful to Dr. Martin (whose role in expanding the educational rights of the handicapped is explored below) for supplying me with a copy.

23. Boggs was a theoretical chemist by training, with a doctorate from Cambridge University. She helped to design the implosion device for the atomic bomb. Soon after discovering that her son was severely retarded, she helped to establish a New Jersey parents' group, and subsequently she became president of the NARC and a tireless advocate for the mentally retarded. On Boggs and other important figures in the early politics of mental retardation (such as Gunnar and Rosemary Dybwad), see http://www.npr.org/programs/disability/ba_shows.dir/revoluti.dir/highlights/subject/ng0002tx.html (accessed January 15, 2005).

24. Generally present at these meetings by the late 1960s were staffers from the appropriations and education subcommittees, together with Patria Forsythe and Edwin Martin of BEH. Frederick Weintraub, telephone interview with author, November 18, 2004. For the legislative accomplishments, consult issues of CEC's excellent monthly magazine, which increasingly supplemented its regular diet of articles about new research and pedagogy for exceptional children with reports on the latest breakthrough. See, for example, "The Morse-Carey Amendment—New Portent for Exceptional Children," *Exceptional Children* 33, no.4 (December 1966): 213–214, and "1966—Special Education's Greatest Year," *Exceptional Children* 33, no.5 (January 1967): 269–271 (featuring photos of two happy-looking CEC executives receiving signature pens from LBJ).

25. *Wall Street Journal*, March 22, 1972, p. 1.

26. House Select Committee, *Education of the Handicapped Act Amendments*, 2.

27. Ibid., 11.

28. Table 8 in LaVor, "You Want to Change the System," 276–277. This re-

flected the growing generosity of the authorizing committees more than the stinginess of appropriators. Appropriations had increased during this period from $28.3 million to $133 million, with the bulk of the increase occurring since 1968. But at least three congressional friends of the disabled with power on the appropriations committees had recently died or retired: John Fogarty, Melvin Laird, and Lister Hill.

29. See, for example, the "white cane" laws that started to be enacted at the state level in the 1930s. (These required motorists to stop for visually impaired pedestrians carrying a white cane who wished to cross the road.) Doris Zames Fleischer and Frieda Zames, *The Disability Rights Movement: From Charity to Confrontation* (Philadelphia: Temple University Press, 2001), 20–21. See also Kathleen W. Jones, "Education for Children with Mental Retardation: Parent Activism, Public Policy, and Family Ideology in the 1950s," in Steven Noll and James W. Trent, eds., *Mental Retardation in America: A Historical Reader* (New York: New York University Press, 2004), 322–350.

30. Compassion and good works indeed represented thoroughly advanced and enlightened positions, given the tendency of others to see these afflictions as marks of divine disfavor or moral turpitude.

31. When the new association came up with a "bill of rights for the retarded" in 1952, its spokesman noted that "there is nothing comparable to Braille or a hearing aid for those who are feeble in mind. They are shadow people—except for being hurt—in a world of words, needing a continual interpreter and counsellor, a continual defender, not of their faith, but of their foibles." See Richard H. Hungerford, "A Bill of Rights for the Retarded," *Children Limited* (August 1952), reprinted in *American Journal of Mental Deficiency* 63, no.6 (May 1959): 937–938.

32. This rights talk differed markedly from the debate of the early 1970s, inasmuch as the failure of the United States to fulfill these "rights'" was not presented as an indictment of society, but rather as a consequence of the newness of the discovery that the life chances of the mentally retarded could be improved. Although the 1957 Senate hearings uncovered a startling failure to train teachers and furnish educational facilities for the mentally retarded, the tone was consistently even and upbeat, perhaps reflecting the assumption that all this was about to change. Senate Committee, *Mentally Retarded Children*, 5. On the new promise of rehabilitation during the 1950s, see Edward D. Berkowitz and Kim McQuaid, *Creating the Welfare State: The Political Economy of Twentieth Century Reform* (New York: Praeger, 1988).

33. President's Panel on Mental Retardation, *A Proposed Program for National Action to Combat Mental Retardation* (Washington, D.C.: Government Printing Office, 1962). President Kennedy, whose retarded sister Rosemary had been institutionalized following an unsuccessful lobotomy, took some personal interest in this subject, although the main impetus came from their sister, Eunice Shriver. See Edward Shorter, *The Kennedy Family and the Story of Mental Retardation* (Philadelphia: Temple University Press, 2000); Edward D. Berkowitz, "The Politics of Mental Retardation in the Kennedy Administration," *Social Science Quarterly* (June 1980): 128–142.

34. President's Panel on Mental Retardation, *Proposed Program*, 14.

35. President's Panel on Mental Retardation, Task Force on Law, *Report* (Washington, D.C.: Government Printing Office, 1962), 17 and passim. They did not

elaborate on this point, returning immediately to the need for protective legislation, which was the main focus of the report. The task force was chaired by federal judge David Bazelon, who had a particular interest in the related but distinct area of mental illness. The vice-chair was Elizabeth Boggs.

36. Cited by Alan Abeson, Nancy Bolick, and Jayne Hass, "Due Process of Law: Background and Intent," in Weintraub, *Public Policy*, 23.

37. Letter to *New York Times*, March 15, 1964, p. E8.

38. For a detailed examination of the growth of a new "liberal legal network" during the 1960s and early 1970s, see chapter 2 of Steven M. Teles's forthcoming book, *The Rise of the Conservative Legal Movement: Organizational Mobilization and Political Competition*.

39. On the Yale Law School during this era, see especially Laura Kalman, *Yale Law School and the Sixties: Revolt and Its Reverberations* (Chapel Hill: University of North Carolina Press, 2005). Their professors—who included Alexander Bickel and Robert Bork and had in many cases been appointed by Dean Eugene Rostow prior to his 1965 departure for Washington—were generally unsympathetic, with the exception of Charles Reich. See Laura Kalman, "The Dark Ages," in Anthony T. Kronman, ed., *History of the Yale Law School* (New Haven, Conn.: Yale University Press, 2004), 154–237.

40. See Peter Milius, "Feeling the Sting of Legal Aid," *Washington Post*, February 6, 1972, p. A8. The growth of clinical law during this period, like so many of the other developments treated in this chapter, was stimulated to a large degree by the Ford Foundation. See Philip G. Schrag and Michael Meltsner, *Reflections on Clinical Legal Education* (Boston: Northeastern University Press, 1998), 3–14.

41. William Raspberry, "Young Lawyers Shun Big Firms," *Washington Post*, October 6, 1969, p. C1.

42. From the beginning, community action leader Edward Sparer and social welfare lobbyist Elizabeth Wickenden had favored this approach, but they were outgunned initially by those who adhered to a more bottom-up, individual-centered ethos, as promoted by Edgar and Jean Cahn (Yale law graduates both) in "The War on Poverty: A Civilian Perspective," *Yale Law Journal* 73, no.8 (July 1964): 1137–1152. On this ongoing tension, see Earl Johnson Jr., *Justice and Reform: The Formative Years of the OEO Legal Services Program* (New York: Russell Sage Foundation, 1974). Another useful source on the growth of public interest law is Joel F. Handler, Ellen Jane Hollingsworth, and Howard S. Erlanger, *Lawyers and the Pursuit of Legal Rights* (New York: Academic Press, 1978), 17–47.

43. *Goldberg v. Kelly*, 397 U.S. 254 (1970). Here, the court ruled that the Constitution requires due process hearings before welfare benefits are terminated. See Melnick, *Between the Lines*, 83-84.

44. That public interest law and antipoverty law sprouted with such vigor during the early 1970s owed much to the fact that the Nixon administration backed down from a number of fights with these constituencies. This fascinating story still awaits its historian.

45. See Gordon Harrison and Sanford M. Jaffe, "Public Interest Law Firms: New Voices for New Constituencies," *American Bar Association Journal* 58 (May 1972): 466.

46. 325 F. Supp. 781 (M.D. Ala, Mar. 12, 1971), at 784.

47. Ibid., at 784 (first three items), 785 (due process; individualized plan), 786 (least restrictive environment).

48. Alan Abeson, "Litigation," in Weintraub, *Public Policy*, 240.

49. David and Sheila Rothman, *The Willowbrook Wars* (New York: Harper and Row, 1984), 66.

50. The lawyer, George Dean, might have assumed that the state court would side with Governor Wallace, who had ordered the cutbacks.

51. See Tinsley Yarbrough, *Judge Frank Johnson and Human Rights in Alabama* (Tuscaloosa: University of Alabama Press, 1982), 159. The plaintiffs pursued their employment case in the state court and won.

52. Stonewall Stickney, "The Inception of *Wyatt* and the State's Response," in L. Ralph Jones and Richard R. Parlour, eds., *Wyatt v. Stickney: Retrospect and Prospect* (New York: Grune and Stratton, 1981), 16. Jack Bass notes that Judge Johnson admired Stonewall Stickney, socialized with him, and considered him "a party to the suit only in the most technical sense." Jack Bass, *Taming the Storm: The Life and Times of Judge Frank M. Johnson and the South's Fight over Civil Rights* (New York: Doubleday, 1991), 296. Although Stickney's behavior is understandable, it is not obvious why his lawyer—presumably appointed by the state of Alabama—did not offer a more robust defense.

53. Jack Drake, "The Development of *Wyatt* in the Courtroom," in Jones and Parlour, *Wyatt v. Stickney*, 36. Drake, a lawyer involved in the case, argued that "had the defendants adopted a different posture, the district court may have reached a different conclusion or not reached the question at all." For the reference to *Rouse*, see Yarbrough, *Judge Frank Johnson*, 160. His citation is *Rouse v. Cameron*, 373 F. 2d 451, 452 (D.C. Cir., 1966).

54. 325 F. Supp. 781, at 784.

55. 344 F. Supp.387, at 390.

56. 325 F. Supp. 781 (M.D. Ala, Mar. 12, 1971), at 785.

57. See DeMent to Johnson, "personal and confidential" memo, January 18, 1971, papers of Frank Johnson, Library of Congress, box 70. A year later, and a week before Johnson handed down his second ruling, DeMent wrote to Elliot Richardson to ask for a stronger HEW role in alleviating "this dire and continuing tragedy." He sent a blind copy to CEC. See DeMent to Richardson, letter, April 6, 1972, in CEC Archives, Government Relations files, RG2.5.2.2, box 17.

58. Bass, *Taming the Storm*, 289.

59. Former Supreme Court justice Goldberg was seeking a new political role and struggling to overcome the perception of New Politics types that he was an old-guard New Deal liberal. According to one enjoyable muckraking account, he was embracing all manner of radical causes in this period (including that of the Black Panthers). See Victor Lasky, *Arthur J. Goldberg: The Old and the New* (New Rochelle, NY: Arlington House, 1970).

60. See Harrison and Jaffe, "Public Interest Law Firms," 462. For an early overview of CLASP's activities, see Charles R. Halpern and John M. Cunningham, "Reflections on the New Public Interest Law: Theory and Practice at the Center for Law and Social Policy," *Georgetown Law Journal* 59 (1970–1971): 1095–1126.

61. Rothman and Rothman, *Willowbrook Wars*, 50. They recount that Ennis's interest in NYCLU stemmed from having watched its director Aryeh Neier "get the best of William Buckley, whom Ennis admired for his wit," in a television debate.

62. Ibid., 53–54.

63. Leonard Roy Frank, "An Interview with Bruce Ennis," in Sherry Hirsch et al., eds., *Madness Network News Reader* (San Francisco: Glide Publications, 1974), 162–167. In the event, Alabama did invest an enormous amount of money in reforming its institutions but ended up closing them anyway, as deinstitutionalization gained ground. See http://www.psychlaws.org/LegalResources/CaseLaws/Case5.htm.

64. *New York State ARC v. Carey*, 393 F.Supp. 715 (E.D.N.Y., 1975). In early 1972, the young ABC television news reporter Geraldo Rivera presented a dramatic television exposé of conditions at Willowbrook. See Rivera, *Willowbrook* (New York: Vintage Books, 1972). For a full analysis of the case, see Rothman and Rothman, *Willowbrook Wars*.

65. Some of the information in this paragraph comes from two Web sites: a brief biography appears at http://www.ciec.org/Ennis_bio.html; an obituary at http://www.alum.dartmouth.org/classes/62/ennis.htm.

66. See 344 F. Supp. 373 (M.D. Ala.) and 344 F. Supp. 387 (M.D. Ala.), both handed down on April 13, 1972. The orders went into extraordinary detail, covering—among other things—precise staff ratios, toilet facilities, and rights to regular hair styling. Stonewall Stickney found the rulings "exhilarating" but was fired shortly thereafter by Governor George Wallace, who, not for the first time, found his old adversary's opinion infuriating. See Yarbrough, *Judge Frank Johnson*, 172, and Bass, *Taming the Storm*, 299.

67. Haggerty explains that Boomer was so named "because he was a head-banger . . . boom, boom, boom against the wall for 20 out of 24 hours." All details in this paragraph come from Haggerty's testimony before a joint hearing of the subcommittee on disability policy of the U.S. Senate Committee on Labor and Human Resources and the subcommittee on early childhood, youth, and families of the U.S. Senate Committee on Economic and Educational Opportunities, May 9, 1995, *Twentieth Anniversary of the Individuals with Disabilities Education Act (Part B)*, 104th Cong., 1st Sess., 25–26.

68. Haggerty explains that "I did not fault them for trying to teach retarded kids to be barber[s], but I did not think this person was a good candidate."

69. In their account of Willowbrook, the Rothmans emphasized that individual staff members, far from being sadistic brutes, were generally people of goodwill faced with very trying working conditions and a chronic lack of resources. In addition, parents sought cooperative relationships in the hope that this might result in staff's looking out for their child (Rothman and Rothman, *Willowbrook Wars*). The other material in this paragraph is drawn from Weintraub, telephone interview, November 18, 2004.

70. This quote is from Dennis Haggerty's prepared statement, *Twentieth Anniversary of the Individuals with Disabilities Education Act*, 78. Previous quotes came from his spoken testimony.

71. Weintraub, telephone interview, November 18, 2004.

72. *New York Times*, August 6, 1964, p. 19; October 5, 1969, p. 68. Leopold Lippman and I. Ignacy Goldberg, *Right to Education: Anatomy of the Pennsylvania*

Case and Its Implications for Exceptional Children (New York: Teachers College Press, 1973), 20. A historian of the Philadelphia New Left explains that it had a revolutionary wing, but associated Gilhool with the faction that believed meaningful change to be achievable through the system. See Paul Lyons, *People of This Generation: The Rise and Fall of the New Left in Philadelphia* (Philadelphia: University of Pennsylvania Press, 2003), 170, 178.

73. Weintraub, telephone interview, November 18, 2004.

74. Lippman and Goldberg, *Right to Education*, 18–19.

75. For a summary of all five options, see ibid., 20–22.

76. For an article that places *PARC* in the context of this wider debate, see Paul Dimond, "The Constitutional Right to Education: The Quiet Revolution," *Hastings Law Journal* 24 (May 1973): 1087–1128. For an earlier, general exploration of the issue, see Philip B. Kurland, "Equal Educational Opportunity: The Limits of Constitutional Jurisprudence Undefined," *University of Chicago Law Review* 35 (1967–1968), 583–600. For an example of the new approach to educability, see Stanley S. Segal, *No Child Is Ineducable: Special Education—Provision and Trends* (Oxford, Eng.: Pergamon, 1967).

77. The logic here was that the institution existed because the public schools refused to educate its residents. If the right of all retarded children to an education provided in the "least restrictive setting" were affirmed by the court, there would be no need for places like Pennhurst to exist. Weintraub, telephone interview, November 18, 2004.

78. Pennhurst remained open until 1987. Gilhool went back to court in 1974 with a more direct bid to have it closed down on constitutional grounds. *Halderman v. Pennhurst* went all the way to the Supreme Court and is one of the most significant of the deinstitutionalization cases. The Eastern District of Pennsylvania again endorsed his case, but the U.S. Court of Appeals for the Third Circuit disagreed, and the Supreme Court upheld the appeal. See 446 F.Supp. 1295 (E.D.Penn., 1977); 612 F.2d. 84 (3rd CCA, 1979); 451 U.S. 1 (1981).

79. 334 F. Supp. 1257 (E.D.Penn., Oct.8, 1971)

80. 343 F. Supp. 279 (E.D. Penn., May 5, 1972), at 295.

81. Melnick, *Between the Lines*, 143. *Colorable* is defined in the Oxford English Dictionary thus: "Capable of being presented as true or right; having at least a *prima facie* aspect of justice or validity."

82. *Mills v. Board of Education of the District of Columbia*, 348 F. Supp. 866 (D.C., Aug. 1,1972), at 878.

83. See ibid., at 869 and 871. The facts laid out on behalf of the plaintiffs were extraordinarily damning. Their case is reproduced in full in House Committee on the District of Columbia, hearings, *Mentally Ill and Handicapped Children*, March 14, 1972, 92nd Cong., 2nd Sess., 323–353. For the wider crisis surrounding both special education and general education provision in the District of Columbia, see William Raspberry, "Disturbed Child: Where to Now?" *Washington Post*, August 27, 1970, p. A21; Raspberry, "Retardates Face Extra Handicaps," ibid., September 10, 1970, p. A19; Bart Barnes, "Contempt Charge Is Urged on Handicapped Services," ibid., July 22, 1972, p. B6; and David Kirp, William Buss, and Peter Kuriloff, "Legal Reform of Special Education: Empirical Studies and Procedural Proposals," *California Law Review* 62, no.1 (January 1974): 82–96.

84. 348 F. Supp. at 876.

85. Ibid. at 874–875. No reference is made to either *Wyatt v. Stickney* or *PARC v. Commonwealth of Pennsylvania.* Waddy's main citation is to a District of Columbia segregation case with which he would have been very familiar, *Hobson v. Hansen.* In that opinion, his colleague J. Skelly Wright relied not just on the due process clause of the Fifth Amendment but also on the equal protection clause of the Fourteenth Amendment, even though the Fourteenth Amendment applies only to states and not to the District of Columbia. Waddy reproduced the relevant section of Wright's decision without comment. For Judge Wright's rationale, which seems strained, see 269 F. Supp. 401 (D.C., 1967) at 493.

86. Kirp, Buss, and Kurilof, "Legal Reform," 83.

87. HCLE had been established in 1969, as one of a number of "legal backup centers" (others specialized in welfare and food aid, housing, and consumer affairs). Nick Kotz, "Fate of Mass. Center Called Key to Nixon Plans on Legal Aid," *Washington Post,* January 25, 1973, p. A2. Kotz noted that conservative critics blamed the backup centers for "providing the intellectual ferment and brainpower that has helped legal services challenge local, state and federal government, with frequent success."

88. NLADA's role had expanded in line with the general trend in antipoverty law since the mid-1960s, and in 1969 it made the decision to shift its emphasis in civil cases "from handling individual cases to concentrating on group representation and test cases." See *New York Times,* October 30, 1969, p. 49.

89. Besides Herr, the other NLADA lawyers involved in the case were Patricia Wald, another Yale product who subsequently joined the Mental Health Law Center before embarking on a distinguished career as a federal judge, and Julian Tepper, a recent Cambridge University graduate in criminology who had just made the news as a citizen mediator during the Attica prison riot. In 1973, at thirty-one, he would take on the job of managing the District of Columbia's neighborhood legal services program. *Washington Post,* February 26, 1973, p. A2.

90. For copies of these affidavits, see CEC Archives, Governmental Relations Advocacy Files, RG2.5.2.2, box 12.

91. CEC's other contribution to *Mills* was to facilitate cooperation between prosecution and defense. As with Ohrtman in *PARC,* many of the defendants were members of CEC. They worked with NLADA and the other public interest law groups to identify suitable plaintiffs. Weintraub, telephone interview, November 18, 2004.

92. Frederick J. Weintraub and Alan Abeson, "New Education Policies for the Handicapped: The Quiet Revolution," *Phi Delta Kappan* 55 (1974): 526–529, 569; Frederick J. Weintraub and Alan Abeson, "Appropriate Education for All Handicapped Children: A Growing Issue," *Syracuse Law Review* 23, no. 4 (1972): 1037–1058.

93. Had they been confident, of course, they would have welcomed the prospect of an appeal, which—if successful—would have given the constitutional rights broader geographic reach, national in the event that the case went all the way to the Supreme Court and was won. Weintraub, telephone interview, November 18, 2004.

94. "Nearly all States Now Have Mandatory Law," *Insight,* May 1973, 3; Alan Abeson, "Movement and Momentum: Government and the Education of Handi-

capped Children—II," *Exceptional Children*, October 1974, 114, 110. Their other top priority also had to do with education funding: the legal campaign to overhaul school financing arrangements. (See Chapter 8.)

95. For a review of these laws, see Alan Abeson and Joseph Ballard, "State and Federal Policy for Exceptional Children," in Weintraub, *Public Policy*, 83–95, and additional sources cited therein.

96. Weintraub and Abeson, "New Education Policies for the Handicapped," 526.

97. Abeson, "Movement and Momentum," 113.

98. It may be that defeat had been narrowly averted in the case of one Tennessee lawsuit. In that case, however, disability advocates who worried that they had drawn an unfriendly judge managed to persuade the state legislature to enact the CEC's model law, which provided by statute all the gains that the plaintiffs were trying to win through the courts. The legal challenge was accordingly withdrawn. Weintraub remembered the CEC's appealing to state legislators in Knoxville by arguing: "You don't want judges telling you what to do, do you? Why not pass our model statute instead." Weintraub, telephone interview, November 18, 2004. Soon after the state law was passed, a fresh round of litigation began, on the grounds that the new law was being flouted. For documentation relating to this case, *Rainey v. Tennessee*, see CEC Archives, Government Relations Advocacy Files, RG2.5.2.2, box 15.

99. See, for example, the remarks of Blair Lee III, lieutenant governor of Maryland, who told senators in 1975 that his state might successfully have appealed the state circuit court's ruling in *Maryland ARC v. Maryland*, but "we didn't feel like appealing it. It was an area where we felt an obligation to do . . . what the court thought we should do." Senate Committee on Labor and Public Welfare, Subcommittee on the Handicapped, hearings, *Education for All Handicapped Children*, April 8, 1975, 94th Cong., 1st Sess., 142.

100. The state with the most comprehensive measure was Massachusetts. For an account of its Chapter 766 program, enacted in 1972 but not implemented until 1974, see Richard A. Weatherley, *Reforming Special Education: Policy Implementation from State Level to Street Level* (Cambridge, Mass.: MIT Press, 1979), and Adam Nelson, *The Elusive Ideal: Equal Educational Opportunity and the Federal Role in Boston's Public Schools, 1950–1985* (Chicago: University of Chicago Press, 2005), 132–135, 169–190.

101. Senate Committee on Labor and Public Welfare, Subcommittee on the Handicapped, *Education for All Handicapped Children*, 40.

102. Weintraub, telephone interview, November 18, 2004.

103. Cited by Melnick, *Between the Lines*, 116. The context was the effort to impose a stronger AFDC work requirement on the states.

104. While in the Minnesota legislature, Quie had served on a committee that overhauled state provision for special education. Quie, interview with author, Minneapolis, Minn., August 11, 2004.

105. *Education for All Handicapped Act of 1975*, PL 94-142, sec. 611 (a) (1) (B). Reproduced in Erwin L. Levine and Elizabeth M. Wexler, *PL 94-142: An Act of Congress* (New York: Macmillan, 1981), 194.

106. Cited by Scotch, *From Good Will to Civil Rights*, 48.

107. Cited in *Exceptional Children*, November 1969, 213.

108. For a lucid overview of these developments, see Julian Zelizer, *On Capitol*

Hill: The Struggle to Reform Congress and Its Consequences, 1948–2000 (New York: Cambridge University Press, 2004).

109. Jack Duncan to author, e-mail, November 13, 2004.

110. The Brademas subcommittee predated these changes, having been in existence since early in Adam Clayton Powell's tenure as chairman of the full committee.

111. Randolph had a longstanding interest in the problems of the blind. According to one aide, Anne Hocutt, it dated from an accident back in the 1930s that had detached his retina and left him bed-bound for six months with a sandbag over his eye. Hocutt to author, e-mail, November 8, 2004.

112. Patria Winalski had previously worked in the small branch of HEW that then handled education for the handicapped; she had a deaf son. A forceful and resourceful advocate of a larger federal role in education for disabled children, she had good connections on the Hill (she had worked for Abraham Ribicoff, before going to HEW, and was partner and then wife of Senate staffer Jack Forsythe) and was an indomitable advocate for the handicapped in general, and the deaf in particular. She was responsible for the inclusion of a speech and language title in PL88-164, and in 1965, Fogarty and Carey had introduced the legislation that created a National Technical Institute for the Deaf on her birthday, as a present. Edwin Martin, interview with author, December 26, 2004, Venice, Fla.; Martin LaVor, interview with author, November 22, 2004, Alexandria, Va.; Samuel Halperin, interview with author, February 16, 2005, Washington, D.C.

113. The material in the next two paragraphs is drawn from Anne Hocutt (a staff member on the Randolph subcommittee) to author, e-mail, November 8, 2004.

114. Quie, interview, August 11, 2004.

115. The opening statement of purpose, for example, referred not to the requirement that all states provide a "free, appropriate public education" but to the desire that "all handicapped children" would "receive maximum special education services." Senate Committee on Labor and Public Welfare, Subcommittee on the Handicapped, *Education for All Handicapped Children Act of 1975*, 94th Cong., 1st Sess., May 16, 1972, S. Rep. 3614, sec. 2, introduced by Senator Williams. Records of Senate Committee on Labor and Public Welfare, Subcommittee on the Handicapped, RG 46, National Archives I, Washington, D.C., box 2.

116. As chair of the Labor and Public Finance Committee, Williams would be an important player in any debate about school finance. Weintraub, telephone interview, November 18, 2004. For the outcome of that debate, see Chapter 8.

117. Weintraub, telephone interview, November 18, 2004.

118. For a general overview of BEH's impact, see "BEH Celebrates 5th Birthday," *Insight*, January 1972, 4. See also Martin, "A Golden Age for Special Education," pt. 2.

119. Martin's activist, rights-oriented sympathies had been evident since early in his career. When he was codirector of the University of Alabama's speech and hearing clinic, during the early 1960s, he and his wife participated in a civil rights protest and found themselves being harassed by the local Klan and by Al Lingo's highway patrol. Martin took pride in having desegregated his clinic, at a time when the rest of the university system was still all white. Martin, interview, December 26, 2004.

120. See *Insight*, November 1970, 2. Martin says that this appearance generated

20,000 to 30,000 letters to his bureau. Martin, "A Golden Age for Special Education," 35.

121. See *Insight*, May 1971, 1–2; November 1971, 2.

122. For example, Martin made creative use of a $1 million earmark under Title VI, designed to encourage parents of handicapped children to contact BEH for advice. Martin used it to establish regional centers of parents, and they lobbied at the state level for better state legislation, including the Massachusetts law mentioned above. Another seed money grant from BEH helped the National Association of State Directors of Special Education to establish a Washington office. And a third grant, to CEC, helped it to put together a model state education for the handicapped law that was widely adopted during the early 1970s. Martin, interview, December 26, 2004.

123. Weintraub, telephone interview, November 18, 2004.

124. On Mathews's Alabama background, see David Mathews, interview with author, November 2, 2004, Alexandria, Va. See also John Mathews, "Ford Signs Handicap Measure," *Washington Star*, December 3, 1975, p. A-32; Mathews to Jennings Randolph, letter, October 7, 1975, box 801, Office Files of Commissioner of Education, RG 12, National Archives II, College Park, Md., box 801.

125. Had Ford sacked him for disloyalty, Martin recalls, he would have "welcomed the publicity." But this would have been difficult, since he was a civil servant rather than a political appointee.

Chapter 8. Compensatory Education through the Courts: The Politics of School Finance

1. The exception was Hawaii, where the school finance system was centralized.

2. 487 P.2d 1241.

3. See editorial in *New Republic*, October 2, 1971, 9–10. See also Note, "*Serrano v Priest:* The End of an Era in Public School Financing," *Hastings Law Journal* 23 (1972): 365.

4. 411 U.S. 1.

5. William Greider and Nick Kotz, "Justice—An Elusive Jewel: Counter-Currents Slowing Legal Activism," *Washington Post*, April 14, 1973, p. A1.

6. See J. R. Pole, *The Pursuit of Equality in American History*, 2nd ed. (Berkeley: University of California Press, 1993), 433.

7. These efforts are reviewed at the end of the chapter.

8. In 1968–1969, the local property tax provided the largest share of revenue receipts in thirty-one states. The states most reliant upon this form of taxation were New Hampshire (86.0 percent), Oregon (75.6 percent), Nebraska (74.8 percent), South Dakota (73.7 percent), Massachusetts (70.7 percent), and Wisconsin (69.4 percent). The other nineteen states derived more revenue from statewide taxation. See U.S. Department of Health, Education, and Welfare, *Digest of Educational Statistics 1969* (Washington, D.C.: National Center for Educational Statistics, 1970), 49, table 66.

9. Cited in Arthur Wise, "The California Doctrine," *Saturday Review*, November 20, 1971, 78. These figures include the state contribution.

10. Because the extreme examples distorted the picture, education economists

tended to compare per pupil spending in districts that were in the 75th percentile in terms of wealth with spending in districts that were in the 25th percentile. The ratio varied from a low figure of 1.11:1 in Utah to a high of 1.87 in Missouri. Figures cited in John E. Coons, William H. Clune III, and Stephen D. Sugarman, *Private Wealth and Public Education* (Cambridge, Mass.: Belknap Press, Harvard University Press, 1970), 498. The national ratio was 1.70:1. See Arthur Wise, *Rich Schools, Poor Schools: The Promise of Equal Educational Opportunity* (Chicago: University of Chicago Press, 1968), 126.

11. For example, they passed laws that granted rebates to seniors, or—responding to the broader antitax animus—set maximum tax rates or established maximum interest rates for bond issues. See Robert Boyden Lamb, "The Taxpayers' Revolt Against Rising School Costs," *Current History* (July 1972), and Robert Bendiner, *The Politics of Schools: A Crisis in Self-Government* (New York: Harper and Row, 1969), pt. 4.

12. *McInnis v. Shapiro*, 293 F.Supp.327 (N.D. Ill., 1968), at 329 and 329n4.

13. Coons, Clune, and Sugarman, *Private Wealth*, 2.

14. When thirty attorneys general presented a brief to the Supreme Court in 1972, objecting to the idea, they described Wise darkly as the "founder of the new cult." Brief of Amici Curiae in Support of Appellants, filed July 22, 1972, in the case of *San Antonio I.S.D. v. Rodriguez*, 30; Available at www.curiae.law.yale.edu (accessed May 16, 2005).

15. Arthur E. Wise, "Is Denial of Equal Educational Opportunity Constitutional?" *Administrator's Notebook* 13 (February 1965): 1–4.

16. A. E. Wise, "The Constitution and Equality: Wealth, Geography, and Educational Opportunity" (Ph.D. diss., University of Chicago, 1967); Wise, *Rich Schools*.

17. Philip B. Kurland, "Equal Educational Opportunity, or The Limits of Constitutional Jurisprudence Undefined," in Charles U. Daly, ed., *The Quality of Inequality: Urban and Suburban Public Schools* (Chicago: University of Chicago Press, 1968), 48. A strong conservative critic of Warren Court jurisprudence, Kurland did not view this prospect with enthusiasm.

18. Wise was later told that George Bushnell, the Detroit lawyer who represented the city school board in that case, had waved a copy of the dissertation at his clients, imploring them to believe that litigation might be the answer, even though nothing like this had ever been tried before. Arthur Wise, interview with author, May 4, 2004, Washington, D.C.

19. *McInnis v. Shapiro; Burruss v. Wilkerson*, 310 F. Supp. 572 (W.D. Virginia, 1969). For a report on the Detroit case, which was brought in the Wayne County circuit court, see *New York Times*, February 3, 1968, p. 16.

20. The author of the Illinois opinion found the case "non-judiciable," observing that "there are no 'discoverable and manageable standards' by which a court can determine when the Constitution is satisfied and when it is violated." *McInnis v. Ogilvie*, 293 F. Supp. 327, at 335. The judge in the Virginia case found that the circumstances of the *McInnis* case were "scarcely distinguishable from the facts here." 310 F. Supp. 572, at 573.

21. *McInnis v. Ogilvie*, 394 U.S. 322 (March 24, 1969); *Burruss v. Wilkerson*, 397

U.S. 44 (February 24, 1970). These were per curiam decisions. Because the initial cases had raised federal constitutional questions, they had been heard by a special three-judge court. In such cases, appeals went straight to the Supreme Court, which had to render a decision but did not have to hear arguments. In the *McInnis* case, only William O. Douglas favored hearing arguments. In *Burruss*, he was joined by Byron White.

22. On Title VI, see obituary of Horowitz in the UCLA's *Daily Bruin Online;* http://www.dailybruin.com (accessed May 10, 2005).

23. Asked about his prior interest in poverty, Horowitz replied: "I became aware of it in my career at HEW. I was an academician . . . and, really, aside from a generalized liberal interest in the programs of the New Deal and the New Frontier, I had not thought about the question." Harold W. Horowitz, February 23, 1968, oral history for LBJL, 4. He went on to describe the legal services idea as "a magnificent development in social programs in the United States" (21), and one obituary said that he "helped found" WCLP; http://www.law.harvard.edu/alumni/bulletin/2001/spring/memoriam_main.html (accessed May 10, 2005).

24. Gerald C. Lubenow, "The Action Lawyers," *Saturday Review,* August 26, 1972, 37.

25. Ibid.

26. The first was Horowitz, "Unseparate but Unequal—The Emerging Fourteenth Amendment Issue in Public School Education," *UCLA Law Review* 13, no.4 (May 1966): 1147–1172. When Judge Skelly Wright handed down his decision in *Hobson,* the following year, Horowitz's article was cited three times (see 269 F. Supp. 401). The second was Horowitz and Diana L. Neitring, "Equal Protection Aspects of Inequalities in Public Education and Public Assistance Programs from Place to Place within a State," *UCLA Law Review* 15, no.3 (April 1968): 787–816.

27. Horowitz and Neitring, "Equal Protection Aspects," 812, 816. This emphasis on geography was new: for Wise, the key constitutional issue was discrimination between individual children, and for lawyers in the three early cases it had been failure to meet educational "need."

28. See Wendy Madnick, "On Being an Advocate," an interview with Sid Wolinsky, *Olam Magazine,* issue 7, n.d., http://www.olam.org/issues.php (accessed March 14, 2007).

29. Bell provided this biographical material to the Web site http://www.thehistorymakers.com/biography (accessed December 20, 2006). For the Mississippi arrest, see *New York Times,* February 11, 1962, p. 18, and *Washington Post,* February 11, 1962, p. 25. When he left WCLP, Bell became the first tenured black professor at Harvard University Law School.

30. Lubenow, "Action Lawyers," 39. The material in the rest of this section is drawn mainly from this excellent journalistic account of the origins of the *Serrano* suit, supplemented by Robert Reinhold, "John Serrano Jr., *et al.,* and School Tax Equality," *New York Times,* January 10, 1972, pp. E1, E26.

31. Paraphrased by Reinhold.

32. David L. Kirp, "Judicial Policy-Making: Inequitable Public School Financing and the *Serrano* Case," in Allan P. Sindler, ed., *Policy and Politics in America: Six Case Studies* (Boston: Little, Brown, 1976), 84.

33. LCCR transcript, 154.

34. Kirp, "Judicial Policy-Making," 98. Wolinsky and Horowitz had retained the "need" standard, along with all the other complaints.

35. The material in this paragraph is drawn primarily from John E. Coons, telephone interview with author, May 11, 2005.

36. Coons noted that "the rationale protecting such differentials in the provision of a governmental service is by no means clear." John E. Coons, "Chicago," in U.S. Commission on Civil Rights, *Civil Rights U.S.A.: Public Schools, Cities in the North and West, 1962* (Washington, D.C.: Government Printing Office, 1962), 184.

37. Lubenow, "Action Lawyers," 37.

38. Coons, Clune, and Sugarman, *Private Wealth*, xix, xxii.

39. See John Silard's remarks, LCCR transcript, 155, and George E. Bushnell Jr., Richard A. Jones, and David J. Olmstead, "Litigation and the Quest for Equal Educational Opportunity," *Inequality in Education*, no.3 (March 17, 1970): 15. They would have drawn encouragement from judges such as Skelly Wright, who blithely acknowledged: "I guess I am an activist, but I want to do what's right. When I get a case, . . . the first thing I think of [is] what should be done—and then you look at the law and see whether or not you can do it. . . . If you don't take it to extremes, I think that it's good to come out with a fair and just result and then look for law to support it." Quoted in Jeffrey Brandon Morris, *Calmly to Poise the Scales of Justice: A History of the Courts of the District of Columbia Circuit* (Durham, NC: Carolina Academic Press, 2001), 196.

40. At the Chicago conference on Arthur Wise's dissertation, the dean of the New York University Law School argued that local control should always yield to justice, where the two values were in conflict. See Robert B. McKay, "Defining the Limits," in Daly, *Quality of Inequality*, 77.

41. David L. Kirp, "The Poor, the Schools, and Equal Protection," in Harvard Education Review, *Equal Educational Opportunity* (Cambridge, Mass.: Harvard University Press, 1969), 140, 146, 169.

42. Coons, Clune, and Sugarman elaborated on what they meant by this with citations drawn from Popes Pius XI and John XXIII. *Private Wealth*, 15n8.

43. In a characteristically waspish aside, Coons, Clune, and Sugarman observed at one point that "educational administration is not noticeably overpopulated with philosopher kings." Ibid., 18.

44. Ibid., xxii.

45. The final section of the book has a distinctly tentative, probing, speculative air that presents a vivid contrast to the certitude of earlier sections. This is striking given that this was the one section of the book that focused on the authors' home turf, namely the law (the first 286 pages of *Private Wealth* are devoted to the history and inadequacy of the existing system and to an explication of "district power equalizing").

46. This was a reference to Franklin Roosevelt's angry denunciation of the "nine old men" of the Hughes Court.

47. Coons, Clune, and Sugarman, *Private Wealth*, 2.

48. For an extended discussion of Proposition I, see ibid., chapter 11.

49. Ibid., 461–462.

50. The reception of the book is all the more striking, given that it assessed the

Detroit, Illinois, and Virginia suits and the theoretical work of Wise and Kirp with a mixture of lofty disdain and biting sarcasm. See especially pp. 304–306, particularly the footnotes.

51. David L. Kirp and Mark G. Yudof, "Whose Priorities for Educational Reform?" *Harvard Civil Rights–Civil Liberties Law Review* 6 (1971): 619–630, quote from 621. Arthur Wise acknowledged that the book "provided an excellent exposition and analysis of public school finance," in *Saturday Review,* April 17, 1971, 76. For perhaps the most perceptive analysis, see the review by Stephen R. Goldstein in *California Law Review* 59 (1971): 302–313.

52. As Wolinsky told the *New York Times,* "the major strategy was to ask for a very restrained principle. We avoided concepts like 'need' and 'educational opportunity'—all those garbage terms that education has become overburdened with." *New York Times,* January 10, 1972, p. E26. (Such "garbage terms" had been central to the original *Serrano* complaint, back in 1968.)

53. *Serrano v. Priest* (Calif. Supreme Court, 1971), 487 P.2d 1241, at 1250, 1258.

54. See Kirp, "Judicial Policy-Making," 100–101. See also A. Alan Post, oral history interview conducted by California State Archives, April 23 to June 4, 2002, Center for California Studies, California State University, Sacramento, 139–143. I am grateful to Rebecca Wendt for supplying me with Post's oral history. For the legislative debate over reforming the property tax, see "Statewide Property Tax for Schools," *California Journal,* March 1971, 72–73, 85.

55. See Joann S. Lublin, "Trailblazing Bench: California High Court Often Points the Way for Judges Elsewhere," *Wall Street Journal,* July 20, 1972, pp. 1, 18. The state court overturned a ban on racially mixed marriages in 1948, nineteen years ahead of the U.S. Supreme Court. The state court banned use of evidence gathered in illegal police searches in 1955, six years before *Gideon.* It ordered the California police to warn criminal suspects of the rights to remain silent and to have an attorney in 1965, a year before *Miranda.* It also pioneered expanded definitions of standing to sue and did much to encourage class-action lawsuits. The occasion for the *Wall Street Journal's* article was the U.S. Supreme Court's abolition of the death penalty in the case of *Furman v. Georgia.* That decision too had been anticipated in the California court, one month earlier.

Governor Reagan had hoped to stop the rot in 1970 when he appointed Donald Wright, a Los Angeles Republican, to replace Roger Traynor as chief justice. According to one of Wright's new colleagues, there had been some suspicion that he would be "a bit of an Archie Bunker type." But by 1972, that expectation had yielded to a new conventional wisdom: this might be "the Earl Warren of Reagan's administration."

56. Lubenow, "Action Lawyers," 42.

57. Cited by Kirp, "Judicial Policy-Making," 104.

58. This is based on comprehensive notes that Elliot Richardson took during the meeting, held on September 30, 1971. Richardson papers, folder entitled "Memcon Sept. 1971," box 126.

59. The first of them was *Van Dusartz v. Hatfield* (USDC, Minnesota, 2nd Division, 1971), 334 F.Supp. 870. According to Coons, the suit originated when district judge Miles W. Lord buttonholed an activist lawyer at a cocktail party and urged

him to put a case together. He did so, and it was Lord who heard the case. When it came to writing an opinion, Lord phoned Coons and invited him to draft one, which he did, after having consulted a legal ethicist. Unsurprisingly, the opinion found the logic of *Private Wealth* to be unassailable. Coons, telephone interview, May 11, 2005.

60. LCCR Transcript, 161, 162, 165.

61. Ibid., 160, 164, 153, 156. The final speaker was Abraham Sofaer, law professor at Columbia.

62. This was in 1968, and MALDEF had only recently been established. Although its headquarters were in San Antonio, it had not yet started getting involved in class-action lawsuits. For an account of the origins of the case, see Caroline Wagstaff, "Race, Class, and Federalism: A History and Analysis of *San Antonio Independent School District v. Rodriguez*" (Ph.D. diss., University of Kent, England, September 2001), chapter 1. See also Paul A. Sracic, *San Antonio v. Rodriguez and the Pursuit of Equal Education: The Debate over Discrimination and School Funding* (Lawrence: University Press of Kansas, 2006); Peter Irons, *The Courage of Their Convictions* (New York: Free Press, 1988), 283–285, 298–300; and William Allen, "The Case of Demetrio Rodriguez," *Saturday Review*, September 9, 1972, 6–12. In suggesting a lawsuit, Gochman was influenced not by the Detroit suit, filed some six months earlier, but rather by *Hobson v. Hansen*, the 1967 case having to do with race-based discrimination within school districts.

63. Mark G. Yudof and Daniel C. Morgan, "Rodriguez v. San Antonio Independent School District: Gathering the Ayes of Texas—The Politics of School Finance Reform," *Law and Contemporary Problems* 38 (1973–1974): 392–393.

64. 337 F. Supp. 280, December 23, 1971. The opinion was written by Judge Adrian Spears, a Kennedy appointee who lived not far from Edgewood. For his unhappiness with the state, see also Irons, *The Courage of Their Convictions*, 286. Gochman received advice from Coons, who flew in from the West Coast, and Mark G. Yudof, formerly of the Harvard Center for Law and Education, now a professor at the University of Texas.

65. "A Decade after *Rodriguez*: An Interview with John Coons," *Phi Delta Kappan*, March 1983, 479.

66. Earl Warren was replaced by Warren Burger, Abe Fortas by Harry Blackmun, John Marshall Harlan by William Rehnquist, and Hugo Black by Lewis Powell.

67. The cases were *Roe v. Wade* (1973), *Furman v. Georgia* (1972), *Swann v. Charlotte-Mecklenburg* (1971), and *Griggs v. Duke Power* (1971). Only one of them was decided by less than a 7–2 majority.

68. Attention here will focus on Lewis Powell and Potter Stewart, but note that Harry Blackmun described it as a "very difficult case" and that William Brennan told colleagues that "few cases have troubled me more." See Harry Blackmun to Lewis Powell, letter, February 13, 1973, in Blackmun papers, box 161; Lewis Powell, notes on June 5, 1972, conference, in Powell papers, docket sheet, No. 71–1332, folder labeled "1972, June-Sept." (There are no box numbers for the Powell papers, which are organized by docket number.)

69. Powell told a clerk that this finding "cast considerable doubt upon the rationality of the district court judges." Powell to Larry Hammond, memo, October 12,

1972 (but dictated October 7), Powell papers, folder entitled "1972 Oct. 2 (bench memo)." As interpreted by the Supreme Court, the equal protection clause allows state legislation to make classifications, so long as they bear some "rational" basis to the purposes of the law. If the classification concerns a group to which the court grants a higher degree of constitutional protection, however, the state has to demonstrate a "compelling" rationale.

70. Powell believed that "the local school board . . . has been the most dynamic force behind the overall effectiveness of our public school system." Powell to Larry Hammond, memo, October 12, 1972 (dictated October 7).

71. In Powell's own state of Virginia, the city of Richmond was rich in property but had a large poor population. Powell to J. Harvie Wilkinson III, memo, August 30, 1972, Powell papers, folder entitled "1972, June–September." (Wilkinson, a fellow Virginian, clerked for Powell between 1971 and 1973.)

72. "There is, of course, a relationship between resources devoted to education and its quality. But it is equally true that money alone can't buy educational quality." Powell to Hammond, memo, August 31, 1972, Powell papers.

73. These were the briefs of Charles Alan Wright, on behalf of the state of Texas, and of the Maryland attorney general (on behalf of a group of thirty attorneys general), both July 22, 1972. All the briefs for this case save for that of Wright are reproduced on microfilm in U.S. Supreme Court, "Records and Briefs," and are also available at http://www.curiae.law.yale.edu. I am indebted to the University of Texas Law Library for furnishing me with a copy of Wright's brief. The only brief on the other side to have been submitted by this time was by Arthur Gochman, but it was shoddily constructed.

74. See Powell to J. Harvie Wilkinson, letter, March 11, 1976, in Powell papers, folder entitled "1973 March 22–1976." According to one of Blackmun's clerks, a very high proportion of them favored affirmance. See "Jim" to Blackmun, memo, n.d. (but between October 12 and 17, 1972), Blackmun papers, box 161. "Jim" noted that he was "in a very small minority among the clerks" in favoring reversal.

75. Larry A. Hammond, "Bench Memo," October 2, 1972, 14, 15. (The Powell memo had opened by noting that the Texas court was "following almost slavishly the California case of *Serrano v Priest*, which in turn adopted almost literally the 'activist scholarship' theory of Professors Coons and Sugarman." Powell to Wilkinson, memo, August 30, 1972, Powell papers, folder entitled "1972, June–September.")

76. For example, Powell applauded the brief submitted by the Maryland attorney general but also recognized that it was "advocacy" and urged Hammond: "Please help me judge it fairly." Powell to Hammond, memo, October 9, 1972, Powell papers, folder entitled "1972, October 9–28" (second of two memos, each dated October 9, and with identical headings). Hammond reports that "I have never worked with a more honest and open-minded lawyer." Hammond, e-mail to author, July 24, 2006.

77. Powell to Hammond, memo, October 12, 1972 (dictated October 7), 10.

78. See Hammond, "Bench Memo," October 2, 1972, 14–15, and Powell's approving annotations.

79. Powell to Hammond, memo, October 12, 1972 (dictated October 7), 15.

80. Unless otherwise cited, material in the next three paragraphs is drawn from a profile by Christopher Lydon, "The Man Who Said 'No' for Nixon: Charles Alan Wright," *New York Times*, July 24, 1973, p. 18. Lydon described Wright as having a

"sparkling intellect," and a reputedly partisan Democrat on the Federal Communications Commission who had studied with Wright felt that he had "perhaps the most brilliant mind I have ever encountered." He also recounted that Wright "is something of a celebrity in Austin, Tex—a standing-room only law lecturer, as well as an Episcopalian vestryman, a trustee of the Austin symphony, an excellent golfer, and a flamboyant party-giver." He was also a "passionate coach of the law school touch-football team."

81. For Brennan, see Library of Congress inventory to Part 2 of the Brennan papers (which contain private correspondence and are not open for research), listing three folders of correspondence with Wright, stretching over three decades (one of the larger nonfamily series). For Powell, see Wright to Powell, letter, April 25, 1973, Powell papers, and Powell's admiring references to "Charlie" Wright in his correspondence with Hammond. For Stewart, see Wagstaff, "Race, Class, and Federalism," 118n57. Wright also knew William Rehnquist. Mark Yudof, telephone interview with author, June 5, 2005.

82. Wright revered the Supreme Court and its traditions. Friends liked to recall the occasion when he was looking to fulfill a lifelong aspiration: to buy a Cadillac. He changed his mind when the Texan auto dealer whom he had approached remarked: "Isn't it a shame what the Supreme Court is doing to the country." Shocked, Wright had asked the man for directions to the nearest Lincoln Continental dealership, and that was the model that he had been driving ever since.

83. The case was *Hughes Tool Co. v. TWA*. The source for the material in the first half of this paragraph is L. A. Powe Jr., "Charles Alan Wright: Supreme Court Advocate," in Roy Mersky, ed., *Charles Alan Wright: A Tribute—The Man and the Scholar* (Austin, Tex.: Jamail Center for Legal Research, 2000). According to Powe, the outcome of the Hughes suit was considered "extraordinary," for Wright's client had expected nothing more than a reduced penalty.

84. Coons, telephone interview, May 11, 2005. Identity of lawyer kept confidential at request of interviewee.

85. Wagstaff, "Race, Class, and Federalism," 121–122, 148; Coons, telephone interview, May 11, 2005. (Archibald Cox was a celebrated law professor at Harvard and former solicitor general in the Kennedy and Johnson administrations. The following year, he would find himself on the opposite side to Wright in another context, as Watergate special prosecutor.) Among school finance experts, the hope was that Gochman would step aside in favor of Coons. Yudof, telephone interview, June 5, 2005.

86. James A. Kelly, telephone interview with author, June 3, 2005.

87. Coons, telephone interview, May 11, 2005. He considered Gochman's performance "calamitous." for a fuller account of the oral arguments, see Sracic, *San Antonio v. Rodriguez and the Pursuit of Equal Education*, 83-98.

88. Handwritten notes, "71—1332–San Antonio Independent School District v Rodriguez, October 12, 1972," Blackmun papers, box 161, folder 4. He offered no description of Wright, with whom he was after all already well acquainted. This habit of making unflattering notations on the appearances of witnesses was apparently characteristic. See Linda Greenhouse, *Becoming Justice Blackmun: Harry Blackmun's Supreme Court Journey* (New York: Times Books, 2005), 105–106.

89. In particular, see Paul Dimond, "Serrano: A Victory of Sorts for Eth-

ics, Not Necessarily for Education," *Yale Review of Law and Social Action* 2 (1971); Stephen R. Goldstein, "Interdistrict Inequalities in School Financing: A Critical Analysis of *Serrano v Priest* and Its Progeny," *University of Pennsylvania Law Review*, 120 (1972), 504–544; Note, "A Statistical Analysis of the School Finance Decisions," *Yale Law Journal* 81 (1972): 1303–1341; Joel S. Berke and John J. Callahan, "*Serrano v Priest:* Milestone or Millstone for School Finance," *Journal of Public Law* 25 (1972), 23–71.

90. Wright had made the same point to Coons in private, one month earlier: "I am going to do my best to beat you in *Rodriguez*, but regardless of the outcome of the case, I have nothing except admiration for the thoughtful and incisive attention you and your associates have brought to this very important question." Cited by Wagstaff, "Race, Class, and Federalism," 151.

91. Oral Arguments, *San Antonio v. Rodriguez*, October 12, 1972, reproduced in microfiche form in *The Complete Oral Arguments Of the Supreme Court of the United States: A Retrospective, 1969 Term through 1979 Term* (Frederick, Md.: University Publications of America, 1980), fiche no. 76, 42.

92. "Notes for Conference—Rodriguez—71-1332," (October 17, 1972), Powell papers.

93. Blackmun and Douglas each indicated regretting that the case had come before them.

94. See William Douglas's conference notes, Papers of William O. Douglas, Library of Congress, box 1575; and Blackmun's conference notes, Blackmun papers, box 161. Potter Stewart's papers are not yet available for research. Stewart's jurisprudence has not received much attention. See, however, Gayle Natalie Binion, "The Evolution of Constitutional Doctrine: The Role of Justice Stewart on a Changing Supreme Court" (Ph.D. diss., UCLA, 1977). For his ambivalent attitude to the rights of the poor, see 209–228.

95. This is according to Bob Woodward with Scott Armstrong, *The Brethren: Inside the Supreme Court* (New York: Simon and Schuster, 1979), 258. This book is based for the most part on anonymous sources.

96. See Powell to Stewart, letter, December 21, 1972, Powell papers, folder entitled "1972-November-December." Reminiscing about the case in a 1976 letter, Powell noted that "revisions were made to accommodate the thinking of another Justice." Powell to Wilkinson, letter, March 11, 1976, Powell papers, folder entitled "1973 March 22–1976."

97. Stewart to Powell, letter, February 26, 1973, Powell papers. Powell visited Marshall to compliment him on his opinion, according to Woodward and Armstrong, *Brethren*, 258–259.

98. Preparing possible conference remarks a day before oral arguments in the case, Blackmun was impressed by the arguments that both Wright and Coons had outlined in their briefs, but he feared that "this would be far worse than . . . reapportionment" and was "really a non-judiciable controversy." He wished that he had not been put in the position of having to vote on the matter: "I would like to see what happens in California under their state court's ruling of unconstitutionality. The step for us to take is a gigantic one that has ramifications of unknown dimensions." Draft conference speech, "71-1332—San Antonio ISD v. Rodriguez," , October 11, 1972, Blackmun papers, box 161. Chief Justice Burger agreed with his friend that the

issues here were "more overwhelming than *Baker v Carr.*" Blackmun handwritten notes on Burger's comments at conference, October 1, 1972, ibid.

99. 411 U.S. 1, at 44.

100. See Larry W. Yackle, "Thoughts on *Rodriguez:* Mr. Justice Powell and the Demise of Equal Protection Analysis in the Supreme Court," *University of Richmond Law Review* 9, no.2 (Winter 1975): 181–247; David L. Kirp, "Law, Politics, and Equal Educational Opportunity: The Limits of Judicial Involvement," *Harvard Educational Review* 47, no.2 (May 1977): 117–137.

101. The classic example of a protracted suit is *Robinson v. Cahill* in New Jersey, eventually resolved as *Abbott v. Burke.* But see also the case of Texas. Edgewood Independent School District, the district at the heart of the *Rodriguez* suit, went back to court in the 1990s, precipitating a saga that has been well told by Mark Yudof, "School Finance Reform in Texas: The Edgewood Saga," *Harvard Journal of Legislation* 28 (1991): 499–505.

102. The Supreme Court has continued to maintain that silence, with the intriguing exception of *Plyler v. Doe* (1982), authored by Justice Powell, which concerned the right of the child of illegal immigrants to an education. In that case, the "right" had been withheld entirely.

103. Michael A. Rebell, "Educational Adequacy, Democracy, and the Courts," in Timothy Ready, Christopher Edley Jr., and Catherine E. Snow, eds., *Achieving High Educational Standards for All: Conference Summary* (Washington, D.C.: National Academy Press, 2002), 240 (emphasis added).

104. Peter Enrich, "Leaving Equality Behind: New Directions in School Finance Reform," *Vanderbilt Law Review* 48 (1995): 125.

105. Some constitutions mandate "an adequate public education" or an "ample" education. See ibid., 232.

106. Douglas S. Reed, *On Equal Terms: The Constitutional Politics of Educational Opportunity* (Princeton, N.J.: Princeton University Press, 2001), 10. This new egalitarianism was possible in part because many state constitutions had recently been amended to include an "equal protection" clause. See William J. Brennan, "State Constitutions and the Protection of Individual Rights," *Harvard Law Review* 90, no.3 (January 1977): 489–504.

107. See, for example, Robert Berne and Leanna Stiefel, *The Measurement of Equity in School Finance: Conceptual, Methodological, and Empirical Dimensions* (Baltimore, Md.: Johns Hopkins University Press, 1984).

Chapter 9. Teacher Power: Carter, NEA, and the Creation of the Department of Education

1. *NEA Journal,* October 1964, 1, 12–13.

2. "Teacher-Opinion Poll: Teachers and Politics," *NEA Journal,* October 1965, 64. By 1965, however, 65 percent favored political participation by teachers.

3. In 1965, 57 percent of its members considered themselves to be conservative. Ibid.

4. Terry Herndon, interview with author, August 21, 2003, Germantown, Md. Herndon was executive secretary of NEA during the 1970s.

5. For fuller analyses of this process, see Wayne Urban, *Why Teachers Organized* (Detroit, Mich.: Wayne State University Press, 1982) and *Race, Gender, and the Na-*

tional Education Association (New York: Routledge Falmer, 2000); Maurice Berube, *Teacher Politics: The Influence of Unions* (New York: Greenwood, 1988); Marjorie Murphy, *Blackboard Unions: The AFT and the NEA, 1900–1980* (Ithaca, N.Y.: Cornell University Press, 1990); and William G. Carr, *The Continuing Education of William Carr: An Autobiography* (Washington, D.C.: NEA, 1978).

6. Lambert also clearly saw the need to extricate himself from his mentor's unfashionable coattails. Compare Carr's farewell to the NEA at its 1967 convention with Lambert's speech as executive secretary-designate. NEA, *Addresses and Proceedings of the 115th Annual Meeting: 1967* (Washington, D.C.: NEA, 1968), 8–24, 33–39. At the same meeting, president-elect Braulio Alonso (NEA's first Hispanic president) declared that "for too long we teachers have been seen as the meek, mild, passive, acquiescent teachers who will take whatever is given us. But this is a new day—the day of the new teacher." Ibid., 43.

7. Stanley McFarland, interview with author, May 31, 2006, Potomac, Md.

8. Fischer took office in 1969, when Koontz resigned to become one of the highest-ranking black officials in the Nixon administration (head of the Women's Bureau). In taking office, Fischer promised to "speak in a clear, militant voice." *NEA Journal*, February 1969, 3. For the Morrison quote, see NEA, *Addresses and Proceedings of the 110th Annual Meeting: 1972* (Washington, D.C.: NEA, 1973), 8.

9. The willingness of the activist-dominated national convention to take such positions was arresting, given that the mass membership remained sharply divided in partisan terms. One survey suggested that, by a ratio of 3:2, NEA teachers categorized themselves as being conservative rather than liberal. *NEA Journal*, May 1972, 17.

10. *Today's Education/NEA Journal*, November 1971, 51.

11. Herndon, interview, August 21, 2003. At the 1971 NEA convention, Lambert characterized "Mr. Nixon" as "a hear-nothing, say-nothing, do-nothing education President." NEA, *Addresses and Proceedings: 1972*, 16.

12. In 1972, NEA-PAC supported thirty-two candidates for national office, and twenty-six of them won. NEA, *Addresses and Proceedings of the 111th Annual Meeting: 1973* (Washington, D.C.: NEA, 1974), 8.

13. These other unions included the Association of Federal, State, County, and Municipal Employees and the Service Employees International Union.

14. *Today's Education*, November–December 1975, 5.

15. See Helen Wise, presidential address, NEA, *Addresses and Proceedings: 1973*, 20.

16. For the standard account, see Byron Shafer, *Quiet Revolution: The Struggle for the Democratic Party and the Shaping of Post-Reform Politics* (New York: Russell Sage Foundation, 1983).

17. Herndon, interview, August 21, 2003; Stanley McFarland, interview with author, August 19, 2003, Potomac, Md. For Governor Carter's difficulties with the Georgia Education Association, see Betty Glad, *Jimmy Carter: In Search of the Great White House* (New York: Norton, 1980), 200–201.

18. Carter also committed himself to the NEA's other two core political objectives, even though (as McFarland and Herndon were happy to acknowledge in interview) neither of them was politically realistic: a federal collective bargaining law for public sector workers and a one-third federal contribution to school funding.

19. Herndon, interview, August 21, 2003.

20. Robert Stephens, "President Carter, the Congress, and the NEA: Creating the Department of Education," *Political Science Quarterly* 98, no.4 (Winter 1983–1984): 644; Byron Shafer, *Bifurcated Politics: Evolution and Reform in the National Party Convention* (Cambridge, Mass.: Harvard University Press, 1988), 120. In an aside that captures the dramatic speed with which NEA had come to the fore in Democratic Party politics, Shafer observes that "there may actually have been some NEA delegates at the 1972 convention too, but they had been unrecognized as an organized bloc and uncounted even by their official leadership." Shafer, *Bifurcated Politics*, 119–120.

21. Herndon, interview, August 21, 2003.

22. Address to National Education Association, July 5, 1977, Minneapolis, Minnesota, in Office of Congressional Liaison: Les Francis office files, JCPL, box 162, folder: "Education: Correspondence." The "labor coalition" referred to here was the Labor Coalition Clearinghouse, a group of nine unions, including NEA, the United Automobile Workers, and the Communication Workers of America, who worked with one another during the 1976 campaign.

23. *New Republic*, October 11, 1980, 10; *Today's Education*, January–February 1977, 5.

24. Ibid.

25. John Ryor, "A Victory for Teacher Power," *Today's Education*, January–February 1977, 5.

26. Jimmy Carter, *Keeping Faith: Memoirs of a President* (New York: Bantam Books, 1982), 88.

27. Ibid., 80–81 (emphasis added).

28. As governor of Georgia, when Carter created a broad Department of Human Resources, he had retained a separate Department of Education. As president, he had a strong tendency to use his governorship as a template, and this precedent presumably helped him to think that his campaign pledge to NEA had been about more than just politics. See Stephens, "President Carter, the Congress, and NEA," 646.

29. Beryl Radin and Willis Hawley, *The Politics of Federal Reorganization: Creating the U.S. Department of Education* (New York: Pergamon, 1988), 45–46.

30. The director of the PRP was Harrison Wellford, who had previously worked for Ralph Nader and had no prior executive branch experience. Its "human resources" team, whose responsibilities included HEW, was headed by Patricia Gwaltney, a thirty-one-year-old OMB official. And Gwaltney's ED task force was led by Willis Hawley, a professor of political science at Duke University who had headed an "educators for Carter-Mondale" group during the 1976 campaign.

31. For Lance's "serious doubts," see Robert V. Heffernan, *Cabinetmakers: Story of the Three-Year Battle to Establish the U.S. Department of Education* (San Jose, Calif.: Writer's Showcase, 2001), 65, 78. For Califano's position, see Joseph Califano, *Governing America: An Insider's Report from the White House and the Cabinet* (New York: Simon and Schuster, 1981), 273–293.

32. See James Fallows, "The Passionless Presidency," *Atlantic Monthly*, May 1979, 41–42.

33. Herndon to Carter, letter, March 29, 1977, in NEA Name File, JCPL.

34. Califano, *Governing America*, 276.

35. The other members of the review group were Lance, who opposed a depart-

ment, and Stuart Eizenstat, head of the Domestic Policy Staff, who at this time was neutral.

36. Gail Bramblett, Bramblett MS, 3. I am grateful to Stan McFarland for supplying me with a copy of this document.

37. Heffernan, *Cabinetmakers*, 86. Heffernan, a junior staffer to Senator Abraham Ribicoff, worked closely with his boss, Marilyn Harris, on the legislative effort to create a Department of Education. Although his account is detailed and vivid, it lacks citations and should be used with caution. In this case, Bramblett confirms that NEA had no contact with the OMB team for two months after the meeting, despite repeated phone calls. Bramblett MS, 4.

38. For some of these contradictions, see Walter S. Mossberg, "Can Carter Deliver on His Promises?" *Wall Street Journal*, January 11, 1977, p. 20.

39. Joseph Califano recalls only one occasion when Carter exhibited the kind of passion for the subject that Califano had routinely encountered in conversations with LBJ. See *Governing America*, 293. Carter's 600-page memoir devoted only one page to education (by way of comparison, he spent six pages discussing environmental issues, four on health, and thirty on energy policy). When he made his only reference to ESEA, he got its title wrong. In mid-1977, DPS staffer Beth Abramowitz warned Eizenstat that "on the Hill, the general feeling is that the White House is not concerned about education." Abramowitz to Eizenstat, memo, September 27, 1977, Eizenstat office files, box 196.

40. Jordan to Carter, memo, n.d. (but September or early October 1977), in Jordan office files, box 34.

41. The aide was Mark A. Siegel. The *Washington Post* story is cited by Radin and Hawley, *Politics of Federal Reorganization*, 65.

42. They convey well the growing enthusiasm with which Hawley and his colleagues on the President's Reorganization Project discharged their task, conceiving elaborate new visions of executive reorganization in which the labor, health, education, and welfare responsibilities of the federal government were comprehensively reshuffled. Ibid., 63.

43. According to Bramblett, NEA placed a call to Hamilton Jordan, resulting in a second meeting with OMB at which the question had shifted from "whether" to "how." Bramblett MS, 4. On Jordan's intervention, see also a passing reference in Radin and Hawley, *Politics of Federal Reorganization*, 64.

44. Ribicoff, secretary of HEW under Kennedy, had long argued that the department was unmanageable and had been trying to break it up ever since he had joined the Senate.

45. Bert Carp to Eizenstat, memo, with Eizenstat's handwritten comments appended, Eizenstat office files, box 195.

46. Jordan to Carter, memo, n.d., Jordan office files, box 34 (emphasis in original). It is unclear whether Jordan genuinely believed that the Ribicoff bill would be so easy to pass. If so, then he badly misread the politics of the issue.

47. Radin and Hawley, *Politics of Federal Reorganization*, 74.

48. See McIntyre and Eizenstat to Carter, thirty-two-page memo, with Carter's responses appended, n.d. (but April 1978), Office of Congressional Liaison: Les Francis Files, JCPL, box 162. In endorsing a narrower bill, Bert Carp had earlier conceded that it "would not consolidate either training or social services, and is

at best uninspired from a policy point of view." Carp to Eizenstat, memo, November 23, 1977, Eizenstat office files, box 195.

49. NEA's preference was for a narrow department within which elementary and secondary education interests would dominate. It feared that education, and its own voice, would be lost in a broader human development department. As McFarland observed at one point: "Politically, the narrower the department is, the better off we are. . . . I'd be damn happy if they took the education division and made it a department." Cited by Califano, *Governing America*, 282.

50. That is the principal focus here. For accounts that pay greater attention to other aspects of the story, see Heffernan, *Cabinetmakers*; Radin and Hawley, *Politics of Federal Reorganization*; Califano, *Governing America*; and Stephens, "President Carter, the Congress, and the NEA," 641–663.

51. *Today's Education*, January–February 1977, 5; *Today's Education*, February–March 1980, 27.

52. In interviews, both McFarland and Herndon claimed that they had never expected having a new department to transform NEA's political power. Herndon, interview, August 21, 2003; McFarland, interview, August 19, 2003.

53. Bramblett MS, passim.

54. McFarland, interview, May 31, 2006.

55. Heffernan, *Cabinetmakers*, 283. Heffernan, as a Senate staffer, presumably did not witness this outburst in person. He does not provide a source.

56. Ibid., 321. Also active in making these claims was Ralph Nader's group, Public Citizen, Inc.

57. See, generally, Julian Zelizer, *On Capitol Hill: The Struggle to Reform Congress and Its Consequences, 1948–2000* (New York: Cambridge University Press, 2004).

58. Both of these examples come from Heffernan, *Cabinetmakers:* O'Neill is quoted on 284, Brademas on 302. McFarland confirms that O'Neill resented NEA power; interview, May 31, 2006. For another hint of Brademas's lukewarm feelings toward NEA, see his book, *The Politics of Education: Conflict and Consensus on Capitol Hill* (Norman: University of Oklahoma Press, 1987), 47.

59. For House Speaker Tip O'Neill's poor relationship with Moore, see John A. Farrell, *Tip O'Neill and the Democratic Century* (Boston: Little, Brown, 2001), 452–453. In interviews, both Herndon and McFarland expressed disdain for Carter's congressional staff and claimed that their feelings were widely shared on Capitol Hill. Herndon, interview, August 21, 2003; McFarland, interview, August 19, 2003.

60. Bramblett noted: "The committee was totally organized and financed by NEA, but we carefully kept our name out of the forefront." Bramblett MS, 5.

61. McFarland felt that NEA-PAC had been a tremendously successful innovation, but appeared in our interview to regret the growing involvement of NEA in extraeducational affairs. McFarland, interview, August 19, 2003.

62. Ibid. One of his moles was Bert Carp, of the DPS, who had previously been an aide to Senator Mondale. "Big Six" gatherings were generally attended by each organization's chief executive officer, but McFarland went along in lieu of Herndon, who had little interest in their deliberations.

63. Bramblett MS, 13.

64. Eugene H. Methvin, "The NEA: A Washington Lobby Run Rampant," *Reader's Digest*, November 1978, 97–101, quotes at 101, 97.

65. Allan Cohen, telephone interview with author, September 16, 2006.

66. The Scottsdale meeting is discussed in Heffernan, *Cabinetmakers*, 321, and Radin and Hawley, *Politics of Federal Reorganization*, 130. White resigned his lobbying position at NAVA shortly after Edith Green made him a poster child for the "education-industrial complex." He was appointed to the California position by Governor Reagan shortly thereafter, at the recommendation of school superintendent Wilson Riles. (By the late 1970s, most large state education systems maintained a lobbying presence in Washington, as indeed did a number of large cities.) Donald White, interview with author, August 6, 2005, Annapolis, Md.

67. Bramblett MS, 13. Ribicoff's staffer Heffernan goes further, suggesting that "many NEA people looked upon the idea with disdain" and remained "afflicted with the mentality that we can do this by ourselves." Heffernan, *Cabinetmakers*, 322.

68. Radin and Hawley, *Politics of Federal Reorganization*, 130. Reston housed the headquarters of the National Association of Elementary School Principals. Bramblett MS, 13.

69. Heffernan recalls that "four NEA lobbyists showed up, somewhat like CIA agents, to monitor everything." Heffernan, *Cabinetmakers*, 322.

70. Radin and Hawley, *Politics of Federal Reorganization*, 130.

71. See Les Francis to Frank Moore, memo, April 12, 1978, Office of Congressional Liaison: Les Francis Files, JCPL, box 162. In this memo, the former NEA staffer complained of the administration's "noticeable lack of enthusiasm" about the ED bill and asked if Carter still supported the measure.

72. In one memo, Beth Abramowitz of the DPS told her boss that higher education groups opposed to the ED bill "have Joe Califano's assurance that the . . . bill is not priority legislation for the President." See Abramowitz to Eizenstat, memo, November 22, 1978, in Eizenstat office files, box 195.

73. Heffernan, *Cabinetmakers*, 305–307.

74. Stephens, "President Carter, the Congress, and the NEA," 654.

75. Califano, *Governing America*, 291.

76. Radin and Hawley, *Politics of Federal Reorganization*, 138.

77. Even to the extent that the emphasis remained on governing, moreover, Carter needed the approbation of the NEA, which was a strong supporter of the Panama Canal treaty, his strongest legislative priority for 1979. In an interview, Herndon recalled with amusement that he had made one of his rare appearances in Congress to testify on behalf of the treaty. (He explained that he "hated" the world of Capitol Hill politics, which he saw as parochial and unprincipled.) See Herndon, interview, August 21, 2003. See also David Broder's interview with Herndon in *Washington Post*, July 9, 1980, p. A17.

78. According to one poll, Democrats preferred Kennedy to Carter by a margin of 62 percent to 24 percent. Heffernan, *Cabinetmakers*, 439.

79. OE had been upgraded to a division in 1972.

80. Radin and Hawley, *Politics of Federal Reorganization*, 129.

81. Ibid., 134, 140.

82. Bramblett MS, 14. See also Heffernan, *Cabinetmakers*, 413.

83. Heffernan, *Cabinetmakers*, 396, 457.

84. So were two fiery young House Republicans: Newt Gingrich of Georgia and Trent Lott of Mississippi. It may be that some of these legislators were influenced by

the power of (relatively conservative) NEA chapters in their states and by the disproportionate share of federal education dollars that went to poor and rural states. To some, too, the notion of "breaking up HEW" might have been attractive.

85. Samuel Halperin, letter to author, July 7, 2006. By this time, Halperin was director of the Institute for Educational Leadership at George Washington University and a participant in Allan Cohen's ad hoc coalition.

86. See Stephen Halpern, *On the Limits of the Law: The Ironic Legacy of Title VI of the 1964 Civil Rights Act* (Baltimore, Md.: Johns Hopkins University Press, 1995).

87. Radin and Hawley, *Politics of Federal Reorganization*, 66.

88. Allan Cohen considers that his eventual victory owed more to Mondale's efforts than to those of Carter. Cohen, telephone interview, September 16, 2006.

89. Bramblett MS, 26; Heffernan, *Cabinetmakers*, 393–394. The other crucial vote was that of Lyle Williams, a freshman Republican from Ohio. He had voted for the ED bill in 1978 but was leaning against the following year, until NEA and Carter swung into action. The NEA promised to support him in his next election, and the White House intervened on behalf of an underwriting application that a commuter aircraft business in his district had made to the Economic Development Agency. See Bramblett MS, 26–28; Heffernan, *Cabinetmakers*, 392, 402; McFarland, interview, May 31, 2006.

90. Bramblett MS, 30; Heffernan, *Cabinetmakers*, 411 (quote from Heffernan).

91. Bramblett MS, 40–41. She notes that NEA had to rent a helicopter to get Republican supporter John Anderson of Illinois to interrupt a campaign trip in New Hampshire.

92. Former congressman Lloyd Meeds, by then a K Street lawyer-lobbyist, acted as middleman. On St. Patrick's Day 1979, the McFarlands, the Meeds, and the O'Neills all went out to dinner together, and in McFarland's view the symbolism of the occasion meant a lot to O'Neill. McFarland, interview, May 31, 2006.

93. At the same time, O'Neill tried to maintain his relationship with Democratic opponents of the ED bill by appointing Lucien Nedzi of Wayne County, Michigan, as floor manager. He was a strong labor Democrat who opposed the bill and duly helped to complicate its passage by permitting votes on all manner of barely germane but hard-to-oppose amendments, having to do with such matters as racial quotas, busing, abortion, and prayer in schools.

94. Radin and Hawley, *Politics of Federal Reorganization*, 144.

95. *Wall Street Journal*, October 1, 1979, p. 22.

96. Ibid., August 13, 1980, p. 2.

97. *National Journal*, July 9, 1983, 1450.

98. Moynihan, an ally and admirer of Albert Shanker, described Carter's bill as "a backroom deal born out of squalid politics." Quoted in Chester A. Finn Jr., "A Federal Department of Education?" a chapter in his memoir, provisionally titled *Hard Lessons: A Personal History of Public Education in America since Sputnik*, forthcoming from Princeton University Press. (Finn was Moynihan's legislative assistant during the Carter presidency.)

99. Shafer, *Bifurcated Politics*, 120–121.

100. An especially articulate statement of this case was made by Terrel Bell, who had been commissioner of education under Gerald Ford and would be secretary of education under Reagan. See Senate Committee on Governmental Affairs, hearings,

Department of Education Act of 1977, 95th Cong., 1st Sess., October 13, 1977, 266–267. See also the testimony of Rufus Miles and Samuel Halperin, at 34 and 38, respectively.

101. See Califano, *Governing America,* 277–278. For the full nineteen-page memo that he summarized, see Califano to Carter, memo, November 26, 1977, in Jordan office files, box 34.

102. Wilbur Cohen's argument was raised by Ribicoff, in colloquy with Stephen K. Bailey, in Senate Committee on Governmental Affairs, hearings: *Department of Education Act of 1977,* 43.

Chapter 10. Education and the Reagan Revolution

1. Reagan went on to praise "the old-fashioned McGuffeys readers that were standard in our school for more than half a century." (During his presidency, they came back into print and were advertised in the conservative periodical, *Human Events.*) Kiron K. Skinner, Annelise Anderson, and Martin Anderson, eds., *Reagan, in His Own Hand* (New York: Free Press, 2001), 344–345. This is one of ten education addresses that the editors have included in their illuminating collection of Reagan's radio addresses. For another, see Kiron K. Skinner, Annelise Anderson, and Martin Anderson, eds., *Reagan's Path to Victory: The Shaping of Ronald Reagan's Vision: Selected Writings* (New York: Free Press, 2004), 473–474.

2. In 1983, Reagan noted "the almost uninterrupted decline in student achievement scores during the past two decades, decades in which the Federal presence in education grew and grew." "Remarks on Receiving the Final Report of the National Commission on Excellence in Education, April 26, 1983," *Public Papers of the Presidents of the United States: Ronald Reagan: 1983,* vol. 1 (Washington, D.C.: Government Printing Office, 1984), 585.

3. Radio address broadcast on October 2, 1979. Skinner, Anderson, and Anderson, *Reagan's Path,* 473–474.

4. *New York Times,* October 14, 1980, p. D22.

5. See Lou Cannon, *President Reagan: The Role of a Lifetime,* 2nd ed. (New York: Public Affairs Press, 2001), 51.

6. She went on to run the gubernatorial campaign of Ron Unz, brainchild of Proposition 227 (which abolished bilingual education in California).

7. Kinder, e-mail to author, September 28, 2005.

8. In this chapter, I refer both to "Reaganauts" and to "Reaganites." In using the former term, I am seeking to characterize people who not only approved of Reagan's ideas but also had a deeply personal commitment to his leadership.

9. For Anderson's view of Nixon's record, see his account of its welfare reform initiative, *Welfare: The Political Economy of Welfare Reform in the United* States (Stanford, Calif.: Hoover Institution Press, 1978). For the tussles with HEW, see Desmond King, *Actively Seeking Work? The Politics of Unemployment and Welfare Policy in the United States and Great Britain* (Chicago: University of Chicago Press, 1995), 182–183.

10. For brief accounts of the work and composition of the Kinder task force, see *Wall Street Journal,* February 6, 1981, p. 20; *American School Board Journal,* January 1981, 43; *Chronicle of Higher Education,* December 15, 1980, 9, 12. I also rely here on Charles W. Radcliffe, interview with author, August 6, 2004, Washington, D.C., and

Radcliffe to author, letter, December 2, 2005. For a copy of the unpublished Pifer task force report, see Keppel papers, box 40.

11. Nancy Reagan, *My Turn: The Memoirs of Nancy Reagan* (New York: Random House, 1989), 240–241.

12. Quoted in *Human Events*, January 17, 1981, 48.

13. On Meese's long-term agenda, see Terrel H. Bell, *The Thirteenth Man: A Reagan Cabinet Memoir* (New York: Free Press, 1988), 2. Max Rafferty, who had been superintendent of schools for California during Reagan's governorship, was another advocate of completely eliminating the federal role in education. See Rafferty, "An Open Letter to Ronald Reagan," *Human Events*, January 24, 1981, 9. For Reagan's different approach, see his interview with *U.S. News and World Report*, January 19, 1981, 26.

14. See *Baltimore Sun*, January 8, 1981, pp. 1, 7.

15. Lou Cannon, *President Reagan: The Role of a Lifetime* (New York: Public Affairs, 2000), 107; Wirthlin's comment, 730.

16. "Reagan's Rx for a Sick Economy," *U.S. News*, January 19, 1981, 23.

17. *National Journal*, October 10, 1981, pp. 1086–1089.

18. David Stockman, *The Triumph of Politics: How the Reagan Revolution Failed* (New York: Harper and Row, 1986), 69.

19. He had come to Reagan's attention already, having played the role of independent candidate John Anderson in a mock debate during the 1980 campaign.

20. Stockman, *Triumph of Politics*, 111–112.

21. Ibid., 127, 120.

22. For Bell's account of how he saved bilingual education, see *Thirteenth Man*, 69. For Stockman's account of how he "shackled" Bell, see *Triumph of Politics*, 113. Emerson Elliott, a career budget official at ED, recalls having helped to craft a more moderate consolidation proposal and seeing it "alter[ed] beyond recognition" by OMB. Elliott to author, letter, January 20, 2007.

23. Chester E. Finn Jr., "Tinkering with U.S. Education Policy," *Wall Street Journal*, January 13, 1981, p. 30. Finn, a professor of education at Vanderbilt University, was denied a job in Reagan's ED department in 1981 because of his previous position as an aide to Senator Daniel Patrick Moynihan, a Democrat. Before that, he had been an education specialist in the Nixon White House.

24. John A. Farrell, *Tip O'Neill and the Democratic Century* (Boston: Little, Brown, 2001), 555.

25. *Education Week*, September 7, 1981, 12.

26. Stanley M. Elam, ed., *Phi Delta Kappa Gallup Poll of Attitudes Toward Education, 1969–1984: A Topical Summary* (Bloomington, Ind.: PDK, 1984), 29.

27. See "NEA's Political Activism Seems to have Backfired," *Phi Delta Kappan*, May 1981, 622. For NEA's response to such criticism, see "NEA, 'In' during Carter Administration, Must Adjust to Being 'Out' under Reagan," *Chronicle of Higher Education*, April 20, 1981, 1, 22, including an interview with Terry Herndon.

28. Quoted in *Education Week*, September 21, 1981, 2.

29. The next few paragraphs are drawn primarily from Radcliffe, interview, August 6, 2004, and Radcliffe, letter, December 2, 2005.

30. Christopher T. Cross, e-mail to author, December 9, 2005.

31. Stockman, *Triumph of Politics*, 211, 209.

32. Recollection of Richard DiEugenio, in marginal comments on an earlier draft of this chapter. Dr. DiEugenio was a GOP staffer on the House Education and Labor Committee.

33. Stockman, *Triumph of Politics*, 228. For the glum reaction of movement conservatives, see *Human Events*, August 15, 1981, 1, which deplored how the administration's block grant proposals had been "decimated," weakened "virtually beyond recognition." It blamed "Congressional liberals" and lobbyists rather than people like Ashbrook for this "travesty."

34. Radcliffe's leading role is confirmed by Jack Jennings, the top Democratic staffer on the House Education and Labor Committee. Jennings, interview with author, August 3, 2005, Washington, D.C.

35. According to Radcliffe, the Title I reforms were drawn up in consultation with Rep. Goodling, the ranking Republican on the subcommittee that handled ESEA. He had been a public school teacher and a principal, as well as a superintendent, before coming to Congress in 1975.

36. This was John Charles Houston, director of congressional affairs for the Washington-based Public Service Research Council. See *U.S. News and World Report*, July 20, 1981, 33.

37. These two appointments generated some adverse publicity from journalists who doubted their educational credentials. The *Wall Street Journal* reported sniffily that Billings had a "'Ph.D.' from Clarksville school of theology, primarily a correspondence school" that was currently "under investigation by the state higher education commission"; October 14, 1981, p. 56. And Lou Cannon noted that Oliver's background appeared to leave him largely "unfamiliar with national education policy": *Washington Post*, March 1, 1981, p. A7.

38. For details, see *Education Week*, September 28, 1981, 13.

39. Bell, *Thirteenth Man*, 2.

40. Following his departure in 1982, Uzzell denounced Bell for leading "the permanent bureaucracy, dedicated to the sabotage of the Reagan Presidency." Quoted in *American School Board Journal*, November 1982, 55.

41. David Savage, "Washington Report," *Phi Delta Kappan*, February 1981, 411.

42. Bell, *Thirteenth Man*, 90.

43. *Wall Street Journal*, October 14, 1981, p. 56; *U.S. News and World Report*, July 20, 1981, 33; *Chronicle of Higher Education*, October 28, 1981, 21.

44. Even when there was no significant clientele, it could be hard: Nixon had famously been unable to abolish the federal Board of Tea-Tasters. See William Safire, *Before the Fall: An Inside View of the Pre-Watergate White House* (New York: Ballantine, 1977), 319–320.

45. Behind the scenes Bell advised NEA's Stanley McFarland on how to increase GOP support for the ED bill. McFarland, interview with author, May 31, 2006, Potomac, Md.

46. For Herndon's response, see *Human Events*, January 17, 1981, 48; for the organizational endorsements, see Senate Committee on Labor and Human Resources, *Nomination: Hearings on Dr. Terrel H. Bell*, January 15, 1981, 97th Cong., 1st Sess., 5–6, 114.

47. Ibid., 27.

48. Unnamed ED staffer, cited in *Human Events*, January 17, 1981, 48.

49. Ibid.

50. Also, he was consulted by Meese during the transition and asked who he thought might be approached. But that meeting had not gone well and neither encounter had encouraged Bell to believe that he was under consideration. Elam K. Hertzler, interview with author, June 4, 2006, Charlottesville, Va. Hertzler was Bell's Chief of Staff.

51. Sweet, interview with author, August 6, 2005, Strasburg, Va.

52. Doubtless it helped that Bell's appointment was strongly supported by his conservative home state senators: Jake Garn and Orrin Hatch. They admired his performance as head of the Utah higher education system, which he had managed with distinction.

53. This is according to Joseph Gerard, "Down with the Department of Education," *National Review*, October 30, 1981, 1271.

54. For copies of both speeches, see General Correspondence and Administration Files, 1979–1983, RG 441, NARA II, box 200.

55. Edwin Meese, *With Reagan: The Inside Story* (Washington, D.C.: Regnery, 1992), 69.

56. *Human Events*, February 14, 1981, 6.

57. Ibid., July 25, 1981, 17.

58. Worried educators were kept abreast of Bell's efforts to protect their programs via intermediaries, including state lobbyists on the Hill, such as Don White (California) and Allan Cohen (Illinois). They would frequently share this information with Jack Jennings, chief education staffer on the House Education and Labor Committee. Hertzler, interview, June 4, 2006.

59. *Education Week*, November 2, 1981, 9.

60. Bell told Edward Kennedy that "title I of ESEA is one of the best programs that we have in the Department" and that its record was "very, very encouraging." See Senate Committee on Labor and Human Resources, *Nomination*, 25.

61. Hertzler, interview, June 4, 2006.

62. *Phi Delta Kappan*, May 1981, 622.

63. *New York Times*, March 15, 1981, p. 27.

64. Andrew Mollison, "After 25 Years, ED Is Here to Stay," *Phi Delta Kappan*, May 2005, 871.

65. One conservative charged that "career people" were "hoping that the Republicans will lose control of the Senate next year, and that public opinion will turn against us." *Wall Street Journal*, October 14, 1981, 56. Eventually, Hertzler overplayed his hand and was replaced on the committee by Charles Heatherley, a strong conservative. Hertzler, interview, June 4, 2006.

66. "Death Warrant for a Department," *Newsweek*, September 14, 1981, 95.

67. *Wall Street Journal*, October 14, 1981, p. 56.

68. Its members were drawn from OMB and Anderson's Office for Policy Development as well as from ED. See "Reagan Weighing Much Deeper Education Cuts and Faster Dismantling of Federal Department," *Education Week*, September 28, 1981, 1.

69. See "Reagan Task Force Divided on Fate of U.S. Agency," ibid., November 2, 1981, 1; Bell, *Thirteenth Man*, 90–91.

70. For a fuller examination of this decline in political fortunes, see Gareth Davies, "The Welfare State," in W. Elliot Brownlee and Hugh Davis Graham, *The Reagan Presidency: Pragmatic Conservatism and Its Legacies* (Lawrence: University Press of Kansas, 203), 214–219.

71. "The Baker Network—Reagan Revolution—or Bush Rebellion," *Human Events*, January 23, 1982, 15. The titles of other *Human Events* stories during the months that followed give a vivid impression of the declining morale of conservatives during this period. See, for example, "Conservative Leaders Find Administration Officials Undermining Reagan Mandate," January 30, 1982; "Where Is the Revolution? Reagan Government a Mystery to Conservatives," June 26, 1982; "What's Behind the Attack on Ed Meese?" July 17, 1982; and culminating the series, "White House Vipers Spit Venom at Ed Meese," August 7, 1982.

72. Bell, *Thirteenth Man*, 92.

73. "Address to the Nation on the Program for Economic Recovery," *Public Papers of the Presidents of the United States: Ronald Reagan: 1981* (Washington, D.C.: Government Printing Office, 1982), 833. For a critical insider's assessment of the speech, see Richard Darman, *Who's in Control? Polar Politics and the Sensible Center* (New York: Simon and Schuster, 1996), 100–101.

74. *Education Week*, January 12, 1982, 9. See also "Breaking Up the Education Department: School Aid May Be the Real Target," *National Journal*, October 24, 1981, 1909.

75. Meese told California school administrators that Reagan had no plans for "drastic cuts." See "President Reagan Values Education, Meese Proclaims," *Education Week*, December 21, 1981, 1.

76. David Gergen, *Eyewitness to Power: The Essence of Leadership, Nixon to Clinton* (New York: Touchstone, 2001), 190; *Education Week*, March 10, 1982, 10.

77. Cochran to Reagan, letter, November 21, 1981, Correspondence and Administration Files, RG 441, NARA II, box 266. Both of Cochran's parents had been teachers in Mississippi.

78. Hayakawa to Bell, letter, December 30, 1981, in ibid.

79. The following four paragraphs are based on Bell, *Thirteenth Man*, 94–98.

80. Roth had even spoken in a publicity film that Don White created for Allan Cohen's pro-ED coalition in 1979. I am grateful to Mr. Cohen for supplying me with a copy of the film.

81. The few legislators who felt strongly about abolishing ED—such as John Erlenborn and Senator Dan Quayle (R-Ind.)—would not sponsor Bell's proposal because it did not go far enough. On the decision to pull the bill, see *Congressional Quarterly Weekly Report*, April 10, 1982, 783–786.

82. See "Backers Gird to Defend Cabinet-level Education Department," *Chronicle of Higher Education*, September 2, 1981, 19, 23; *Wall Street Journal*, February 3, 1982, p. 8; *Congressional Quarterly Weekly Report*, April 10, 1982, 786; and *National Journal*, October 24, 1981, 1910.

83. President Reagan did not mention the effort to abolish ED in his memoir, and there is no evidence that he viewed the failure of the venture with anything other than equanimity.

84. *Human Events*, June 19, 1982, 5. See also Bell, *Thirteenth Man*, 97.

85. See Joe Wright to Dave Stockman, memo, January 6, 1985, Records of Office of Management and Budget—Education Branch, 1981–1988, RG 51, NARA II, box 3.

86. See Barry White to Director [Stockman], memo, October 2, 1985, in ibid. White was deputy associate director at OMB.

87. Moderate career civil servants played a leading role in running most ED agencies at first, as Bell and Meese struggled over appointments. When Bell vetoed Lorelei Kinder as his deputy, Meese retaliated by vetoing Bell's choice, Christopher Cross (a scholarly, moderate Republican and former member of Albert Quie's staff). Bell then managed to secure the appointment of another moderate, William Clohan. In 1982, the White House forced him out, but his conservative replacement, Gary L. Jones, was loyal to Bell and was regarded within his circle as "a powerful force for good." See Bell, *Thirteenth Man*, 40–41; Cross, telephone interview with author, August 4, 2005; Hertzler, interview, June 24, 2006; Milton Goldberg, interview with author, August 4, 2006, Arlington, Va. (quote from Goldberg).

88. *Human Events*, July 17, 1982, 7.

89. See Maris Vinovskis, *Revitalizing Federal Education Research and Development: Improving the R&D Centers, Regional Education Laboratories, and the "New" OERI* (Ann Arbor: University of Michigan Press, 2001), 101–105.

90. Iserbyt to Reagan, letter, July 7, 1982. This letter, which is very long, is reproduced by Iserbyt in an Internet article, entitled "Background Paper on President Reagan and the U.S. Department of Education"; http://deliberatedumbingdown. com/pages/articles/letter_reagan.html (accessed July 19, 2006). According to Iserbyt, she too was supplied with a secret code that ensured that it reached the president's desk, but Reagan declined her request for a personal meeting. See also Charlotte Thomson Iserbyt, *The Deliberate Dumbing Down of America: A Chronological Paper Trail* (Ravenna, Ohio: Conscience Press, 1999). Iserbyt was sacked when she leaked details of an ED grant of which she disapproved to *Human Events*.

91. See "Election Results Seen as Helping the Position of Education: Democratic Gains in Congress, States, May Stymie Reagan Plans, Lobbyists Say," *Education Week*, November 10, 1982, 4.

92. They included Robert Stafford of Vermont, chair of the education subcommittee, and Lowell Weicker of Connecticut, also a member of that subcommittee. See *Wall Street Journal*, November 12, 1982, p. 7.

93. See "House, Rejecting President's Budget, Urges Funds Increase for Education," *Education Week*, March 30, 1983, 9. Bell made no effort to conceal his satisfaction. See "Committee Praises ED Shift on Budget," *Education Week*, March 9, 1983, 8.

94. In terms of the federal share of total spending on schools, meanwhile, there was no recovery from 1981. The proportion shrank quite dramatically during Reagan's first year, from 9.2 percent to 7.4 percent, and then continued to worsen. See Appendix. These statistics reflected the strong growth in local and state spending on education during the 1980s.

95. ECIA was formally repealed by the Hawkins-Stafford Act of 1988, which preserved the Chapter 2 block grant but destroyed its raison d'être by insisting that the funds be spent on six particular program areas (mainly ones that had enjoyed

their own categorical program prior to ECIA). See Deborah Verstegen, "Education Fiscal Policy in the Reagan Administration," *Educational Evaluation and Policy Analysis* 12, no. 4 (Winter 1990): 365.

96. *National Journal*, July 9, 1983, 1452–1456.

97. *Congress and the Nation: 1981–1984* (Washington, D.C.: Congressional Quarterly, 1985), 555.

98. "Deluge of new programs" was a considerable overstatement. What OMB mainly had in mind was a new Mathematics and Science Education program that Congress passed in 1984, as part of the grand-sounding, but in truth cosmetic, Education for Economic Security Act.

99. *Education Department: 1986 Budget: Director's Review*, n.d. (but shortly after the 1984 election). In Records of OMB—Education Branch, 1981–1988, RG 51, NARA II, box 3. For another critical account of the first term record from a conservative perspective, see Eileen M. Gardner, "The Department of Education," in Stuart Butler et al., eds., *Mandate for Leadership II: Continuing the Conservative Revolution* (Washington, D.C.: Heritage Foundation, 1985), 49–62.

100. See *Education Week*, September 28, 1981, 13.

101. Milton Goldberg, telephone interview with author, July 10, 2006. For a profile of Gardner, see *Chronicle of Higher Education*, September 9, 1981, 11.

102. The other three were Glenn Seaborg (Nobel laureate and former chancellor of the University of California–Berkeley), Donald Baker (Bell Telephone executive), and Gardner.

103. Goldberg was struck by the growing attention that governors started to pay during this period to education (for example in their annual "state of the state" addresses) and speculates that commission hearings might have contributed to this development. Telephone interview, July 10, 2006.

104. Bruce Boston, e-mail to author, July 5, 2006.

105. David P. Gardner, *Earning My Degree: Memoirs of an American University President* (Berkeley: University of California Press, 2005), 114.

106. Otis L. Graham Jr., *Toward a Planned Society: From Roosevelt to Nixon* (New York: Oxford University Press, 1975), 201.

107. Gardner, *Earning My Degree*, 118–119.

108. By contrast, Harvey says, "the movement conservatives thought it was wonderful," perhaps thinking it "would contribute to the end of the department." James Harvey, e-mail to author, June 30, 2006.

109. Gardner, *Earning My Degree*, 124.

110. Hertzler, interview, June 24, 2006; Goldberg, telephone interview, August 4, 2006.

111. Hedrick Smith, *The Power Game: How Washington Works* (New York: Ballantine, 1988), 412. According to polls in early 1983, Reagan trailed both Walter Mondale, his eventual opponent, and John Glenn, another possible candidate, by as much as 15 percent. See Darman, *Who's in Control?* 115.

112. Cabinet Commission on Excellence in Education, *A Nation at Risk* (Washington, D.C.: Department of Education, 1983), 1. The dramatic sentence beginning "If an unfriendly foreign power . . ." came from Seaborg, but he wanted it to end ". . . we would have declared war on that country" rather than "we might well have

viewed it as an act of war." Goldberg and some of the commissioners felt Seaborg's version too inflammatory, and it was in this context that Seaborg threatened to withhold his signature from the report. Goldberg, telephone interview, August 4, 2006.

113. The next sentence after those cited above read: "Our society and its educational institutions seem to have lost sight of the basic purposes of schooling, and of the high expectations and disciplined effort needed to attain them."

114. For an account of this occasion, see Bell, *Thirteenth Man*, 127–131; Gardner, *Earning My Degree*, 126–127; Glenn Seaborg, *A Chemist in the White House: From the Manhattan Project to the End of the Cold War* (Washington, D.C.: American Chemical Society, 1998), 274–275.

115. For assessments of its impact, see Dick Kirschten, "The Politics of Education," *National Journal*, July 9, 1983, 1447–1448; Bell, *Thirteenth Man*, 131–43; Gerald Holton, "'A Nation at Risk' Revisited," in Holton, *The Advancement of Science, and Its Burdens* (Cambridge, Mass.: Harvard University Press, 1998), 268–270; Department of Education, *The Nation Responds: Recent Efforts to Improve Education* (Washington, D.C.: Department of Education, 1984); Glenn Seaborg, *A Scientist Speaks Out: A Personal Perspective on Science, Society, and Change* (Singapore: World Scientific, 1996), 400–405.

116. Smith, *Power Game*, 412.

117. Ibid.

Conclusion

1. Godfrey Hodgson, *More Equal Than Others: America from Nixon to the New Century* (Princeton, N.J.: Princeton University Press, 2004), 24, 301.

2. Dan T. Carter, *From George Wallace to Newt Gingrich: Race in the Conservative Counter-Revolution, 1963–1994* (Baton Rouge: Louisiana State University Press, 1996), xiv.

3. See Steve Fraser and Gary Gerstle, eds., *The Rise and Fall of the New Deal Order, 1930–1980* (Princeton, N.J.: Princeton University Press, 1989), "Introduction," and passim; Gareth Davies, *From Opportunity to Entitlement: The Transformation and Decline of Great Society Liberalism* (Lawrence: University Press of Kansas, 1996).

4. Carter, *From George Wallace to Newt Gingrich*, and *The Politics of Rage: George Wallace, the Origins of the New Conservatism, and the Transformation of American Politics* (New York: Simon and Schuster, 1995).

5. Lisa McGirr, *Suburban Warriors: The Origins of the New American Right* (Princeton, N.J.: Princeton University Press, 2001); Jonathan Schoenbrod, *A Time for Choosing: The Rise of Modern American Conservatism* (New York: Oxford University Press, 2001); Rick Perlstein, *Before the Storm: Barry Goldwater and the Unmaking of the American Consensus* (New York: Hill and Wang, 2001); Stephen Hayward, *The Age of Reagan: The Fall of the Old Liberal Order, 1964–1980* (Roseville, Calif.: Forum, 2001).

6. Fraser and Gerstle, Epilogue, in Fraser and Gerstle, *Rise and Fall*, 294.

7. McGirr, *Suburban Warriors*, 5.

8. James T. Patterson, *Restless Giant: The United States from Watergate to Bush v. Gore* (New York: Oxford University Press, 2005), 90.

9. Ibid., 424.

10. See, for example, William H. Chafe, *Unfinished Journey: America since World War II*, 6th ed. (New York: Oxford University Press, 2007), 414–421; Bruce Schulman, *The Seventies: The Great Shift in American Culture, Society, and Politics* (New York: Free Press, 2001); Edward Berkowitz, *Something Happened: A Political and Cultural Overview of the Seventies* (New York: Columbia University Press, 2006), 133–157.

11. Hugh Davis Graham, *Collision Course: The Strange Convergence of Affirmative Action and Immigration Policy in America* (New York: Oxford University Press, 2002), 66.

12. Hugh Davis Graham, *The Civil Rights Era: Origins and Development of National Policy* (New York: Oxford University Press, 1990), 8.

13. Ibid., 3, 449.

14. See Henry J. Perkinson, *The Imperfect Panacea: American Faith in Education*, 4th ed. (Boston: McGraw-Hill, 1995).

15. See Patrick McGuinn, *No Child Left Behind and the Transformation of Federal Education Policy, 1965–2005* (Lawrence: University Press of Kansas, 2006), 159.

16. Reflecting the growing role of the courts in social policy during the 1970s, Graham refers to "iron quadrilaterals" having taken the place of "iron triangles." See *Civil Rights Era*, 470.

17. Berkowitz, *Something Happened*.

18. The precise contribution of school finance litigation to this development is hard to gauge. There were clearly other factors, including the rising power of the teacher unions within state legislatures and the efforts of "education governors" in both political parties. On the other side of the ledger, some scholars argue that California's effort to implement *Serrano* explains the passage of Proposition 13 in 1978. (By capping property taxes, Proposition 13 greatly added to the difficulty of those seeking to increase spending on schools.) See William A. Fischel, "How *Serrano* Caused Proposition 13," *Journal of Law and Politics* 12 (1996): 607–645.

19. John F. Jennings, *Why National Standards and Tests? Politics and the Quest for Better Schools* (Thousand Oaks, Calif.: SAGE, 1998), 127.

20. See, for example, the bulletin "Some Republican Accomplishments in Federal Education Law," which Roy Millenson, minority staff member on the Senate education subcommittee, prepared for inclusion in the *Congressional Record* in 1974 in order "to illustrate the active Republican interest in education during this period." I am grateful to Mr. Millenson for furnishing me with a copy of this bulletin.

21. The following summary is drawn from Christopher T. Cross, *Political Education: National Policy Comes of Age* (New York: Teachers College Press, 2004); McGuinn, *No Child Left Behind*; Paul H. Manna, *School's In: Federalism and the National Education Agenda* (Washington, D.C.: Georgetown University Press, 2006); Elizabeth DeBray, *Politics, Ideology, and Education: Federal Policy during the Clinton and Bush Administrations* (New York: Teachers College Press, 2006).

22. On the growing role of think tanks, see DeBray, *Politics, Ideology, and Education*, passim. For business, see McGuinn, *No Child Left Behind*, 101, 116, 174, and Jennings, *Why National Standards?* 160–168.

23. The "Contract with America," the platform on which the Republicans had campaigned in the midterm elections, provided them with much of their agenda for the 104th Congress.

24. McGuinn, *No Child Left Behind*, 123.

25. I am indebted to Martha Derthick for this point.

26. Cross, *Political Education*, 122.

27. Ibid., 126–127. Bush noted that "change will not come by disdaining or dismantling the federal role in education."

28. At least, NCLB greatly enhanced the *theoretical* "regulatory capacity of the central state." The difficulty the federal government has encountered in implementing the law suggests that regulatory intent may exceed regulatory capacity. See, for example, Michael Petrilli, "The Problem with 'Implementation Is the Problem': A Short History of No Child Left Behind" (paper delivered at American Enterprise Institute Conference, "Fixing Failing Schools: Is the NCLB Toolkit Working," American Enterprise Institute, Washington, D.C., November 30, 2006): www.aei.org/event 1351 (accessed December 3, 2006). Frustrated by these problems, some "conservatives" called for tougher national standards. See Diane Ravitch, "Every State Left Behind," *New York Times*, November 7, 2005, p. A25; and Jay Mathews, "National School Testing Urged," *Washington Post*, September 3, 2006, p. A1.

29. Halperin to author, letter, March 30, 2006 (emphasis in original).

INDEX